Shops and Shopkeeping

Shops and Shopkeeping in Eighteenth-Century England

HOH-CHEUNG MUI
LORNA H. MUI

McGill-Queen's University Press
Kingston, Montreal, London

Routledge
London

© McGill-Queen's University Press 1989
ISBN 0-7735-0620-9
Legal deposit 1st quarter 1989
Bibliothèque nationale du Québec

Printed in Canada on acid-free paper

Published in the United Kingdom in 1989 by
Routledge
11 New Fetter Lane
London EC4P 4EE
ISBN 0-415-01608-8

This book has been published with the help of a grant
from the Social Science Federation of Canada, using
funds provided by the Social Sciences and Humanities
Research Council of Canada.

Canadian Cataloguing in Publication Data

Mui, Hoh-cheung, 1916–
    Shops and shopkeeping in eighteenth-century England
    Includes index.
    Bibliography: p.
    ISBN 0-7735-0620-9

    1. Retail trade – England – History – 18th century.
    2. Stores, Retail – England – History – 18th century.
    I. Mui, Lorna H. (Lorna Holbrook), 1915– . II. Title.

HF3515.M84 1988   381'.1'0942   c88-090330-9

British Library Cataloguing in Publication Data

Mui, Hoh-cheung
    Shops and shopkeeping in eighteenth-century
    England.
    1. England. Shops, 1700–1800
    I. Title II. Mui, Lorna M.
    381'. 0942

    ISBN 0-415-01608-8

Contents

Tables

Maps

Preface

This book on eighteenth-century shops and shopkeeping studies a neglected period in the history of retailing in England. It is hoped that in so doing the role of retail shops in the pre-industrial economy may be demonstrated in substance rather than in general observations as has hitherto been the case. But the task is not an easy or a straightforward one. Surviving shop records are rare. Of other sources, some are direct such as the excise survey of shops in 1759 and the excise accounts of tea licences. Others yield pertinent information only after labourious examination. Each document required a sustained and detailed analysis of its institutional basis in order to obtain comparable data and to ascertain an interpretation relevant to the subject. Tedious as the work was, the methods employed by traditional historians to collect "scientific facts" often turned out to be necessary and productive. We feel fortunate in being able to offer substantive support for the following conclusions. During the eighteenth century, the number and variety of shops increased considerably. More important, in the distribution and sale of goods, shopkeepers introduced many innovative practices which have been usually attributed to nineteenth-century entrepreneurs. It would be presumptuous to claim a retailing revolution for the eighteenth century. But it is perhaps not too far-fetched to suggest that if a "consumer society" can be said to have been born in that period, a firmly established network of shops, some of whose proprietors actively attracted customers, nourished the new society.

Our first gratitude is offered in memory of the late Professor T.S. Ashton whose stimulating questions about shops encouraged us to explore the subject. We would like to thank Professor D.C. Coleman and Professor Peter Mathias for their encouraring remarks on an earlier draft of this study. The present version has benefitted from their comments and suggestions. Three anonymous readers examined the manuscript with great care. We are grateful for their kind evaluation and helpful advice – especially for calling our attention to a revealing, although limited, survey of Tax on Shops towards the end of the century (buried among many Home Office papers on the police, transportation of convicts, and similar subjects). While we have incorporated most of the suggestions, responsibility for the remaining errors of fact and judgment rests solely with us.

We are grateful to the Earl of Harrowby for letting us consult the collection of eighteenth-century excise and other documents in his possession; the directors of Melroses Ltd, Leith, for the Andrew Melrose Archives; Mr G. Taylor of W.E. Taylor & Son, Ltd, Bishops's Court, Exeter, for the Garratt Papers; the late Robert O. Mennel for the Mennel (Tuke) Archives; and David Lloyd Pigott & Co. for the use of their archives.

It is a pleasure to acknowledge our gratitude to the librarians and their staff of the following depositories for their ready cooperation and frequently laborious searches for sources: the British Library, especially the Manuscript Department and the State Paper Room; the Public Record Office (London); the Scottish Record Office; the Library of HM Customs and Excise; the India Office Records and Library; the Guildhall (London) Library; the National Library of Scotland; the Probate Office, Somerset House (London); the H.E. Huntington Library; the Baker Library at Harvard University; the Stirling Library at Yale University, in particular, the special collection of eighteenth-century newspapers; the University of North Wales Library (Bangor); the local history department of the public libraries at Edinburgh, Glasgow, Liverpool, Manchester, Shrewsbury, and York. Special thanks are due the reference librarians and librarians at the Interlibrary Loans Department of the Queen Elizabeth II Library at Memorial University of Newfoundland for their tireless efforts to obtain obscure material from both sides of the Atlantic.

We are happy to thank the following institutions for their generous grants and assistance: the Vice-President Research Fund at Memorial University; the former Canada Council; the Association of American Learned Societies. Sabbatical leaves from Memorial University facilitated research on several aspects of the subject. We hope the present study may be accepted as an acknowledgment, however inadequate, of their encouragement of scholarly pursuits.

We are grateful to Mrs Denise Lachance, officer of the Aid to Publications Programme of the Social Science Federation of Canada, for her efficient handling of our application. We thank the staff of

McGill-Queen's University Press for their interest and helpful suggestions that spurred us to improve the clarity of exposition.

H.C.M.
L.H.M.

Shops and Shopkeeping

Introduction

Historians have frequently observed that the absence of artificial barriers to the flow of goods within Britain was one of the conditions which facilitated the industrial revolution during the eighteenth century. More recently, it has been proposed that the century witnessed the birth of a consumer society. Little information, however, has been assembled to define the channels through which goods flowed in increasing volume and to specify the institutions that provided for consumption. The present study seeks to offer an answer, even if partial, to these questions. It will demonstrate that by midcentury, there was firmly-established in the country an intricate network of shops, the number and variety of which continued to increase to the end of the century. Among institutions, not the least important was the small back-street shop, the existence and prevalence of which has been ignored. To set these themes in context, it seems desirable first to spell out briefly the views expounded in historical writings about retail shops, the relevant economic changes during the century, as well as the institutional foundations that enabled retail shops to increase.

Despite Westerfield's pioneering study of English middlemen, published over half a century ago, no systematic study of shops and shopkeeping in the eighteenth century has been undertaken.[1] The readily-available studies are either too specific or too general. Concerning individual shopkeepers, two are of special interest: the autobiography of William Stout of Lancaster for the early part of the century, and T.S. Willan's analysis of the activities of Abraham Dent, a midcentury shopkeeper in Kirkby Stephen, Westmorland. Both are good sources for current business practices but too restricted to serve as a basis for a study of the retail network.[2] The survey of shopping practices by Dorothy Davis, on the other hand, sweeps over eight centuries and is not designed as a history of the retail trade. It has almost no information on eigthteenth-century provincial shopkeepers and only brief descriptions of shops in London. With these few exceptions, the retail trade in the eighteenth century "remains a complete historical blank."[3]

In contrast to the paucity of material for the eighteenth century, there are excellent studies on various aspects of the retail trade in the nineteenth century. The result has been a tendency to underrate, if not ignore, developments in the previous century. J.B. Jefferys sees no change either in the structure of the trade or in the techniques of selling and displaying goods until the latter half of the nineteenth century. Prior to 1850, the distributive system "still bore the marks of a pre-industrial economy,"[4] one in which shops, few in number, catered only for the more affluent and workers purchased their goods at markets or from pedlars. A similar view is expressed by Peter Mathias. He links the rise of small grocery shops and "multiple retailing in the food trades" to the increased purchasing power of urban workers during the latter half of the nineteenth century.[5] In several articles on markets and the retail grocery trade, Janet Blackman also stresses the importance of the market for workers, but dates the rise of small back-street shops to the 1830s.[6] David Alexander locates their rise in the 1820s and concludes that the first half of the nineteenth century witnessed major changes in the distributive system.[7] For Alison Adburgham, the Napoleonic wars serve as the watershed, after which a new pattern of retail distribution emerged. She too contends that in the trade of clothing shops no changes occurred during the whole of the eighteenth century.[8] If historians of nineteenth-century retail trade differ concerning the nature and time of change in the system, they agree that the eighteenth century was a fallow period.

Dating the course of change is notoriously difficult. When do increments of change become turning points? Moreover, if the focus is on the nineteenth or twentieth centuries, increments of change occurring in earlier periods are likely to be overlooked or unexplored. Thus, Clapham saw the emergence of a modern system of distribution in the first half of the nineteenth century; Alexander, whose study is based on evidence for the years 1810 to 1850, around 1820; Mathias and Jefferys, for the period they were particularly concerned with. The changes these studies document are not in question. The problem is rather that their comments on the eighteenth century are impressionistic.

Even an increase in the number of shops has been questioned. Clapham's confident assertion of "their very rapid multiplication during the eighteenth century" has been largely disregarded.[9] True, W.G. Hoskins noted the increasing size of the shopkeeping population in Exeter during the eighteenth century. Shopkeepers, he says, formed one of the most prominent groups in the city in 1792, topped only by those involved directly or indirectly in the carrier trades.[10] More recently, Willan essayed the opinion that "shops were more numerous and more important than is commonly realized."[11] But these historians are exceptions.[12] The more commonly held view is expressed by Mathias:

In the eighteenth century, the retailing of beer and spirits was the most widespread form of retailing at fixed points of sale, in established shops. There were, of course, many other shopkeepers who kept permanent establishments apart from their market stall, but they were fewer in number and practically confined to the towns. As a whole, one might say that the main development of retailing at fixed points of sale came only after the birth of the epithet "a nation of shopkeepers."[13]

The implication is that on the eve of the industrial revolution or ca. 1780, shops numbered less than 50,000, an incredibly low figure that has gained currency because of the lack of firm data to refute or confirm it.

It would thus appear that the retail trades stagnated throughout the eighteenth century and, depending upon what is considered sufficiently momentous modifications of the system, until well into the nineteenth. Such a view fits uncomfortably into the general picture of the economic and social life of the country and seems incomprehensible. D. Davis, seeking to explain the apparent lack of innovative activities during the eighteenth century, suggests that "so much of the nation's energy and imagination was being drawn into industry and foreign commerce that none was left to fertilize the retail trades with new ideas."[14] But would either have flourished if the retail network linking producers and merchants to the ultimate consumer had not responded with increased and improved facilities? Indeed, it is a view that has recently been challenged. In a study proclaiming *The Birth of a Consumer Society* and a "Consumer Revolution" in the eighteenth century, Neil McKendrick asks why "so little attention has been given" by historians "to those hordes of little men who helped to boost the demand side and who succeeded in exciting new wants, in making available new goods, and in satisfying a new consumer market of unprecedented size and buying power."[15] The answer lies, in part, in the lack of evidence concerning those "little people." Even McKendrick, who has argued cogently on the importance of fashion and its commercialization in creating and extending demand, has added little significantly new information on the country's shopkeepers.[16]

However important the "compleat English tradesman" may have been to an increasingly commercialized nation, he has left few commercial or personal records of his activities. While contemporaries describe vividly the elegance of the shops and their prosperous proprietors in the fashionable centres of London and some of the leading towns in the provinces, we catch only a glimpse of *mere* shopkeepers whose income and life-style placed them among the lower echelons of the middling groups. And yet such shops performed indispensable services without which a take-off into sustained economic growth would hardly have been possible.

Indeed, with a few exceptions, most notably Defoe, shopkeepers did not receive a good press in the eighteenth century. In 1695, John Carey, a Bristol merchant, described shopkeepers not unfavourably as "the wheel whereon the inland trade turns."[17] But to many eighteenth-century critics, it was a torture wheel exacting blood from the pockets of the poor and one, moreover, that was multiplying far in excess of the needs of the community. It was a judgment based on a *mentalité* that looked back to a mythical Merrie Ol' England, to a past that looked suspiciously at, if not with hostility upon, all those who bought to sell again without altering the object disposed. Few would have agreed with Adam Smith that retailers were "productive labourers" who performed essential services by "breaking and dividing ... rude and manufactured produce into such small parcels as suited the occasional demands of those who want them." Breaking and dividing might not have appeared to Charles Townshend as altering the form of the object sold. Nor would the critics of the village shops have accepted Smith's argument that "nothing can be more convenient" for a poor workman "than to be able to purchase his subsistance from day to day, or even from hour to hour, as he wants it."[18]

"The prejudices ... against shopkeepers and tradesmen" that Smith observed among contemporary writers were not adopted by nineteenth-century political economists. Their attention was focussed on other sectors of the economy, in particular, the supply side of the equation. To classical economists, demand was unproblematic, a response to the supply of goods in the market. The major engines of growth were the factors of production. And historians studying the eighteenth-century economy followed in their footsteps. Improvements in agriculture, the rise of industries, the increase in overseas trade and shipping, changes in inland transportation, the establishment of provincial banks and the extension of credit facilities, and the changing structure of the labour force are among the subjects that have received extended study. Not until Keynes did economists return to the view of Adam Smith and take a serious look at the role of demand in stimulating economic growth.

At the same time, historians, whether debating the standard of living question or the deeper "causes" of the industrial revolution, have been exploring the conditions of the home market during the eighteenth century. Although differences of opinion remain concerning the timing, extent, and significance of the changes, there is a general consensus that the home market was buoyant and expanding during most of the eighteenth century, that demand for imported consumer goods and manufactured commodities was increasing as a result not only of growth in population but also of a rise in real incomes for most if not all groups. But the retail facilities available to distribute that increased quantity of goods has received little attention. They remain, as R.M. Hartwell has noted, a "neglected variable" of the service sector. The "Service Revolution" in advanced economies has however engendered an increased awareness of the importance of the service sector in the processes of economic growth and there has been a growing interest in the time sequence of structural changes.[19] It is hoped the following chapters will provide a rough map of the distributive trades in that century of change and contribute something to the on-going discussion of changes in the structure of the economy. They will show that the growth of fixed-shop retailing, as well as many of the innovations currently attributed to early or mid-Victorian entrepreneurs, had their inception in the eighteenth century.

The major focus will be on the shopkeeping trades with only passing references to market traders and licensed hawkers. The area covered is confined almost exclusively to England and Wales, not by design, but because of the nature of the records used. Only a brief and partial view of shopkeeping in Scotland towards the end of the century can be offered. The study aims to provide some firm evidence and to offer tentative conclusions concerning activities within the shopkeeping world, in particular: the size of this sector of the economy and the geographical distribution of retail shops; the changing functions and types of shops serving the public; and the general business practices adopted to meet the needs of a society undergoing revolutionary changes.

CHAPTER ONE

Response of the Retail Sector to Economic and Social Changes

The business practices of William Stout provide a point of departure for the changes that occurred during the eighteenth century in the retail sector of the economy. Stout commenced business in 1688. To stock the shop he mounted horse and travelled with other shopkeepers of Lancaster to London, a five-day journey. He carried with him almost his whole capital in cash, £120. In London, he purchased from sundry tradesmen to whom he had been recommended goods to the "value of £200 or upwards, and paid each of them about half ready money, as was then usual to do by any young man beginning trade,"[1] the other half to be paid on his return the following year. After collecting his goods and seeing them safely on board a ketch, he and his fellow shopkeepers began their return journey, Stout stopping on his way at Sheffield where he laid out £20 for Sheffield and Birmingham wares.[2] For years Stout made an annual pilgrimage on horseback to London and Sheffield, usually in the spring, to acquire his stock. The whole trip took about three weeks. And if he often had pleasant company on the road, he and his fellow travellers were subject not only to inclement weather, impassable roads, and dubious inns, but also to the greater hazards of highwaymen. They must certainly have been prime targets, carrying as they did, their ready cash with them.[3] Finally, in 1709 on a trip to Sheffield, having bought what goods he needed for ready money, he "took the names of the makers, soe as after to order what I had ocation for; and gave orders to Samuel Shore [an ironmaster and factor] to take them in and pack them and send them to me, allowing him a small sum as commission. And continued so ever after for many years without the trouble or charge of a journey thither."[4] A little later, the annual trip to London come to an end when his cousin set up as a drysalter there. Henceforth, his cousin served as a source of supply for drysaltery and also purchased the other goods Stout needed.[5] How Stout settled his accounts at Sheffield and London after these changes is not clear. He does not seem to have used bills of exchange. Carriers could, of course, have carried money as well as goods, and often did.

Stout did not purchase all his stock so far afield. Cheese he got at the Garstang and Preston fairs. Nails and other ironware were purchased locally as was most of his tobacco and much of the sugar. He also turned to Liverpool and Bristol to supplement his supply of tobacco and sugar. In addition to drysaltery and Sheffield and Birmingham wares, he also stocked earthenware (purchased in London, not nearby Staffordshire) and household utensils. In 1709, tobacco, "the most profitable" of the commodities, represented one-third of his sales; iron, one-quarter, that is, almost 60 percent of his sales. Sugar was, it appears, fairly low in the hierarchy of consumer goods in 1709. Indeed, the proportion of groceries in the total annual sales was probably quite small.

Stout stocked his shop the first year with £300 worth of goods in preparation for the summer fair. For the principal shopkeepers of Lancaster, the annual fair was a major event, serving as a means of attracting potential customers for a considerable portion of their goods, particularly the more durable ones. The weekly market brought in customers for the smaller and the more perishable articles. As a shop apprentice, Stout was principally employed during weekdays in preparing and packaging goods for market day – such things as sugar, tobacco, brandy, nails, and prunes, the latter in packages of 1 and 2 pounds. He tells us that in the summer they sold about 100 pounds of prunes weekly. On market day, he and his fellow apprentices were "fully employed ... delivering goods."[6] The impression one gets is that the periodic fair and market were still vitally important to principal shopkeepers, despite the fact that Lancaster had a sizeable population. One can also presume that the market area for the major tradesmen of Lancaster was fairly widespread. Coward, Stout's master, extended his trade by establishing two branch shops, one at Boulton Holmes, the other at Cockerham. Thomas Green had a branch shop at Burton near Kendal, Westmorland. Stout himself sold iron to customers in Yorkshire.

Stout, like all principal shopkeepers, sold both retail and wholesale to a large number of customers. From 1688 to 1698, his loss by "insolvent debtors" amounted to £220, distributed among 248 debtors.[7] The number of solvent customers must have been considerably higher. During the first year of business, sales for ready money amounted to £450; for credit, £150. If his memory served him right, the average mark-up that year was close to 100 percent, stock having cost him £300.[8] Stout does not state his own mark-up, but the figures he gives for Coward show a mark-up of 200 percent on tobacco and 38 to 55 percent on prunes. These may well have been exceptional examples; they were, as Stout admits, very profitable articles.

It is possible that Lancaster is not representative of commercial activities in other parts of the kingdom, that the winds of change had already opened up commercial avenues in the southern counties. Nevertheless, Stout's autobiography does describe in an unselfconscious manner traditional practices. What strikes one most forcefully is the slow, unwieldy movement of goods from producers and suppliers to the final consumers at the turn of the eighteenth century. Periodicity still dominated the retail trade. Despite the fact that the tradesmen of Lancaster kept "open shop," a *continuous market*, they appear little different than the stallholders in the weekly market or fair. The fair determined the timing of their journey to London and elsewhere for stock. And it was an annual affair. How restrictive or destructive such a practice must have been! To plan for sales one year in advance must have been particularly taxing on the less experienced, resulting in bankruptcy for the overoptimistic and reduced sales for the more cautious and conservative by nature. One may also wonder how much satisfaction such a system gave to consumers. Were they always able to obtain what they were prepared and willing to pay for, or did they have to restrict their desires to what was available, wait for the annual restocking or just save their money?[9]

Moreover, throughout the system of distribution, in striking contrast to later decades in the eighteenth century, buyers sought suppliers. The shopkeepers of Lancaster not only had to travel to London to purchase goods from their fellow tradesmen, they also had to seek manufacturers for the goods they required. Stout even appears to have acted as his own shipper. Changes occurred during Stout's business career, but they were minor and fortuitous – a cousin in London and an ironmonger and factor whom he got to know in Sheffield. Both eased his burden somewhat. In one respect, the tradesmen of Lancaster were very fortunate compared to their inland brethren. They were close to the small creek, Poulton le Fylde, a customs port. As a consequence, Stout was able to purchase much of his tobacco and some of his sugar at mercantile prices. A ready stock of tobacco was probably always on hand at the customs port. Ironware was also easily obtained from nearby manufacturers. Is it then surprising that these two products formed an important source of trade and profit? Indeed, with respect to Stout's transactions in tobacco, the line distinguishing the merchant and shopkeeper was blurred.

Just as tradesmen of Lancaster sought suppliers, so too did the final consumers and small shopkeepers from outlying areas. Customers were drawn by the market, fair, and the *continuous market*, not by any particular inducements proffered by the shopkeepers of Lancaster other than their wares. Stout even disdained "inviting" to his new shop "any of my master's or neighbour's customers," a practice he claimed was "much then used." Nonetheless, he "had good encouragement ... at Midsummer Fair." And wherein lay his success? Stout appears to think it was due to his policy of setting "the price at one word" without bargaining or abatement, that "such plaine dealing obliged worthy customers and made business goe forward with few words."[10] Perhaps, but the impression conveyed is that the shopkeeper was a passive seller of his wares, offering no enticements to incite demand. The goods rested in chests and drawers, ready to be shown and priced on request. One may even doubt if shopkeepers competed in any real sense. The friction between the drapers and hatters, who "envied the drapers for their selling hats," expresses an attitude reminiscent of the restrictive practices of the guilds.[11]

The sources of supply and the transport of goods followed traditional patterns, although changes were occurring. London remained the major source of supply for groceries, household wares, and drysaltery. But the increase in the import and consumption of sugar was shifting at least a portion of the trade to the more convenient ports of Bristol and Liverpool, both were to become increasingly important as wholesale centres. With the exception of ironmongery, most goods came by coastal vessels. In this respect, England, as Willan has pointed out, was particularly fortunate in having "more usable coastline per square mile" than any other major European country,[12] undoubtedly contributing not a little to England's later fame (or infamy) as a nation of shopkeepers. Stout provides less information on inland transport. He and his fellow travellers used horses. And he mentions iron being brought from Leeds by pack horses. In 1689, due to war with France, Lancaster received its London merchandise by land carriage, shipped by wagon first to Standish from where the Lancaster tradesmen arranged its carriage home. They paid "3s. to 5s. a hundred bringing them from Standish to Lancaster."[13] Stout does not say whether or not there were any local carriers to distribute wares from Lancaster. Perhaps most goods were carted home by the purchasers themselves.

Some information on wholesale prices was available to Lancaster tradesmen on their annual buying expeditions to London and elsewhere. However, there is little evidence of any general commercial awareness that would have enabled Lancaster shopkeepers to buy at the most favorable market. On the other hand, Stout appears to have been well informed on the import prices of tobacco and sugar at Liverpool, Bristol, and Poulton le Fylde, and he took full advantage of it. But these transactions were basically mercantile and the information was easily available at Lancaster. On the whole, one has the impression that Stout and his fellow shopkeepers remained staunch customers after their initial introductions to their suppliers and did little shopping around. Could they have done otherwise given their purchasing practices – practices conditioned by a system of distribution and communication that had changed little in the preceding century and were largely dominated by the market and fair?

During the eighteenth century, many economic and social changes were effected that gave rise to a better integrated and structured system of retail trade. Inland transport was facilitated by improvement in the condition of the roads, more navigable rivers, and the construction of canals. Although London remained the most important single centre of trade, the rise of outports as distributive centres enabled shopkeepers to escape the dominance of the metropolis. By midcentury, it was complaining loudly against competition of the outports that attracted "retailers in their neighbourhood," who "instead of repairing to the London market ... furnish themselves at those which are nearer and cheaper."[14] The new facilities enabled shopkeepers in areas remote from London to save both time and money.

Equally important was the emergence of a nationwide carrier system that brought within the circuit of trade many out-of-the-way communities. In the 1760s, Kirkby Stephen, a small market town in Westmorland, was extraordinarily well served. It had regular carrier service to Newcastle, Stockton, Barnard Castle, Lancaster, Kendal, Sedbergh, and Kirkby Lonsdale, and via Kendal to London. The unsung heroes of this inland trade were the carriers. Eight, not including the London carriers, plied the service from Kirkby Stephen to points north, south, east, and west, connecting this remote market town to all parts of the kingdom.[15]

At the same time, demand for consumer goods increased. The expansion of the home market was the result of a number of interrelated forces. The quickening of industrial activities and changes in the organization of agriculture brought about an ever-larger number of workers almost wholly dependent on wages. Most experienced an improvement in their disposable income. The margin between

income and expenditure for subsistence enabled all but the most
deprived to purchase some imported consumer goods and the
cheaper manufactured articles. The workers were at least free to
spend their money on what critics of the "poor" considered extravagant "luxuries," such as tea and sugar. In addition, the proportion
of the population in the middling ranks increased. Their incomes
were well above the subsistence level. It has been estimated that by
1780 some 20 to 25 percent of the population had incomes sufficient
to allow an average household expenditure of thirty pounds per
annum on manufactured goods and commercial services.[16] These
changes were accompanied from midcentury onward by a sustained
increase in population.

Throughout the century, the proportion of people living in urban
settlements increased strikingly. According to P.J. Corfield, 68 towns
in England and Wales had a population of 2,500 or more in 1700;
104, in 1750; and 188, in 1801 – an increase of 176 percent. When
the century opened, 18.7 percent of the population of England and
Wales were living in towns of 2,500 or more inhabitants; at its close,
urban inhabitants numbered 2.7 million or 31.6 percent of the total
population. The growth of urban population in the provinces was
even more remarkable. In 1700, urban inhabitants in the provinces
accounted for 7.5 percent of the total population; in 1801, 19.9
percent, almost a threefold increase. By then, the total provincial
urban population was almost double that of London; in 1700, it was
only 68.7 percent. The increase in the number and size of towns was
not, however, distributed evenly throughout the provinces. Much of
the growth took place in the Midlands and the industrial north. By
the end of the century, the former urban predominance of the south
was overtaken by that of the newer industrialized areas. Wales, on
the other hand, remained far behind the rest of the country. In
1700, no town qualified as an urban settlement; in 1750, 2. But
during the latter half of the century, urbanization quickened, at least
in South Wales. In 1801, 3 Welsh towns were in the 5,000–10,000
category, and 4, in the 2,500–5,000. Of the 8 towns, only 2 were in
North Wales. The level of urbanization in England was relatively
high even in 1700; by 1801, it had become, as Corfield notes, "one
of the most densely populated countries in the world."[17]

The rising level of demand was expressed by increased consumption of home manufactured goods and foreign imports. During the
period 1709–11, the average annual retained imports of sugar was
40.9 million pounds; during 1799–1801, 322 million pounds. Tea
increased from 122,600 pounds per annum to 16 million pounds;
rum, from 18,341 gallons to 2.3 million gallons; tobacco, from 10.6

to 15.3 million pounds. Figures for home industries are less easy to document but all economic indicators point upward, the most striking of which is that of printed goods. In 1713, 2.03 million yards were charged with duty; in 1800, 34.13. During the same period, the amount of candles and soap charged with duty merely doubled. However, the figures for both are somewhat suspect because of smuggling and the ease of evasion, as well as a drawback for soap used in the textile industry. No reliable figures for hosiery, silks, handkerchiefs, ribbons, and lace are available, but there is little doubt they formed an increasingly important part of the inland trade. The same is true for watches, cheap Birmingham wares, Sheffield plate, and chinaware, to name the most obvious.

The faster tempo of industrial and mercantile activities was accompanied by a quickening of the transmission of commercial information through a more efficient and extended postal system and by the rise of newspapers. At the same time, commercial transactions were eased by the rise of country banks and the more extended use of inland bills and promissory notes. This was the social and economic environment in which the shopkeepers of the kingdom operated and to which they responded.

By midcentury, the retail trade was being pursued with more vigour by both manufacturers and dealers. No longer did they wait passively for buyers to knock on their doors. The Birmingham and Sheffield manufacturers sent patterns with lists of prices to shopkeepers and other dealers who were expected to return the cards with their orders within a month.[18] It was a well-established custom by the 1770s. Walthal Fenton of Woodhead near Cheadle received pattern cards "of the newest and best oval gilt and plated with the prices."[19] The firm informed him that "we shall be glad to receive your commands – any of them may be had cheaper but will be much inferior in quality."[20] Such pattern cards enabled small shopkeepers to extend their range of goods. Fenton, a draper by trade, did not stock ironmongery but ordered specific items requested by his customers. Much of his trade in breeches and waistcoats was conducted in a similar fashion. Presumably his London dealers supplied him with patterns. In 1770, "Jackson's Habit-Warehouse" was selling ready-made masquerade dresses and had available, for its customers, "a book of several hundred prints coloured, which contains the dresses of every nation."[21]

Just as manufacturers sent out pattern cards, the major shopkeepers of London and the larger provincial towns sent circulars to their customers. The earliest printed circular we have been able to locate is 1778, but the formats indicate they had been in use for a number of years. The London firm of Smith, Nash, Kemble and Travers, wholesale-retail grocers, informed its customers in 1779 that "unfortunately we have just received information of the loss of Grenada ... which has caused an advance in Raw sugar ... Refined sugars are very scarce and dear, but will be more Plenty in a Month or six Weeks, and hope cheaper ... We shall be glad to see you in Town if it suits your convenience, but if otherwise, shall endeavour to execute any Orders you may favour us with, on the same terms and with equal Attention."[22] There followed a list of prices for sugars, dried fruits, teas, coffees, pepper, spices, Spanish juice, and rice. Walthal Fenton received printed circulars from Charles Brewster, a London wholesale-retail tea dealer. Among tea dealers it was customary to send out circulars after the East India Company Sales. Brewster's May 1781 circular lists a range of prices for various kinds of tea, coffee, chocolate, and cocoa: for example, "congou teas – 5s. 9d., 6s. 6d., 7s. to 7s. 6d." Fenton, having determined the needs of his customers, remitted an order to Brewster in June specifying the quality, kind, and price of tea, coffee, chocolate, and cocoa required.[23] But not only London dealers circularized their customers. William Tuke and Son of York regularly informed its customers on the state of the market and prices of tea, coffee, and cocoa. In April 1785 customers were advised that "Congous and Souchongs have sold higher than expected; other sorts are very reasonable. Thy orders, as occasion offers, will be executed on good terms, and oblige."[24] William Tuke was certainly not exceptional. Abraham Dent of Kirkby Stephen undoubtedly received circulars from some of his suppliers. The circular, usually one printed page, was ideally suited for the grocery trade as it allowed the listing of many different goods in a minimum of space. Its origin may have owed something to the printed catalogue issued by the East India Company throughout the century for its quarterly auctions. The printed catalogue had, of course, been used by the book trade for many years.[25]

By the 1780s, enterprising publishers were supplying tradesmen with the names, occupations, and addresses of the principal inhabitants of the country so "that no merchant or trader may be at a loss where to apply for any article or to establish a proper correspondence."[26] The appearance of commercial directories that aimed at a national coverage was no fortuitous event. They fulfilled a well-recognized need for those engaged in the inland trade and provided a ready list for the more aggressive tradesmen. The directory was to become a regular feature in the office of established tradesmen.

But more personal methods were also adopted to reach customers. Early in the century the outrider or commercial traveller made his appearance. The iron merchants, the Birmingham toy manufacturers, the West of England clothiers, the Manchester warehousemen, and the hat and smallware manufacturers among others sent their personal representative to solicit orders from shopkeepers and other dealers, and sometimes to collect money due. It was, one might say, a small shift from travelling with samples to the fairs to meeting the major shopkeepers at their doors; but it certainly quickened and eased inland distribution and generated demand. The traveller not infrequently was an owner of the firm. In the 1750s, John and Nathaniel Philips, Staffordshire smallware manufacturers, made the rounds themselves, pushing, along with their tapes, hats made by their uncles in Manchester.[27] John Fothergill, a partner of Matthew Boulton, sought orders from London shopkeepers in 1762 but found it no easy task as other Birmingham toy manufacturers were also canvassing the dealers. He informed Boulton that Cantrell, a London jeweller, told him that "Taylor Gimblett Ward and Rabone had been with him like so many wolves for orders, the former offer'd him any encouragement he would accept of for the sake of a little business.[28]

The major wholesale-retail grocers, tea dealers, and drysalters quickly followed suit. By midcentury, commercial travellers were being employed by many London tradesmen, and no doubt by the larger provincial dealers.[29] The purpose was to drum up business. Francis Garratt, who commenced trade as a London tea dealer in 1760, told Henry Dundas that "at this time I was in the habit of travelling the kingdom for the purpose of selling tea, but [due to the largescale smuggling] found it was almost impossible to do any business within 30 miles of the sea coast."[30] In addition to obtaining orders, the traveller, particularly if he was a partner in the firm, frequently settled accounts and assessed the customer's credit worthiness. Various members of the Twining family on their tours of the country remitted orders to the London shop, collected money, and reported on the business of their customers and the general state of the trade.[31] Highly respectable and well-established firms, such as the Twinings, Garratts, and Travers, disdained the use of hired commercial travellers, preferring a more personal and dignified approach by occasionally visiting their customers themselves, a method that no doubt served to cement the tie between supplier and buyer. The more agressive, rising firms had no such scruples in their search for new customers. That the hired traveller represented an intrusive force, one which was encroaching upon the trade of the older, traditional firms, can be seen by the reaction of Smith, Kemble, Travers and Kemble. In a postscript to a circular, the firm observed: "it is possible some in the Trade may offer Teas, etc., at lower prices, in particular those who keep Riders, but you may depend upon it that no House of Credit shall undersell us of the same good quality."[32]

According to recent studies of the retail trade, the eighteenth-century shopkeeping world was characterized by extraordinary passivity, constrained by traditional methods of retailing and the socio-economic milieu. Advertising, window display, price-ticketing, and other methods of attracting new customers and creating demand were not adopted until the midnineteenth century. Such aggressive sales techniques were, from the shopkeeper's point of view, self-defeating because demand was inelastic and the retail market, restricted. Traditional fair-trade norms abjured competition and enjoined cooperation, or at the least an equitable sharing of the limited market. Permeating the system was a "live-and-let-live attitude"; to encroach upon another shopkeeper's bailiwick was little short of poaching. The goal of the shopkeeper was to maintain a regular and steady clientele; the means, "his reputation and skill" in providing desired goods and services.[33]

It is a picture redolent of a genteel trade catering to the leisure class, of shopkeepers who took pride in their aristocratic patronage and whose mode of conduct conformed to the norms of their clientele. It is not completely false but it is a partial picture and illuminates only one type of shop. Moreover, many of the generalizations are simply wrong. Then as now, there were shopkeepers who confined their trade to "ladies and gentlemen" and who disdained the use of "vulgar advertising." But they represented an ever-diminishing proportion of the trade. Within the shopkeeping world, there was room for many different sales techniques which largely depended upon the clientele served. If some looked askance at "open advertising," others pursued it with vigour, and still others used it hesitatingly. Such diverse attitudes were not confined to shopkeepers. One finds them among those innovating entrepreneurs, the manufacturers.

Matthew Boulton and Josiah Wedgwood each established salesrooms or shops in London to promote his wares. One might say that in this area of activity, they were functioning as shopkeepers. Both were fully aware of the sales value of aristocratic patronage and assiduously pursued it by gifts, personal relations, and letters. It was, one might say, a multisided sales campaign to attract buyers who set the fashion. Both resorted to signed advertisements in newspapers as well as anonymous articles about their wares.[34] Nonetheless, certain differences are apparent in their view of what constituted an appropriate form of salesmanship. From the beginning, Wedgwood aimed primarily at the aristocratic market. Pall Mall was excluded as a site for a showroom because it was "too accessible to the common folk."[35] Although he advertised extensively, he did so with some reluctance, fearing it would cheapen his wares in the eyes of those whom he sought to attract. And he resolutely banned the use of handbills from his showroom. They would, he told Thomas Bentley, "sink us exceedingly. We have hitherto appeared in a very different light to common shopkeepers."[36] Boulton, on the other hand, had no scruples about advertising and his marketing techniques for "toys" were designed for the widest possible market. The London agent, Richard Chippendall, was roundly criticized for attempting to restrict the trade to the more exclusive outlets. Boulton informed him in no uncertain terms:

We think it of far more consequence to supply the People than the Nobility only; and though you speak contemptuously of Hawkers, Pedlars and those who supply *Petty shops*, yet we must own that we think they will do more towards supporting a great Manufactory, than all the Lords in the Nation, and however lofty your notions may be, We assure you we have no objection against pulling off our Hats and thanking them 4 times a Year and must beg you will allow us to do it. It is certain that Buckles ... will sell, and therefore let it be understood, once for all, that we mean to follow the fashion of all Countries and confine our Sales to *this World alone* and to such members of it as will pay their debts and do their Business peacably, rationaly, genteely and without incessant squabbling.

We have Agents in most parts of Europe, as well as in most of the great Towns in England, and we have considered London and its environs as your province; provided you take pains to supply every safe and respectable Dealer in Buckles from St. Jame's Street down to Wapping.[37]

Such contrasting views and actions were echoed within the retail trade. It should also be noted that without a receptive shopkeeping system, even a Boulton or a Wedgwood would have found it extremely difficult to market his wares. The problem for the historian is, of course, evidential. No single great retail entrepreneur of the stature of a Boulton or even a Lipton emerged during the eighteenth century, at least none has left his correspondence and business records. The changes occurring in the system have to be pieced together from scattered sources.

Indeed, eighteenth-century shopkeepers were competing for trade far more vigorously than is generally conceded. The traveller and the circular provide incontrovertible evidence that the principal shopkeepers of the kingdom were not depending solely upon "reputation and skill" to attract custom, but were actively seeking to

extend their trade. There was, in the first place, considerable jock-
eying for position between the leading shopkeepers in London and
those in the rising provincial centres of the country. Bristol, Liverpool, Hull and Glasgow became increasingly important as wholesale
centres for inland manufactured goods and legal imports, particularly sugar, tobacco, and rum. To these goods should be added the
flourishing trade in illicit tea, tobacco, and brandy. In these trades,
London dealers were, as they claimed, placed in a very disadvantageous position. They were required to pay the high duties strictly
enforced at the London port, while traders in the outports could
obtain goods considerably cheaper due to the widespread "connivance of customs officers."[38]

Londoners fought the battle against provincial dealers on two
fronts: by seeking the assistance of the government for stricter control of the provincial trade and by more aggressive sales techniques.
For example, in 1751 London tobacconists proposed that no tobacco
or snuff be removed below a line running through Carlisle, Hexham,
and Newcastle (unless from those towns) without a proper certificate
showing all duties had been paid. Not surprisingly, the proposal was
opposed by provincial dealers. Those in Leeds observed that orders
were "commonly brought by Carriers, Watermen, Howmen and
Bargemen, who came to town after, and return before the usual
Office Hours, and sometimes on holidays when certificates are not
to be had in which cases it may not be possible to comply with the
order till the next return which frequently does not happen in seven,
sometimes not in fourteen days."[39] They feared such "inconveni-
ences, delays and disappointments" would force their customers to
repair to London dealers who were not so restricted. There was,
moreover, a further hazard. As the permit was to list the supplier
and buyer, "it will discover the names of his customers and the extent
of his trade to the Officer who by communicating the same to others
may detriment [sic] him in his business" – little sign here of the
much-lauded cooperation of tradesmen. Indeed, the reaction of the
dealers in Leeds bears the mark of a highly competitive market.

Tea was an even more valued commodity of the illicit trade. While
a major portion of the legal trade went through the hands of London
dealers who had easy access to the East Indian Company auction,
illicit tea was largely a provincial trade, even if at times financed by
Londoners. As the century advanced, the illicit tea trade constituted
an increasingly greater obstacle to the sale of legal tea, one that the
the East India Company, the government, and the London dealers
in particular were only too well aware of. In 1767, after repeated
requests from the company and the London dealers, the government

lowered the duty on tea for a period of five years. It was an ill-fated experiment that cost the company dearly and left the fair-trade dealers of London as besieged as before.[40] In the 1770s, the Association of London Tea Dealers was formed to institute measures to protect the legal trade and was instrumental in effecting a number of new excise restrictions. The most important law was the act of 21 Geo. 3 c. 55 (1781), which was specifically designed to protect the London fair-trade dealer. By this act, no tea above six pounds could be moved into the London Bills of Mortality and no tea exceeding forty pounds (not in the original chest in which it was imported) could be removed at any one time from one dealer to another between places outside the limits of the Bills. The following year the quantity permitted to be removed outside the limits was reduced to twenty pounds.

The restriction was a mortal blow to the provincial tea dealers, licit or illicit, and caused an uproar of opposition, particularly from Bristol and Hull. The Bristol dealers observed that the "City of Bristol is the principal market for the greater part of Wales" but the restriction would make it exceeding difficult, if not impossible, for Bristol to supply satisfactorily the shopkeepers in Wales. Vessels came from Cardigan "but once in three or four months"; from Neath and Haverfordwest, once in six weeks to two months; and from Pembroke and Newton, once a month or six weeks. The vessels will not now be able to "take a sufficient quantity to supply the demand from one voyage to another." And although "a vessel arrives from Cardiff every fortnight, that place and the country round it cannot now be sufficiently supplied notwithstanding" the Bristol tea dealers have sufficient in their warehouses "to supply all ... [their] country dealers." Moreover, while there were several carriers for the counties of Gloucester and Somersetshire, "it is hard that the shopkeepers who may want about 80 to 100 pounds ... must be at the extra expense of several packages when one might do and employ many carriers when one might bring the whole."[41] Bristol reminded their lordships that "Parliament is the guardian of all people" and trusted it "will not encourage those who reside in one part of the kingdom to the prejudice of those who reside in another." But, if the clause "respecting the quantity of tea ... is not repealed, it will of necessity transfer the customers of every trader in Bristol who will not be limited to 20 pounds weight to London."

The dealers of Hull informed their lordships that they and other "dealers in tea in many cities and large towns in the kingdom without the Bills ... of London frequently sell large parcels of tea from 50 to 100 pounds weight and upwards at one time but are apprehensive that they shall sustain a considerable loss by being totally deprived of that trade." While they and the other fair dealers in the country are "subject to so great a restraint on their trade, the dealers ... in ... London enjoy an unlimited privilege of sending to their correspondents tea in any quantity and in any package." They feared the restriction would "divert the channels of trade from them wholly to the dealers ... in London."[42] The Board of Trade admitted the act would create "some inconvenience, particularly at Hull and Bristol," but agreed with Excise that it was necessary in order to prevent smuggling.[43] The large quantities of tea illicitly landed all along the coast opened up new channels of distribution which enabled provincial dealers to offer stiff competition to their counterparts in London.[44]

What is too frequently overlooked in the conventional description of the retail trade in the eighteenth century is the dual role played by the principal shopkeepers of the kingdom. Almost all served both the wholesale and retail trade. The picture of the "high-class luxury trade" of the grocer "drawing its customers from the middle and higher income groups" ignores completely the wholesale side of the counter, which for many was as important, if not more important, than the retail counter.[45] One suspects that some of the innovative marketing techniques employed by eighteenth-century shopkeepers owed not a little to their role as wholesalers where the forces of competition were keener. The riders and circulars sent out by the London grocers were not specifically designed for their "high-class" retail customers.

Indeed, in contrast to the somewhat restrictive facilities available to William Stout, by midcentury country shopkeepers could obtain their stock from a wide list of suppliers who were both willing and able to supply goods at frequent intervals. And shopkeepers took advantage of the choice open to them. This can be seen in the records of Abraham Dent of Kirkby Stephen who, between 1756 and 1777, purchased goods from 190 suppliers. In 1763 alone, there were 47 suppliers situated in various parts of the country. It is interesting to note that Dent purchased almost all his groceries from provincial dealers.[46] His comments seem to indicate that he kept a close check on the quality and prices of goods from different suppliers and shifted his trade or reduced orders when dissatisfied.

The wholesale-retail shopkeepers dealing in drapery, haberdashery, and "toys" experienced a different type of competition. The records of Dent and Fenton show that country shopkeepers were able to obtain their wares directly from the manufacturers and not necessarily in large quantities. In 1767 Lillington and Penfold of

Norwich supplied Dent with 168 yards of crape for a total cost of £12 14s.[47] Abraham Dent was not a largescale shopkeeper, but he would have been a valued customer to the principal drapers and mercers in London and the major provincial centres. In 1763, the total cost of his stock amounted to £677, a considerable portion of which was for clothing materials. For these goods, Dent appears to have given most of his business to manufacturers rather than other shopkeepers. Such undercutting of the once-powerful drapers by the manufacturers must have created considerable disturbance in the trade and led to a highly competitive market. It would be interesting to know what discounts were allowed by the manufacturers for larger purchases.

The problem for the wholesale-retail dealers is exhibited in a somewhat different context by Matthew Boulton. The principal London jewellers controlled the fashionable trade of jewellery. Although Boulton was eager to promote the sale of his ormolu, he feared there was not "the least probable prospect of obtaining an extensive sale" of it through the London shops. He therefore relied primarily on his London agents to sell direct to the nobility and gentry. Not surprisingly, the jewellers disapproved. Messrs Wooley and Heming claimed he was ruining their own trade in ormolu. Boulton did not agree and reminded them that he allowed the trade "a 20 per cent discount (15 per cent with credit and a further 5 per cent on the net amount for prompt payment) and that when the shopkeeper had added his 10–15 per cent profit, this made a very reasonable profit."[48] Presumably Boulton charged private customers some 20 per cent more than the trade. In this instance, the competition was distinctly retail. But a similar competition must have arisen wherever manufacturers assumed some of the distributive functions formerly handled by factors or wholesale-retail shopkeepers. The shopkeeper would at least be forced to moderate his mark-up for the country trade. The competition engendered by illicit tea had, in fact, reduced the mark-up on legal tea to the point that on some sorts the London dealers claimed to have incurred a loss.[49] Indeed, shopkeepers throughout the system were becoming increasingly sensitive to both their cost and selling prices.

Price sensitivity reflected both the forces of competition and the more rapid flow of commercial information by trade circulars, newspaper reports, and business correspondence. In 1765, Abraham Dent was informed by his Lancaster supplier of sugar: "you'll no doubt think the prices are high, but are the lowest we are selling at and I do think they'll go a deal higher, that if you can at Newcastle do better you'd do well to lay in a stock."[50] How quickly market

information was transmitted and how it affected the pricing policy
of shopkeepers is shown in the letters of Richard Twining. During
the French Revolutionary Wars, there was always the possibility that
the annual June arrival of the East India Company's China ships
would be long delayed. Any suspicion that the fleet would not arrive
at the usual time sent shock waves throughout the tea trade. In June
1802, Richard Twining observed: "I see nothing in the newspapers
as to the arrival of the China ships: and if they should not arrive
before the Sale, some people may be eager to buy, and teas may sell
higher than they ought to do." Twining argued that there was no
reason to suppose they would not arrive or that there would be any
"scarcity of tea." He, therefore, advised his son to "buy sparingly"
anticipating a greater "scarcity of money than of tea."[51] As Twining
said later, he never desired "that sort of temporary benefit which,
upon some occasion, we might derive from the fleet's non-arrival."[52]
Not all dealers held the same opinion. In 1804 rumour spread that
the China ships would be detained and the prices of tea shot up –
unnecessarily as it turned out. By August, Richard Twining II reported to his uncle that he and his father "are pleased at the well-
timed arrival of the Chinese fleet. My father thinks it will not be
necessary to alter the prices of the green teas going this week as the
quality is so good and the tea is also sifted."[53] The problem the
Twinings faced with the prices of green teas is illustrated in the
father's description of the plight of the "Misses B," regular customers
of the Twinings:

Misses B told me this morning that they were plagued by the expectation,
which many people entertained, of an immediate and considerable reduction
in the Prices of Teas in consequence of the arrival of the China Ships and
of "the vast quantity of tea which there is in this kingdom." Some dealers
indeed had raised their prices beyond anything which was reasonable so as
to sell no green under 8s. and these Dealers have room for getting down.
But Misses B, not having advanced with them, cannot afford to fall with
them; and of this they are convinced.[54]

Apparently even small dealers in places far removed from the East
India Company's warehouses on Leadenhall Street responded rapidly to news about the China ships. The "Misses B" were country
shopkeepers, possibly in Norfolk and not, one gathers, in a large
town. At one point they "were obliged to buy some tea in Norwich
as the carrier disappointed them." Twining "advised them not to let
their stock be so low."[55] And yet they, like the Twinings, had to keep
a sharp eye on the pricing policy of their fellow shopkeepers. After

an East India Company June Sale, Richard Twining advised his son that "as the general account will be that common Congous are cheaper, we must, I think, lower the sort which we usually recommend – such as the 4s. 11d. of last sale – 1d. a pound."[56]

A rather intriguing form of competition one which also reveals pricing policies, is reported from Colchester. Richard Twining sent up an order to London for John Mills whose tea shop was on the High Street. It consisted of one chest of green tea at 7s. 6d. a pound, one chest of souchong at 7s. 4d., and one chest of hyson. The price and quality of the latter, however, were creating problems. Twining asked if it were "possible to send any of a worse quality than his last at 8s. 8d. and at a lower price – even a worse quality would be something – for his 9s. now is so good that it interferes with the sale of his 10s. – so then any Bloom fine enough to mix with and reduce his Hyson?"[57] Retail customers too, it would seem, were alert to price differentials. The "Misses B ... were plagued" that customers would desert them for shops that high-lighted reductions; John Mills found his customers bypassing the 10s. tea for the cheaper but almost-as-good 9s. hyson. And his was one of Colchester's high-class shops.[58]

Credit remained characteristic of commercial relations but the period allowed shortened as the century advanced. By the last quarter three months credit appears to have been the norm in the grocery trade. Davison Newman and Company advised a Norwich shopkeeper that "if you can be well recommended to us as paying punctually in three months we shall be ready to deal with you or sending a bill at that date with your order. You may depend on the best services."[59] The Travers firm also appears to have conducted its business on a quarterly basis. An 1805 circular offered "three months credit. Such of our friends who remit in One or Two months will be fully compensated either in quality or price."[60] The quarterly auctions of the East India Company may have been one of the forces leading to a shortening of credit in the grocery business. After the Commutation Act of 1784, the buyers of tea at its auctions were required to pay both the cost of the tea and the duty on prompt day, usually one or two months after the end of the Sale.[61] At the same time, manufacturers were offering inducement for ready payment. As early as 1753, J. and N. Philips and Company gave 5 percent discount for bills at one month from the dispatch of the goods, or no discount and payment at six months. When business was tight they occasionally allowed two and a half percent discount with six months credit.[62] Other manufacturers were doing the same, Peter Stubs gave discounts for early payment to trade customers and to his agent and he himself received similar discounts.[63] Sometimes the initiative came from the shopkeepers. In 1793, Archibald Turner of Glasgow asked Peter Stubs "for 10 per cent for payment within one month, and Sorley and Stirling for 20 per cent for immediate payment."[64]

Even in areas remote from the main centres of trade, shopkeepers appear to have effected shortening of credit terms, at least for their trade customers. The ledger of a relatively small shopkeeper near Bangor gives the date of purchase and the time and form of payment of his customers, a number of whom are identified as grocer, hatter, mercer, linen-draper, druggist, or bookseller. A few accounts specify the items charged, for example, tea, ribbons, hats, and indigo, but most debits are "to goods." Of the twenty-eight customers charged in 1784, eighteen paid within three months. There were the usual slow payers but not many went beyond six months. The accounts were largely settled by "bill" or "draft," with one customer regularly remitting half-pennies in part payment. Some customers received discounts, presumably for early payment, although not all who paid within three months were so fortunate, at least the discount was not recorded.[65]

Not only were credit terms shortening but dealers were also becoming more cautious in extending credit to trade customers. In January 1756, John Latham clockmaker of Wigan, sent a small order of £4 4s. 1d. to Abraham Dent for payment on delivery, "which I hope you cannot take amis. But before you'l want any more I shall enquire your charrecter which, if good, as I hope it is, I will alow you Comon Credit with the next."[66] The inquiry must have proved satisfactory as Dent received credit on his next shipment. Davison Newman and Company informed a Norwich shopkeeper that we

are much obliged to Messrs Butler and Hammond for recommending you to us and had a letter from them accompanied yours it would have been satisfactory. But were we to send goods to persons who write to us as verbally recommended by Gentlemen travelling the country, we should frequently get into indifferent hands. Our intention is to use our friends well but before we can open an account upon credit we must have some knowledge of the character and circumstance of the person.[67]

When business was slow and money scarce, credit accounts were scrutinized even more closely, at least by the more experienced and established tradesmen. In 1802–3, tea dealers suffered a decline in their trade, largely due to hefty increases in duty. As early as September 1802, Richard Twining was lamenting the decline in profits and foreseeing "the necessity of a diminution of expenses."[68] It took the form of a reduction in purchases at the East India Company's auctions and a retraction of sales to doubtful correspondents. In December 1803 Richard Twining stated he was "very glad that our trade with Scotland is *at this time* reduced within narrower bounds, i.e. that we do not send *so much tea* to Scotland as we did. And I think we shall do well *in these times* to confine our dealings *beyond the Tweed* to those persons whom we have reason to consider as undoubtedly good and punctual."[69] Tightening of credit continued for several years. In 1805, Twining informed his son that "McDougall wrote another letter desiring to have his lot of tea and saying that he always had paid regularly and would pay regularly for what he still owed. Nevertheless I did not send his teas; but repeated the susbstance of your letter."[70] Sales, however, began to improve; purchases at the auctions increased and little was said concerning the hazards of credit accounts. By 1807 trade was buoyant and optimism reigned; gone are the dismal prognostications of past years and also the memory. The Twinings, like their fellow businessmen past and present, responded to the current economic environment. "Nothing," said Twining, "can check the disposition of teas to keep up, if not to get up! And yet what trade there has been for some years past, or is there [anything?] so desirable as our Trade?"[71] As C.R. Fay once expressed it, capitals "rush around, like electrons, in search of profit: deny them their reward, and they will vanish, to reappear in a more congenial atmosphere. They are at once nervous and importunate."[72]

The Twinings and the Newmans were reacting like their forbears. No astute businessman in earlier centuries willingly extended long credit to dubious correspondents. The difference was a matter of degree of control. By the latter part of the eighteenth century, the tempo of the inland trade had quickened, due in no small part to a vastly improved carrier service. Shopkeepers were now able to buy in small quantities at more frequent intervals and keep on hand a smaller stock. As a consequence, suppliers were in a much better position than their predecessors to insist upon regular payments and to shorten the period of credit. McDougall would have to settle his accounts more promptly with the Twinings or find another supplier. At the same time, inducements were being offered to those who paid under three months. The shortening of credit by the major suppliers had a rippling effect throughout the retail trade. It may not yet have reached such remote areas as Penmorfa in North Wales, but on the main thoroughfares of the country it was fast becoming the standard mode of conducting business. Indeed, well before the end of the century, shopkeepers were taking pride in paying ready money. James McGuffog of Stamford, Lincolnshire, who specialized in apparel for ladies and "made all his purchases with ready money" was certainly not unique.[73] Peter Davenport Finney ran a profitable grocery and confectionary shop in Manchester in the 1750s. One of the reasons for Finney's success, according to his brother, was his "custom of buying with ready money."[74] Thomas Griggs of Ballingdon, Essex, was a typical mideighteenth-century pluralist. He was at once clothier, grocer, and malster; his grocery wares were purchased with the promissory notes received from the sale of textiles. And he appears to have always paid cash for his London purchases "possibly because he was allowed a discount off the purchase price."[75] Finney and Griggs were undoubtedly exceptions to the general custom of their day. But by the last two decades of the century, ready-money purchases and sales were being featured by shopkeepers in various parts of the country.

By the end of the century, the wholesale functions once performed by the fair had long since fallen into desuetude. All that remained of the great fairs was the trade in livestock and some foodstuffs. Gone too was the packman merchant. Both had been replaced by pattern cards, circulars, and commercial travellers that allowed the shopkeeper to order goods when and as he needed them and from whomever he wished. This, we suggest, was a momentous change in the methods or channels of distribution, one that introduced into the trade a far greater measure of competition than the old ponderous system engendered. The retail trade had also shifted. In the seventeenth century, the fair was still an important source of supply for the great houses, but the eighteenth century witnessed the demise of almost all its retail trade except for trifles. Shops, which had begun to encroach upon the trade at the fairs even in the seventeenth century, were firmly established by the eighteenth century.[76] The weekly market remained the most important source for butchers' meat, poultry, vegetables, and fruit throughout the eighteenth century; shops were, however, beginning to retail some of these items, particularly poultry and fruit and, in the larger centres, vegetables. Itinerant traders continued to peddle their wares, but the number of licensed hawkers declined. They were, however, an active group of competitors to the drapers and haberdashers in small towns. There was another type of small pedlar who hawked his wares within the town. The pedlars sold bread, vegetables, fruits, and a variety of other small items. How large a group they were is impossible to say. As they were basically an urban phenomena, their numbers probably increased in the nineteenth century. But, with the exception of meat and vegetables, there seems little doubt that by the end of the eighteenth century the retail trade was largely in the hands of shopkeepers, many of whom were petty chandlers.

When William Stout first set up shop in Lancaster, the retail trade, confined within narrow limits, still bore the marks of an agricultural society. By the end of the eighteenth century, England had broken through the barriers of a pre-industrial economy and was emerging as the first industrialized nation. The growth in demand for consumer goods that accompanied the social and economic changes stimulated the retail trade and in the course of the century more and more shopkeepers responded to the opportunities now opened to them. Methods to secure supplies were modified; more efficient means of transportation employed; credit facilities improved and terms shortened; customers enticed to buy; and competition throughout the system intensified. The changes effected during the century facilitated the movement and sale of an ever-increasing quantity of imported and manufactured goods. Indeed, many of the innovations that revolutionized retail distribution in later centuries were conceived and executed in the eighteenth century. For their full realization, however, further changes were necessary in the economic and social structure. The retail system marched in tandem with the other changes occurring in society. The following chapters will demonstrate how this was accomplished.

CHAPTER TWO

Number and Geographical Distribution of Retail Shops, 1759

Contemporary estimates have hitherto served as a basis for determining the proximate size of the retail sector of the economy. Unfortunately, their numbering of shopkeepers and tradesmen inspires little confidence. From King's modest figure of 50,000 in 1688,[1] the number rises to 100,000 in Postlethwayt's 1757 estimate, 162,500 in Massie's account for 1759, and then drops to 74,500 in Colquhoun's 1803 estimate (see table 1). King and Colquhoun have both been acknowledged as careful and cautious political arithmeticians.[2] Certainly, Massie's very high estimate contrasts uncomfortably with that of Postlethwayt, a difference of over 60 percent in two years! But even more so is the contrast between the estimates of Massie and Colquhoun. Did the number of shopkeepers decline during the famed "take-off into sustained economic growth"? Was there a drain from retailing into industrial entrepreneurship? That hardly seems likely. In fact, Mathias, to whom we are indebted for unearthing Massie as a worthy member in the rostrum of eighteenth-century calculators, is himself extremely skeptical of this particular estimate. At the same time, few historians question Colquhoun's incredibly low figure. If King's and Colquhoun's estimates are accepted, there had been little growth in shopkeeping during the eighteenth century. Indeed, the number of persons per shop had increased from a ratio of 110 in 1688 to 125 in 1803. The categories may not, of course, be comparable. Did Gregory King intend his figure to include publicans? If so, his estimate for shopkeepers is very low. In 1700, Excise recorded 39,469 victuallers and 746 common brewers.[3] Colquhoun does recognize the distinction, and his numbering of publicans is substantially correct. But what kind of shop had he in mind whose proprietors earned an average income of £150 a year? As shall be shown, such a high average income leads one to suspect that

Table 1
Estimates of Shopkeepers and Merchants, 1688–1803

	Shopkeepers and Tradesmen	Merchants
Gregory King, 1688	50,000	10,000
M. Postlethwayt, 1757	100,000	15,000
Joseph Massie, 1759	162,500	13,000
P. Colqulhoun, 1803	74,500	15,000

Source: King and Colquhoun, see Colquhoun, *Treatise on Indigence*, 23; Massie, see Mathias, "Social Structure," 43; Postlethwayt, see his *Britain's True System*, 321.

Colquhoun's enumeration was largely confined to major shopkeepers. In short, without further corroborating evidence, the estimates are questionable.

Excise accounts and papers form one of the richest sources of information on tradesmen. Their reliability is attested by the organization and administrative procedures devised for collecting excise duties. Since the seventeenth century, the revenue under the administration of Excise had been increasing with the number of commodities taxed. By mideighteenth century Excise had a relatively efficient organization that succeeded in escaping some of the more reprehensible abuses current in other collecting agencies. Indeed, towards the end of the century, it featured many of the bureaucratic characteristics of Max Weber's ideal type so antithetical to the ambitions and temperament of the ebullient Tom Paine.[4] By the early nineteenth century, Excise was serving as a model for the reorganization of Customs and for a corresponding establishment in Ireland. In fact, some of its officers were seconded for the latter task. Acting within the boundaries defined by acts of Parliament, Excise, through its local, regional, and national organization, was able to keep a firm hand on the pulse of an increasingly commercialized nation.

The chief office in London had at its disposal a vast amount of information concerning the activities of traders and shopkeepers in England and Wales. How detailed and accurate that information was can be shown by a brief description of the regional organization and the accounting controls enforced by the chief office.[5] The whole country was divided into collections (see map 1), each under the direction of a collector whose major responsibility was to collect and transmit the revenue to London at stated intervals. The geographical area covered by a collection varied enormously, depending largely upon the amount of revenue-producing activities within the area.

For the whole of Wales there were only four collections, whereas four were required for Devonshire and Cornwall. Rarely were the boundaries of a collection conterminous with a county. Often a collection included small contiguous areas of several counties.[6] Starting at the southwest corner of Cornwall, the collections, each consecutively numbered, moved east and west across the country to their northern terminus in Northumberland. The last number was reserved for the most important revenue-producing collection, the Bills of Mortality of London.

Each collection was subdivided into districts numbering from four or five to eight or more. The supervisor of the district was mainly a disciplinary officer. He checked the activities of the inferior officers; recorded in his diary the names, places of abode, and description of the traders in his district, and transmitted the information at regular intervals to the chief office. A district was further divided into six to eleven rides, the size of which was determined by the number of traders a ride officer could conveniently survey. For each ride a scheme was drawn up with the names of every place to be surveyed and the number and description of the traders. In the country collections, the ride officers were stationed in small towns or villages centrally located within the area under their survey. It was the duty of the ride officer to survey the rooms, places, and ustensils of every manufacturer of, and dealer in, an exciseable commodity, and to record the various charges due from each trader. Eight times a year the ride officer submitted a return to the chief office in London of the various charges levied upon each person under his survey. These vouchers, as the returns were called, formed the foundation for the charges raised at the chief office against the collector of the area. After completing the vouchers, the ride officer drew up an abstract listing the total amount of the commodities charged to every trader in the ride. Having been duly inspected by the supervisor of the district and checked against both the supervisor's and ride officer's diaries and account books, the abstract was forwarded to the collector. On the basis of the amounts posted in the abstract, the collector levied the duties charged against each individual trader. It was the responsibility of the collector to attend at every market town eight times a year at specified dates to receive the duties payable by the traders.

Unfortunately, very few reports and accounts have survived. Only after an immense amount of search was a detailed description of the geographical boundaries of excise collections discovered, and even then the excise map originally accompanying the account had apparently been lost.[7] If fire had not destroyed a large portion of the records of Excise, its documents would provide a far more comprehensive account of inland trade during the eighteenth century.

It would be folly to assume that each excise officer performed his duties diligently and faultlessly, although, as Paine observed, negligence was soon followed by discharge. Nevertheless, Excise was the most efficient collecting agency at the time, effectively enforcing checks and double checks on all officers responsible for the revenue. Equally important, stored at the chief office in London was very precise information on every individual in the country required to pay any of the numerous duties. Fluctuations of activities within an area were duly registered and, if necessary, changes in the boundaries of a ride were effected. Major changes, such as those occurring in the industrial northwest and the Midlands, required a redrawing of the boundaries of the collections. In the 1740s, there were only fifty collections, by the 1780s, fifty-five, due primarily to the additional collections created in the newly industrialized areas.

In addition to serving as a revenue-collecting agency, Excise also had policing functions. To the inland trader, that diligent rider must have appeared as an omnipresent evil spirit ready to pounce on the unwary at the slightest mis-step. If the ostensible aim of the multifarious laws was to protect the revenue from fraudulent use or abuse of exciseable commodities, they also gave Excise the means to observe the movement of a great number of goods within the kingdom. Those governing the sale and distribution of tea illustrate how minute and specific the regulations were.

As early as 1724, detailed and specific regulations of the tea dealers' trade were enacted by Parliament. In subsequent years, especially 1745, 1748, 1779, and 1780, new legislation added to or repealed various sections of earlier laws. The following account summarizes regulations enforced by Excise on dealers in tea at the turn of the century. Many of the laws also applied to the sale of coffee, cocoanuts, and chocolate. Sellers or dealers in tea, cocoanuts, chocolate, and coffee were required to make "entry in writing of the several and respective warehouses, storehouses, rooms, shops ... to be made use of ... with the nearest officer for inland duties." No coffee, tea, etc. "shall be sold, uttered or exposed to sale, either by wholesale or retail" except from such entered places (10 Geo. 1, c. 10, sec. 10, 14). Every seller or dealer was required to have "painted in large, legible character, over the door of every shop" the words "dealer in coffee, tea, cocoa-nuts or chocolate, as the case may be" (19 Geo. 3, c. 69, sec. 18). In 1780, dealers were required to take out a licence clearly specifying the location of the shops used for trade (20 Geo. 3, c. 35). No tea, coffee, etc. were allowed into entered places without a written permit issued by an excise officer of the originating district and without first giving notice of the arrival of the tea to the officer of the receiving area. The permit specified the quantity, quality and, if tea, the colour – black or green – of the goods shipped (10 Geo. 1, c. 10). No tea above six pounds was allowed to be moved even to a private dwelling unaccompanied by a permit (12 Geo. 3, c. 46). Every dealer was required to enter each night in an account book provided by Excise the total quantity of tea sold that day in amounts under six pounds; and in a second book, each parcel of tea above six pounds. When the books were filled they must be returned to the excise office in exchange for new ones (10 Geo. 1, c. 10, sec. 35). Dealers in cocoanuts were not allowed to sell less than twenty-eight pounds at a time and were required to enter an account of the name and address of the purchaser (12 Geo. 1, c. 28, sec. 29). Along with all these regulations went the right (and duty) of the excise officer to inspect the stock on hand and to check the accounts to ensure there had been no fraudulent addition or reduction of the commodities under surveillance.

Without presuming a perfect record, the excise accounts of commodities taxed, if correctly interpreted, can be accepted as representing the minimum quantity available in the country.[8] Nor is there reason to doubt the reliability of data compiled by Excise concerning the numbers of licensed tea dealers, tobacconists, common brewers, victuallers, and shopkeepers, among others. When the government requested information, the chief office in London had recourse to its voluminous records or, if not immediately available, could order a survey by its army of officials. In 1784, William Pitt needed to know the amount of legal tea in the dealers' shops. Excise immediately compiled a survey of one-third of the collections, giving the quantity of black and green tea on hand in each collection and in the principal towns.[9]

Data on inland trade and traders were frequently sought by government when looking for new and fruitful sources of revenue. Just such a need gave rise to what is probably the most exhaustive coverage of inland traders for the mideighteenth century. The Seven Years' War created an unprecedented drain of government finances. As early as 1757, the Duke of Newcastle was receiving various proposals for new or additional taxes. One suggested a "tax on signs."[10] One proposed that a duty be laid on all "open shops and retailers" either at the rate of twenty shillings per annum or by a tax ranging from five shillings to twenty shillings in proportion to the rent of the house.[11] An even more elaborate plan was suggested ca. 1758 that "all merchants, wholesale and retail dealers" be required to take out licences ranging from ten shillings per annum to two pounds sterling, rated according to the land tax. "Public Marts, Markets and Fairs," were however "to be open for all sellers as before" and untaxed.[12]

Indeed, a tax on shops was being seriously considered.[13] On 13 January 1759 James West, secretary to Treasury, wrote to Excise requesting information concerning the number of shops or houses selling by retail in the Bills of Mortality and other parts of England and Wales.[14] The suggested tax on merchants and wholesalers had apparently been dropped. Within less than a fortnight, Excise submitted an account of the "number of shops within the Bills of Mortality and the Parish of Marylebone which sell by retail (alehouses excepted), without counting more than one shop to a house or including those that sell by retail on bulks or in sheds."[15] By April, Excise had prepared a full listing for each of the remaining forty-nine collections of the "number of shops or houses wherein anything whatever is sold by retail exclusive of alehouses and farmers' and labourers' houses unless they keep shops. Shops above stairs are not reckoned and double shops are reckoned but as one, in this account."[16] These two documents form the most detailed account of the number and distribution of retail shops for the eighteenth century. Confidence in the reliability of this enumeration of the nation's shopkeepers is attested by the methods Excise adopted to collect such information and by the trustworthiness of other excise accounts that can be verified. To interpret it correctly, however, requires some understanding of the scope of its coverage.

What was excluded by design is clear: alehouses and the bulks, stalls, sheds, and stands that dotted the streets of London and some of the larger market towns. Nor does the enumeration include market stalls. As James West specifically requested "retail shops," one may with reasonable certainty conclude that those who sold only by wholesale were also excluded. But as very few wholesalers outside London (and except for the warehousemen even in London) did not at the same time sell by retail, the distinction is perhaps more nominal that real. As "double shops" were reckoned "as one," Excise presumably counted only one shop to a building.

Why "shops above stairs" were excluded is somewhat puzzling. In 1775 a committee of unfree shopkeepers at York unsuccessfully contested the right of the city to require them to obtain their freedom claiming, among other things, "that the custom extended only to shops opening to the street and not to inward rooms."[17] The test cases particularly chosen for trial at York all concerned various places not immediately accessible from the street: "the door of which shop opened into an entry"; "the door of which was made up"; and "keeping an inner room" or "inward shop." Most of the cases cited in the report appear to be evasions of the by-laws of York, but there may have been current a subtle distinction between what was commonly considered a *shop* and selling by retail from an *inner room*.[18] It is possible Excise defined a shop narrowly as one the door of which opened directly to the street. Certainly, "inner" and "secret" places would have been difficult to identify and the officers may well have inadvertently overlooked such rooms. But that hardly explains the specific reference to "shops above stairs," a phrase not used for the enumeration of the Bills of Mortality. Possibly, it refers to a rather common eighteenth-century practice in the provinces where rooms, generally above a shop or in an inn, were used occasionally as a means of selling by auction or at an under-price.[19] It was a frequent complaint against licensed hawkers that among other "vile" practices they "take rooms and hold temporary auctions."[20] Such rooms were temporary places for the sale of goods and not shops in the ordinary sense of the word.

Similarly excluded were the houses of farmers and labourers "wherein anything whatever is sold by retail ... unless they keep shop."[21] The phrase reveals that Excise had attempted to distinguish those who sold by retail occasionally or in the course of their work from those who *kept* shop. In deciding who should be included in the enumeration, Excise was anticipating the intent of the forthcoming law and its enforcement. Certainly Excise had a vast fund of information on various types of tradesmen and was in a position to identify what might more properly be considered a retail shop. To excise officials, keeping shop had in all probability similar connotations to present-day usage – a shop "open" to the public at regular and continuous intervals where the merchandise on sale is displayed. The terms generally used in the York report on unfree tradesmen were showing, displaying, or putting to sale. The report on Joseph Williamson, a cordwainer residing in the Bedern, who was not free of the city of York and who had "doubtful" claims to exemption, particularly noted that he "exposed shoes to sale in his window next Goodramgate."[22] The precise criteria Excise adopted to differentiate a "shop" from other places where items could be purchased is not known, but the account submitted to Treasury was compiled with considerable care and deliberation.

Nevertheless, the excise compilation does include a few ambiguous areas. In the 1785 shop tax, bakers were specifically excluded, presumably because the price of bread and therefore profits were controlled by the assize. How Excise treated bakers is not known for sure. One suspects that those who not only baked for hire but also sold bread from their shops were counted; not, however, the much larger group of hucksters who sold in the market or elsewhere.[23] Artisans who worked for hire obviously did not qualify for inclusion, but in certain trades the shopkeeping aspect was beginning to predominate, particularly in the larger towns. For example, among the tailors, whipmakers, jewellers, watchmakers, and cabinetmakers were some who quite distinctly kept shop, and who displayed and advertised their wares and who were in many respects proprietors rather than artisans. Such shops were unquestionably included – so too the large shoe shops in London serving a high-class clientele and the "Yorkshire Shoe Warehouses," the *rendezvous* of the "night-men, penny-postmen and slaughter-house men" on a Saturday night search for cheap ready-made shoes.[24] But what of the village cobblers or the translators from whom the workers got their second-hand patchep-up shoes? Were they also included? Some perhaps – those like Joseph Williamson, who "exposed shoes to sale" and could be seen to "keep shop," or like Roger Hynd, shoemaker, who sold other sundries.[25] But it is unlikely that ride officers would look upon small cobblers as shopkeepers. Village cobblers probably escaped enumeration as did most village tailors. Many tailors were itinerant, working in the homes of those they sewed for, and could not remotely be considered shopkeepers.

Admittedly, no rigid line distinguishes working and shopkeeping artisans. There were certainly borderline cases. Similar ambiguities apply to the tradesmen listed in Pigot's directories and continue to plague classifiers. The problem was undoubtedly more acute in the eighteenth century, but Excise was not unmindful of it. In all, one can be sure the excise account included a wide range of shops from the elegantly fitted-out shops of the London mercers to the small chandlers whose shops consisted of little more than a scale and a few sundries. But despite the difficulties, the excise enumeration of retail shops in England and Wales in 1759 may be accepted as a fairly accurate account.

The number of shops within the London Bills of Mortality and the parish of Marylebone totalled 21,603; the remaining forty-nine collections, 120,097; or a total of 141,700 shops in England and Wales (see table 2, summary). It is perhaps no mere coincidence that Joseph Massie's figure of 162,500 shopkeepers in Great Britain corresponds so closely to the excise account, further corroborating Mathias's view that Massie had access to government papers. And as shall be shown, the excise account proved far more reliable than the data upon which Colquhoun presumably based his estimate.[26]

In addition to enumerating the total number of shops in the kingdom, the excise account of 1759 contains uniquely important information. By listing the number of shops in each collection, it enables one to reconstruct a hitherto unobtainable picture of the geographical distribution of the retail trade. As there is no map of the boundaries of the collections for 1759, it has been necessary to rely on the description accompanying the excise account of 1795–6. Fortunately, there were few changes in the collections during the intervening years and the information provided by Excise is quite detailed. It is, therefore, possible to draw the boundaries of a collection with a reasonable degree of accuracy. But in no instance does the administrative area of an excise collection coincide with the county it partially covers. Occasionally a collection covered a small part of an adjacent county. The collection of Barnstaple, for example, included a small coastal area in Somersetshire. The excise collections were designed to facilitate the efficiency of their administrative units, and while the county remained the principal organizing factor, awkward portions were incorporated within the more convenient collection. In the few instances where such small protrusions occurred, they have been ignored. The effect on the calculations would in any case be minimal.[27] More frequently, the collections straddle two or three counties. One cannot, therefore, ascertain the exact number of shops in a county. However, if one traces the boundaries of a group of contiguous collections and counties, it is possible to delineate an area within which the two different administrative units are conterminous, or almost. As the accompanying map shows (map 1), the areas distinguished differ considerably in size. The collections of Cornwall, Barnstaple, Tiverton, and Exon fall within the boundaries of Cornwall and Devonshire (Region I). A similar, almost perfect, fit occurs on the eastern coast (Region IV), the collections of Suffolk, Norwich, and Lynn coinciding with the counties of Norfolk and Suffolk. In order to equate the collections and counties for Region II, on the other hand, it was necessary to follow the boundaries of eleven collections (from Sussex to Gloucester) and eight counties (for the collections and counties in each region, see appendix 1).[28] Nonetheless, significant regional differences in the density of shops can be identified.

The ratios of population per shop are based on county population figures for 1751.[29] No attempt has been made to adjust for population increases during the intervening years, a refinement not warranted by the raw data.[30] The derived ratios will, therefore, understate the number of persons per shop by a factor of three or more.[31]

Map 1
Excise Collections of England and Wales, 1759

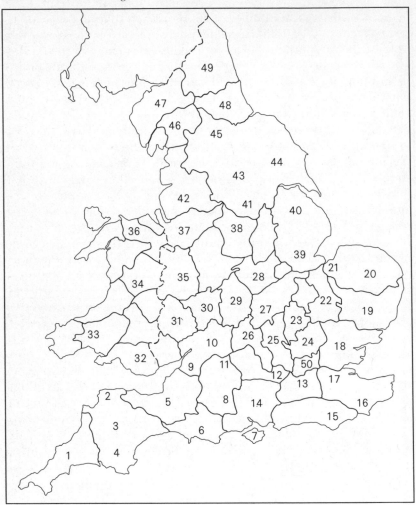

Note: Numbers indicate the approximate location of each collection.
Collections are identified in appendix 1.

In table 2, the collections are grouped into eleven regions. For England and Wales, the ratio of population to shop is 43.3; for England alone, 41.4. Far more revealing are the strikingly different ratios from one part of the country to another. The heaviest concentration of shops is in an area lying south of a line drawn across Lincolnshire on the northeast coast through Leicestershire, Warwickshire, and Gloucestershire to Somersetshire on the southwest

Map 2
Counties of England and Wales, ca. 1787

Source: John Cary, *Cary's New and Correct English Atlas* (London 1787).

coast (see map 2). Within this zone were 97,890 retail shops for a total population of 3,357 million, an average ratio of a little over 34 persons per shop. Excluding London, the ratio is slightly higher, 35.5 persons. For the rest of the country the average ratio is 63.5; omitting Wales, it drops to 58.8. Even if the estimates of population for individual counties are inaccurate, it is hard to believe they are

Table 2
Geographical Distribution of Retail Shops in England and Wales, 1759[1]

		Number of shops	Population 1751	Ratios – Population /Shop
London: Bills of Mortality & St Marylebone		21,603	650,000	30
Country Collections				
South of line:				
Region II		27,464	1,074,717	39
Region III				
(minus London)		22,775	636,323	28
Region IV		8,085	380,832	47
Region V		2,850	102,932	36
Region VI		15,113	512,384	34
	Total	76,287	2,707,188	35.5
North of line:				
Region I		6,037	438,425	73
Region VII		5,596	337,060	60
Region VIII		8,736	542,399	62
Region IX		16,077	746,626	46
Region X		3,275	269,102	82
	Total	39,721	2,333,612	58.8
Summary				
Wales		4,089	449,200	110
Total (excluding London)		120,097	5,490,000	45.7
Total (England and Wales)		141,700	6,140,000	43.3

Source: Same as appendix 1.

Note: [1]See appendix 1 for identification of regions.

so widely off the mark or so biased that they could possibly account for differences of such magnitude.[32] There is, moreover, some corroborative evidence that the difference in the ratios are not produced by inaccurate population figures. If one calculates the density of shops per square mile, the same striking contrast appears. For the area south of the line, excluding London, which would tend to distort the figure, there were just over 3 shops per square mile; for the rest of England, 1.6. Even Devonshire and Cornwall (Region I) fit the pattern for the northern counties, although it has been suggested that the estimated population for Devonshire "may well overstate its *level* by something like 30 percent."[33] For these two counties, the number of shops per square mile is 1.5. Note that their ratio is also higher than the average for the northern counties (see appendix 1).

However tentative the various calculations, it seems clear that shopkeeping was more advanced in the counties south of the line. Why that should be so is less clear. An agricultural map shows that these counties, with a few exceptions, lie within the lowland zone, an area characterized by mixed husbandry. In the lowland zone, the nucleated village was the predominant type of settlement, in contrast to the isolated farmhouse and small hamlet of the pastoral zone.[34] The lowland zone was also an area well served by market towns. The average market area in England was seventy square miles. With the single exception of Cambridgeshire, all the counties south of the line were at or below the average.[35] Both these conditions, ancient in origin, would tend to facilitate the spread of shopkeeping as the means of inland communication improved, as commercial activities quickened, and as an ever-larger proportion of the working and consuming population became increasingly dependent upon local markets *and* shops for their daily "necessaries" and "luxuries."[36] Counties outside the lowland, with their hamlets and isolated farmhouses, lacked an economically viable settlement pattern and in these areas shopkeeping lagged behind the rest of the country. Even by the end of the century, Lancashire had not achieved parity with the counties south of the line.

It is perhaps no mere accident of fortune that during the eighteenth century the largescale capitalistic hawkers were still known as "Manchester Men" or "Travelling Scotchmen," although both had changed the nature of their activities. North of the line, itinerant traders served the needs of the hamlet and isolated farmhouse, and their relations to shopkeepers in the larger market towns were, by and large, complementary rather than competitive. In the south, with its higher density of shops, most shopkeepers looked upon hawkers as dangerous rivals whose activities should be drastically curtailed or, better still, completely suppressed.

Of the two facilitating mechanisms for the spread of shops, the village seems to have played a more significant role than the market town. Lancashire, with a very high ratio of persons to shops, was better served with market towns than Cambridgeshire, Hampshire, or Surrey. Indeed, the village settlement pattern was even more important than density of population. Very sparsely inhabited areas such as Wales and the three northern counties obviously inhibited the development of shopkeeping, but a high density of population was not necessarily accompanied by a corresponding density of shops. Again Lancashire is a prime example although it is by no means the sole one.[37] In 1751, with a population density of 170 persons per square mile, Lancashire was surpassed only by Surrey and Middlesex. But until the rise of the cotton mills, "the increase in the population of Lancashire was not so much an urban increase as a thickening of the population over the countryside,"[38] a thickening, that is, of the hamlets and small farmsteads. It is revealing that until 1766 the parish register of Oldham in Lancashire, an area of farmer-weavers, records no trace of shopkeepers except the usual bakers, butchers, tailors, and shoemakers.[39] On the other side of the divide, fenland Cambridgeshire, with a population density half that of Lancashire — 84 persons per square mile — had an ancient and cherished village tradition. It also had a high density of shops.

It is not necessary to attribute a causal role to the village; other forces were at work. For centuries the fielden villages of the Midlands had been conservative institutions functioning according to traditional norms. The village provided only a potential market. To be translated into an effective demand that would make the shop a viable economic unit required a sufficiently large wage-earning population. And here too the lowland zone appears to have made the transition to a wage-earning population earlier than the pastoral areas and to a much greater extent, with a far larger proportion of its rural workers dependent almost wholly upon wages for their livelihood.

Did village life also encourage a spirit of emulation among the cottagers and labourers, a desire to own (or consume) a few shop-bought items sported by the resident squire, the yeoman, or the more prosperous craftsmen? In short, did village life also facilitate the diffusion of urban values? Questions can be raised and suggestions made, but until a great deal more is ascertained about local conditions, the answers remain tentative. One thing is clear. At mid-century, shopkeeping outside the lowland zone was, relatively speaking, in a primitive stage. An increase in the number and variety of shops in these counties awaited a more favourable economic and social environment, which the rise of industry in the latter half of the century would make possible.

Ratios of population per shop within each of the major divisions vary from one region to another (table 2). Wales, with the highest ratio, requires little special explanation. It lacked all the conditions necessary to sustain a high density of shops. Nor is it surprising that the two northern counties, Durham and Northumberland (Region X), ranked second. However, a legitimate question can be raised concerning the location in the northern zone of Region IX, comprising the counties of Derbyshire, Nottinghamshire, Yorkshire, and the northern half of Lincolnshire. The ratio for this area (forty-six) is slightly below that (forty-seven) for Norfolk and Suffolk (Region IV). It is possible that something more than half the population of Lincolnshire should have been allocated to this area (see notes 4 and 5, appendix 1). But if one takes as much as three-quarters, somewhat more than seems reasonable, the ratio would only rise to forty-nine not much above East Anglia. In fact, it is a moot question whether the line should not have extended from Teesmouth. Certainly the eastern half of Yorkshire and Nottinghamshire and most of Lincolnshire are within the mixed husbandry zone with its characteristic settlement of the nucleated village. But Western Yorkshire and Derbyshire are in the pastoral zone (see appendix 1 for the counties included in Region X). The region is a borderline case in every respect and the density of shops is likely to reflect its overall economic characteristics.

But what are we to make of East Anglia (Region IV) with a higher ratio than the southwest counties? True, the actual ratio is lower than that calculated; some Suffolk shops are listed in the Cambridge collection. But even if Cambridge and East Anglia are combined – a combination not warranted by the excise description of boundaries[40] and one that would present a distorted picture of shopkeeping in this area – the ratio is still high, a little over forty-four persons per shop. Possibly, population figures are on the high side. But it would require an overestimate of some 20 percent to bring it into line with other southern regions. Neither seems the answer. The average density of shops for Suffolk and Norfolk is 2.286 shops per square mile, which is 33.1 percent lower than the average for the counties south of the line. Could it be a mere coincidence that the average ratio of population per shop is also 32.7 percent higher? That hardly seems likely. Given the uncertainty of population figures, it would be folly to assume that a ratio for any one region was exact. But there is no reason to suppose that they are not measuring differential levels of shopkeeping between various areas. It seems reasonable to accept the ratio as an indication that shopkeeping in East Anglia was below that of other adjacent areas. Perhaps the explanation lies in part in the decline first in Suffolk and later in Norfolk of the old textile industries. At least they were not flourishing. And although the two counties were well dotted with market towns and substantial villages, in the wood-pasture areas "small hamlets and dispersed farms were generously sprinkled between the villages."[41]

For an explanation of the low ratio in the Home Counties (Region III, see appendix 1 for the counties included), we need look no further than the great Wen whose tentacles had long since reached into the countryside. Nor is the low ratio for the Midlands (Region IV) surprising (see appendix 1 for counties included). In addition to the village settlement pattern, the Midlands commenced early in the century those industrial changes which were to label the area the "Black Country." Did trucking, a practice not uncommon in the area, also increase the number of shops? We suspect so. Surely, Excise would have included in its enumeration shops such as those described by Peter Stubs.[42]

Perhaps more surprising is the relatively low ratio of population to shops for the country as a whole. By Gregory King's estimates, the average ratio in 1688 was 110 persons per tradesman. By 1759 it had dropped to 46 persons per shop.[43] During the intervening seventy years the population had increased roughly one-fifth (18.2 percent) while the number of shops had almost trebled, increasing 183.4 percent. It would appear that by the mideighteenth century, several decades before the famed "take-off," the shopkeeping world had already achieved a maximum growth rate, at least in terms of numbers. With the exception of the northern counties, and Wales in particular, which lagged well behind the national average, future growth in most areas would almost by necessity be tied to an upward movement in population. Indeed, as population increased in the fast-growing urban centres, a rise in the ratio of persons to shops could be expected. The densely populated London Bills of Mortality may well have reached that stage by 1759. The ratio of population to shops charged with assessed taxes in 1797 is very little below that of 1759.[44] True, the estimated population for the first period may be understated, and the number of shops not charged assessments in the 1797 accounts may be so large that their inclusion would reduce the ratio. But it is hard to believe that outside the City and Westminster, whose principal shops serviced a far wider area reaching out into the country, the metropolis could have supported a ratio much below the 30 persons per shop recorded in 1759 – neither in 1797 nor for that matter in 1897.

What difference the excise figures might make to the estimated proportion of the national product allocated to the commercial sector of the economy in the eighteenth century is difficult to say. But they do cast doubt on the customary timing of structural changes for at least one component of the service sector. Convention links a great increase in retail shops with industrialization, either concomitant or trailing after, and with urbanization. In England, at least, that increase appears to have taken place before the industrial sector had achieved revolutionary changes and when the proportion of the population living in urban centres of 5,000 or more may have been no more than 20 percent.[45] Unfortunately, there are no adequate enumerations of all retail shops in the nation for the late eighteenth or early nineteenth centuries. What is certain is that sometime, probably during the nineteenth century, the ratio of persons to shops began to rise. By 1950 there were ninety-two persons per shop.[46] What changed drastically in the two centuries since the excise survey was the annual turnover per shop. In 1950 the average annual sale per shop was £6,000.[47] In 1759, many petty chandlers probably sold no more than £200 worth of goods.[48] Nor are the two retail units comparable in terms of numbers employed. In 1759 few of the major shopkeepers in the market towns or even the larger cities, with the exception of London, would have had more than one apprentice and the business handled by the many small shops was hardly sufficient to fully employ one person. These were the areas of future growth in the retail trade, but a firm basis for their expansion had already been laid in 1759 by a complex network of shops, whose general features the following chapters will explore.

CHAPTER THREE

Functional Distribution of Shops

Economic historians have described the early eighteenth century as a period of substantial economic activities and changes. At the same time, prices, particularly for cereals, declined. For at least some workers, there was a rise in real wages that may have encouraged a greater demand for domestic and imported commodities. The consumption of tea and sugar, some of which found a place in the workers' diet, certainly increased considerably. And whereas the home trade in British manufactured goods is less easy to document, most signs point to an upward movement. Despite contemporary complaints of extensive voluntary underemployment, not all workers eschewed higher earnings in favour of more leisure. The excise survey suggests that many adopted new consumption patterns with their higher incomes and that the demand was met by an increasing number of shops. This chapter depicts the range of specialized shops called into existence by the consuming public and attempts to determine the changing proportions of each type during the second half of the eighteenth century.

For the first part of the nineteenth century, James Pigot's classified trade directories provide a guide to the range of specialized shop trades and their varying proportions in major cities and towns. No such easily accessible information is available for the eighteenth century. Without undertaking a far more extensive search into local depositories than has seemed feasible for a study of this scope, only a rough map of the general contours of the shop trades can be drawn. It does, however, cast some light on the subject and will enable us to compare the structure of major shop trades in the eighteenth century with that presented by Pigot for the early decades of the nineteenth century.

In both periods, shops varied enormously in terms of turnover, in degree of specialization, and in the range of commodities handled. At the most humble level were shops similar to the one described by "Mary Smith, chandler of Flixton, Suffolk, a widow," who sold "candles, bread, small beer and diverse other small articles." In 1752, 108 pounds of run tea were found in her shop and, having no money to pay the fine, she went to jail.[1] In the mideighteenth century, shops such as Mary Smith's may well have outnumbered all other types, although they hardly qualify as one of the specialized shop trades. Petty shopkeepers were not entered in Pigot's first national survey of 1822–3 and are not included in our classification. On the other hand, some of the larger village shops carried a relatively wide range of commodities in the grocery and household line. William Wood (1720–90) of Didsbury,[2] who owned the Ring O'Bello Inn, dealt in coal, and ploughed for his neighbours, was also a shopkeeper. At his shop, customers could purchase most of their daily needs: several kinds of flour (wheat and barley), meal, berm, bread, manchets (small loaves of wheaten bread), tea, coffee, sugar, treacle, currants, raisins, figs, salt, pepper, cloves, mustard, rice, candles, soap, starch, blue, and pitch sands. Such goods, with the exception of bread, formed the basic stock of small grocers, one restricted to the more commonly required goods. Few luxury articles were stocked. Wood did not, however, confine himself to groceries. He also had available for his customers potatoes, apples, plums, peas, and, in the dairy line, butter, cheese, eggs (very infrequently), and milk occasionally. Some of his more affluent customers could purchase fresh meat – beef, veal, mutton, lamb, and pork – as well as the more common bacon. He had on hand tobacco, snuff, and pipes, probably items stocked by the inn. Wood even provided his regular customers with "cash" for trips to Stockport, Manchester, and other nearby places.[3] In short, it was a fairly well-stocked village shop. In view of its narrow range of commodities and relatively small turnover, one would hesitate to rank it with the more specialized grocery shops. For William Wood, the shop was probably a sideline to the inn and his various other activities. One wonders how many such shops were sheltered under the wings of inns and public houses.

But while one can identify the specialized shop trades and distinguish the commodities handled by each, classifying the great diversity of shops scattered throughout the country is not so simple. Outside London and the larger market towns and cities few shopkeepers in the early eighteenth century could afford to confine themselves to one trade. At Lancaster ca. 1680, Henry Coward, master of William Stout, was grocer, ironmonger, and brandy merchant. When Stout opened his first shop in 1689, he too set up as grocer and ironmonger. (Stout did not mention brandy – perhaps his Quaker principles militated against retailing alcoholic beverages.) And both dealt extensively in tobacco. During Stout's lifetime, the sale of sugar increased enormously. In the 1740s, he estimated that in 1709 "not above one-quarter part of the sugar consumed here as has been since."[4] Tea, the consumption of which was beginning to increase during the last decade of Stout's business life (1719–28), was not mentioned and probably did not form one of his grocery items. With the rise in the consumption of tea and sugar in later decades, the specialized grocery shop would become a more viable unit in the larger towns. How many grocer-*cum*-ironmongers Henry Coward fathered is difficult to determine. Stout carried on the traditional combination, as did his apprentices.

If Lancaster shopkeepers combined iron with spices – a rather profitable combination in a largely agricultural area – those in other localities added groceries to draperies and not always by apprenticeship. Shopkeepers were no less venturesome than their fellow countrymen in grasping opportunities. Indeed, adding a new line of goods required very little additional capital or specialized knowledge. Their suppliers, who were just as eager to extend trade, provided both credit and trade information. Walthal Fenton, a draper at Woodhead near Cheadle, Staffordshire, took no chances with his transactions in tea. Customers placed their orders with him specifying the kind and quantity desired, which he in turn remitted to his London supplier, Charles Brewster, grocer and tea dealer.[5] Fenton does not seem to have sold tea from his shop. Rather he acted as an agent for Brewster who supplied him with price lists of tea, coffee, cocoa, and spices. Abraham Dent, on the other hand, was a full-fledged, grocer, draper, and book dealer. At his shop in Kirkby Stephen, a small market town in Westmorland, customers could purchase a wide variety of goods from the finest silk to lamp black. He even kept on hand flour, barley, hops, and bread, although the town had a flourishing weekly market. He does not seem to have sold any dairy products, not even cheese; and with the exception of gunpowder, no ironmongery. His was in truth a general shop and, in terms of the range of commodities and turnover, on a different level to Wood's shop at Didsbury.[6]

Across the hills in Penmorfa, Caernarvanshire, "Roberts" ran a very different style shop. In this remote Welsh village, groceries, even sugar, were a very minor part of the trade. And, as one might expect, there were no provisions or dairy products. He dealt, however, in a wide variety of dyes, drugs, ironmongery, as well as the usual household wares, and all kinds of goods in the drapery and haberdashery line, from pins to petticoats and breeches.[7]

While general shops of varying types and sizes formed the broad base of retail trade, at the head of the chain of distribution were the specialized shops, particularly the old and well-established trades of the draper, mercer, hatter, hosier, grocer, ironmonger, bookseller, and chemist. Pre-eminent were the opulent London shopkeepers who, like their lesser counterparts in the more important provincial towns, carried on a brisk wholesale trade from their elegantly furnished retail establishments. No analysis of the structure of the eighteenth-century retail trade would be complete without attempting to determine the relative proportion and importance of these various specialized shop trades.

Publicly announced bankruptcies provide an initial source of information. The announcements record the name, trade, and abode of those whose economic failures were sufficiently significant to creditors to warrant action. In that sense, bankrupts represent the more important, albeit insolvent, members of the business community. No such action would have been instituted against petty shopkeepers and chandlers – they simply languished in debtors' prisons or vanished without traces. Nor can it be assumed that all the important commercial failures were registered in the list. Bankruptcy in the eighteenth century was the court of last resort, a procedure devoutly to be avoided by all concerned. Until well into the century, even creditors, unless vindictive, might prefer to compound with debtors privately rather than seek redress by expensive commission proceedings that all too often consumed the greater portion of the available assets. The increase in the number of reported bankruptcies during the eighteenth century may, in part, reflect changes in the response of the business community to commercial failures.

The bankruptcy list is, admittedly, a selected sample of the commercial failures during any one year. However, for our purpose, the omission of petty grocers and chandlers is not important; and the reports do display a greater range of shop trades dispersed over a more extensive area than other available sources, particularly for the mideighteenth century. It may be argued that the quantitative data derived from such a source can hardly be accepted as representative of the commercial population. Surely, no sample, random or selected, perfectly reproduces the population from which it is drawn. But unless it can be demonstrated that the selective processes, economic or otherwise, involved in bankruptcy grossly distort the numbers reported for particularly shop trades, there is no compelling reason why they cannot be made to yield valid information concerning the relative proportion of the major shop trades in England and Wales. At the very least, the bankruptcy lists provide an easily available yardstick by which to test figures derived from other sources.

Tables 3, 4 and 5 summarize the results. They are constructed from the bankruptcy reports in the *Gentleman's Magazine* for the years 1748 and 1750, 1759 and 1760, and 1768 and 1770.[8] Three periods, each a decade apart, were chosen partly to see if any changes emerged, but primarily to provide a sufficiently large sample. Such a method, it was hoped, would dampen the effect of economic fluctuations on the incidence of bankruptcy for particular shop trades in any single year. The time span was centred on 1759, because it was the year of the excise survey and thus of particular interest. The year 1759 was, of course, a war year. But avoiding the possible effects of war would, in any case, have been difficult. Ideally an analysis of each year from 1748 to 1780 would have provided a less vulnerable sample, but it is questionable if the results would have warranted the amount of work involved in such a compilation – spot checks of nearby years revealed no remarkable differences.

We have classified the bankruptcies by broad occupational categories on the reasonable assumption that the trades listed in the reports are those in which insolvency occurred. One needs, however, to be aware that some shopkeepers may be hidden behind other trades. This is particularly true of those identified as merchants, a title which carried a higher status than shopkeepers. If a person became free of a city through a merchant company, he tended to retain the title whatever his current trade. This was certainly occurring in York. A number of individuals identified in the directories as *merchants* were in fact established shopkeepers. And in 1785 it was the Merchant Company of York which organized the protest against the shop tax.

In distinguishing shopkeeping from other occupational categories, a few trades have been included among shopkeepers which do not fully qualify as one of the old established shop trades. Most are artisan trades in which shopkeeping was assuming greater importance. The bankrupt tailors, breechesmakers, staymakers, and milliners were almost all Londoners with very fashionable addresses and undoubtedly shopkeepers. Also included among shopkeepers were those identified as cabinetmakers. Indeed, it would be surprising if cabinetmakers against whom bankruptcy proceedings were instituted were working artisans or journeymen. The cabinetmaker's shop "so richly set out that it looked like a palace" had long been a fixture in London and was beginning to make its appearence in the provinces.[9] True, artisan proprietors continued to repair and to make some furniture sold to their customers, but the eighteenth century witnessed a surprising amount of inland trade in ready-made, as distinct from factory-made, furniture. The larger shops in London also supplied the colonial market, although no cabinet-maker, to our knowledge, dealt exclusively in the export trade. It was from such shops that many provincial cabinetmakers obtained their more elegant furniture. There had been a brisk trade in ready-made chairs since the seventeenth century. The master tradesmen who organized their production and distribution were not, however, shopkeepers. It is possible, although highly unlikely, that they have been labeled cabinetmakers in the bankruptcy reports. If so, the occupational distribution of bankrupt tradesmen will be slightly distorted. But to have excluded cabinetmakers from the shopkeeping group because of this possibility would have equally falsified the picture.

Also assumed as shopkeepers were bankrupt jewellers, gold and silversmiths, and watchmakers. Again they were almost all Londoners with very fashionable addresses far removed from the journeymen's quarters in Clerkenwell and elsewhere. Shopkeeping was only one of the roles of these highly skilled artisans.[10] The only other artisan-shopkeepers about whom one might have some doubts are two London whipmakers.

Dealers in wine and spirits are omitted as retailers in some lists of nineteenth- and twentieth-century shops.[11] Whatever justifies the omission for the later period does not seem to apply to the eighteenth century. However, eighteenth-century dealers in wine and liquor clung tenaciously to the title merchant as the pompous advertisements in London newspapers and directories indicate. And similar dealers certainly existed in large provincial cities and towns. True, their trade was largely confined to customers who ordered in large quantities, usually not less than two gallons at a time. Perhaps because dealers in wine and liquor did less trade over the counter than the grocer or draper, and dealt more exclusively with customers who purchased by order, the proprietors considered themselves far above *mere* shopkeepers. They sought to retain the aura of the great merchant importers. But outside of London, Bristol, and Liverpool, with its West Indian rum, very little legal wine or brandy was brought into the outports.[12] One suspects that few of the so-called *wine merchants* in the provinces were importing their supplies, or for that matter all those listed in the London directories. Certainly many kept shops from which they retailed their ambrosia. We have, of course, included in the shopkeeping category only those clearly labeled wine and brandy merchants or dealers.

After some hesitation, pawnbrokers were included among shopkeepers. It is perhaps a doubtful entry. Also included is the lone Bristol "fruiterer," more as a token. The fruit stall was the norm, although the specialty fruit and vegetable shop had been creeping into London for some time. By 1770, such shops were appearing in provincial towns. It is not impossible that the Bristol fruiterer was a shopkeeper. His presence will certainly not distort the figures.

The baker is the most questionable entry in the shopkeeping category. Baking was an old, skilled trade. In London and in many provincial towns the assize continued to control the prices bakers were allowed to charge the public. They thus occupied a unique position in the shopkeeping world that Pitt recognized when he excluded them from the shop tax. They have been included among shopkeepers in part because of their changing role – in the provinces many bakers were beginning to retail other consumable goods.

The total number of bankruptcies for all categories during the six years surveyed amounted to 1,569; for shopkeepers alone, 586 (see table 3). The figures for individual counties are too small to allow a county by county comparison, but certain broad geographical distinctions are discernible. Not surprisingly, London leads the country with 43 percent (1759 and 1760) to 59.7 percent (1768 and 1770) of all bankruptcies, and 45 percent to 58 percent respectively of bankrupt shopkeepers. The breakdown for the provinces reveals significant differences between the counties north and south of the line drawn for the excise survey. In 1751, 43 percent of the provincial population resided in the northern counties but their proportion of bankruptcies was considerably less – ranging from 30.5 percent in 1748 to 34.9 percent for the years 1768 and 1770. The figures for bankrupt shopkeepers in the provinces are even more revealing. The counties north of the line contributed only 31.9 percent during the first period, 32.3 percent in 1759 and 1760, but rose to 36.4 percent in 1768 and 1770. In the 1759 excise survey, 31.5 percent of the provincial shops were in the area. It would seem more than a coincidence that the percentage of bankrupt shopkeepers echoes that of the excise enumeration. (Bankrupt shopkeepers in Wales reveal a similar correspondence to the excise figures – 2.5 percent versus 3.4 percent.) One may well wonder if the increase in the proportion of bankruptcies in the northern counties in 1768 and 1770 signals a corresponding increase in shopkeeping during the decade of the sixties. Certainly by 1797, the density of shops north of the line more closely approximated that of the south.

Table 3
Bankruptcies in England and Wales by Occupation, 1748 and 1750, 1759 and
1760, 1768 and 1770

	Number of Bankruptcies			Percentage Increase (+) or Decrease (−) Between Periods		
	1	*2*	*3*	*1 & 2*	*2 & 3*	*1 & 3*
	1748 & 1750	*1759 & 1760*	*1768 & 1770*			
Finance[1]	8	7	8	− 12.5	+ 14.3	—
Commerce[2]	146	157	204	+ 7.5	+ 29.9	+ 39.7
No. of merchants in this group	(77)	(69)	(116)	− 10.4	+ 68.1	+ 50.6
Manufacture[3]	70	43	94	− 38.6	+118.6	+ 34.3
Building Trades[4]	18	22	46	+22.2	+109.1	+155.6
Public Houses[5]	24	21	26	− 12.5	+ 23.8	+ 8.3
Brewing[6]	24	12	19	−50.0	+ 58.3	− 20.8
Miscellaneous[7]	5	9	20	+80.0	+122.2	+300.0
Subtotal	295	271	417	− 8.1	+ 53.9	+ 41.4
Shops	129	169	288	+31.0	+ 70.4	+123.3
Total	424	440	705	+ 3.8	+ 60.2	+ 66.3

Source: *The Gentleman's Magazine* for the relevant years.

Notes: [1]Finance – those included were identified as money scriveners or simply scriveners.

[2]Commerce – merchants, brokers, factors, packers, warehousemen, dealers, chapmen, salesmen, and carriers, including bargemen, etc.

[3]Manufacture – "manufacturers," clothiers, bay and sergemakers, hosiers and glovers (manufacturers), calico printers, dyers, clothworkers, sacking, button, paper, glass bottle, coach and engine makers, ironmasters, sugar refiners, as well as artisan trades such as shoemakers, saddlers, furriers, sword-hilt makers, etc.

[4]Building Trades – builders, carpenters, joiners, plasterers, masons, bricklayers, plumbers as well as the ship-building trades, such as the shipwrights, sailmakers, shipscrapers, etc.

[5]Public Houses – in the provinces those identified as innholders outnumbered the victuallers, twenty-nine to twelve; in London, on the other hand, there were twenty-five victuallers to five innholders.

[6]Brewing – brewers, malsters along with a few distillers.

[7]Miscellaneous – butchers represent slightly over one-half of this group (eighteen) and the number of bankruptcies increased from two in the first period to eleven in the third. In addition, three gardeners and three farmers were included. Presumably they were involved in trade. No occupations were given for ten of the bankruptcies and they have been included in this group.

Bankruptcy was not, of course, evenly distributed throughout the provinces. South of the line, Bristol, as one might expect, stands out; and the county of Norfolk contributed more than its share in terms of population. But the concentration in the counties north of the line is far more striking. In 1759 and 1760, Yorkshire and Lancashire accounted for 67.9 percent of all bankruptcies in the north

Table 4
Bankruptcies in London, 1748 and 1750, 1759 and 1760, 1768 and 1770

	Number of Bankruptcies			Percentage Increase (+) or Decrease (−) Between Periods		
	1	*2*	*3*	*1 & 2*	*2 & 3*	*1 & 3*
	1748 & 1750	*1759 & 1760*	*1768 & 1770*			
Finance[1]	5	3	7	− 40.0	+133.0	+ 40.0
Commerce[2]	84	69	137	− 17.9	+ 98.6	+ 63.1
No. of merchants in this group	(45)	(31)	(84)	− 31.1	+170.9	+ 86.6
Manufacture[3]	36	16	44	− 55.6	+175.0	+ 22.2
Building Trades[4]	13	13	39	—	+200.0	+200.0
Public Houses[5]	13	5	12	− 61.5	+140.0	− 7.7
Brewing[6]	9	5	7	− 44.4	+ 40.0	− 22.2
Miscellaneous[7]	1	2	8	+100.0	+300.0	+700.0
Subtotal	161	113	254	− 29.8	+124.8	+ 57.8
Shops	60	76	167	+ 26.7	+119.7	+178.0
Total	221	189	421	− 14.5	+122.8	+ 90.5

Source and *Notes*: See table 3.

and 66.6 percent of the shopkeepers. And most of the latter, 43.3 percent, were located in Yorkshire.[13]

Almost all bankrupt shopkeepers came from the industrial or commercial centres of the kingdom, county seats, or large market towns. For the first two periods, only 8 percent were located in nonmarket places. Moreover, some of these, such as Deal and Chatham, were sizeable towns well able to support specialized shops. By 1768 and 1770 the proportion of bankruptcies in nonmarket places had increased to 14.6 percent; very few, however, were obscure places. (These bankrupts were usually identified simply as "shopkeepers.") Apparently, bankruptcy proceedings were reserved for those shopkeepers located in the more important centres of the country.

The geographical distribution of bankrupt shopkeepers bears some correspondence to the density of shops in 1759. There are also some striking and thought-provoking differences in the number and proportion of bankrupt shopkeepers compared with other tradesmen. Tables 3, 4 and 5 list the number of bankruptcies by occupational category for each of the three periods surveyed. Of the total number of bankruptcies in England and Wales, the proportion for shopkeepers rose from 30.4 percent (1748 and 1750) to 40.9 percent (1768 and 1770). More revealing is the increase in the number of

Table 5

Bankruptcies in the Provinces, 1748 and 1750, 1759 and 1760, 1768 and 1770

	Number of Bankruptcies			Percentage Increase (+) or Decrease (−) Between Periods		
	1	*2*	*3*	*1 & 2*	*2 & 3*	*1 & 3*
	1748 & 1750	*1759 & 1760*	*1768 & 1770*			
Finance[1]	3	4	1	+ 33.3	− 75.0	− 66.7
Commerce[2]	62	88	67	+ 41.9	− 23.9	+ 8.1
No. of merchants in this group	(32)	(38)	(32)	+ 18.8	− 15.8	—
Manufacture[3]	34	27	50	− 20.6	+ 85.2	+ 47.1
Building Trades[4]	5	9	7	+ 80.0	− 22.2	+ 40.0
Public Houses[5]	11	16	14	+ 45.5	− 12.5	+ 27.3
Brewing[6]	15	7	12	− 53.3	+ 71.4	− 20.0
Miscellaneous[7]	4	7	12	+ 75.0	+ 71.4	+200.0
Subtotal	134	158	163	+ 17.9	+ 3.2	+ 21.6
Shops	69	93	121	+ 34.8	+ 30.1	+ 75.4
Total	203	251	284	+ 23.6	+ 13.1	+ 39.9

Source and *Notes*: See table 3.

shopkeepers compared with other trades. Between 1748 and 1750 and 1759 and 1760, the number of bankrupt shopkeepers increased by 31 percent while the number of bankruptcies in all other trades declined by 8.1 percent (table 3). London registered an increase for bankrupt shopkeepers of 26.7 percent (table 4); the provinces, 34.8 percent (table 5). Interestingly, the counties north of the line showed a slightly higher increase for the period: 36.4 percent in contrast to 34 percent for those south of the line. The contrast was even greater between 1759 and 1760 and 1768 and 1770: 46.7 percent versus 22.2 percent for the counties south of the line. Comparing the first and third periods for the country as a whole, the number of shopkeepers increased by 123.3 percent; all other trades, 41.4 percent (table 3).

Differences of this magnitude cry for an explanation. Admittedly, it is premature to conclude that the 1750s and 1760s witnessed a wave of new shops and provided a larger base on which the normal course of business failures could operate.[14] And yet it seems difficult to accept other possible explanations – that shopkeeping experienced greater commercial hazards than other trades, or that shopkeepers who failed were more likely than other traders to have insolvency dragged through bankruptcy proceedings. It has been said that a "substantial increase in the number of bankruptcies may be taken as evidence of a change of economic weather." Are the figures registering an increase in the activity of shopkeeping in an economic climate encouraging new ventures in retailing and thereby creating a more intensive competition that "squeezes out the weaker producers and traders"?[15] It is perhaps not without significance that 1759 also marked the date of the attempt to tax retail shops. One can hardly resist the thought that the government was, in part, reacting to the increasing importance of this sector of the economy. As the estimates show, the government anticipated a rich yield from the tax. Moreover, an analysis of the specialized shop trades shows that changes were occurring in the general structure of the retail trade, with some trades assuming greater significance and new ones arising.

Distinguishing by shop trade those clearly identified in the bankruptcy reports – the drapers, grocers, ironmongers, etc. – raised a pertinent question. Did John Doe, "draper," confine his trade to draperies or was he also retailing groceries, books, and other goods? No positive answer can be given to this knotty problem. There are, however, reasons to believe that the title fairly represents the line of goods carried. Some, in fact, were very specifically identified. One bankrupt, for example, was listed as a "peruke maker and dealer in rums and brandies." A few shopkeepers were listed as "draper and grocer," a clear recognition of the combined trades. They have been included among those identified as "shopkeepers." Quite a number, particularly in the provinces, were reported simply as "shopkeepers," presumably one who had a general shop. Most of the bankruptcies outside London occurred in large cities or towns that could support the major line of activity of the bankrupt. Pigot faced similar problems in compiling his classified directories; the bankruptcy reports are probably no less accurate.

An analysis of the 586 bankrupt shopkeepers is presented in table 6. The shop trades are grouped according to the major type of goods retailed. The classifications are not ideal: chemists, for example, could have been subsumed under "special services" and those identified as "shopkeepers" resist specific categorization. But whatever else they sold, one can presume that consumable household goods and wearing apparel were the staple items retailed. Thus, in considering the proportion of shops in each of these two classes, some allowance should be made for those subsumed under "general shops." The oil-and colourmen proved an awkward group, but as none were titled "Italian oilmen" who did indeed sell groceries, it has been presumed they were retailing paints and similar articles.

Tallow-chandlers, on the other hand, may well have retailed groceries, a very common combination in the eighteenth century. In Norwich in 1783, for example, almost half the grocers were entered in the directory as "tallow chandlers and grocers."

However one juggles the classification, it is quite evident that the retailing of wearing apparel was the predominant shopkeeping trade, particularly in the provinces where it represents almost one-half of all shops or a little over 53 percent, if the "general shop" is included. Even in London, the wearing apparel group ranked first; the average for the three periods was 38.6 percent of all shops. But there are signs of change. The proportion of shops in this class for the first two periods was 44.1 percent (60 shops out of a total of 136); for the third period, 34.1 percent (57 shops out of a total of 167). No similar movement is registered in the figures for the provinces. The average proportion for the first two periods was 44.4 percent (72 shops out of a total of 162); for the third period, 44.6 percent (54 out of 121). There is, however, an enormous difference between the metropolis and the provincial towns with respect to the types of specialized clothing shops. In the provinces, drapers far outnumbered all other types of shops selling wearing apparel. Out of a total of 126 shops selling wearing apparel, 78 percent were drapers. In London, on the other hand, out of a total of 117, only 37 percent were drapers. Nevertheless, the proportion of drapers steadily declined in both places. In the first period (1748 and 1750), there were 30 shops selling wearing apparel in the provinces. Of these, 90 percent were drapers. By 1768 and 1770, the proportion had declined to 68.5 percent (37 drapers out of a total of 54). In 1748 and 1750, London drapers comprised 45.8 percent of the wearing apparel group (11 out of 24); in 1768 and 1770, 26.3 percent (15 out of 57). By then, the number of haberdashers, hatters, and milliners in London was almost double (29) that of drapers, or 51 percent of the shops in Class I. Although the proportion of haberdashers, hatters, and milliners in the provinces increased from 6.7 percent (1748 and 1750) to 27.8 percent (1768 and 1770) of shopkeepers in Class I, drapers easily outranked them for obvious reasons. Few towns outside London could provide a sufficiently numerous and wealthy clientele to support such highly specialized shops. In the less populous market towns, drapers or even general shops carried a small range of haberdashery goods.[16]

Milliners – they were all women – formed a very insignificant proportion of the clothing group. Before 1768, no bankrupt milliner was reported for the provinces. That year there were three, one each in Devonshire, Huntingdonshire, and Lancashire. However, there is reason to suspect that the small number reported for both London and the provinces is not representative. Millinery was one shop trade within the domain of women. The association once formed was strengthened not only by the inhibition of men to enter a trade so closely related to women, but also by the practices of apprenticeship. From the meagre evidence available, the trade appears to have been a haven for widows and orphaned daughters of shopkeepers in other trades, a rather genteel occupation for those with little capital but some knowledge of shopkeeping. The insolvency of such a shop, a very small ripple in the business world, would rarely have been registered in bankruptcy proceedings. Perhaps creditors gallantly came to the rescue of their weaker sisters. Like the small village shopkeepers, milliners have left few records of their activities.

No slop shops appeared in the bankruptcy reports for the provincial towns, although there was undoubtedly a brisk market in second-hand and ready-made clothing. At the end of the century, Evesham, with a population just under 3,000, had at least three "dealers in ready-made clothes." The *Universal British Directory* of 1799 listed one dealer, John Reese, as a "butcher and dealer in ready-made clothes." He probably sold his clothes in the market; others may have hawked their goods. Few places in the provinces could support slop shops on the scale of London. There the owners were sufficiently important to be listed in the directories.

The second largest group were shops selling consumable household goods (Class III). But even with the addition of "shopkeepers," the proportion of shops retailing food was less than that of the clothing trades. It was very much less in London. What is perhaps startling is the small number identified as grocers. In London, the average for the three periods is 6.3 percent, ranging from 4.2 percent (1768 and 1770) to 11.7 percent (1748 and 1750); in the provinces, 15.2 percent, ranging from 12.4 percent (1768 and 1770) to 18.3 percent (1759 and 1760). If cheesemongers and tallow-chandlers, both of whom were likely sellers of groceries, are included, the average for London is 11.9 percent; for the provinces, 16.6 percent. If we add to the group those identified as "shopkeepers," then one-quarter of the total number of shops in the provinces might be said to have some groceries available for customers. In the light of the fact that the vast majority of people expended some 70 percent or more of their income on food and probably no more than 10 percent on clothing, the proportion of shops in each of these two categories appears either inexplicable or totally inaccurate. It should, however, be remembered that the analysis does not comprehend all shops but only the more important shopkeepers, those who would tend to be listed in the directories as "principal inhabitants" and whose business was sufficiently extensive to allow a degree of specialization in the items stocked. Now, groceries, unlike wearing apparel, were not confined to specialized shops. Until well into the nineteenth century, the traditional grocery shops formed a relatively small proportion of shops retailing a narrow range of consumable household goods. Draperies and haberdasheries, however, were rarely stocked by petty chandlers or small village shops. Very few petty shopkeepers had sufficient capital to stock even a small selection of draperies and, given the little money available for clothing by their customers, it would not have been profitable to do so. On the other hand, groceries and other household wares, unlike draperies, were in high demand and easily divisible into small units. Chandlers could purchase from their suppliers as much or as little as they could afford. Thus, with the exception of the licensed hawkers, the specialized clothing shops and the larger general shops were by and large the main source of wearing apparel, even by the workers. Viewed in that light, their proportion of the *total* number of all shops in the kingdom would be very much less than indicated in the table and more commensurate with their share of the retail trade. Conversely, the full-fledged *grocer* was only one of the sources for the worker's food-basket, and not the most important.

It is hardly surprising that only one provincial cheesemonger was recorded in the bankruptcy reports. Cheese was sold in the local markets and by a great variety of retailers. It was certainly a staple article of the small village shop and petty chandler. Cheesemongery as a shop trade was only feasible in a large urban setting, and was well established in London. Nevertheless, those reported for the metropolis may include some who were only wholesale dealers. Chemists, on the other hand, were a necessary and standard feature in provincial towns. With the exception of patented drugs, medicinal goods were only obtainable from the chemist. Indeed, his was a highly skilled art or profession. Chemists were held in high esteem by the community and generally ranked a shade above other retailers. As the figures show, there is little difference between London and the provinces in the proportion of shops selling drugs.

For shops selling household furnishings, the figures for London raise serious doubts concerning their reliability. In 1770, an unusually large number of bankrupt cabinetmakers were recorded. Interestingly, there was also an unusually large number of bankrupt oil-and colourmen. They might well have been supplying the cabinetmakers.[17] Economic indicators give no evidence of an unfavourable movement in the consumers goods industries. True, American

resistence to the Townshend Duties had almost put a stop to exports
to the colonies in 1769. It was a temporary condition and trade
revived in 1770. But it is highly possible that the stoppage of trade
the year before had created credit difficulties for cabinetmakers
accustomed to supplying the American market.[18] However, the export problem does not explain the unusual number of bankrupt
upholsterers in 1768 or the slight increase of cabinetmakers and
upholsterers in provincial towns. There was also an increase in the
number of china shops and the appearance of a new shop trade,
the carpet warehouse. Shops dealing in household furnishing catered, of course, to the more affluent and have never been very
numerous. As questionable as the London figures for 1770 may be,
one has the impression that the overall picture reflects increased
activity in this area, that the number of such shop was increasing.

Among the shop trades subsumed under "hardware" (Class V),
ironmongers clearly predominated in the provinces. There, 4.6 percent of all shopkeepers were ironmongers compared to 2 percent
in London. Not surprisingly, ironmongers were far more numerous
in the provinces than cabinetmakers and upholsterers. Nevertheless,
the proportion of shops dealing in hardware was relatively small –
5.2 percent in the provinces. (The figure for London is, we fear,
distorted by the unusually large number of bankrupt oil-and colourmen in 1770.)

The last class (Class VI), "special services," contains a miscellaneous
collection of shop trades offering primarily luxury items. In these
trades, London led the way with almost 20 percent of its shops in
this category compared to 8 percent for the rest of the country. With
the exception of tobacconists, the proportion for all other trades in
the provinces fell below that in London, particularly the jewellery
trades. Gold-and silversmiths, watchmakers, and jewellers formed
8.3 percent of all shops in London, 1.7 percent in the provinces.
The difference was considerably less in the proportions of booksellers and stationers, 4.3 percent in London compared to 2.8 percent
in the provinces.

As suggested earlier, the bankruptcy reports provide some evidence, however slight, of the areas of growth in the shopkeeping
trades. The relative decline in the proportion of drapers and the
increase in haberdashers are most distinct. The average increase
for all shop trades was 123 percent; for drapers only 37 percent
compared to 290 percent for haberdashers. Among the shop trades
subsumed under "consumable household goods," the most noteable
increase was for chemists, particularly in the provinces. There were

no chemists in the first period (1748 and 1750); in the last period (1768 and 1770), there were six or 5 percent of all shops in the provinces. Grocers, like drapers, fell behind with an average increase of 22.2 percent for the country as a whole and 36.4 percent in the provinces. The only other particularly noteworthy areas of change, aside from household furnishings, were the striking increase in the proportion of book shops and jewellers in London, and the appearance of a new shop trade, the carpet warehouse.

It has been argued that bankrupt shopkeepers form a sufficiently reliable sample to chart the quantitative distribution of specialized shop trades in mideighteenth-century England and Wales. If the mirror is not perfect, neither does it grossly distort. We believe it reflects the general contours of the shopkeeping world, at least its principal representatives. Moreover, evidence drawn from other sources, albeit for a later period, corroborates the figures derived from bankruptcy reports. In 1783–4, Bailey compiled directories for many towns and cities in which he listed the "principal inhabitants" alphabetically along with their occupations or status. Entries into the directory were confined to those of "established credit." Although he claimed to have "been particularly careful to make the list of names complete," it is to be feared that even within his own restricted terms of reference many credit-worthy tradesmen escaped his net.[19] The coverage is relatively good for London but varies enormously for the provincial towns. The listing for some places is excellent – that for Norwich, for example, appears to be as good or even more adequate than the one prepared by James Pigot in 1822–3.[20] The same is true for Bristol. Other places are very poorly served, for example, Birmingham and Liverpool.[21] Despite their limitations, Bailey's commercial directories provide evidence of the type and number of shop trades considered sufficiently important to be listed in 1783–4.

In 1822–3, James Pigot compiled the first classified trades directories for the country. His was a far more ambitious project, aiming at nothing less than a full listing of all tradesmen in the towns and cities included in his survey. Pigot's directories have been universally acclaimed, rightly so, for their accuracy and reliability, and are certainly far more comprehensive than Bailey's. Although the 1822–3 directories failed to include small shopkeepers,[22] they are an excellent source of information on the number of specialized shop trades in major towns and cities, offering a profile of principal shopkeepers comparable to those in the bankruptcy reports. Together with Bailey's directories, they provide a means of checking the figures de-

Table 6
Major Shop Trades in London and the Provinces, 1748 and 1750, 1759 and 1760, 1768 and 1770

	London					Provinces				
	Number of Shops					Number of Shops				
	1748 & 1750	1759 & 1760	1768 & 1770	Total	%	1748 & 1750	1759 & 1760	1768 & 1770	Total	%
Class										
I Wearing Apparel										
Drapers	11	17	15	43	14,2	27	34	37	98	34.6
Haberdashers	5	4	13	22	7.3	1	1	6	8	2.8
Hatters, Hosiers, etc.	3	2	14	19	6.3	1	6	6	13	4.6
Milliners	—	2	2	4	1.3	—	—	3	3	1.1
Breeches & Staymakers	1	1	1	3	.9	—	—	—	—	—
Tailors	4	8	10	22	7.3	1	1	2	4	1.4
Clothesbrokers	—	2	2	4	1.3	—	—	—	—	—
Subtotal	24	36	57	117	38.6	30	42	54	126	44.5
II General Shop										
Shopkeepers	—	1	—	1	.3	5	6	14	25	8.8
III Consumable Household Goods										
A Food										
Grocers	7	5	7	19	6.3	11	17	15	43	15.2
Cheesemongers	3	5	3	11	3.6	1	—	—	1	.3
Bakers	—	1	5	6	2.0	2	3	8	13	4.6
Fruiterer	—	—	—	—	—	—	—	1	1	.3
Subtotal	10	11	15	36	11.9	14	20	24	58	20.5
B Drinks										
Wine & Brandy Merchants	4	7	10	21	6.9	5	5	4	14	4.9
C Sundries										
Chemists	4	1	6	11	3.6	—	3	6	9	3.2
Tallow-Chandlers	1	2	3	6	2.0	—	3	—	3	1.1
Subtotal	5	3	9	17	5.6	—	6	6	12	4.3
Total Consumables	19	21	34	74	24.4	19	31	34	84	29.7
IV Household Furnishings										
Cabinetmakers	1	—	11	12	3.9	1	—	2	3	1.1
Upholsterers	—	1	6	7	2.3	1	—	2	3	1.1
China & Earthenware Dealers	2	2	5	9	3.0	—	2	2	4	1.4

Table 6 (continued)

	London					Provinces				
	Number of Shops					Number of Shops				
	1748	1759	1768			1748	1759	1768		
	&	&	&			&	&	&		
Class	1750	1760	1770	Total	%	1750	1760	1770	Total	%
Carpet										
Warehouse	—	—	1	1	.3	—	—	—	—	—
Subtotal	3	3	23	29	9.5	2	2	6	10	3.6
V Hardware										
Ironmongers	1	1	4	6	2.0	5	2	6	13	4.6
Drysalters	—	—	1	1	.3	—	1	—	1	.3
Oil-&										
Colourmen	3	1	9	13	4.3	—	1	—	1	.3
Toy Dealers	1	—	1	2	.7	—	—	—	—	—
Subtotal	5	2	15	22	7.3	5	4	6	15	5.2
VI Special Services										
Booksellers &										
Stationers	1	2	10	13	4.3	3	4	1	8	2.8
Perukemakers	2	4	1	7	2.3	1	1	1	3	1.1
Jewellers	1	1	11	13	4.3	1	—	—	1	.3
Watchmakers	—	1	6	7	2.3	—	1	—	1	.3
Gold-&										
Silversmiths	—	—	5	5	1.7	1	—	2	3	1.1
Pawnbrokers	3	1	1	5	1.7	—	—	—	—	—
Tobacconists	1	3	4	8	2.6	2	2	3	7	2.5
Whipmakers	1	1	—	2	.7	—	—	—	—	—
Subtotal	9	13	38	60	19.9	8	8	7	23	8.1
Total Number										
of Shops	60	76	167	303		69	93	121	283	

Source: Gentleman's Magazine for the relevant years.

rived from the bankruptcy reports and of charting the course of change in the structure of the shop trades during the intervening years.

The places selected for comparison include, in addition to London, three populous provincial towns well represented in the bankruptcy reports: two south of the line, Bristol and Norwich, both old established cities; and one, Manchester, a fast-growing industrial town in the north.[23] Although the sample, unlike the bankruptcy reports, is restricted to a few large places, the cities chosen differ considerably in their social and occupational structures, and each served as a redistribution centre for the surrounding towns and villages. Unfortunately, a perfect comparison of shop trades is not feasible. Bailey's professed purpose was to supply merchants and tradesmen with a properly identified list of names so that none "may be at a loss where to apply for any article, or to establish a proper correspondence."[24] As a consequence, minor shop traders such as bakers, fruiterers, tailors, staymakers, and pawnbrokers whose customers and suppliers were generally locally based are omitted. Nor are milliners included in the list for London, although they do appear in the provincial towns, perhaps to allow London tradesmen "to establish a proper correspondence." In Pigot's directories, there is some ambiguity in the classification for tailors, many of whom were working rather than shopkeeping tailors. Consequently, only those labeled tailor-drapers were counted, and included in the figures for drapers. Some shopkeeping tailors may have escaped enumeration. Pigot was also rather cavalier in his listing of bakers. As they are not one of the trades covered by Bailey, and form a very small proportion of bankrupt shopkeepers, bakers have been excluded. Pawnbrokers, milliners, and staymakers were, however, listed by Pigot and are entered among the shop trades. The total effect of these differences is not sufficient to invalidate the comparison, although they should be kept in mind.

One heading, "warehouses" may appear inappropriate in a list of shopkeepers. However, "Yorkshire Shoe Warehouses," shops retailing ready-made shoes, were a well known feature in mideighteenth-century London. The use of the term *warehouse* as an alternate for shop made its appearance in the provincial towns in the 1770s, generally to designate places selling low-priced articles. By the 1780s, "warehouses" of various types were springing up all over. In 1785, London tea dealers – their shops metamorphosed into "warehouses" – engaged in a veritable battle of advertisements displaying in bold type their specially priced "cheap" teas, a practice quickly adopted by the more enterprising provincial dealers.[25] In the 1780s and 1790s, there are many advertisements in London and provincial papers by "Ready-made and Child-bed Linen Warehouses," "Muslin" or "Manchester Warehouses," and "carpet" or "Blanket Warehouses." The advertisements clearly indicate they were in fact shops parading under a term that implied cheap wholesale prices. Other types of warehouses established or supported by the Staffordshire potters and the Birmingham and Sheffield toy manufacturers were designed for a very different clientele. No one would accuse Josiah Wedgwood of offering cheap wares at his "Staffordshire Warehouse" on Greek Street, but his was no less a shop than the Child-bed Linen Warehouse. That Wedgwood's shop served as an advertising gimmick to extend his wholesale and retail sales in no way distinguishes it from other London shops whose proprietors were just as concerned with their trade as with their retail customers.

Another euphemism for shop that appeared in London and provincial papers in the 1780s and earlier is "repository" or "fancy repository," generally designating a shop retailing fancy draperies, haberdasheries, or other special articles. It was apparently applied originally to rooms used for the sale of a specific lot of goods on a temporary basis. John Christie's salerooms in Pall Mall used by Matthew Boulton to such great advantage served as a repository.[26] The term was not, however, widely adopted as an alternate for shop.

One other heading may appear incongruous. For the provincial towns, confectioners and fruiterers are entered as one category. They were often so designated in the directories, and the advertisements show that confectioners often combined the two trades.

Table 7 gives the proportion of shops in each trade for the four cities. The classifications are broadly similar to those adopted for bankrupt shopkeepers. Several new types have been added and one, "shopkeepers," is dropped. Neither Bailey nor Pigot has an entry for mere "shopkeepers." As the 1783 figures for London show, the proportion of shops in each of the five major divisions is strikingly similar to the bankrupt London shopkeepers (see table 6). Trends observed for the earlier period have continued: a slightly smaller proportion of shops retailing wearing apparel with drapers representing less than half of the clothing group; an increase in the proportion of book dealers and china shops; and even an increase in upholsterers and cabinetmakers, if one excludes the figure for 1770. True, the proportion of shops in "special services" is slightly lower. Bailey did not enter pawnbrokers and very few perfumers were listed. The one noticeable difference is in the proportion of various shops retailing food. There is a slight increase in the percentage of grocers and tea dealers along with several new types of food shops.[27] Some confectioners were certainly present in London in the 1750s and 1760s, but if Bailey listed only twenty-three as principal shopkeepers, their absence from the bankruptcy reports is not surprising. The same is true for fruiterers. As to wine and brandy *merchants*, although many kept shop and sold by retail, as explained earlier, they remain difficult to identify, particularly for London. The London directories, unlike Bristol's, do not distinguish between retailers and genuine merchants. In all, the figures for these *merchants* are the least credible in both this and the bankruptcy reports.

A comparison of the figures for 1822–3 with those forty years earlier shows that trends commencing in the 1750s and 1760s continued. The proportion of shops retailing wearing apparel declined even more, and drapers now formed less than one-third of the group. On the other hand, the proportion of warehouses increased. A new type of milliner specializing in straw hats appeared. Among shops retailing food, only the proportion of cheesemongers, confectioners, and fruiterers increased. There was little change in the figures for grocers and tea dealers. By 1822–3, shops retailing household furnishings represented 10 percent of all shops. The proportion of shops subsumed under "special services" went up to 20.5 percent. Dealers in books, stationery, maps, prints, etc. now formed 10 percent of all shops. And a new trade appeared – the umbrella- and parasolmakers: one appeared in Bailey's directory; Pigot listed ninety-nine. As it is not clear whether they were artisans, shopkeeping-artisans, or just shopkeepers, they are not included in the enumeration.

In the analysis of bankrupt shopkeepers, the proportional distribution of shop trades in the provinces differed markedly from that of London. The distribution in 1783–4, particularly for Bristol and Norwich, appears to belie that distinction and offer little support to the bankruptcy figures. With a few exceptions, Bristol conforms to the London pattern and Norwich is moving in the same direction. True, the proportion of shops subsumed under "special services" in Bristol and Norwich is less than London. (Jewellers and dealers in books etc. were not well represented in either city.) And both cities had a greater proportion of grocers and tea dealers, particularly Norwich where many are identified by Bailey as "grocers and tallow chandler." The figures for cabinetmakers and upholsterers in Norwich are suspiciously high, due possibly to the fact that the city was a centre for chairmaking. Chairmakers hardly qualify as shopkeepers; we have, therefore, not counted those identified in the directory as "cabinet makers and makers of chairs." Nevertheless, some listed only as "cabinet maker" may have been chairmakers. Norwich, incidently, was one of the few towns that listed furniturebrokers, generally retailers of used furniture, among its "principal inhabitants." Such shops existed in all large towns; perhaps those in Norwich were in fact "brokers" or agents for chairmakers. But on the whole, the profile of shops trades in these two old established cities is little different to that of London.

The distribution of shop trades in Manchester in 1783 is, on the other hand, almost a replica of the bankrupt shopkeepers. Nor is it singular. The shop trades in Lancaster and other small towns show a similar pattern.[28] However, by 1822–3 the distribution in Manchester was not radically different from that in Bristol, although Manchester still lagged behind in the household furnishing category and special services. Without the large number of pawnbrokers, the

Table 7
Major Shop Trades: London, Bristol, Norwich, and Manchester, 1783 and 1822-3
(in percentages)

	London		Bristol		Norwich		Manchester	
	1783	1822-3	1783	1822-3	1784	1822-3	1783	1822-3
Class I Wearing Apparel								
Drapers	17.0	8.5	17.6	11.1	10.5	8.8	26.3	12.2
Haberdashers, Hatters, etc.	16.6	10.2	10.7	8.9	10.9	7.9	17.9	7.3
Lace Dealers	—	1.7	—	.4	—	.2	—	—
Milliners & Straw Hat Makers	—	3.2	1.0	6.3	4.5	8.8	.6	2.8
Breechesmakers & Glovers	—	—	—	—	4.1	1.7	—	.2
Staymakers	—	.7	—	1.0	—	.6	—	1.1
Warehouses: Muslin & Child-bed Linen	1.3	1.7	1.0	1.3	1.6	.4	—	2.0
Ready-made Clothes, Shawls, etc.	—	.6	—	—	—	—	—	—
Shoe & Cheap Stocking	—	—	1.7	—	—	.4	—	2.1
Fancy Repositories	—	.1	—	—	—	—	—	—
Clothesbrokers	.4	.7	.7	—	—	2.1	—	2.3
Subtotal	35.3	27.4	32.7	29.0	31.6	30.9	44.8	30.0
Number of Shops	1,021	3,142	95	321	78	145	70	285
Class II Consumable Household Goods								
A Food								
Grocer and Tea Dealers	7.6	8.2	11.4	10.2	20.6	11.1	13.5	9.7
Tea, Cocoa & Coffee Dealers	1.8	1.5	1.4	1.7	.8	.9	1.9	2.4
Dealers in Flour & Sundries	2.5	2.0	1.7	7.0	.4	1.1	7.1	5.3
Cheesemongers	3.3	5.8	1.7	1.7	—	.2	—	1.2
Confectioners & Fruiterers	.8	2.2	1.7	2.9	1.6	6.2	.6	3.2
Ham & Tongue Dealers	.1	.1	—	—	—	—	—	—
Subtotal	16.1	19.8	17.9	23.5	23.4	19.5	23.1	21.8
B Drinks								
Wine and Spirit Merchants	8.3	5.7	6.2	4.1	8.1	4.5	5.8	1.6
Lime Dealers	—	—	—	—	—	—	—	.2
Liquor and Porter Dealers	—	—	—	—	—	—	—	3.3
Subtotal	8.3	5.7	6.2	4.1	8.1	4.5	5.8	5.1

Table 7 (continued)
Major Shop Trades: London, Bristol, Norwich and Manchester, 1783 and 1822-3

	London 1783	London 1822-3	Bristol 1783	Bristol 1822-3	Norwich* 1784	Norwich* 1822-3	Manchester 1783	Manchester 1822-3
C Sundries								
Italian Oil								
Dealers	1.2	.5	.3	.4	—	—	—	—
Tallow-								
Chandlers*	.5	3.2	1.7	—	—	3.2	3.8	1.1
Chemists	3.8	3.0	9.0	4.3	3.2	3.8	2.6	5.5
Subtotal	5.5	6.7	11.0	4.7	3.2	7.0	6.4	6.6
Total: Consumables	29.9	32.2	35.1	32.3	34.7	31.0	35.3	33.5
Number of Shops	866	3,699	102	358	86	145	55	316

*Many grocers in Norwich were
identified as "grocers and tallow-
chandlers."

Class III Household Furnishings								
Upholsterers &								
Cabinetmakers	3.7	5.5	3.1	6.8	4.5	7.9	3.2	4.1
Upholsterers	—	—	—	—	4.0	1.5	—	—
China &								
Earthenware								
Dealers	2.9	2.5	2.8	3.3	4.0	3.4	.6	2.8
Musical								
Instrument								
Dealers	—	.7	—	—	—	—	—	—
Warehouses:								
Carpet, Blanket,								
Paper, etc.	.9	.6	1.0	—	—	1.5	.6	1.2
Specialties:								
Desks, Dressing								
Cases, etc.	—	.7	—	—	—	—	—	—
Subtotal	7.5	10.0	6.9	10.1	12.5	14.3	4.4	8.1
Number of Shops in Group	217	1,145	20	113	31	67	7	77
Not included in this class were furniture brokers	(—)	(98)	(—)	(25)	(11)	(27)	(—)	(36)

Class IV Hardware								
Ironmongers &								
Hardwaremen	6.0	3.6	7.6	5.4	6.5	4.1	4.5	3.7
Drysalters	.8	.4	1.7	.4	—	—	4.5	4.3
Oil-& Colourmen	3.1	4.0	.3	2.1	—	—	—	1.4
Seedsmen &								
Florists	.9	.8	1.7	2.9	4.0	.2	.6	.8

Table 7 (continued)
Major Shop Trades: London, Bristol, Norwich and Manchester, 1783 and 1822-3

	London		Bristol		Norwich		Manchester	
	1783	1822-3	1783	1822-3	1784	1822-3	1783	1822-3
Toy Dealers	.4	.7	1.4	.8	—	.9	—	.6
Warehouses: Sheffield & Birmingham	.3	.3	—	—	—	—	—	—
Subtotal	11.5	9.8	12.7	11.6	10.5	5.2	9.6	10.8
Number of Shops in Group	330	1,136	37	128	26	24	15	103
Class V Special Services								
Booksellers & Stationers	6.2	8,5	2.4	6.9	4.5	5.6	4.5	3.6
Sellers of Music, Pictures, etc.	—	1.5	—	.5	—	1.1	—	.6
Perfumers	.6	1.9	.3	1.0	.4	1.3	—	.7
Jewellers, Gold- & Silversmiths	6.7	4.5	3.5	4.4	5.3	6.2	—	3.6
Dealers in Fans, Pens, etc.	—	.7	—	—	—	—	—	—
Opticians	—	.1	—	.3	—	.9	—	.4
Pawnbrokers	—	1.8	—	2.9	—	2.6	—	6.5
Tobacconists	2.3	1.5	6.2	1.3	.4	1.1	1.3	2.4
Subtotal	15.8	20.5	12.4	17.3	10.6	18.8	5.8	17.8
Number of Shops in Group	458	2,352	36	191	26	87	9	170
Not included in this class were umbrella & parasolmakers	(1)	(99)	(—)	(10)	(—)	(6)	(—)	(18)
Total Number of Shops in Survey	2,892	11,474	290	1,111	247	468	156	951

Sources: 1783, London, Bristol, Manchester: *Bailey's Western and Midland Directory*; 1784, Norwich: *Bailey's Eastern Directory*; 1822/3, London, Bristol, Norwich, Manchester: Pigot, *London and Provincial Directory*.

proportion of shops in the latter category would have been paltry – dealers in books, music, etc. form only 4 percent of the total number of shops.

Is it necessary, then, to conclude that the bankruptcy figures for provincial towns are totally unreliable? We do not think so. First, the bankruptcy figures were based on shops located in Welsh counties and every county in England with the single exception of

Rutland. They include areas least advanced in shopkeeping facilities, counties that had a very high ratio of population to shops in 1759. Secondly, the figures cover the two middle decades. Between the bankruptcy figures and Bailey's, there is a difference of roughly a quarter of a century, a period of considerable movement in the shopkeeping population. One observes it most noticeably among the bankrupt shopkeepers in London, but a similar trend is also discernible in the figures for the provinces. There is a further important consideration: the differences in the social and economic life of the cities included in the sample.

F.J. Fisher describes the enormous influence of London as a market for agricultural production. Its tentacles reached far out into the hinterland drawing in men and goods.[29] Some would say devouring both with equal voracity. But the traffic was not one-way. London was also the fashion centre, as Josiah Wedgwood well understood when he established his warehouse there.[30] Its patterns of consumption radiated over a wide area and it sent back to the country all the newest articles of food, clothing, household furnishings, and other stylish goods. If the London population was dependent upon the countryside for its food, the principal London tradesmen or shopkeepers were equally dependent for their economic well-being on the orders of their country correspondents. The great increase in the number of shopkeeping watchmakers and jewellers in London, for example, was made possible in part by their ability to stimulate demand and to establish a "proper correspondence" with shopkeepers in towns and cities up and down the country. As extensive as the London market was, the principal shopkeepers in Westminster and the City neither did nor could rely solely on retail sales. Thus, changes in the structure of the shop trades first registered in London would, almost by necessity, be followed by similar changes in provincial centres of distribution. In turn, the principal shopkeepers of such places were dependent upon an ability to establish connections in their own market area, and, as noted elsewhere, were sometimes in the position of competing against London suppliers.[31] The functions performed and the influence exerted by such regional centres were no less important to their hinterland than those accomplished by London for the country as a whole. Thus, an impetus first generated in London and radiated outward was invigorated in the provincial centres and fed back to the metropolis to nourish its commercial population. Some of the major entrepôts were in fact little Londons. The sugar, wine, and tobacco trade of Bristol opened up opportunities for its principal shopkeepers. It is not surprising that William Stout established a correspondence in

Bristol. As a commercial centre, Bristol was for the greater part of the eighteenth century the second city in England. But the rise of the outports with their own import trade, a matter of considerable concern to London tradesmen, is another subject. London was pre-eminent and set the fashion.

The sway of London was not, however, evenly distributed over the country. Distance from the centre played a part; the Home Counties were early drawn into the commercial life of the metropolis. Equally, if not more, important was the particular social and economic structure of provincial centres. It determined the receptiveness of an area to London patterns of consumption and allowed the shopkeeping population to multiply and to specialize. In mideighteenth century, the counties north of the line lacked an appropriate structure and thus lagged behind the rest of the country in the number and types of shops. And is that not what Bailey's directories for 1783–4 indicate? The structure of shop trades in Manchester, with a population surpassing that of Bristol, was no further developed than the pattern that emerged from the analysis of all bankrupt shopkeepers in the provinces. And the latter were drawn from all parts of the country. Bristol and Norwich, very different types of cities, follow the lead of London. It took Manchester several decades to catch up.[32]

The evidence extracted from the bankruptcy records and early directories hardly supports a view of stagnation in the retail sector of the economy. During the fifty years or more after the excise survey, some significant changes in the structure of the retail trade were occurring. There was a greater diversity in the type of shop trades, changes in their proportions, and more provincial centres were adopting the London pattern. Not surprisingly, changes appeared first in areas most densely populated with shops. As later chapters will indicate, these changes were accompanied by innovative practices in the sale and distribution of goods. The delineation of the retail structure is, however, only partial, a truncated pyramid restricted to principal shops. Although their numbers would appear to be increasing, they still represented a relatively small proportion of the shops surveyed by Excise. At the base of the pyramid were shops similar to Mary Smith's of Flixton. Wholly dependent upon market-street shops, they carried little weight in the political affairs of the country compared to their suppliers. But they were by no means unimportant and formed an essential link in the chain of distribution, as necessary to the principal shops as to the small consumers they served. Before dealing with the problem of their number and business practices, it will be helpful to identify and describe the shopkeepers who were required to pay the shop tax of 1785, and whose voices were by no means unheard by their representatives in Parliament.

CHAPTER FOUR

Politics of Shopkeeping: Shopkeepers vs. Hawkers, 1785-9

Pitt's tax on retail shops was not a success. It was short-lived (1785–9), failed to yield the anticipated revenue, and, more damaging, alienated a considerable portion of the London commercial community. But the whole proceedings form a fruitful source of information on the retail traders of the kingdom, particularly their business practices and principles. The bill presented to Parliament in 1785 was a modified version of the 1759 proposed tax on retail shops. Pitt, however, sweetened the pill of the forthcoming tax by promising in his budget speech to eliminate one source of competition, the licensed hawkers and pedlars.[1] By so doing, he placed in public opposition two major retail sellers whose subsequent actions reveal the particular position of each in the commercial and political life of the country. The evidence suggests that by the last decades of the century, the shop trades had become an important and valuable sector of the retail trade of the economy, well able to exert political pressure to effect legislation on behalf of the principal shopkeepers.

The aborted shop tax of 1759, which was designed to include all retail shops, gave rise to one of the most exhaustive surveys of shops. Ironically, the tax of 1785 has not proved as rich a source: much of the valuable statistical information assembled by the tax office and presented to Parliament has been destroyed.[2] There are, however, a few accounts of the number and rental value of shops taxed as well as a full listing by counties of the number of licensed hawkers. Together they provide some information on the state of the retail trade in various parts of the country a quarter of a century after the first full survey. However, to interpret the data correctly it is essential to know what was being counted. For that information one must turn to the laws governing the collection of taxes on shopkeepers and hawkers and to the debates and petitions.

To make the burden of the tax on shopkeepers more equitable, Pitt suggested a rising scale of rates based on the rent paid, "which rent, he should suppose, always bore a proportion to the profit of the business and to the traffic carried on within it."[3] The following are the rates he proposed in his budget speech: 1s. in the £1 for an annual rent of £4 to under £10; 1s. 3d., from £10 to under £15; 1s. 6d., from £15 to under £20; 1s. 9d., £20 to under £25; and 2s. for an annual rent of £25 or more. In setting the minimum annual rent for taxing purposes at £4, Pitt had presumably intended to excuse from the tax the petty retailer whose income hardly sufficed to maintain a family and was not sufficient to bear the cost of even the lowest rate of tax. When the bill was presented to Parliament, further protection from the burden of the tax was extended to small shopkeepers. As amended, the bill raised the minimum annual rent for taxing purposes to £5 and lowered the rates for the first two categories: 6d. in the £ for an annual rent of £5 to under £10 and 1s. from £10 to £15; the three other categories remaining unchanged. The bill reduced the potential yield of the tax considerably. However, with the exception of the adjustments in the rates, something Pitt did not actively oppose, the bill sailed relatively smoothly through Parliament. Charles Fox, joined by Sir William Pulteney, William Windham, and Alderman Newnham of London spoke against it.[4] The only petition opposing the bill came from the "Lord Mayor, Aldermen and Commons of the City of London."[5] The bill passed the Commons on 30 May and received royal assent on 13 June 1785.

Who and what was affected by the act (25 Geo. 3 c. 30)? The tax was levied "upon every house, or other building ... any part of which shall for the time being be used as a shop, publicly kept open for carrying on any trade, or for selling any goods, wares or merchandize by retail, and upon every building or place used as a shop only," the rental value of which was five pounds or more (sec. 1). The assessed value was to be the same as that used to determine the duties on inhabited houses or if no duties were being paid on the full yearly rent or value of the building (sec. 6). That is, the annual rent was to be based not on the value of the shop alone, but the whole building. Specifically excluded from the tax were warehouses "employed solely for the ... lodging ... or sale of goods by wholesale only"; also excluded were places used only for "carrying on some manufacture, although the same may adjoin to or have an internal communication" with a shop (sec. 7). It was, in other words, a tax levied on *retail* shops, the definition of which may not have been drastically different from what guided the excise enumerators of 1759.

Two groups, presumably counted in 1759, were excluded from the tax. Section 9 states that "nothing in the act shall extend, or be construed to extend, to any shop, house, or place where bread, flour, meal, bran, and rubbles only are made or sold." The number of shops excused by this provision may not have been very large, but their number was not insignificant, particularly in the southern counties where the baker's shop was a common feature even in relatively small villages. It is the second group – shops with an annual rent less than five pounds – that is far more important. As the number of such shops probably equalled or surpassed those assessed, no valid information on the total number of shops in the country can be derived from the yield of the tax.

When Pitt promised to abolish the licensed hawkers, he did so with the intention of lessening the possible outcry against the tax on shopkeepers. It was just here that his nicely calculated plans went awry. Voices were already raised during the debate on the budget and swelled to a chorus as he moved to fulfill his promise. On 10 May 1785, the Committee of the Whole House resolved that the duties payable by hawkers were to cease.[6] Opposition was immediate and intense. Between 19 May and 14 June, eighteen petitions were submitted to Parliament supporting the hawkers. Their provenance is instructive: five came from Lancashire, from four different places;[7] two each from Shropshire, Westmorland, Yorkshire, and Scotland;[8] one each from Staffordshire and Cumberland; and three from London and Westminster. That is, with the exception of London, the petitions supporting the hawkers all emanated from counties north of the line. At the same time, the petitioners represented a wide variety of business interests. They included the manufacturers or printers of silk, linen, cotton, handkerchiefs, calicoes, thread, etc.; the journeymen silkweavers; merchants; wholesale dealers; and even some shopkeepers. The licensed hawkers were of course materially and immediately threatened, but only four petitions originated with them.[9] In addition, petitions were submitted from two Shropshire firms – one from Shrewsbury, the other from Bridgnorth. Each firm called itself the "Society of Travelling Scotchmen" and was a supplier of licensed hawkers.[10]

The most eloquent and revealing petition was submitted by the hawkers from the parish of Alstonfield, Staffordshire. As Hawkins Brown, MP claimed, they "had converted some thousand acres from a barren wild spot to a rich fertile circuit."[11] The hawkers noted, as did many petitioners, that the act of Queen Anne had held out a promise of permanence and stability to the trade. Having "conducted themselves with industry, reputation and propriety," they had "gained credit with a great number of manufacturers in many principal towns" and, in turn, "have likewise been under the necessity of giving great credit" to their customers. They and their creditors would be beggared if "trade is discontinued." Had the legislators "thought it expedient" to place an additional charge on the licence they "would have exerted their utmost endeavours to have complied." The hawkers concluded with a stinging rebuke. It was, they thought, "particularly hard that out of the great number of different trades ... they only should be selected for destruction" and "conceive that it is contrary to the spirit of Justice and the rights of humanity to abolish an avocation which has hitherto been countenanced by successive acts of the legislators, by a law whose principle is pregnant with as many dreadful consequences to the rights of property as that which makes an *ex post facto* law so greatly inimical to the liberty of the subject."[12]

The hawkers and pedlars of London and Westminster heard "with the utmost astonishment and affliction" that a measure was introduced "for their utter extermination, uncensured, unsummoned, unheard, untried and uncondemned" and claimed their "birthright ... as free citizens ... to be confronted with their accusers." The licensed hawkers of Halifax and neighbourhood claimed to have owing to them "no less than £40,000 and now stand indebted in large sums to merchants and manufacturers of London, Glasgow, Manchester, Leicester, Nottingham, Carlisle, etc."[13]

The hawkers as well as their suppliers all stressed the large sums of money employed in the trade and the long chain of credit. Nor should it be supposed that all the licensed hawkers were freelance pedlars purchasing their wares haphazardly as they travelled from place to place with their packs. The trade was far better organized than one might suspect. The Society of Travelling Scotchmen of Shrewsbury stated that the "said society hath been settled in Shrewsbury ever since the Act for licensing hawkers and pedlars and that the petitioners, William Corrie and James Craig,[14] are the two principals of the said society and purchase goods in the silk, linen and hosiery ware from the several manufacturers in ... Great Britain and Ireland to furnish the Travelling Scotchmen therewith." They claimed to have "a capital of £20,000 and upwards in the said trade" and to have owed to them for goods sold upon credit some £16,000. "The Travelling Scotchmen, their debtors," all licensed hawkers, had in turn "due to them £10,000." The society at Bridgnorth operated on a smaller scale. William Macmichael, "one of the principals," had invested a capital of £5,000 and upwards"; his licensed hawkers had owing to them "from their country customers, £1,500 and upwards."[15]

Judging from the many petitions submitted to Parliament, the merchandise most frequently sold by licensed hawkers was in the silk, linen, cotton, and calico line. Worsted was mentioned only once, appearing after a long list, almost as an afterthought. Handkerchiefs and hosiery were often mentioned; lace, occasionally. Thread was particularly noted in the petition from Paisley. But, as the merchants and wholesale dealers of Liverpool observed, the licensed hawkers dealt "in almost every article of female attire, whether for use or ornament."[16] Nevertheless, the singular absence of petitions from the older woollen textile centres leads one to suspect that woollens were not frequently hawked.[17] Were they too heavy to carry in bundles or had domestic distribution long since established a chain of shops headed by the woollen drapers, while the newer textile manufacturers of the north pushed their wares by any available means? Or had the particular market serviced by the hawkers determined the type of goods? Did their customers find the newer, less costly articles more attractive? The petitions particularly emphasized the importance of hawkers in extending the sale of manufactured goods. Indeed, the manufacturers of linen, cotton, and calico appear to have mounted a campaign against abolishing the hawkers. Their petitions were suspiciously similar – that of Wigan (Lancashire) was identical to the one submitted from Liverpool,[18] But that does not necessarily disqualify their assessment of the trade or their judgment that the hawkers "by their industry and perseverance," as the Scottish petitioners expressed it, "have contributed greatly to the extension of the manufactories both of England and Scotland." The Glasgow petitioners were convinced that if the bill should pass, it would "very materially injure the manufacturers of Scotland in general and the City and neighbourhood of Glasgow in particular."[19]

The campaign proved effective, at least in part. On 14 June 1785, a new proposal was introduced. In lieu of abolishing licensed hawkers, the licence fee was to be raised. Such a move was like waving a red flag in the face of the shopkeepers. Their reaction was immediate and as intense as the campaign waged to save the hawkers. From 16 June to 12 July, twenty-three petitions were submitted from twenty-two places.[20] Ten English counties were represented and two Welsh. Scotland remained quiet and so did London. No pattern emerges with respect to counties north or south of the line. Indeed, the controversy divided the business community in several places. From Kendal (Westmorland), two petitions supported the hawkers; two urged their suppression. In Halifax the "retail shopkeepers and inhabitants," in contrast to the manufacturers and wholesalers, wanted the hawkers abolished. Lancashire, one of the strongest supporters of hawkers, was torn apart over the issue. The retail shopkeepers of both Lancaster and Warrington sought the suppression of hawkers, hinting strongly that they dealt in contraband goods. Even Staffordshire, the famed centre of a large group of hawkers, submitted a petition. The shopkeepers of Wolverhampton reminded the minister that he had promised to abolish the licensed hawkers to compensate for the shop tax.[21] But Cornwall is the one county that stands out as the most vigorous and embittered opponent of the hawkers, and as we shall see, the shopkeepers there may well have had reason for their hostility. The retail shopkeepers in five towns – Falmouth, Penryn, Penzance, Redruth, and Truro – and the "Mayor, Commonalty and principal inhabitants of Launceton" requested the annihilation of the licensed hawkers or, as Penzance suggested, that "such considerable duties be imposed on their licence" to "prevent them from underselling ... the shopkeepers." In the eyes of the shopkeepers, the hawkers "paid no taxes having no settled abode" while they themselves were burdened with "the house tax, window tax, commutation tax, insurance tax, and the taxes on bills of exchange and receipts," not to mention the parochial rates and now the shop tax.[22] As compensation for the heavy burden of taxes, the shopkeepers of Exeter demanded that hawkers be completely suppressed or "at the least" not be allowed "to sell in or within two miles of cities, towns corporate or market towns."[23]

At this point the shopkeepers were not actively opposing the shop tax. They were, however, demanding relief from the competition of their unworthy rivals. It is evident from the petitions that licensed hawkers were injecting into the retail trade competitive sales practices that appeared to traditional shopkeepers as wholly uncalled for and unjust. The principal shopkeepers of Sussex, for example, had the "mortification to see their neighbours inveigled away by fallacious advertisements."[24] Those in Carmarthen having just "laid in an assortment of goods which they have a certainty of disposing in a reasonable time see their hopes blast and too often their credit also ... by a pompous advertisement" of a hawker who had made his unexpected and unwelcome appearance. They had sustained heavy losses "from unfair practices of hawkers and pedlars who generally sell some articles at or under prime cost to delude the unwary while on other articles they take exorbitant profits." Hawkers were also charged with taking rooms in towns where they were not resident and holding temporary sales. According to the shopkeepers of Scarborough, the itinerant traders, in order to sell their wares "more speedily ... put them up by lottery, raffle and other games of chance" thereby "corrupting the morals" of the people.[25] Sir Edward Astley, MP, *accused* the hawkers of selling cheaper than country shops.[26]

Coupled with the charge of cheap prices was the complaint that while shopkeepers were compelled to give "long credit to their customers," the hawkers "carry off the ready money" which should have been used to discharge book debts.

If one looks at the list of places submitting petitions, one is struck by a certain similarity. With the exception of Leeds and Halifax, they are the smaller centres of population or cities like Exeter that were either declining or had lost their relative importance in the economic life of the country. One may also presume that the shopkeepers organizing the campaign were drapers and haberdashers. Many, particularly in the smaller market towns, may indeed have felt the pressure from their more enterprising competitors. The welter of petitions for and against the hawkers clearly shows that hawkers, in contrast to the more passive shopkeepers, pushed their sales by every possible means: selling their wares at prices below those of shopkeepers; offering specially low-priced goods for "ready money"; and attracting customers by "pompous advertisements" or even games of chance. Such practices not only disturbed the customary relations among shopkeepers, where cooperation rather than competition was the ideal norm, but also unsettled the usual relations between seller and buyer. True, some shopkeepers in the larger cities were adopting similar sales techniques, but open price competition was alien to the more traditional shopkeepers who viewed their potential market as relatively stable and restricted. Such a view almost required stable prices if the shopkeeper was to maintain his standard of living. A policy based on such premises might conform to the traditional trade in woollen draperies, but did not appeal to the more aggressive textile manufacturers of the north. Perhaps that is why they so strongly supported the hawkers.

A large number of petitions had been remitted from widely scattered areas. Pitt had, therefore, to steer a narrow course between accommodating the supporters of the hawkers and removing some of the major objections of the shopkeepers, particularly if he was to prevent opposition to the shop tax. After considerable haggling over various amendments, the hawkers' bill received royal assent; but its passage was far stormier than the shop tax. The new act (25 Geo. 3, c. 78) applied only to hawkers travelling in England and Wales (sec. 1). It was insinuated in Parliament that a special indulgence had been granted Scotland as the new duties on hawkers had not been extended to that country. In fact, as the attorney-general noted, had the duty been a new one it could have been applied to Scotland "but being merely an addition to an old one it could not be extended to those who had before felt no such duty."[27]

The new act levied an additional duty of four pounds per annum on all hawkers; for those travelling with horse or other beast, an additional charge of eight pounds per beast (sec. 1). That is, from 1 August 1785, hawkers travelling by foot were to pay eight pounds for their annual licence; those travelling with one beast, sixteen pounds – a considerable levy and far heavier than the taxes paid by most shopkeepers. In addition to the increased charges, several new restrictions were placed on the activities of the hawkers. For the first time they were specifically forbidden to sell by auction; the penalty for so doing was not light – fifty pounds for every offence (sec. 2). And the demand from Exeter was heeded. Henceforth, no licensed hawker was permitted to sell or expose to sale any goods by retail in any city or market town in England and Wales or "within the distance of two miles from the middle of the most central market place" (sec. 9) except on market day at the public mart (sec. 10). Finally, the most devastating potential exclusion: a county could lawfully deny licensed hawkers the liberty to vend any goods what-soever at any time if the justices at the quarter sessions so ruled and a public notice to that effect had been posted for nine months (sec. 11). For all these restrictions, the Commons finally agreed, after considerable debate, to offer the hawkers compensatory employ-ment. A licensed hawker, whether apprenticed or not, was permitted to set up any business or exercise any trade in the place where he was a resident inhabitant, from where he could not be removed until he became "actually chargeable" to the parish for poor relief (sec. 13).

The hawkers and their supporters accepted with good grace the additional levy on their licence as well as the prohibition on selling by auction. They were, however, bitterly opposed to sections 9 to 11, which restricted where they might vend their goods. Indeed, when the bill was first introduced, the London wholesale dealers immediately lodged an objection on the grounds that such restric-tions would "prove highly detrimental to the business of the peti-tioners and injurious to the state."[28] Early the following year, petitions began arriving. Between 24 February and 30 March, twelve were submitted, their provenance similar to the earlier ones. The hawkers threatened to give up their trade unless the restrictions and "the unmerited imputation of their trade being unfair" were re-moved. And the manufacturers loudly bewailed the loss of business. Those from Manchester claimed they were forced to discharge half of the many thousands employed and "if sections 9 and 11 were not repealed the rest will have to go."[29] The hawkers found numerous supporters in Parliament, many claiming to speak on behalf of the shopkeepers. Alderman Sawbridge (London) said his constituents, burdened with the shop tax, considered the restrictions an additional injury as the hawkers "took off remnants and goods not very saleable in the shops of the metropolis and sold them in the adjacent villages." Sir Watkins Lewes (London) and Alderman Newnham (London) expressed the same view. The Lord Advocate of Scotland had been "instructed by several of his constituents who were shopkeepers to obtain the repeal of the severe restrictive clauses."[30] The hawkers' trade was indeed being threatened. By April, the Quarter Sessions of at least three counties – Norfolk, Kent, and Cornwall – had ruled that hawkers and pedlars keep out of their counties.

But the hawkers had to await the repeal of the shop tax in 1789 before receiving relief. The act, 29 Geo. 3, c. 26, restored the old charges, and justices of the peace were no longer empowered to rule against hawkers and pedlars entering the county. However, the restriction on selling in cities and market towns was retained until 1795 when it too was removed (35 Geo. 3, c. 9). By that time, with the exception of the prohibition on auctioning,[31] the hawkers' trade had returned to its old channels and old rivalries. Even after the shop tax had been repealed, the shopkeepers in Cornwall and Devonshire continued to oppose their hated competitors.[32]

By early 1786, the shopkeepers knew what the annual tax would be. For the next several months, their opposition to the shop tax dominated the political scene. Some of the opposition may have arisen spontaneously but the London shopkeepers, who had opposed the shop tax even before it became law, were certainly the prime instigators. Early in January 1786, the London Common Council appointed a "Shop Tax Committee" with a drawing fund of £200 and directed the committee "to correspond with such counties, cities and towns as they may think proper to co-operate in obtaining a repeal of the shop tax."[33] The appeal met willing ears. At York on 25 January, the Merchants Company and other retail shopkeepers held a general meeting at which they resolved that the "tax on retail shops is a partial and oppressive Impost" which should be repealed. A committee was formed of the leading shopkeepers and instructed "to correspond with the committees appointed in other places."[34] The campaign was successful. Between 25 January and 6 March 1786, forty-one petitions were submitted to Parliament. They came from twenty-two counties in England and two in Scotland. None came from Wales, probably the shopkeepers did not find themselves particularly burdened – with their low rents, many would not have been taxed, and very few assessed at the higher rate. Interestingly, although the Cornish shopkeepers had been the most vigorous opponents of the hawkers and had complained bitterly of the decay of trade, they were apparently unmoved by the shop tax. Throughout these years, no petition opposing the shop tax came from Cornwall, presumably few shops were heavily assessed. Those who might have felt the pinch were the principal shopkeepers in the larger centres where rents were comparatively high. But not all complained. The shopkeepers in Suffolk, another county that sent no petitions, may not have paid cheerfully; but those in the "two largest towns" were, according to Mr Grigsby, MP, "generally satisfied with the tax ... and if it were extended ... to other traders, e.g. warehousemen and bankers, they should be still more satisfied."[35] Compared to London shopkeepers, as shall be demonstrated, they had little reason to complain.

Unlike the campaign against the hawkers, almost all the places submitting petitions were county towns, fashionable resorts, or large industrial or commercial centres: places such as Birmingham and Coventry in Warwickshire; Liverpool, Manchester, and Preston in Lancashire; Halifax, Leeds, Sheffield, and York in Yorkshire; Glasgow and Edinburgh; Norwich, Southampton, Bristol, and Bath. There were a few exceptions, for example, Oxford City, Chipping Wycombe, and New Sarum. Political considerations may have activated some places, but it is not our impression that this was a campaign organized by Charles Fox and the opposition. Rather, Charles Fox made political capital out of it and, given the situation in Westminster and London, that was not a difficult task. Five petitions were submitted from the metropolis: one each from the retail shopkeepers of the City, the county of Middlesex adjacent to the City, the borough of Southwark and the city of Westminster, and one from the Lord Mayor, Aldermen, and Commons of the City of London.

The general burden of their arguments can be summarized briefly. The tax was a "personal" one, and could not be passed on to the consumer, as Pitt had assumed. That would be very "unfair" as it would increase "the price of almost every necessary of life."[36] It was, moreover, "impossible to calculate a proportionate advance ... without adopting a line of conduct totally incompatible with the object of the fair trader." Liverpool looked at the mechanics of competition. It was, they said "a known fact, that there are in every town ... men of bad principles and desperate fortunes (besides itinerants) who, regardless of paying their credit, undersell the fair trader, and to these any advance in the established price of goods would be an advantage and accelerate the ruin of the honest dealer." The Londoner called on the authority of Adam Smith for support. It was false reasoning to argue, as did Pitt,[37] that the tax would fall eventually on the consumer, "it being a notorious fact that the prices of all commodities are regulated by the natural force of the supply at

market combined with demand."[38] Implicit in all the arguments was
the acceptance of an "established" or "fair" price, the changing of
which would wreak havoc on dealer and customer alike. It is basically
the same refrain expressed in the complaints against hawkers selling
their wares "cheaper than country shops." Open price competition
was a distasteful and destructive practice in the eyes of traditional
shopkeepers.

A further set of charges was levelled at the injustice perpetrated
by the act. In the eyes of the petitioners, the tax was *partial, unequal,*
and therefore *unfair* and *oppressive*, phrases that crop up in almost
all the petitions. Partial, because they alone among all traders were
taxed; the merchants, the wholesale warehousemen, and the bankers, who were in a far better position to bear the burden of additional
taxes, were exempt. The complaint was almost universal. Even the
shopkeepers in Suffolk who were apparently "satisfied" with the tax
would have been "even more satisfied" had the other traders been
taxed. The bitterness of the shopkeepers on this score can be de-
tected in the lament from Liverpool. Having noted that their stocks
in trade were purchased "chiefly upon credit to pay at a certain date
and mostly sold upon credit, the payment uncertain" with many
disappointments, they concluded that their hard life was torn between "humouring the public taste for a precarious subsistence ...,
by provision for the stated returns of rent and taxation and the
periodical arrival of their untaxed wholesale tradesmen." But the
tax was partial and unequal for another reason – it fell "unequally
upon shopkeepers" themselves.[39] Even for approximately similar
habitations, rents varied not only from place to place, but within the
same community. Thus, if prices were increased commensurate with
the tax imposed on particular shopkeepers, the level of prices would
be distorted and, more devastating, some shopkeepers would have
a differential advantage. It was, therefore, an unfair and unjust tax.
The most aggrieved in this respect were the London shopkeepers
whose rents and taxes were the highest in the kingdom. The retail
dealers of Westminster noted in particular that "several hundreds
of the shopkeepers in the City and Liberty of Westminster are in
circumstances so low as to be rendered incapable of discharging both
the public and parochial taxes, and many of that description are
relieved from payment of the parish rates," which in turn increased
the rates on the petitioners.[40]

Indeed, the plight of the small shopkeepers was a refrain in all
the petitions from the metropolis. The retailers of the county of
Middlesex adjacent to the City observed that "there are many persons
keeping retail shops by which they maintain families with decency
and credit, yet their expenses are so extremely heavy it becomes

necessary for the parish officers to excuse them their rates, but the collectors of parliamentary taxes being activated by different motives ... will insist on being paid."[41] This was not a complaint frequently voiced by petitioners in the provinces, probably because few such shops had to pay the tax. The City of Oxford and Bath were exceptions. The petitioners from Bath reminded the minister that "a small retail shop, with the rigid expedient of letting out the other parts of the house, has heretofore been found an asylum for the poor and industrious." But as they also noted "the notorious increase of retail dealers beyond all proportion with the increase of trade," one wonders why they would wish to have such shops protected. The shopkeepers at Oxford, having observed the "great number of retail shops the profits whereof are ... barely sufficient to support the industrious owners," warned that the tax would "reduce to want a description of men who have long been considered the strength of this nation."[42]

Pitt bowed to the pressure and on 6 March 1786 a bill was introduced amending the act of 1785. Within less than three weeks it received royal assent (26 Geo. 3, c. 9). The amended act offered relief to shopkeepers in the lower rental range by reducing the duties for all shops the annual rent of which was less than £30. The new rates were: 4d. in the pound for an annual rent of £5 to under £10; 8d. for the £10 to £15 category; 1s. for the £15 to £20; 1s. 3d. for the £20 TO £25; and 1s. 9d. for an annual rent of £25 to under £30. Shops renting for £30 and upwards continued to pay 2s. in the pound. The effect was to widen the difference between the lower rented shops and those in the higher category, and offered little relief to London shopkeepers. In addition, the act also excluded from the tax a further group. Henceforth, no assessment was to be imposed on shopkeepers who were excused from paying the parish rates for church and poor (sec. 3).

Judging from the paucity of complaints during the next several years, the amendments removed much of the sting of the tax for the shopkeepers in the provinces. During 1787, four petitions were remitted, one each from Birmingham, Exeter, Lincoln, and New Sarum; in 1788, two, Lincoln and Liverpool; and in 1789, one only, Coventry. London, however, continued to press for repeal of the hated tax and succeeded in obtaining the support of the London tax commissioners. It was the commissioners' opinion, based on experience, that the "middle and inferior order of traders" in London were "suffering" from the tax assessments.[43] By March 1789, the commissioners submitted a long list of indictments against the tax. The assessments were "very partial and severe" and imposed "hardship" on many; there were "numerous evasions" and differences of opinion on contested and "intricate cases"; and finally, it was "impossible for them to execute" with due regard to the commissioners' oaths.[44]

After 1786 the struggle over the shop tax was reduced to a battle between Pitt and London and owed little to political opposition. At the same time, Pitt must have been aware that the shopkeepers of London had every reason to feel they were being unduly and unequally burdened by the tax. As Alderman Newnham noted, "by the amendment to the shop tax few country shopkeepers would be required to pay."[45] He was eminently right. In 1787, the assessment for the whole kingdom was approximately £59,000, of that amount £42,709, or 72.4 percent, came from Middlesex. The shopkeepers of Westminster and the City paid £29,897; the other "cities, boroughs, towns corporate and market towns" of Middlesex, £175.[46] The remaining £12,637 was shared by adjacent areas outside the City. The assessment, for example, of Marylebone was £2,545; St Andrew and St George the Martyr, £1,843.[47] And since the assessments were for Middlesex and did not include the outlying areas in Surrey, the proportion paid by the whole of the metropolis was even more.

The controversy over the hawkers and the shop tax illustrates the power wielded by extraparliamentary forces to influence the course of legislation. Not all might accept the Oxford pronouncement that retail shopkeepers were "the strength of this nation," but they, no less than manufacturers, had demonstrated ability to organize their forces. And their voices were heeded. It would have been uncharacteristic of Pitt to persist in a tax the returns of which could not justify antagonizing a substantial portion of the London business community. Moreover, as a source of revenue, the shop tax had not proved as fruitful as Pitt had at first planned and the amendments of 1786 further reduced the yield. He could certainly have maintained a majority had he so chosen. In 1788 when a bill was introduced to repeal the two acts, he mustered a majority of 141 to 98, figures not very different to previous years. But in 1789 Pitt was prepared to accept the verdict of the London tax commissioners and his bill to repeal the acts had a smooth passage. Only once did he intervene to delete the words condemning the shop tax as "partial and oppressive."[48]

The politics of the shop tax has been well recorded. The accounts submitted by the assessors have not been as well preserved. No figures have been discovered on the total number of shopkeepers taxed during the four years. However, a series of accounts have proved a

rich source of information on the number and rental value of assessed shops in different types of cities. The earliest, drawn up in
1785 prior to the passage of the act, was an attempt to determine
"the probable amount of the tax" according to the rates first suggested by Pitt in his budget speech. To arrive at the estimate, a survey
was made of the number of shops in each rental category in London
and thirty-one provincial towns.[49] The second series of accounts
appears to have formed part of the report submitted to Parliament
by the tax office in 1787 showing the assessments made on all shops
in each county.[50] But only three of these accounts have survived: a
seemingly complete list of the number of shops by rental category
in the towns and parishes of Northamptonshire; an incomplete list
for Suffolk; and an "account of the number of shops and their rents
within the Cities of London and Westminster."[51]

Where relevant, a comparison of the two series has been made.
The accounts reveal several significant dimensions of the country's
shops. The most obvious is that the burden of the tax did indeed
fall "unequally" upon shopkeepers, particularly those in London who
benefitted little by the 1786 amendments. It is also clear that the
assessed rental value of a large proportion of shops in the provinces
was low. And, although the evidence is scanty, there seems little
doubt that many shops in the provinces escaped the tax altogether.
Relatively few petty shopkeepers in London were as fortunate.

Table 8 summarizes by rental categories the number of shops in
the 1785 account of "London, Westminster, Southwark, and part of
Middlesex." The account is very specific, listing by intervals of £5
the number of shops, the rate of duty, the average assessment per
shop, and the amount of estimated revenue for that rental category.
Of the 23,083 assessed shops, the annual rent of 10,184, or 44.1
percent, was £25 or over. Shops with a rental value of £25 or more
were rated at 2s. in the pound. For some shopkeepers it was a heavy
additional tax. Among the 283 shops in the last two rental categories
(£90 to £305), the rent of 159 ranged from £100 to £185;[52] nine,
£200 to £300; and one in the highest category, £300 to £305, the
tax for which was £30 6s. The estimated assessment of the 10,184
shops was £44,134 8s., or 73.6 percent of the total for the metropolis
and 35.6 percent of the estimated yield of the tax for the whole of
England, Wales, and Scotland. In fact, the proportion paid by the
London shopkeepers was considerably higher, especially after the
amendments of 1786. Moreover, compared to the figures for provincial towns, the proportion of London shops in the two lowest rental
categories was particularly small: 7.8 percent were in the £5 to £10
category; 17.8 percent, £10 to £15. The two groups were assessed

Table 8
Assessed Shops by Rental Category[1] in London, Westminster, Southwark, and Part of Middlesex, 1785

Rent	Average Tax per Shop			Number of Shops	%
	£	s.	d.		
£5 to under £10		8		1,797	7.8
10 " " 15		16	3	4,102	17.8
15 " " 20	1	6	6	3,383	14.6
20 " " 25	2	0	3	3,617	15.7
Subtotal				12,899	55.9
£25 to under £30	2	16	0	2,064	8.9
30 " " 40	3	10	0	3,773	16.3
40 " " 50	4	10	0	1,999	8.7
50 " " 60	5	10	0	943	4.1
60 " " 75	6	14	0	859	3.7
75 " " 90	8	4	0	263	1,1
90 " " 120	10	10	0	225	1.0
120 " " 305				58	.3
Subtotal				10,184	44.1
Total				23,083	

Source: "Tax on Shops, 1785," HO 42/7, PRO.
Note: [1]Thirty-seven rental categories listed ranging from £5 to £10 to £300 to £305.

£4,051 13s. 6d. or 6.8 percent of the total tax for the metropolis. Shops in rental categories £15 to £25 number 7,000 or 30.3 percent of all shops. Their estimated assessment was £11,701 13s. 9d., almost triple that of the two lower categories. There were undoubtedly many petty shopkeepers in these four categories who could ill afford to pay the shop tax. Very few London shopkeepers (25.6 percent) benefitted from the lower rates finally enacted in 1785. Even the amended act of 1786, which lowered the rates for shops with annual rents under £30, failed to benefit at least 35 percent of the London shopkeepers.

What parts of Middlesex were not covered by the account is not known, probably the towns and boroughs never considered part of London. On an estimated population of 850,000, the ratio of persons to assessed shops in the metropolis is almost thirty-seven. In view of the fact that bakers, provision dealers, and shopkeepers with rents below five pounds were not assessed, the total number of shops in the metropolis must have been considerably greater. Clearly, the number of shops since the excise survey of 1759 had not declined.

Appendix 2, and tables 9 and 10 are compiled from the 1785 accounts of provincial towns. The formats are identical to the London account. The proportion of provincial shops in each rental category is in marked contrast to that of London: a much smaller portion in the high rent categories and a much larger portion in the lower categories. Of the 8,784 shops listed, the annual rent of only 967 or 11 percent was twenty-five pounds or over (see appendix 2). Among the 967 shops were 95 with a rent of fifty to seventy-five pounds, and 19, seventy-five pounds and up. Together they comprise 1.29 percent of all shops. By far the greater number of provincial shops were in the two lowest rental categories: 3,117 or 35.5 percent in the five to ten pound category; 2,412 or 27.5 percent, ten to fifteen pound (see table 10). That is, 62.9 percent of all provincial shops were assessed annual rents of five to fifteen pounds (see appendix 2) compared to 25.6 percent in London. Some variation occurs from town to town, but surprisingly few departed from the norm. Unfortunately, there are no obvious explanations for the particular rent structure of these towns. Neither size nor economic importance appears to be a determining factor. Birmingham, for example, follows the average pattern for provincial towns (see tables 9 and 10). On the other hand, the distribution for Worcester, with a population of only 11,000 in 1801, is almost identical to that of Bath and Bristol with a combined population of about 89,000 (see table 9). Nor does the social or cultural significance of a town appear to bear any relation to the level of rents. The highest rent recorded for York, the capital of the north, falls within the thirty to thirty-five pound category; for Nottingham, eighty to eighty-five pound (see appendix 2). In fact, only four shops in York had a rental value of thirty to thirty-five pounds; there were forty-nine in Nottingham with rents ranging from thirty to eighty-five pounds. In York, the rent of 69.6 percent of assessed shops was under fifteen pounds; in Nottingham, 56 percent (see table 9). Whatever may have been the underlying cause, seven of the listed places diverged noticeably from the average rent structure: Bath and Bristol, Liverpool, Nottingham, Salisbury and Southampton, and Worcester. The remaining twenty-four towns had far fewer shops in the higher rental categories and many more in the lower categories. In these towns, the assessed rent of 72.9 percent of shops was under fifteen pounds and 6.1 percent over twenty-five pounds; the figures for the seven towns are respectively, 51.1 percent and 16.9 percent (see table 10). It is perhaps not surprising that after the initial outcry against the shop tax, few provincial towns sent petitions to Parliament.

Table 9
Distribution of Shops in Select Provincial Towns, 1785 (in percentages)

	Assessment Categories			Total Number of Shops
	£5-£15	£15-£25	£25 and up	
Bath & Bristol	47.2	37.0	15.8	1,769
Birmingham	69.1	19.7	11.2	780
Nottingham	56.0	25.9	18.1	393
Worcester	46.0	39.0	15.0	602
York	69.6	25.9	4.5	486

Source: PRO, HO 42/7, fols. 3-11.

The 1785 survey covered twenty-three counties, from Northumberland in the northeast to Devonshire in the southwest, and included towns ranging in size from Liverpool with a population over 77,000 to small market towns such as Aylesbury, Buckinghamshire, with a population under 4,000. The survey can, therefore, serve as a guide to the approximate ratio of persons to assessed shops in towns of various sizes and types (see appendix 2 for ratios). The average ratio of persons per assessed shop was 54.8; for the towns north of the line, 69.7; for the south, 46.6.[53] However, there is an enormous difference in the ratios, ranging from 141 in Liverpool to 19 in Worcester. True, more populous centres tend to have a higher ratio of persons to shops, and in fast-growing towns a ratio based on census figures for 1801 would exaggerate that tendency. It should also be remembered that not all shops were subject to the tax. In addition to bakers and provision dealers, any shop with an annual rent under five pounds was exempt. Perhaps rents were considerably lower in those towns with high ratios, and there were many shops not assessed. Until much more work has been done on the local level no definitive answer can be given. What is startling is the relatively small number of persons per *assessed* shop in many of the towns. In a recent study which calculated the number of persons per shop for nine towns in 1822, the ratios ranged from a low of 70 for York to 400 for Merthyr Tydfill; for Leeds, 225; Manchester, 195; Liverpool, 170: Norwich, 135; Nottingham, 130.[54] And for four of the towns – York, Leeds, Norwich, and Nottingham – bakers and dealers in flour have been included in the number of shops. There were seventy-three bakers and provision dealers in Nottingham; fifty-seven, in York. If these shops are excluded the ratios

Table 10
Distribution of Shops in Select Groups of Provincial Towns, 1785 (in percentages)

	Assessement Categories				Total Number of Shops
	£5-£10	£10-£15	£15-£25	£25 and up	
Seven Towns[1]	27.5	23.6	32.0	16.9	3,999
Remainder	42.2	30.7	21.0	6.1	4,785
All Towns	35.5	27.5	26.0	11.0	8,784

Source: PRO, HO 42/7, fols. 3-11.

Note: [1]These include: Bath and Bristol, Liverpool, Nottingham, Salisbury and Southampton, and Worcester.

rise to 174 for the former and 85 for the latter.[55] That is, the general level of the 1822 ratios is very much higher for the nine towns than for the thirty-one places listed in appendix 2. In fact, the ratios bear little resemblance to the ratios of persons to *assessed* shops in 1785. The number of shops assessed was certainly less than the total number of shops. Either the number of shops declined drastically during the thirty-seven years following the shop tax or, as we shall argue, the trade directories which formed the basis for the 1822 calculations are not a reliable source for numbering shops, at least not until midnineteenth century or later.[56]

The 1787 accounts list by rental categories the number of shops actually assessed by the tax office and in that respect are a somewhat more reliable source than the 1785 survey, which was conducted before the assessors had sufficient experience to determine what should or should not be taxed. However, by 1787 a further group of shopkeepers were exempt from paying the tax, those who by reason of their poverty were not required to contribute to the usual assessments for church and poor. Judging from the 1787 account for Bury St Edmunds, the number of shopkeepers relieved of the tax was not small, at least in the provinces.

Table 11 sets out the figures for London. Unfortunately, the account covers only Westminster and the City, and is not fully comparable to table 8. It does, however, make possible a rough estimate of the rental value of shops in the rest of London. Not surprisingly, Westminster and the City had a very small proportion of shops in the lower rental categories. Of the 6,579 shopkeepers assessed in the City, only 5.7 percent were paying a rent of £5 to £10 and 12.5 percent, £10 to £15. The annual rent of 58.6 percent was £25 or over. The breakdown is no less striking for Westminster: 1.4 percent

Table 11
Assessed Shops by Rental Category in Westminster and the City of London,
ca. 1787.

Rent[1]		Average Tax Per Shop[2]			Number of Shops:	
					City	Westminster
		£	s.	d.		
£5 to under £10			2	4	376	81
10 " " 15			8	0	825	475
15 " " 20			17	0	719	807
20 " " 25		1	7	6	807	1,108
25 " " 30		2	7	3	650	638
	Subtotal				3,377	3,109
£30 to under £40		3	10	0	1,135	1,209
40 " " 50		4	10	0	766	734
50 " " 60		5	10	0	521	272
60 " " 75		6	14	0	446	307
75 " " 90		8	4	0	148	93
90 " " 120		10	10	0	149	66
120 " " 305					37	19
	Total				6,579	5,809

Source: "An Account of the Number of Shops Showing the Rents Paid by the Possessors of the Same, viz. @ £5 and Under £10, @ £10 and Under £15 ... and so on in the same gradation as follows: In the City of London and Westminster." ca. 1787, 30/8/281, fol. 141, PRO.

Notes: [1]In the original document twenty-six rental categories are listed ranging from the first group, £5 to under £10, and rising by £5 to the last group which includes all shops with rents £130 to under £305.

[2]The average tax per shop is a very approximate figure based on the assumption that the average rent of shops in each rental category falls mid-way. No meaningful average can be calculated for the last category.

(£5 to £10); 8.2 percent (£10 to £15), and 57.5 percent (£25 and over). In 1787 only shops with an annual rent of £30 or over paid the highest rate of duty, 2s. in the pound. In the City, 48.7 percent of the shops were so rated; in Westminster, 46.4 percent. Of the total number of shops assessed in Westminster and the City, only 457 or 3.7 percent paid the lowest rate, 4d. in the pound. If the 23,083 shops enumerated in the 1785 account paid the tax in 1787, then the other areas of the metropolis contained 10.695 assessed shops. Of these, a very large proportion were in the lower rental categories: 12.5 percent (£5 to £10) and 26.2 percent (£10 to £15). The annual rent of only 2,218 or 20.7 percent was £30 or over. But with the exception of Marylebone and parts of Southwark, few areas outside Westminster and the City could support many high-class shops. For shopkeepers in such poor districts as Bethnal Green, Spitalfield, and the Tower Hamlets whose total assessment was £2,156, the tax was undoubtedly a very heaven burden.[57]

As one might expect, the ratio of persons to assessed shop was much lower for Westminster and the City than for the metropolis. Based on the resident population of 1801, the ratio for the City within and without the Walls was 22.4; for Westminster, 26.4. Given the changes in population in the intervening fourteen years, the ratio for Westminster in 1787 was probably somewhat lower and that for the City, a little higher. It would appear that in these areas few shopkeepers, with the exception of bakers, provision dealers, and those excused parochial rates, escaped the tax. Of the total number assessed, many were little better than petty chandlers with very low incomes for whom the tax was indeed a "hardship."

The picture that emerges from an analysis of the rental value of shops in Northamptonshire and Suffolk fully supports the rental structure depicted in the 1785 survey (see tables 12 and 13). There is, in fact, an even larger proportion of shops in the lower rental categories. Either rental values were particularly low in these two counties, or the amendments of 1786 had drastically reduced the number of shops subject to the tax. Certainly the yield of the tax for the provinces was well below that estimated in 1785. The total contribution of the thirty-nine counties in England, the twenty-two in Wales, and the thirty-three in Scotland was only £16,000 compared to the £42,709 from Middlesex. Alderman Newnham may have exaggerated slightly when he stated that "by the amendment to the shop tax few country shopkeepers would be required to pay," but he was probably not far from the mark. Certainly many small shops must have escaped the tax in Northamptonshire and Suffolk.

The survey of Northamptonshire appears to include all places contributing to the shop tax. Not only has the tax office summed up the total, but the places named covered the whole geographical spread of the county.[58] And yet only thirty-two towns or parishes are listed. Of the fifteen generally recognized market towns, one, Rockingham, did not make the list. It is difficult to believe that Rockingham could not boast even one shop. The total number of shops assessed in Northamptonshire was 476. Of these, 354 or 74.4 percent fell in the first rental category (£5–£10); 90, in the second (£10–£15), and 28 in the third (£15–£20). Of the remaining four, all in Northampton, only one shop was rated above £30, with a rent between £40 and £45 (see table 12). That is, 93.3 percent of all shops assessed were paying rents less than £15, a striking contrast to the 14.2 percent for Westminster and the City. The total assessment for

Table 12
Population per Assessed Shop and Number of Shops by Rental Category:
Northamptonshire and Selected Towns, ca. 1787

| | Number of Assessed Shops | | | | | | | |
Place	£5-£10	£10-£15	£15-£20	£20-£25	£25-£30[1]	£40-£45[1]	Total	Ratio[2]
Northampton	86	24	17	2	1	1	131	54
Peterborough	74	34	8				116	30
Daventry	31	8					39	66
Kettering	26	7	2				35	86
Wellingborough	28	4	1				33	101
Oundle	25	3					28	70
Towcester	16	4					20	101
Thrapstone	15	2					17	40
Brackley	10	4					14	107
Northamptonshire	354	90	28	2	1	1	476	286
Percentage	74.4	18.9	5.9	.4	.2	.2		

Sources: Shops: PRO, 30/8/281, fol. 143; Population: Census, 1801.

Notes: [1]No shop paid rent between thirty and forty pounds.

[2]The ratio represents the number of persons per assessed shop.

Northamptonshire was approximately £110 with some 74 percent of the shopkeepers paying an annual charge of roughly 2s. 4d. each and 19 percent, 8s. Only four shopkeepers would have been required to pay over £1. Determining a proportionate increase in prices would certainly have been difficult for these shopkeepers! Judging from the form used by the tax office, the highest rent anticipated was £40 to £45 – no provision was made for a higher rent.

While there is no way of knowing how many shops escaped the tax, the proportion was probably less in the larger centres. It is possible, therefore, to form some idea of the *maximum* number of people per shop in a few of the more populous centres. Table 12 sets forth the results of our calculations. As in the 1785 survey, there is a considerable difference in the ratios even for towns of approximately the same population. The ratio for Wellingborough with a population in 1801 of 3,325 was 101 persons per shop; for Peterborough (population 3,449), 30. Nor are the ratios correlated with the size of the town. The ratio for Thrapstone, the smallest town (population 675), was 40; for Northampton, the largest (population 7,020), 54. Some of the variations in ratios may be the result of population changes since 1787. It is also possible that the area surveyed by the tax assessors did not correspond to that of the census. On the other hand, variations many mean nothing more than differences in the rental value of shops, that rents, for example, in Wellingborough were on the whole much lower than in Peterborough and that a larger number of shops were excused from paying the tax. What is surprising is the relatively small number of persons per *assessed* shop in these sparsely populated towns. The actual ratios must have been considerably lower, given the types of shops not subject to the tax.

The account for Suffolk (table 13) is only part of what was originally submitted. There is no grand total for the county and Ipswich is conspicuously absent. Indeed, a number of active market towns within a narrow strip of land running north of Ipswich are not included in the list.[59] We cannot be sure that this is the only area for which there are no figures, but no other market towns are omitted from the list. Even this incomplete account indicates that there were many more towns with taxable shops in Suffolk than in Northamptonshire. Listed for Suffolk are 112 towns in contrast to the 32 for Northamptonshire. The total number of assessed shops in Suffolk is 655. As table 13 shows, the breakdown by rental categories is almost the same as Northamptonshire. There were 482 shops or 73.6 percent in the first category (£5–£10); 113 or 17.3 percent in the second (£10–£15). No shops were recorded in the two highest categories (£35–£40, £40–£45), and only one shop with a rent between £30 and £35. Individual towns varied slightly in the proportion of shops in each of the rental categories. The most marked departure from the norm was not, however, Bury St Edmunds, but the town of Newmarket. Either rents were particularly high at Newmarket or a large number of shops had a rental value below £5.

Table 13 gives the ratio of population per assessed shop for ten Suffolk towns and an estimate for the county. Saxmundham, (population 855) had the lowest ratio, 32; Sudbury, (population 3,283), the highest, 96. The calculated ratio for Bury St Edmunds, the largest town in the 1787 account, (population 7,655), was 61. Indeed, the figures for Bury St Edmunds are most revealing. In 1785, 285 shops were assessed, but only 125 paid the tax in 1787 (see appendix 2 and table 13). Apparently, the 1786 amendment enabled 160 shopkeepers to escape the tax. Almost all were in the lower rental categories. The 1785 account for Bury St Edmunds lists 140 shops in the first rental category (£5–£10) and 89 in the second (£10–£15). The figures for 1787 are respectively, 63 and 38. That is, of the 160 shopkeepers who escaped the tax, 128 appear to have been in the two lowest rental categories. Interestingly, the proportions of shops

Table 13

Population per Assessed Shop and Number of Shops by Rental Category: Suffolk and Selected Towns, ca. 1787

	Number of Assessed Shops							
Place	£5-£10	£10-£15	£15-£20	£20-£25	£25-£30	£30-£35[1]	Total	Ratio[1]
Bury St Edmunds	63	38	19	5			125	61
Bungay Burgh	30	9	4	2			45	52
Beccles	22	13	6	2			43	65
Halesworth	31	6	3	1			41	41
Sudbury	25	7	2				34	96
Hadleigh	28	5					33	71
Stowmarket	25	3					28	63
Saxmundham	18	7	2				27	32
Newmarket	7	3	7	2	2	1	22	81
Botesdale	14	1					15	38
Suffolk	482	113	45	12	2	1	655	332
Percentage	73.6	17.3	6.9	1.8	.3	.15		

Sources: Shops: PRO, 30/8 281, fols. 145-46b; Population; Census 1801.

Note: [1]The ratio represents the number of persons per *assessed* shop. The figure for the county is inflated as it is based on the total population for Suffolk, while the number of assessed shops does not include Ipswich and other nearby towns.

in each rental category are almost identical for both accounts. In 1785, 80.4 percent of shops were in the two lowest categories; in 1787, 80.8 percent. If Bury St Edmunds is representative of the country at large, over half of the provincial shopkeepers assessed in 1785 were relieved of the tax. But even by this incomplete count of shops, the ratios for the Suffolk towns are well below those calculated for the nine towns in 1822.

The average number of persons per assessed shop in Northamptonshire was 286; in Suffolk, 332. Even if the missing towns in Suffolk had 200 assessed shops, the ratio would still be high, 254. In 1787, just three years after the reduction of duty on tea, there were 48,263 licensed tea dealers in England and Wales, or an average of 166 persons per dealer. No one would argue that all shopkeepers paid a licence fee of 5s. 6d. for the right to sell tea. And yet the average ratio for tea dealers was almost half that for the assessed shops in the counties of Northampton and Suffolk. Moreover, a decade later, when the total number of tea licences for the country had increased by 10 percent, 1,194 were issued for the "greater portion of Suffolk," an area that did not include the northern parts adjacent to Norfolk.[60] In short, Suffolk had almost twice as many *tea dealers* as the number of assessed shops. Available information does not allow a definitive pronouncement, but it certainly suggests that less than half the retail shops in the provinces were paying the shop tax. Indeed, the proportion not taxed may well have been considerably greater, particularly in the smaller towns.

As a source on the number of shops in individual towns, eighteenth-century directories are less reliable than Pigot's later series. Generally, only the principal shopkeepers are listed in the eighteenth-century directories. There are, however, a few interesting exceptions. The *Universal British Directory* (1799) gives a very detailed description of shopkeepers in the small market town of Lavenham, Suffolk. In the 1787 account for Suffolk, five retail shops were assessed in Lavenham – three in the rental category £5 to £10 and two, £10 to £15. The *Directory* listed sixteen shopkeepers.[61] The five assessed in 1787 were probably the four grocers and drapers and the one apothecary shop identified in the *Directory*. But in addition to the five, the *Directory* listed: one perfumer and perukemaker; one staymaker; one ironmonger, brazier, and clockmaker; and one identified simply as a "shopkeeper." The remainder were tradesmen-*cum*-shopkeepers: two "yarn makers and shopkeepers"; one "yarn maker and slop seller"; one "woolcomber and shopkeeper"; one "tailor and shopkeeper"; one "bricklayer and shopkeeper"; and "one shopkeeper and barber." It is difficult to believe that during the decade following the shop tax, eleven tradesmen had opened shop in Lavenham. They were, one suspects, the "country shopkeepers" Alderman Newnham referred to, those not required to pay the tax and whose trade was trifling. But however small or large the proportion of such shops may have been, few shopkeepers in the provinces were heavily assessed.

Licensed hawkers fared less well than provincial shopkeepers. Not many shopkeepers outside London were justified in complaining of the heavy burden of taxes compared to the so-called untaxed licensed hawkers. If some three-quarters of the shops paid an annual rent under £10, the house and window taxes could rarely have amounted to £1. It is doubtful if parochial rates were much higher; and the shop tax, as we have seen, could add only 2s. 4d. Moreover, the assumption of the irate shopkeepers that hawkers "paid no taxes having no settled abode" was a fiction of overheated envy. Of course licensed hawkers had permanent abodes, some of which may well have qualified for the assessments on houses and windows. They were by no means paupers, not if licensed to hawk. It would be strange indeed if the manufacturers of Manchester, Glasgow, and

Paisley, and the wholesale dealers of such enterprising towns as Liverpool, Halifax, and London were extending credit to impecunious or unreliable travellers about whom they knew little. On the contrary, one has the impression that the connection between supplier and hawker had long since been firmly established and the trade "thereby reduced and brought into a regular channel."[62] Credit, often on a large scale, was extended to known hawkers who, in turn, gave credit to their regular customers, a practice that continued well into the nineteenth century. In fact, the additional £4 fee for hawking by foot was a far heavier assessment than that imposed by the shop tax.[63] The sad truth is that many shopkeepers, even after almost a century, had not accepted the hawker as a worthy competitor. In addition to capturing potential customers, the hawker was a stranger and as such engendered the hostility and suspicion traditionally felt towards those not part of the life of the community. Perhaps that is one reason why so much opposition against hawkers emanated from small market towns.

The opposition expressed in 1785 is actually little different to that voiced in 1704, when several amendments were made to the laws regulating the hawkers. The "Mayor, capital Burgesses, Shopkeepers and other grieved inhabitants" of Shaftesbury, Dorset, complained in 1704 of the great hardship they "and all other traders of this realm labour under by reason of the licence granted to hawkers and pedlars (most of whom are foreigners never bred up to trades)." There was, they said, "so visible a decay to trade that it renders the petitioners unable to support their families ... and will disable all shopkeepers from paying their rents, taxes and parish duties." The petitioners from Dorchester claimed that many licensed hawkers "privately resort to the said corporation and by their wiles sell great quantities of divers sorts of goods and merchandise" to the great injury of the shopkeepers and traders. Those of East Grinstead, Sussex, prayed for "some effectual remedy ... to suppress their intestine enemies, the hawkers and pedlars." So aggrieved were the shopkeepers that they circulated in various towns and submitted to Parliament a "well-stated printed proposal ... for improving the revenue by suppressing hawkers and pedlars." Available sources do not state the plan, but the petitioners were "heartily" willing to "comply with the conditions therein stipulated" and "to pay their proportions" for the relief of the revenue.[64] Were they suggesting to tax themselves in 1704? Again in 1759, there are signs of opposition to the hawkers – this time, rather suprisingly, from the "merchants, traders and manufacturers of London and Westminster" who "daily suffer by the liberty given by law to hawkers" to impose "their damaged and low priced as well as foreign goods on the ignorant and inexperienced ... to their disadvantage and our great loss." They too suggested that "some other revenue ... be substituted" for the hawker's fee, "more consistent with the nature and circumstances of trade ... [and] more beneficial to the nation."[65] This may have been the first rumbling against the suggested shop tax rather than an attack on the hawkers.

How grave a threat was the licensed hawker to the shopkeepers in 1785? Were they so numerous and so ubiquitous to warrant the hostility expressed? It is doubtful. Licensed hawkers were, it is true, only one of the many types of itinerant traders, those who travelled with packs from town to town. No licence was required of local pedlars whose activities were controlled by town acts or market regulations, often dictated by the interests of the shopkeepers. Also specifically excluded from the requirement to obtain a licence were those who hawked printed papers, fish, fruits or victuals; craftsmen selling their own wares; and travelling tinkers, coopers, glaziers, plumbers, and harnessmenders. By 1785, the licensed hawkers were dealing primarily in drapery goods and other small wares and posed a threat primarily to drapers. And if one can trust the figures, it was a diminishing threat, at least in terms of the number of *licensed* hawkers. How many illegally hawked without a licence during the eighteenth century is impossible to determine. One suspects not many regularly employed hawkers would have exposed themselves to possible discovery and the consequent penalties, particularly as some shopkeepers were eager to find a pretext to hinder the hawkers' activities. Undoubtedly some took the chance, just as some shopkeepers sold smuggled tea from unentered places.

To assess the number of hawkers during the eighteenth century entails a frustrating problem. No account of the *number* of hawkers before 1783 is available. There are, however, two accounts for the gross and net revenue from the hawkers' licenses: one gives the medium revenue for three years, 1723–6; the other, for each year from 1747 to 1757.[66] As the licence fee increased by four pounds for each beast, to convert the gross revenue to the number of licences issued one should know at the least the proportion of hawkers travelling by foot. For the years 1782–5, 75 percent of the total number issued were foot licences. The calculations in table 14 have been based on the assumption that a similar proportion existed during earlier years. By 1817, the proportion of foot licences reached 82.7 percent and continued to increase in later years.[67] It is possible the proportion of hawkers with horse licences was greater in the early part of the eighteenth century. If so, the estimate for those years will overstate the number of licensed hawkers.

Table 14
Licensed Hawkers in England and Wales: 1723–6, 1747–8 to 1756–7, 1782–3
to 1784–5

Year	Gross Revenue £	Net Revenue[1] £	Number of Licences		
			Foot	Horse	Total
1723-6	11,167	8,303	[1,741]	[580]	[2,321]
1747-8	6,692	3,878	[1,043]	[348]	[1,391]
1748-9	6,948	4,010	[1,083]	[361]	[1,444]
1749-50	7,053	4,036	[1,099]	[367]	[1,466]
1750-1	7,329	4,355	[1,142]	[381]	[1,523]
1751-2	7,596	4,709	[1,185]	[394]	[1,579]
1752-3	8,053	5,156	[1,255]	[418]	[1,673]
1753-4	8,426	5,265	[1,313]	[438]	[1,751]
1754-5	8,318	5,358	[1,296]	[432]	[1,728]
1755-6	8,710	5,714	[1,357]	[453]	[1,810]
1756-7	9,666	6,616	[1,506]	[502]	[2,008]
1782-3	6,283	3,496	994	319	1,313
1783-4	6,252	3,049	1,002	311	1,313
1784-5	6,306	3,966	942	348	1,290

Sources: 1723-6 – "Account of the gross and net revenue ... medium of 3 years." 30/8/81, fol. 35, PRO.; 1747/8 to 1756/7 – "Account of the gross and net produce ... 10 Jan. 1759," Add. Ms. 33,039, fols. 177-8, BM; 1782 to 1784-5 – "Account of the gross and net produce ... to 1785," 308/290, fol. 43-7, PRO.

Note: Figures in brackets are estimates as explained in text; the tax year ended at midsummer for all figures.

[1] Net revenue – Amount submitted to Treasury after deducting expenses incurred by the Office for Licensing Hawkers.

The tax on hawkers was not a fruitful source of revenue and the cost of administering it was extraordinarily high, ranging from 25.6 percent of the gross revenue in the first period (1723–6) to 44.2 percent in the third (1782–5). During the tax year 1783–4, it reached an exorbitant 51.2 percent. No wonder Pitt was prepared to sacrifice the hawkers as a palliative to the shopkeepers. What seems surprising is that such a small body of traders loomed so large in the eyes of some shopkeepers. True, the decade of the 1750s, a decade when all economic indicators show an upturn, witnessed a slight increase in their number. But even then they did not achieve the level of 1723–6. And the increase was only temporary. By the 1780s, the number of licensed hawkers was below the figure for 1747–8. In short, whatever cost advantage hawkers had in comparison with shopkeepers, it was not sufficient to attract new entrants – rather a movement out of the trade. Early in the century, Defoe observed a decline in the number of chapmen, many of whom he thought had

Map 3
Distribution of Licensed Hawkers in Wales and each English County, 1782-3

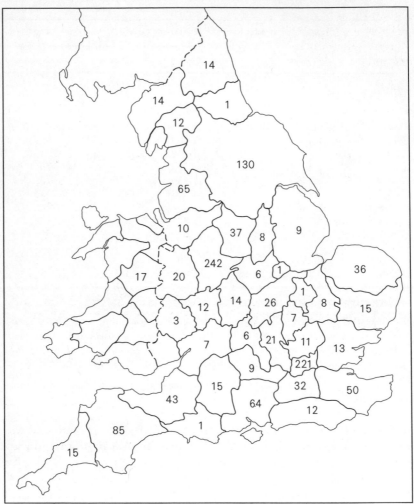

Note: Figures represent the number of licensed hawkers.

become "keepers of shops." The figures suggest he may well have been right. Certainly, shopkeeping was the major area of growth in the retail trade.

The 1785 account lists the number of foot and horse licences issued in each English county and in the principality of Wales for each year from midsummer 1782 to midsummer 1785. Thus, it is possible to sketch the geographical distribution of licensed hawkers.[68] Figures for individual counties range from 242 for Staffordshire to only one each for four English counties (Dorset, Durham, Huntingdon, and Rutland).

Table 15 lists the counties with forty or more resident hawkers. These eight counties accounted for 68.5 percent of all licensed hawkers and 71.1 percent of those travelling by foot. Forty-five percent lived in three counties – Staffordshire, Middlesex, and Yorkshire. A disproportionate number of hawkers resided in certain areas of the country. What had attracted them? Did they settle down near the source of their supplies or had the market potential of the surrounding areas opened up opportunies for the more adventurous? Had they long since established rights of settlement? Or were they wanderers in life as in profession – strangers to the community and to the body politic and fit objects of fear, suspicion, and hostility?

Unfortunately, little information is available on the life and working habits of the hawkers. They are seen most frequently through the eyes of their hostile critics, the shopkeepers and, if one accepts their verdict, the hawkers were indeed homeless. That seems incredible. The petitions supporting the hawkers provide ample proof that their suppliers knew them well and had maintained connections with them for protracted periods of time. Hawkers were no mean businessmen, as their critics grudgingly admitted. They were responsible for introducing to the retail trade novel and dynamic sales techniques that were being slowly adopted by the less tradition-bound shopkeepers in the larger towns. Such skills were not acquired without training and, like many apprenticed trades, were probably handed down from father to son. The petitioners from Staffordshire had been "brought up from infancy" in the trade of hawking and were "totally unacquainted with any other." The promise of "permanence and stability" implicit in the act passed in Queen Anne's reign was a recurring theme in the petitions supporting the hawkers. It is, moreover, unlikely that unsettled hawkers scattered around the country would have been in a position to submit to Parliament exceedingly well-written and argued petitions. It is perhaps not without significance that three of the petitions came from the three major hawking centres – London, Halifax, and the parish of Alstonfield – and they were not carbon copies. Each spoke in its own tongue, in the name of a firmly based local group.

If the 1785 account does register the more or less permanent abode of licensed hawkers, was the settlement pattern a matter of pure chance, or had it arisen in response to economic or other forces? It is certainly curious to find the largest single number of hawkers settled in Staffordshire. The hamlet of Holinsclough in the parish

Table 15
Licensed Hawkers in England and Wales and Selected Counties, 1782-3

Place	Number of Licences			%
	Foot	Horse	Total	Horse Licences
Staffordshire	211	31	242	12.8
Middlesex	166	55	221	24.9
Yorkshire	86	44	130	33.8
Devonshire	63	22	85	25.9
Lancashire	54	11	65	16.9
Hampshire	55	9	64	14.1
Kent	41	9	50	18.0
Somersetshire	36	7	43	16.3
Subtotal	712	188	900	20.9
England & Wales	1,002	311	1,313	23.7

Source: "Account of the Gross and Net Produce ... 1782 ... to 1785," 30/8/290, fols. 43-7, PRO.

of Alstonfield was, it appears, almost entirely inhabited by them. This was the "barren wild spot" that they had transformed into "a rich fertile circuit." It is an area centrally located between two sources of supply, hosiery from Nottinghamshire and Leicestershire, and the cotton, linen, and small wares of Lancashire, all of which were the stock-in-trade of the hawkers. It was also close to potential customers. But it is surely far-fetched to suspect that a group of hawkers some time in the eighteenth century had chosen the county as a location most convenient. Perhaps the Staffordshire hawkers of 1785 were the descendants of those who in earlier years hawked the local pottery.

The large number of hawkers living in or about London is understandable. It was a convenient centre from which they could fan out to the towns and villages in the surrounding area. Welcomed by wholesalers and shopkeepers alike, the hawkers could obtain with ease both supplies and credit. And the manufacturers and wholesalers of Lancashire and Yorkshire had actively promoted the hawking of their wares for many years.

The clustering of hawkers in the south, however, arouses suspicion and speculation. The combined total for Somersetshire, Devonshire, and Cornwall was 143; Hampshire, 64; and Kent, 50. There were and always had been veiled, and sometimes open, accusations that hawkers dealt in smuggled goods. No proof was offered and one doubts that it was true in 1785. But were the accusations wholly unsubstantiated? Were they part of local folklore rooted in the past?

Somersetshire, Devonshire and Cornwall had been, if they were not still, centres for smuggling tea, tobacco, wine, brandy, and even soap from Ireland, to name the most frequently cited items. This is not to suggest that the forbears of the 1785 hawkers were the wild and violent gangs that menaced excise officers. Not all smugglers resorted to force; much of the illicit trade was conducted in a quiet quasi-legal manner and had its regular carriers and contacts with shopkeepers and private families.[69] Shifting from illicit to legal hawking would require very little change in the daily pattern of life or the skills acquired. This, of course, is in the realm of speculation, based on the coincidence of two not completely dissimilar trade practices. But it is perhaps not without significance that despite the large number of hawkers settled in these counties, not one petition, either from the hawkers themselves or from their supporters, was submitted to Parliament while there were many vehement protests against them. Cornwall and Kent were among the first to exclude hawkers from selling within their counties and each submitted many petitions actively opposing hawkers. Devonshire was not far behind.

The usual market area of a licensed hawker is not known. But Wordsworth's Peter Bell who "trod the cliffs of Dover" and lay "beside his asses on lofty Cheviot Hills" was undoubtedly an exception, at least in the late eighteenth century. It is difficult to imagine the cockney-accented hawker of London attempting to sell his wares to Welsh farmers or venturing into the wilds of Northumberland. Why should he go so far afield to compete against homebred hawkers who had long since established connections with customers and suppliers? He could more profitably and with greater efficiency and economy cultivate his own home market, especially if he extended credit to his customers as so many of the hawkers did. To secure payment, he needed to make his rounds at regular intervals and to be known in the communities and farmhouses he visited. A certain familiarity with the people facilitated sales and acted as some protection against bad debts. However industrious a hawker might be, the market area he could serve with satisfaction to his customers and profit to himself must have been considerably more restricted than the romantic view expressed by Wordsworth, particularly if he travelled by foot as three-quarters of the hawkers did. We would suggest that most licensed hawkers confined their activities to well-defined areas within their own regions and made their rounds in nearby counties. Although the number of hawkers resident in any one county may not signify the extent of hawking within that county, figures for groups of counties can give a rough indication of broad regional differences.

It was frequently stated that hawkers sold their wares primarily in country villages and isolated farmhouses remote from market towns and shops, thereby increasing the sales of British manufactured goods. Such statements were bitterly contested by shopkeepers who attested to the hawkers presence in market towns. Some even questioned the necessity for hawkers in remote places, as retail shops were, they claimed, established in all parts of the country. There is reason to believe that in this instance the shopkeepers were not wholly wrong. True, hawkers made the rounds of country districts (what areas outside London could not be so described?). But they certainly did not confine their activities to remote areas, nor were such areas the major scene of their action. The outcry against the law prohibiting hawkers from selling in market towns is incontrovertible evidence that town dwellers were important potential customers of the hawkers. And the regional distribution of hawkers points in the same direction.

If licensed hawkers were concentrating their activities in remote districts far from shops, one would expect to find a greater proportion of hawkers in areas with the lowest density of shops. Table 16 is based on a similar arrangement of counties as that for the excise survey of shops in 1759. It shows quite distinctly that country districts were by no means their major area of activity. In fact, the reverse is true. Given the itinerant nature of the trade, less confidence can be placed in the ratios for individual regions, but the broad differences are too striking to ignore. Wales, with the lowest density of shops in 1759, had the highest ratio of population to hawkers; the Midlands and the Home Counties, on the other hand, with the highest density of shops had the lowest ratio. The ratio for the English counties north of the line was 7,274 compared to 6,250 for counties south of the line. One can only conclude that shopkeeping and hawking were responding to similar economic and social forces.

In contrast to the conservative practices of the traditional shopkeepers, hawkers were aggressive, pushing salesmen. If some still relied on the personal approach at farmhouse doors, many turned to largescale advertising in market towns and cities to attract the eyes of new customers and to increase sales. Advertisements were cunningly designed to appeal to the desire of the middling orders for new fineries at bargain prices. In short, hawkers had developed the art of salesmanship to a fine point. The enterprising manufacturers of Lancashire and Scotland, eager to extend the sales of their ever-increasing production, welcomed such business practices. And they vigorously supported their travelling salesmen. But if hawkers sometimes created a market for British manufactured goods, shops

Table 16
Distribution of Licensed Hawkers, 1782-3

Regions		No. of Licences	Population 1801	Population per Licence
South of Line:				
I & II		257	2,016,425	7,846
III		355	1,949,956	5,493
IV, V & VI		244	1,383,503	5,670
	Subtotal	856	5,349,884	6,250
North of Line:				
VII & VIII		245	1,567,803	6,400
IX		180	1,305,025	7,250
X		15	327,594	21,840
	Subtotal	440	3,200,422	7,274
Wales		17	605,867	35,640
	Total	1,313	9,156,173	6,974

Source: PRO 30/8/281, fols. 145-146b.

Note: Counties included in each region are the same as those in appendix 1. There is, however, one exception. The figures for Cornwall and Devonshire (Region 1) have been allocated to counties south of the line. It would have been unreasonable to suppose that the eighty-five hawkers residing in Devonshire confined their activities to that county or Cornwall. Half the hawkers in Staffordshire have been allocated to Region VI, similar to the arangement of shops in the Lichfield collection (see appendix I, note 3).

quickly followed in their wake. Their relationship within the distributive system was both competitive and complementary: together they extended the home market. However, in the century-long rivalry between these two retail trades, resident traders far outnumbered itinerant hawkers. In the process many shopkeepers began to adopt the practices of their rivals.

CHAPTER FIVE

Shopkeepers in London and York: Analyses of Their Trade, Income, and Site

Of all retail traders, the most difficult to document is the petty shopkeeper. Carrying little weight in the political, economic, and social life of the community, he has largely escaped observation. True, the London commissioners of the shop tax claimed many were assessed in the metropolis, and there is some evidence of their presence in the provinces. But for more information on the number of these lowly tradesmen and on their role in the retail trade, it is necessary to piece together evidence drawn from a number of different sources – a tedious but rewarding exercise. As the following chapters will demonstrate, petty shopkeepers formed a significant proportion of all shops in the eighteenth century and occupied an important and necessary link in the chain of distribution.

Towards the end of the century, Pitt sought information on the ability of various groups within the kingdom to pay additional taxes. Among the accounts remitted to him, those from London and the City of York have proved particularly useful. They not only provide detailed statements of the number, income, amount of assessed taxes, and general economic position of the shopkeepers in 1797, but also describe their geographical dispersion and thus offer a rare opportunity to chart the shopkeeping population for at least two cities. The picture depicted fully supports some of the tentative generalizations drawn from other sources.

LONDON

In 1797, the collectors of assessed taxes submitted to Treasury information on the number of shops and houses charged or paying the assessments within the metropolis[1] Each report identified the district for which the collector was responsible and distinguished "the number of houses in which there are retail shops" from other houses.[2] "Shops" and houses were enumerated according to assessment classes, ranging from the first class "under £1" to the fifth class "£10 to £20."[3] The main purpose of the survey was to determine which of the assessed classes could "bear a single, double or treble rate of assessment." The collectors were, therefore, urged to comment on the financial state "of the different occupiers" within their districts.[4] Not all complied with the request, although some of the reports are fully annotated, particularly with reference to shopkeepers. Many gave the number excused because of poverty from paying the assessment; others merely indicated that there were "many" or "great number excused", or stated the total amount of money foregone. Thus, the collector for the Holleywell Street Liberty in the parish of St Leonard's, Shoreditch, reported "many" shopkeepers were excused from paying the assessments, resulting in a deficiency of £82 1s. 10d. He also noted that "there are 1,200 small houses that pay no taxes," in other words, falling below the minimum assessment rate. He did not mention how many such houses had retail shops. Others made no reference to the number of shops or houses excused. It would, however, be unsafe to conclude that in these wards or districts no shopkeeper was excused from paying. Also recorded are the number having difficulty paying and the number letting lodgings.[5] Even more germane are the comments on the income or trade of the shopkeepers. The objective accuracy of such opinions cannot, of course, be assumed, but they were not idle guesses. Some collectors knew their areas very well. L. Griffin, collector for the Waterside Division of St Olave, Southwark, having "resided 40 years in the parish and served all parish offices" considered himself fully competent to assess the "worth" of retail trades, although he hesitated to express an opinion on their income.[6] The reports thus provide detailed accounts of the number and economic status of shopkeepers in various districts and parishes.

The tables on retail shops in the metropolis are based on this series of reports. Before analysing the figures, however, their limitations should be noted. The reports include only *assessed* shops and, in some instances, only those paying the assessment. But there is a further problem. A number of populous parishes have not been included in the reports.[7] As the collectors identified very precisely the districts for which they were responsible (for example, "Salisbury Court precinct in the Parish of St Brides in the ward of Faringdon Without within the City of London"), it is not likely that the figures for the missing parishes have been inadvertently incorporated in some other area. In fact, in no parish does the number of assessed houses exceed the number of occupied houses in 1801. That would certainly have been the case if the houses of heavily populated parishes such as St James, Westminster, or St Martin's-in-the-Fields had been included in other parishes. Either the collectors of certain districts did not submit the standard forms appearing in the series, or the forms were subsequently lost.[8] Nonetheless, the areas for which figures are available form by far the major portion of the metropolis and include most parishes within the Bills of Mortality. The accounts provide, therefore, a useful set of figures to roughly measure the growth of shopkeeping in the latter part of the century.[9]

Table 17 lists the number of assessed shops for each of the major divisions of the metropolis. In 1759 there were 21,603 retail shops in the Bills of Mortality and Marylebone; the number recorded in 1797 is only 22,017, a deceptively low figure. In Westminster alone at least several thousand shops have escaped enumeration. In 1797, 5,809 shops were charged with the shop tax but only 3,235 are listed in the 1797 accounts.[10] It is inconceivable that over 2,500 shops closed their doors during the decade. And there are no figures for other populous parishes within the Bills. The shop tax assessment for St Giles-in-the-Fields and St George, Bloomsbury, was £2,294, but neither is registered in the 1797 accounts. St Marylebone, with a shop tax assessment of £2,544, had 1,864 shops in 1797. As rents were high in fashionable Marylebone, one can assume there were at least a similar number in the two poorer parishes. Now, if to the 22,017 shops in 1797 recorded, the 4,364 presumably missing is added, an approximate figure of 26,381 is reached, or an increase of 22 percent over the total recorded by Excise in 1759. The approximate increase in population (1750–1801) for the metropolis is in the neighbourhood of 28 percent, somewhat less for the Bills.[11] One may perhaps conclude that there had been no phenomenal increase in shopkeeping during the latter half of the century, rather shops merely followed in step with population. Based on the parishes for which there are reliable figures, the average ratio of population per shop for the Bills of Mortality and St Marylebone is 27, very close to the estimated ratio for 1759.[12] The great increase in shopkeeping, at least for the metropolis, appears to have occurred earlier, a conclusion that is consonant with less tangible, more impressionistic evidence.

Shops were not, of course, evenly distributed throughout the metropolitan area (see table 17). As one might expect, Westminster and the City have particularly low ratios, an average of 21.6 persons per shop.[13] More surprising is the ratio for Southwark, 23.6 if Christchurch, Surrey, is included.[14] On the other hand, the ratio for the

Table 17
Population per Retail Shop in London, 1797

	Number of Shops	Ratio[1]	Wards & Parishes not Reported
The City (within & without the Walls)	6,419	22.4	Bassishaw & Cornhill Wards
Finsbury Division[2]	1,824	36.7	St Mary, Stoke Newington
Holborn Division	2,900	36.0	St George, Bloomsbury; St Giles-in-the-Fields; St John, Hampstead; Paddington; Savoy; Saffron; Hatton Gardens
Tower Division	4,865	36.1	St John, Hackney
Westminster	3,235	19.8	St James; St Martin's-in-the Fields; part of St George, Hanover Square
Southwark (not including Christchurch)	2,662	21.2	
Surrey (including Christchurch)	872	—	None of the areas, particularly Lambeth, appear fully reported.
Outside Bills: Chelsea, Chiswick, Kensington, Fulham	994	—	
Total	23,771		

Source: PRO 30/8/280; Population: 1801, George, *London Life*, 412-4 appendix III B.

Notes: [1]Ratio: For the City, the ratio is based on population for the City within and without the Walls plus the population for St Andrew, Holborn (Middlesex). The shops in the Middlesex part of the parish may be included in those reported for the City. The ratio drops to 19.9 if based on the population of the City alone. For the Tower, Holborn and Finsbury Divisions, and Westminster, ratios are based on the population figures for the parishes reporting the number of assessed houses and shops. In calculating the Westminster ratio, the number of shops recorded for St George, Hanover Square, has not been included. In 1801 there were 4,344 occupied houses in this parish, but the total number of shops and houses recorded by the tax collectors was only 745. No such discrepancy occurs for the other parishes: St Ann had 1,294 houses in 1801, the tax collectors reported 1,010; St Clement Danes, 963 and 858 respectively; St Margaret and St John, 3,635 and 3,256: St Paul, Covent Garden, 598 and 557. No meaningful ratio can be calculated for Surrey.
[2]If St Mary, Islington, is omitted, ratio drops to 33.

other principal divisions is considerably higher: 36 for Holborn; 36.1 for the Tower division; 36.7 for Finsbury (33 if St Mary, Islington, is omitted). It is evident that in the metropolis very few neighbourhoods, rich or poor, were without a few local shops for the residents. Spitalfield had 606 shops, Whitechapel, 528, and St Leonard's, Shoreditch, 713. Such unsavoury districts as St Katherine's, East Smithfield, and Wapping supported a total of at least 895 shops. In St George-in-the-East, a fairly large but relatively poor parish, there were 722 retail shops. Even in these poor districts, a small number of better-stocked shops may have clustered on the main thoroughfares, but the great majority were probably chandler's shops scattered over the area in the many alleys, courts, lanes, and other by-ways.

The economic significance of the shopkeeping trades in any given area cannot be based solely on the sheer number of shops. Of equal if not greater importance is the income derived by their proprietors for services provided. In both these respects, no other city in the kingdom was comparable to London, which had a far greater variety of shops and its shopkeepers had a much wider range of income. Some idea of the different levels of shopkeeping in the various parishes and districts can be deduced from an analysis of the pro-portion of shops in each of the assessment classes.

For shopkeepers, as for most inhabitants in Britian, the two major items determining the house assessment were the annual rent and the number of windows, the rates for which were on an ascending scale. Very few shopkeepers, as far as can be ascertained, were as-sessed for servants, or owned horses, dogs, or carriages.[15] And Pitt was essentially right when he suggested that shop rent "always bore a proportion to the profit of the business and to the traffic carried on within."[16] He was wrong only in assuming that the same yardstick could be applied throughout the country. Rents in London were exceptionally high and the *traffic* and *profit* for an annual rent of £10 in London was certainly not comparable to a similar rent in Suffolk – that was why the London shopkeepers felt so aggrieved at the shop tax. But within the metropolis, there was a correspon-dence between the income of a shopkeeper and his annual rent. Rent was, of course, only one component of the assessment, and not necessarily the most onerous. A far steeper scale of rates was applied to the number of windows in the house. The window tax was a much greater burden on the lower rental group than on those paying an annual rent more than £30. The assessment for a shopkeeper paying £6 rent and fortunate enough to have only six windows was 8s. 3d. (ca. 1797); one additional window raised the tax to 18s. 2d., due primarily to the fact that until the Commutation Act of 1784, houses with six windows or less paid no window tax.[17] Such inequities were a just cause for complaint against the hated window tax. Nonetheless, the assessment is a rough guide to the general value of a house. More important for the purpose at hand, it enables one to identify different income groups of London shopkeepers.[18] One must first, however, determine the range of income associated with the assess-ment classes.

In addition to the survey of London shopkeepers, there are scattered reports that cover small areas in London and other towns and cities.[19] These reports list householders by name, address, occupation, income, rack rent, and the amount of each assessed tax. Interestingly, a few of the parishes not in the general survey of London are represented.[20] Shopkeepers are among the occupations listed, but the areas included in the samples are too small – generally restricted to one street – to draw conclusions on the number of shopkeepers in a parish. Even for such a populous parish as St Marylebone, the number of householders listed is less than 100. However, the reports do provide information on the rent, assessment, and estimated income of different types of shopkeepers. Table 18 has been compiled from these accounts.

In table 18, the shopkeepers are arranged according to the assessment classes adopted by the London collectors. With a few exceptions, such as the oilman in Cornhill (Class 3) and the stationer in Marylebone (Class 1), no major shop trade appears in the first three classes. The chandlers' shop is the predominant type, along with a scattering of petty greengrocers and the less affluent bakers. The annual income of shopkeepers paying an assessment under £2 ranges from £40 to £60, placing them in the same category as journeymen mechanics. Shopkeepers in Class 3 exhibit a wider range of income, but only two earned over £100 and many fall as low as £40. Based on the higher estimated income, the average for shopkeepers in Class 3 is £74 10s. In terms of income and rent, those in the lower range are barely distinguishable from shopkeepers in Classes 1 and 2. Classes 4 and 5 reveal a very different shopkeeping world. Here are the drapers, haberdashers, booksellers, apothecaries, and other specialty shopkeepers who feature in the London directories and whose economic failures were registered in the bankruptcy records. Some have incomes over £500, a few below £100, but the large majority fall between these two extremes. The incomes and rents of the two classes overlap somewhat, but the general level of income is higher for Class 5.

True, the average incomes, particularly for Classes 1 and 2, are based on a very small number of shopkeepers, but the picture depicted is fully supported by the comments of the London tax collectors. None thought any shopkeeper below Class 4 could bear an increase in taxes. In St Botolph without Bishopsgate, 1st Division, the income of the 5 shopkeepers in Class 1, was "barely sufficient to support their families"; in Class 2, there were "many ... trifling shopkeepers" whose incomes were "very small." In the 4th Division, those in Class 1 were "in a very low situation"; there were "very mean shops" in Class 2 and the "usual low shops" in Class 3. Little was said

Table 18
Income and Rent of London Shopkeepers by Assessment Classes, 1797

Shop Trade	Rent £	No. of Windows	Other Items Assessed	Total Assessment £	s.	d.	Income £	Area[2]
Class 1[1]								
Hairdresser	6	6			8	3	40	1
Stationer	10	6			10	9	60	2
Mantuamaker	10	6			10	9	60	3
Greengrocer	10	6			10	9	50	6
Hairdresser	18	6			15	7	50	5
Class 2[1]								
Chandler	8	8		1	5	9	50	8
Baker	8	8		1	5	9	60	8
Chandler	8	9		1	11	9	60	6
Chandler	10	9		1	12	11	40	3
Hat Shop	12	7		1	1	9	50- 60	7
Greengrocer	12	7		1	1	9	40- 50	3
Hairdresser	16	9		1	16	6	50	3
Class 3[1]								
Slop Shop	8	11		2	5	9	70-100	1
Chandler	10	10		2	0	0	40	2
Chandler	12	10		2	1	3	60	2
Chandler	12	14		3	15	0	40	4
Chandler	12	15		4	4	6	40	4
Chandler	14	11		2	9	0	50	2
News Shop	16	11	dog (1)	2	14	0	Very poor (excused parish rates)	3
Greengrocer	18	11		2	11	7	50	5
Chandler	20	10		2	12	0	40	2
Baker	20	12		3	6	7	80	5
Hairdresser	20	12		3	6	7	50	5
Chandler	20	14		4	5	9	60- 70	2
Chandler	20	14		4	5	9	100	2
Chandler	20	14		4	5	9	70	3
Hairdresser	22	9		2	6	9½	80	5
Greenshop	22	14		4	7	6	50	3
Greenshop	23	14	dog (1)	4	11	9	150-200	1
Oilman	24	9		2	8	7	150	5
Baker	24	13		3	18	10	100	1
Hairdresser	25	13		3	19	7	80	3
Baker	25	14		4	10	3	70- 80	1

Table 18 (continued)

Shop Trade	Rent £	No. of Windows	Other Items Assessed	Total Assessment £	s.	d.	Income £	Area²
Class 4¹								
Chandler	20	16		5	4	3	100	4
Baker	20	17		5	14	0	100-150	4
Glover	20	17		5	14	0	120	5
Chandler	22	18		6	4	9	70	3
Apothecary	24	19		6	15	6	150-200	7
Tallow-Chandler	24	19	dog (1)	6	19	2	150	4
Baker	25	17		5	18	7	150	1
Hairdresser	25	17		5	18	7	100	1
Hairdresser	26	17	horse (1)	7	3	4	200	5
Hairdresser	26	18		6	8	4	100	4
Perfumer	28	17		6	18	6	200-250	3
Apothecary	28	21		8	2	0	150	4
Chandler	28	23		9	5	8	150	4
Greengrocer	30	18		6	12	0	300	3
Greengrocer	30	18		6	12	0	100-120	3
Mercer	30	18		6	12	0	130	5
Tailor	30	19		7	1	0	100	4
Mercer	30	23		9	11	0	150	5
Staymaker	32	17		6	4	9	80-100	2
Chandler	32	19		7	2	9	60- 70	2
Grocer	35	16		5	17	9	120-130	2
Grocer	40	16		6	4	9	300	3
Tallow-Chandler	40	17	dog (1)	7	7	6	300-400	2
Draper	40	17		7	4	0	150	5
Fan Shop	40	19		8	2	0	80	5
Milk Shop	42	18		7	13	4	80	2
Draper	45	19		8	8	0	300	5
Draper	48	16		7	0	0	100	2
Greengrocer	48	18		8	2	6	100-120	2
Grocer	48	20		9	3	0	500-600	3
Silversmith	75	18		9	15	0	300	5
Linen-Draper	84	17		9	16	9	400-500	2
Class 5¹								
Apothecary	26	19	servant (1) dog (1)	10	3	4	200	4
Mercer	30	24		10	1	0	70	4
Ironmonger	32	24		10	2	9	500-600	3
Baker	32	29		11	5	7	100	5
Apothecary	32	29	servant (1)	12	15	0	200-300	1
Apothecary	38	23	servant (1)	11	4	6	200-300	2
Grocer	38	26		11	3	9	120-130	2

Table 18 (continued)

Shop Trade	Rent £	No. of Win- dows	Other Items Assessed	Total Assessment £	s.	d.	Income £	Area[2]
Seedsman	40	23		10	1	4	400	4
Apothecary	40	24		11	4	0	200-300	1
Apothecary	40	26	servant (1)	12	7	0	250-300	3
Grocer	44	25		12	0	0	500-600	3
Stationer	45	23		10	14	2	150	1
Stationer	45	24	servant (1)	12	18	0	800-900	1
Baker	45	25	dog (1)	12	4	9	200-300	2
Grocer	48	26		12	7	9	100	2
Hosier	48	36		15	4	2	500	5
Bookseller	48	39		15	11	4	200-300	1
Vintner	50	23	servant (1) dog (1)	12	14	0	200	2
Hardwareman	50	29	horse (1)	14	0	6	200-300	1
Tailor	50	32	dog (1)	14	3	9	200	4
Draper	50	35		15	4	0	350	7
Optician	54	23	servant (1)	12	15	2	400	5
Grocer	60	26		13	1	7	150	2
Bookseller	72	20		10	12	0	600	5
Haberdasher	73	23		12	7	11	300-400	2
Stationer	78	19	carriage (1) horses (2) dog (1)	20	9	7	300	5
Haberdasher	80	27	servant (1)	15	18	0	500	2
Shopkeeper	88	22		12	13	9	300	5
Stationer	90	23	horses (2)	17	6	5	600	5
Hosier	90	26		14	17	7	600-700	2
Silversmith	104	23	carriage (1) horse (1)	19	13	2	500	5
Linen-Draper	130	22	dog (1)	15	4	6	500	2
Chinaman	130	26	horse (1)	18	8	0	400	2

Source: PRO, 30/8/281, fols. 19-43, 52. All those clearly identified as shopkeepers in each of the areas are listed. The tax collectors have apparently taken only a sample of the inhabitants of their districts. The total number of inhabitants listed for Marylebone, was seventy-eight; for St George, Hanover Square, thirty-three, St Giles-in-the-Fields has not been included as the report was very carelessly compiled, particularly with reference to occupation and income.

Notes: [1]Average Income for Each Class in the Sample:

Class 1 – £52 Class 3 – £71 10s–£74 10s Class 5 – £327–£362

Class 2 – £50–£53 Class 4 – £168–£185

[2]Area Symbols: 1 - Rolls Liberty, Holborn

2 - St Marylebone,   "

3 - St George the Martyr and St Andrew's, Holborn

4 - St George, Hanover Square, Westminster

5 - Cornhill Ward, St Michael Street

6 - St Margaret and St John, Westminster

7 - Moorfields

8 - Rotherhithe

about Classes 4 and 5 except to note that these shops were located in high-rent areas. In St Anne, Limehouse, of the 6 shopkeepers in Class 1, "four do not earn more than £50 a year." In the Billingsgate Ward, Upper Division, those paying an assessment under £2 were "not wholly above parochial aid." Many in the £2 to £5 Class in St George, Hanover Square, were having difficult paying their assessment, as were the "trifling small shops" in Walbrook.[21] *Mean, trifling, low* were the descriptive terms applied almost unanimously to the shops in Classes 2 and in some districts to Class 3. The shopkeepers in Clerkenwell were in a deplorable state "scarcely able to live."[22] The collector for St Margaret's, Westminster, thought none of the 36 shopkeepers in Class 1 had incomes as high as £60 and only 6 of the 37 in Class 2. Among the 131 shopkeepers in Class 3, there were, he thought, 45 with incomes ranging from £60 to £75; presumably the rest fell below.[23] A slightly higher range was estimated for St Pancras, North Division.[24] It was the opinion of the collector of St Olave, Southwark, who had resided forty years in the parish that "not one in three retail traders ... are [sic] worth £100 in the world if their [sic] debts are paid."[25] Even in the Aldersgate Ward within the City there were, the collector thought, some in Class 3 with incomes no higher than £60 to £75.

The collectors' comments, together with the detailed information on the shop trade, income, and assessment of householders, leave little doubt that the "profit" and "traffic" of shops in the first two assessment classes were trifling. Nor is there much doubt that most shopkeepers in Classes 4 and 5 were substantial London tradesmen following one or other of the specialized shop trades. Here are the drapers, grocers, and others who dominated the retail trade and whose social and economic position bore little resemblance to their fellow shopkeepers in the two lower-assessment classes. What proportion of those in Class 3 might also qualify as major shopkeepers deriving comfortable incomes from their trade is, however, less easy to determine. The general impression conveyed by the reports is that many, if not most, were little better than chandlers. Certainly, the income of shopkeepers in Class 3 was well below the two upper classes. Admittedly, the classification lacks precision, but it is sufficiently adequate to serve as a rough guide of the shopkeeping population in London.

Table 19 gives the proportion of shops in each assessment class for the major divisions of the metropolis. It is impossible to display all the variations within each division. Tables 20 and 21 illustrate the contrasts for only a few selected areas. Other areas discussed in the following section are not included in these tables. Of the total

Table 19
Shops in London by Assessment Class, 1797 (in percentages)

			1	2	3	4	5
Area	Total No. of Shops	Excused Paying[1]	Under £1	£1– under £2	£2– under £5	£5– under £10	£10– under £20
The City	6,419	5.7	6.6	11.6	34.9	28.2	13.0
Finsbury	1,824	10.7	17,0	19.7	38.1	11.8	2.6
Holborn	2,900	3.6	1.9	5.2	31.5	48.1	9.7
Tower	4,865	12.7	17.3	24.9	35.2	8.1	1.8
Westminster	3,235	5.4	9.4	9.8	28.9	30.6	15.9
Southwark	2,662	6.3	23.1	20.8	29.7	14.7	5.4
Surrey	872	12.8	18.9	27.4	30.3	7.2	3.3
Outside Bills	994	1.8	15.7	20.5	42.9	16.4	2.7
Total	23,771						
Number in Class		1,752	2,872	3,778	7,976	5,424	1,969
Percentage of Total		7.4	12.1	15.9	33.6	22.8	8.3

Source: PRO, 30/8/281, fols. 19-43, 52.

Note: [1]The number excused from paying the tax is reported irregularly. Most collectors merely stated the total number "excused"; only a few reported the number "excused" under each class. In calculating the proportion, all those reported as "excused" are put in the category.

number of shops recorded for the metropolis, 7.4 percent are in the "excused" category, with a further 28 percent falling below the two pound assessment. One-third of all shops are in Class 3, the middling group. The proportion of substantial shopkeepers able to pay an assessment over five pounds is 31 percent. One suspects that well over half of all shops in the metropolis were quite insignificant.

However, individual areas within the metropolis differ markedly from the overall average. In terms of the wealth and importance of its shopkeepers, the Tower Division ranks at the bottom with only 9.9 percent in Classes 4 and 5, and 54.9 percent paying an assessment less than two pounds. At the other extreme is Holborn, with the proportion of its shops almost perfectly reversed – 57.8 percent in the two upper classes and 10.7 percent falling below two pounds (table 19). An even greater contrast is exhibited in the figures for St Mathew, Bethnal Green, 1st and 2nd Division (an area within the Tower Division) and Marylebone (in Holborn). In the hamlet of Bethnal Green (see table 20), one of the very poor areas in the metropolis, there are no shops in Class 5 and only six in Class 4, or 2.2 percent of the total number, while 78.3 percent are rated below

Table 20
Assessed Shops in Bethnal Green and St Botolph without Bishopsgate

	1 Under £1		2 £1– under £2		3 £2– under £5		4 £5– under £10		5 £10– under £20		Total	
	No.	%	No.	%	No.	%	No.	%	No.	%	No.	%
Bethnal Green 1st & 2nd Division												
Houses with Shops Paying												
Assessment	94	33.9	69	24.9	45	16.2	6	2.2	—		214	77.3
Excused	40	14.4	14	5.1	9	3.2	—				63	22.7
Total	134	48.3	83	30.0	54	19.4	6	2.2			277	100.0
Houses[1] Paying												
Assessment	862	37.1	559	24.0	256	11.0	73	3.1	3	.1	1,753	75.3
Excused	378	16.3	158	6.8	26	1.1	11	.5	—		573	24.7
Total	1,240	53.4	717	30.8	282	12.1	84	3.6	3	.1	2,326	100.0
St Botolph without 3rd Division												
Houses with Shops Paying												
Assessment[2]	101	43.2	70	29.9	53	22.6	8	3.4	2	.9	234	
Excused	"Deficiency £40"											
Houses Paying												
Assessment	51[3]	56.0	9	9.9	25	27.5	4	4.4	2	2.2	91	

Source: St Botolph without Bishopsgate, 3rd Division, 30/8/280, fols. 37-8 PRO; St Mathew, Bethnal Green, 1st & 2nd Division, fols. 243-6.

Notes: [1]The collector noted that among the houses assessed in the 1st Division were "37 public houses 6 of which get a decent living the rest can scarce live," fol. 244; in the 2nd Division, "44 public houses 8 of which get a decent living the rest can scarce live," fol. 246.

[2]The collector noted that "this district so poor impossible to give statement of annual income," fol. 37.

[3]The collector stated that "those under this class are all mechanics and labourers," fol. 38.

two pounds. Of the fifty-four shopkeepers in Class 3, nine, 16.6 percent of the group, were apparently too poor to pay the assessment. Even the public houses – eighty-one in the two divisions – were having difficulty getting "a decent living." In Marylebone, a high-class residential area, only 5.8 percent fall below the two pound-assessment, while 71.2 percent are in Classes 4 and 5 (see table 21).

Table 21
Assessed Shops in Marylebone and Clerkenwell, 1797

	Total No. of Shops	Excused Paying		Under £1		£1– under £2		£2– under £5		£5– under £10		£10– under £20	
		1		*2*		*3*		*4*		*5*			
		No.	%	No.	%	No.	%	No.	%	No.	%	No.	%
Marylebone	1,864	33	1.8	26	1.4	48	2.6	430	23.1	1,060	56.9	267	14.3
Clerkenwell	743	127	17.1	152	20.5	136	18.3	278	37.4	45	6.1	5	.7

Source: PRO, 30/8/280.

In view of the small number excused from paying the assessment, even the chandlers in Marylebone were apparently managing to scrape together a living.

On the surface it appears incredible that the proportion of shops in the two upper classes is substantially higher in Marylebone than in the City (41.2 percent) or Westminster (46.5 percent). The explanation lies in the nature of the areas. With a few exceptions, such as the Calmel Buildings off Orchard Street, newly developed Marylebone, unlike the older parts of London, had few really poor districts – the natural habitat for the small shop. In contrast, the City and Westminster had many streets, alleys, and courts notorious for their poverty and ill repute. In such areas, only the petty shop could flourish. The inhabitants of the 3rd Division of St Botolph (the City Without) were as poor as those of Bethnal Green and their shops no better – 73 percent paid an assessment under £2 (see table 20). In Fore and Grub, 2nd Division, of Cripplegate Without the City, "one of the dirtiest and meanest parts of town,"[26] only 2 percent of the shops are in Class 5, while 53 percent are in the lower group. The Portsoken Ward of the City is a picture of contrast: 71 percent of the shops in the Tower Hill precinct in Classes 4 and 5; 5.4 percent, in the Covent Garden precinct. An average based on such variations is therefore somewhat misleading. In fact the retail establishments of the richest and most influential tradesmen in the country remained firmly based in the City and Westminster. Together the two account for 68 percent of the shops in Class 5 and, as we have seen, some had a rental value in excess of £100.

The two largest parishes in the Finsbury Division were St Luke (Old Street) and Clerkenwell. The latter had long been the centre for the watchmaking industry. In 1798, artisan watchmakers in Clerkenwell numbered 7,000, about one-third of the population; in St

Luke, 1,000. The great distress of the watchmakers in 1797 described vividly by the collector for Clerkenwell was exceptional and due in part to the new duty on clocks and watches.[27] Generally their income was sufficient to maintain modest comfort. Clerkenwell and, to a lesser extent, St Luke's were industrial enclaves and their shop-keeping population was representative of areas inhabited by respectable journeymen. There was in fact no shortage of shops in either place. The ratio of persons per shop for Clerkenwell is thirty-one; for St Luke's, thirty-five. However, most were petty shops, catering for the daily necessities of the inhabitants. Nevertheless, like most areas however poor, Clerkenwell had a few substantial shops – 6.8 percent in Classes 4 and 5. The temporary distress of the watchmakers in 1797 is reflected in the plight of the shopkeepers, which was due most probably to a decline in trade, as well as bad debts. Out of 743 shopkeepers, 127 were excused from paying the assessment, and a further 437 were, according to the collector, having great difficulty paying – all in the first two classes and about one-half in the third class. Even a few in Class 4 were experiencing difficulty in meeting their expenses.

Clerkenwell is interesting for another reason. Letting lodgings was a common practice among London shopkeepers largely due to the high rents and to the customary requirement to rent the whole house. Of the total number of shopkeepers in the metropolis, at least 42 percent were letting lodgings. The proportion varied for different districts. In Southwark and the outlying parishes in Surrey, it drops to about 15 percent. In the congested areas in the heart of London, the proportions tend to be lower in the poorer districts. For the Tower Division, it is 36.5 percent and drops as low as 11 percent for areas like Wapping and Whitechapel, and none in Bethnal Green. In the more prosperous parishes of Westminster, however, the range is from 51 percent in St George, Hanover Square, to 76 percent in St Clement Danes. The proportion reaches a high of 84 percent in Marylebone. It is thus rather curious to find the lowly shopkeepers of Clerkenwell in the same class as the more prosperous parishes, with 82.5 percent letting lodgings.[28] Nor can high rents be accepted as the explanation. In Class 1, the proportion of shops letting lodgings is as high as 94 percent. No house paying an assessment under one pound could possibly have a high rental value. Indeed, the proportions vary inversely with assessment: only 62 percent in Class 4 and none in Class 5 had lodgers. Whatever may have been the reason – a great need by the journeymen watchmakers for lodgings or long-existing tradition – it is clear that most shopkeepers in Clerkenwell were covering their major overhead expenses by this means.

If the profits from shopkeeping were still so inadequate, the traffic within must indeed have been very small. How could the trade have been otherwise with an average ratio of thirty-one persons to a shop?

Across the river in the Borough of Southwark, of the 2,662 shops, only 20.1 percent are in Classes 4 and 5. But the five parishes of the borough differed enormously in the style of their shops. The two poorest parishes were St John and St George, the latter a very populous area containing almost half the shops (1,302) in the borough. In each of these parishes, 60 percent of the shops fall below the two pound assessment. And, as one might expect, there were few substantial shopkeepers – 9 percent in St John and 14.5 percent in St George, almost all in Class 4.[29] In St Thomas, St Olave, and St Saviour's, on the other hand, almost one-third of the shops are in the upper two assessment classes, with about the same proportion in the two lower classes.[30] The collector for St Olave thought conditions in his parish were "very unfavourable to retail trade."[31] One suspects they were far worse in St George and St John. Forty percent of the shops in St George are in Class 1 or excused, compared to 10.5 percent in St Olave.

On the face of it, the parishes in Surrey had few high-class shops – only 10.5 percent are in Classes 4 and 5. But as the figures for too many districts are missing, there is no means of knowing whether those reported are representative.

It was suggested earlier that by 1759 the ratio of persons to shops in London in particular could hardly fall lower. The financial straits of the small shopkeepers in London give ample evidence that at this lowly level the shopkeeping trades were overcrowded – swollen well beyond the needs of the society. What was true in 1797 can surely be inferred for 1759, both in London and in many of the counties where the ratio was very little higher. The small chandler's shop was a recognized institution in eighteenth-century London. We suggest that it was as common in the provinces as it was in London; that it was precisely this type of shop counties with a high ratio in 1759 lacked, at least in any considerable numbers. It is noteworthy that in the London Bills of Mortality in 1797 the estimated ratio of population to substantial shops is eighty-six, a figure very close to that recorded for the two northern counties in 1759.

Every taxing area in London, however poor, had a few high-class shops, even Bethnal Green had six. Presumably, most of the shopping requirements of the inhabitants were satisfied by the network of shops in their own district. The particular form of that network depended, in turn, upon the economic and social status of the customers it was designed to serve. London with its congeries of small towns, each with its own particular set of shopping characteristics, was in essence a microcosm of the country at large. Similar networks existed in the many different towns in the provinces.

THE CITY OF YORK

The account submitted from the City of York provides more specific information but is restricted to the major shopkeepers.[32] It is, in substance, a truncated occupational census of householders paying "assessed taxes to the amount of ... £2 to £6 or £7 a year."[33] Those paying less than £2 were not included in the list. As the writer had previously submitted an account of "affluent persons," they too were omitted. In any case, few, if any shopkeepers in York qualified for that category. The estimated annual income of William Tuke, the leading tea dealer, was only £300. Among drapers, William Brown had the highest income with £400 and he was decidedly the exception; the average income was £184. The highest income included in the survey was £800; no shopkeeper even approaches that figure. Moreover, a search of the list of freemen and of the directories for York has failed to reveal any important shopkeeper omitted from the account. It can, therefore, be safely concluded that all the major shopkeepers have been included. It would be strange indeed if a shopkeeper with an income in excess of £800 had not surfaced in one or other of the sources.

In terms of types of shop trades and importance in the commercial life of the city, this group of shopkeepers corresponds broadly to the two upper assessment classes of London. True, no shopkeeper in York could match the wealth of the principal tradesmen of London. And the rent and assessment for York was well below the metropolis. The 1785 shop tax account listed 486 shops in York with rents ranging from five to thirty-five pounds. Only 22 had an annual rent of twenty-five to thirty-five pounds, and 126, fifteen to twenty-five pounds. Most of the principal shopkeepers in the 1797 list are drawn from these two rental categories.[34]

Pitt's correspondent was exceptionally systematic in his survey. Commencing with the parish of St Michael-le-Belfrey, the most populous parish, he listed the householders of each parish by name, occupation or status, estimated income and expenditure, and the assessed taxes paid, along with a running commentary on the presence of lodgers, the number of children, if numerous, and other relevant information bearing on the person's ability to pay increased taxes. In all, thirty parishes are included in the report. The occupations are many and varied, from bricklayers, brushmakers, and joiners to clergymen, schoolmasters, a sculptor, and the manager of the theatre whose estimated annual income was £600. An appreciable number are identified simply as "gentleman" or "widow." Listed are 469 householders with incomes ranging from a low of £60 to a high of £800. Both extremes are exceptional, the bulk falling within a range of £100 to £250. There are 350 with a profession or trade, of which 176 are shopkeepers.[35]

Most of the shopkeepers listed in the account were the principal tradesmen of York, those whose names would most likely be listed in the directories. And, one may add, their insolvency would most probably have resulted in bankruptcy proceedings. The distribution of their shop trades thus forms an interesting comparison with the figures derived from the bankruptcy reports and the directories.[36] Table 22 lists the figures for the years 1784, 1797, and 1822–3.

York was a civic, ecclesiastical, and social centre for the country. Its role in the economy was confined almost exclusively to serving as a regional market centre. It was decidedly not an industrial town. On the contrary, much of the energy and capital of the leading tradesmen were devoted to providing the luxury goods and services demanded by the gentry who flocked to the town. It would not be far-fetched to call York the metropolis of the north. One should, therefore, expect the distribution of its major shop trades to follow more closely the pattern first observed among bankrupt shopkeepers of London rather than the overall pattern for the provinces or the distribution of shop trades for Manchester in 1783. Even Bailey's inadequate coverage reveals a pattern of shop trades similar to the 1797 survey, a far more reliable source.[37] As table 22 shows, the once-powerful drapers formed only 14.2 percent of the total number of major shopkeepers in 1797. And York, like London and Bristol, was well supplied with specialty shops. It could even boast one optician along with six booksellers and stationers and one seller of musical instruments. York lagged behind London in the proportion and variety of shops subsumed under household furnishings, but the number was not negligible – 4.6 percent. In one respect, however, York conformed more closely to the provincial pattern. It is a curious fact that both the bankruptcy records and the directories report a larger proportion of grocers and tea dealers in provincial towns than in London. In 1822–3, only 9.7 percent of the London shopkeepers listed by Pigot were grocers and tea dealers, a figure not vastly different to that derived from the bankruptcy records. Grocers and tea dealers in York, on the other hand, accounted for 16.4 percent in 1797 and 17 percent in 1822–3. In all other respects, York followed the London trend. By 1822 the proportion of shops selling

Table 22
York: Distribution of Major Shop Trades, 1784, 1797, 1822-3

	% in each trade		
Shop Trade	1784	1797	1822-3
I Wearing Apparel			
Drapers	25.0	14.2	10.9
Haberdashers, Hatters &			
Glovers	12.5	9.7	6.5
Milliners & Straw Hat Makers		3.4	4.7
Staymakers		2.3	.9
Tailor/Drapers &			
Breechesmakers		3.4	8.6
Muslin Warehouse		.6	.2
Subtotal	37.5	33.6	31.8
II Consumable Household Goods			
A Food			
Grocers & Tea Dealers	10.2	10.2	17.0
Petty Grocers		1.7	
Tea Dealers		4.5	
Cheesemongers	4.5	2.8	3.5
Confectioners/Fruiterers	4.5	4.0	5.1
Specialty Bakers		4.0	
Subtotal	19.2	27.2	25.6
B Drinks			
Wine and Brandy Merchants	4.5	6.3	3.5
C Sundries			
Tallow-Chandlers	1.1		1.6
Chemists	13.6	5.7	4.7
Subtotal	14.7	5.7	6.3
Total Consumables	38.4	39.2	35.4
III Durable Household Furnishings			
Upholsterers & Cabinetmakers	2.3	2.3	3.5
Dealers in China & Glass		2.3	3.3
Carpet Warehouse			.2
Subtotal	2.3	4.6	7.0
IV Hardware			
Ironmongers & Hardware			
Dealers	5.7	6.8	2.8
Cutlers	2.3		.5
Toy Dealers		1.7	2.3
Colourmen		.6	
Nursery & Seedsmen	1.1		1.2
Subtotal	9.1	9.1	6.8

Table 22 (continued)

Shop Trade	% in each trade		
	1784	1797	1822-3
V Special Services			
Booksellers, Stationers, etc.	5.7	3.4	7.0
Musicseller		.6	.9
Jewellers & Watchmakers	5.7	1.7	4.2
Opticians		.6	.2
Perfumers & Hairdressers		4.0	3.7
Pawnbrokers		.6	2.6
Tobacconists	1.1	1.7	.5
Whipmakers		1.1	
Subtotal	12.5	13.7	19.1
Total number of shopkeepers[1]	88	176	430

Source: 1784: Bailey's Eastern Directory; 1979: PRO, 30/8/281, fols. 72-82b; 1822-3: Pigot, London and Provincial Directory.

Note: [1]Two umbrellamakers in 1822-3 are not included.

household furnishings had increased to 7 percent; dealers in books, stationery, and music now formed 7.9 percent; drapers had declined to 10.9 percent; and the proportion of confectioners and cheese-mongers was 8.6 percent. Although the number of hardware dealers remained the same, their proportion was now only 2.8 percent in contrast to the 6.8 percent in 1797, with toy dealers increasing their share of the market.[38] In short, the structure of the shop trades at York, both in 1797 and 1822–3, was similar to that depicted for Norwich and Bristol, both of which, like York, served as regional centres of distribution.

The 1797 survey also allows us to chart the location of the major shops in York. Map 4 shows the approximate location of each of thirty parishes; the number of shops in each parish is listed in table 23. Quite clearly, the major shops were not evenly dispersed throughout the city. Of the nineteen cispontine parishes lying west of the Foss, thirteen had a total of 153 shops. These parishes formed the central shopping district (see map 4) extending from the Minster (5) in a semicircle to St Mary, Castlegate (11), which barely qualified and marks the eastern limits, around St Michael, Spurriergate (9), and northwest to St Martin, Coney Street (4), to the tiny parish of St Wilfred (2) and up to St Michael-le-Belfrey (1). Across the Ouse, the shopping area centred on two parishes – St John, Micklegate (25), Ousebridge End, with six shops and St Martin-cum-Gregory

(26), with seven.[39] These fifteen parishes contained 166 major shops
– 94 percent of all shops listed. The remaining 10 shops were scattered in six parishes. The size of the area and the density of population obviously determined the number of shops within individual
parishes – St Wilfred (2) for example – but of equal significance was
the social and economic characteristics of the parishes. The fifteen
parishes formed a group with the highest ranking in the socio-
economic scale. Only St Mary, Castlegate (11), one of the more populous parishes, was an exception, and could well have been excluded
from the designated shopping district.[40] The major shopping area
formed a broad swath running south from the Minster and narrow-
ing after it crossed the Ouse Bridge. Parishes bordering the Foss
had very few major shops, and there were none in the Marsh on
the northwest bank. Like similar districts in London, Bethnal Green
for example, such areas were the natural habitat for petty shops.
Few substantial tradesmen chose to set up shops there.

Was there a clustering of shop traders or were they scattered
relatively evenly over the fifteen parishes? Certainly drapers were
ubiquitous – twelve parishes were graced with their shops. There
were, however, specially favoured areas: fifteen of the twenty-six
drapers were located in four parishes – Christ (Holy Trinity), King's
Court, three; St Crux, five; All Saints Pavement, four; St Michael,
Spurriergate, three. Haberdashers were confined to nine parishes
north of the bridge, with only one shop south of the Ouse in St
Martin-cum-Gregory; but again there was a clustering with seven of
the seventeen haberdashers in two parishes – St Michael-le-Belfrey,
three; and St Martin, Coney Street, four. Grocers were located in
eight parishes north of the bridge and two, south. Of the twenty-
one grocers recorded, five were in St-Michael-le-Belfrey, and five in
Christ (Holy Trinity), King's Court. Six of the eight specialized tea
dealers were located in the centre of the shopping district – one in
St Crux; three in All Saints, Pavement; one in St Peter-the-Little;
and one – William Tuke and Son – a little west in St Mary, Castlegate.
Nine of the twelve hardware dealers were in four parishes – St
Martin, Coney Street, two; St Crux, three; All Saints Pavement, two,
Christ (Holy Trinity), King's Court, two. Of the ten druggists, three
were in Christ (Holy Trinity), King's Court, and two south of the
bridge in St John, Micklegate. Even the milliners had their favourite
haunts: four of the six were in St Martin, Coney Street, and two in
St Helen's, Stonegate. No particular locational pattern can be discerned for the other shop trades.

The population south of the Ouse was serviced with a relatively
full complement of shops – a draper, haberdasher, staymakers, up-

Map 4
Parishes of the City of York, ca. 1795

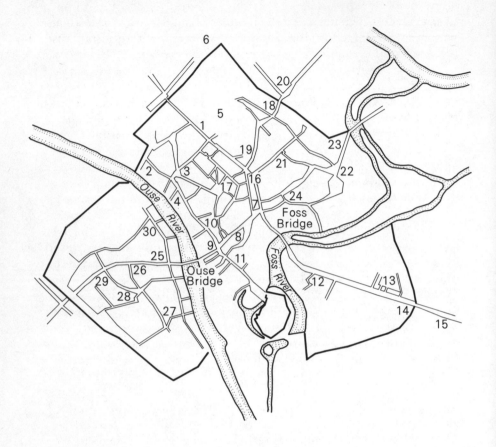

1 St Michael-le-Belfrey	16 Christ (Holy Trinity)
2 St Wilfred	17 St Sampson
3 St Helen, Stonegate	18 St John Del-Pyke
4 St Martin, Coney Street	19 Holy Trinity, Goodramgate
5 St Peter's Liberty	20 St Maurice
6 St Giles	21 St Andrew
7 St Crux	22 All Saints, Peaseholme
8 All Saints, Pavement	23 St Cuthberts, Peaseholme
9 St Michael, Spurriergate	24 St Saviours
10 St Peter-the-Little	25 St John, Micklegate
11 St Mary, Castlegate	26 St Martin-cum-Gregory
12 St Dennis, Walmgate	27 St Mary, Bishophill Low
13 St Margaret, Walmgate	28 St Mary, Bishophill Junior
14 St Peter the Willow	29 Holy Trinity, Micklegate
15 St Lawrence	30 All Saints, North Street

Table 23
Geographical Dispersion of Principal Shops of York, 1797

No. on Map	Parish	No. of Shops	Population Rank	Socio-economic Rank
1	St Michael-le-Belfrey	25	1	High
2	St Wilfred	5	26	High
3	St Helen, Stonegate	14	6	High
4	St Martin, Coney Street	21	9	High
5	St Peter's Liberty	6		High
6	St Giles	2		Low
7	St Crux	17	2	Medium High
8	All Saints, Pavement	20	10	High
9	St Michael, Spurriergate	15	5	High
10	St Peter-the-Little	4	12	Low
11	St Mary, Castlegate	3	3	Medium Low
12	St Dennis, Walmgate	0	13	Low
13	St Margaret, Walmgate	0	19	Low
14	St Peter the Willow	0		Low
15	St Lawrence	0		Low
16	Christ (Holy Trinity)	13	4	Medium High
17	St Sampson	5	7	Medium High
18	St John Del-Pyke	3	21	Low
19	Holy Trinity, Goodramgate	5	16	Medium
20	St Maurice	2	25	Medium Low
21	St Andrew	0	24	Low
22	All Saints, Peaseholme	0	29	Low
23	St Cuthberts, Peaseholme	0	22	Low
24	St Saviours	1	14	Low
25	St John, Micklegate	6	8	Medium
26	St Martin-cum-Gregory	7	20	High
27	St Mary, Bishophill Low	1	23	Medium
28	St Mary, Bishophill Junior	0	18	Low
29	Holy Trinity, Micklegate	0	15	Medium Low
30	All Saints, North Street	1	17	Medium

Sources: Parish locations: Map of the City of York, John H. Harvey, Public Library, City of York; No. of shops: PRO 30/8/281, fols. 72-82b; Population and socio-economic rank: *Victoria County History*, 164, tables 3 and 4; "Hearth tax," 213, table 2, "Baptisms and Burials."

holsterer, a dealer in china as well as two grocers, two chemists, and two wine merchants. Except to shop for special luxury articles such as books, toys, jewellery, spectacles, or perfume, the residents had no need to cross the bridge. There was even one butcher resident in St Martin-cum-Gregory. Did he sell only in the market or had he established a small shop across the river?

Pitt's correspondent had no precise data on the income and expenditure of householders paying assessed taxes. He appears, however, to have been exceedingly well informed on the general circumstances of the occupants. Confidence in his estimates is further enhanced by the relatively wide range of income that emerges for each of the trades – a range that is not based simply on the amount of assessed taxes. Thus, the estimated income for Simeon Gray, a grocer in St Crux, was £350; his estimated expenditure, £200; his assessed tax, £2 10s. On the other hand, the assessed tax of a grocer in All Saints, Pavement, was £6 15s., but his estimated income was only £200 and expenditure, £150. The three linen-drapers in St Michael, Spurriergate, were paying assessed taxes of £8 7s., £2 8s., and £2 3s.; their estimated income was £150, £150 and £100 respectively. Furthermore, the incomes for different shop trades overlap considerably. The lowest income for chemists, whose average income was in the upper echelon, was £100. This is the highest income for the lowest-ranking group, the petty grocer. However he arrived at his estimates, Pitt's correspondent did not base them simply on the type of shop trade or on the value of the dwelling place. If they are not in all respects objectively accurate, they are the considered opinion of someone who had taken great pains to determine the ability of various householders to pay additional taxes. One may wonder if modern income tax records are any more accurate.

In table 24, the shop trades are ranked by level of income. The optician heads the list, but as a group, dealers in china and glass have the highest average income, followed by chemists, and wine and brandy merchants. Grocers, it will be observed, rank higher than drapers, and the latter have a higher average income and a higher range than haberdashers. The proprietor of the muslin warehouse was not among the more affluent shopkeepers. It has sometimes been assumed that specialized tea dealers, like grocers, were engaged in a "high-class luxury trade."[41] The figures for tea dealers in York tend to belie that view. Two of the so-called tea dealers had estimated incomes below £100 – one as low as £60 and the other, £80. If these 2 are omitted, the average rises to £180. At the bottom of the list with an average income of £77 are the 3 petty grocers. The average income for all shopkeepers is £163, ranging from a low of £60 to a high of £400. Among the 176 shopkeepers, 24 have incomes under £100 and 13 over £250. Some shopkeepers lived up to their income, especially those in the lower range, although 1 upholsterer, 1 ironmonger, and 1 grocer, each with an income of £200, were expending their annual incomes. But they are exceptions. The figures for most shopkeepers show an annual surplus. The style of life of only 2 shopkeepers required an expenditure of £300 – a chemist with an income of £400 and Robert Spence, a bookseller,

Table 24
Principal Shopkeepers of York: Income, Expenditure, and Assessed Taxes, 1797
(arranged by average income)

Shop Trades	Number	Income Average £	Income Range £	Expenditure Average £	Expenditure Range £	Assessed Taxes Average £ s.	Assessed Taxes Range £ s. £ s.
Optician	1	300		200		4:10	
Dealers in China	4	225	200-300	168	120-200	6:18	2: 4- 9:13
Chemists	10	218	100-400	163	80-300	4: 0	2: 6- 7: 4
Wine & Brandy Merchants	11	218	150-300	144	100-200	3:10	2: 1- 6: 0
Grocers	18	200	100-350	153	100-200	4: 5	2: 0- 6:15
Pawnbroker	1	200		150		7: 5	
Colourman	1	200		200		7: 1	
Drapers	26	184	100-400	137	80-200	4: 2	2: 3- 8: 7
Toy Dealers	3	183	150-200	153	130-180	4: 3	3:17- 4:10
Book Dealers etc.	6	180	80-350	159	80-300	3: 3	2: 0- 5: 0
Cabinetmakers	4	163	100-200	120	80-200	5: 0	2:17- 6: 2
Jewellers	3	150	150	107	100-120	4:10	3: 3- 5: 9
Muslin Warehouse	1	150		120		3: 0	
Tea Dealers	8	149	60-300	123	60-250	4:18	2: 0-11: 2
Haberdashers	17	149	60-250	116	60-200	4: 4	2: 1- 6: 7
Hardware Dealers	12	149	70-200	112	70-200	3:14	2: 3- 8:10
Whipmakers	2	130	60-200	105	60-150	2:12	2: 3- 3: 1
Milliners	6	128	100-150	103	80-130	3:16	2: 4- 5:16
Specialty Bakers	7	123	80-150	103	80-150	3:12	2: 4- 4:19
Staymakers	4	120	80-150	95	80-100	3: 5	2: 6- 5: 5
Confectioners & Fruiterers	7	119	80-150	111	80-150	4: 0	3: 0- 5:11
Tailors & Breechesmakers	6	111	70-150	98	60-150	2:14	2: 1- 4: 8
Tobacconists	3	110	70-150	95	70-120	3: 1	2:10- 3: 9
Perfumers & Hairdressers	7	94	60-200	87	60-150	3: 9	2: 4- 6: 3
Cheesemongers	5	85	80-100	83	80- 90	3: 7	2: 0- 4:16
Petty Grocers	3	77	60-100	77	60-100	2:18	2: 7- 3: 7
All Shopkeepers	176	163	60-400	127	60-300	4: 0	2: 0-11: 2

Source: PRO, 30/8/281, fols. 72-82b.

whose estimated income was £350. For shopkeepers as a whole, the excess of income over expenditure is 22 percent. It they were, in fact, hoarding their savings, the shopkeepers of York were indeed a frugal lot.

The shop tax was surely a very small burden for most of the shopkeepers listed in the account. It is small wonder that after the 1786 amendments few complaints emanated from the provinces. The highest assessment is that of William Tuke, who was paying £11 2s., but he had a carriage and horse. Only twenty-two shopkeepers were rated £6 and over, six of whom paid over £8. But there were fifty-two rated under £3. The average assessment for all shopkeepers is £4. In terms of assessment and therefore rent the major shopkeepers of York are roughly equivalent to the London shopkeepers in Class 3 (£2–under £5; see table 19). Their average income is, however, much higher – £163 versus £74 10s. for their London counterparts (see table 18).[42] The income of the major shopkeepers in York is well below Class 5 (£327–£362) in London, but it is very close both in range and average to the shopkeepers in Class 4 (£168–£185; see table 18).[43]

Like the Londoners, many of the major shopkeepers of York were reducing their overhead expenses by letting lodgings. Some fifty-six, or 31.8 percent, were listed as so doing, and the practice was not confined to those in the lower-income bracket. Shopkeepers letting lodging can be found in all income groups from £60 for a petty grocer to £300 for the optician, and, with the exception of chemists, in all shop trades. They were not, however, evenly dispersed throughout the city. In the four central parishes – St Michael-le-Belfrey, St Wilfred, St Helen, Stonegate, and St Martin, Coney Street – thirty-nine or 60 percent of the total number of shopkeepers were letting lodgings. A further eleven were distributed in All Saints, Pavement, and St Michael, Spurriergate. That is, 89 percent of the shopkeepers letting lodgings were located in six parishes. Were the houses they inhabited larger and the rents higher than those in other parishes, or were such centrally located areas in demand by lodgers?

In the 1797 surveys, the ratio of population to principal shops in London was 86; in York, 96.6, not very far behind. In London, 31.3 percent of all shops listed were in the two highest assessment classes. Of the 486 shops listed in the 1785 account for York, only 176 or 36.2 percent were sufficiently important to be included in the 1797 survey. For information concerning the remaining 310 shopkeepers whose annual rent was under fifteen pounds, we have to turn to other sources. Indeed, one suspects that a number of the petty shopkeepers described in the following account escaped not only the heavy charges levied by the city, but also the shop tax.

Throughout the eighteenth century, the corporation of York waged an unremitting, often losing, battle against unfree tradesmen. In November 1775, a special committee was appointed "to enquire into the names, number and circumstances" of all such persons. Its report gives a detailed account of small shopkeepers and other tradesmen who had hitherto eluded the grasping hands of the city fathers.[44] The committee performed the task with exemplary diligence but confessed: "as it always hath been so it will ever continue impossible to find out or if found to compel every individual who may be liable to purchase his or her freedom from the various causes of poverty, contrivances, secretion, connivance and deceit."[45] Some of those contrivances, such as selling from "inward rooms" have been noted earlier.[46] Many such shops were probably little more than parlour shops, affording by-employment for the wife. David Phillips, for example, was charged with "keeping an inner room" for the sale of goods by "A. Phillips his wife in her own name."[47] The greater problem lay not with such evasive measures, but with the inability of poor shopkeepers and other tradesmen to pay the twenty-five pound fee for the right to practise their trades. It is perhaps not without significance that among the offenders only one, an apothecary, could claim his freedom by patrimony, and one merchant had a "doubtful" right by reason of apprenticeship. The majority appear to have emerged into the business world without recognized training or the support of an established family. One is tempted to say that here indeed is the "rising middle class" except that very few seem to qualify for that august label.[48]

Of the 239 offenders listed by the committee, 164 were in the distributive trades, many of whom were very small shopkeepers too poor to pay the twenty-five pound fee to obtain their freedom. There were, for example, five "brokers" of second-hand furniture or clothes. Four were so poor that the committee agreed to accept ten shillings as a small acknowledgment of their willingness to pay. The fifth gave up his business and went to Leeds. Three "apple shops" were in similarly straightened circumstances, as were the two butter-sellers and two of the four "meal sellers." Of the four "bacon sellers," two promised to give up the business. One was too poor and was allowed to pay twenty shillings as acknowledgment. The fourth claimed he sold only in the market but the committee was skeptical.[49] The one cheesemonger listed promised to give up his business. Of the two "pot shops," that of William Sturdy in the Shambles was apparently prospering; at least the committee was preparing to sue him. John Bollan in Goodramgate, on the other hand, claimed exemption "by serving in the militia when drawn out in actual service."[50] Ann Finney claimed an exemption for her "fruit shop," because the business was conducted by the children of her late husband who had served in the militia. Whether "sellers" of butter, bacon, and so forth were hawking their wares or had small shops is difficult to say with certainty. But as the committee identified "hucksters" as such – there were seventeen – one suspects they were petty shopkeepers scraping together a meagre living.

Even those following the more specialized shop trades were not in a very much better state. Only one of the five "drapers" paid the fee; the others were either giving over the business or had doubtful claims of exemption. One of the five hardwaremen was allowed to pay a small acknowledgment, as was one of the six milliners. Another promised to stop trading and a third was moving. One of the three booksellers was charged only ten shillings. Of the six hatters, hosiers and glovers, only two purchased their freedom. One pawnbroker was allowed to postpone the purchase of his freedom. A "soap dealer" had a doubtful exemption as the widow of a distiller. In 1784, Excise listed her as a licensed tea dealer. There was even one baker so poor that the committee recommended he be allowed to pay only ten shillings. But the most surprising cases are those identified as grocers, the so-called high-class shopkeepers. Of the five listed, one promised to give over the business; another was to be sued by the corporation; and one was recognized to be too poor to pay more than twenty shillings. But poor Thomas Bowen who "carried on the business of a grocer in Goodramgate" was treated more harshly. Having been sued, he suffered judgment by default and was cast into prison for his debt to the corporation and only secured his discharge on "giving up his effects." Needless to say, he subsequently gave over the business.[51] The committee was also taking action against George Thompson, "a papist without Micklegate Bar," who had recently set up as a grocer and was "keeping a shop ... the door of which ... opened into an entry." Thompson stated he was quite unable to purchase his freedom and was "hired to Mr. Fermer of Bishophill as a menial servant." He promised, however, to give over the business as soon as his wife had sold the goods on hand. The committee held off action for the time being, but the threat remained.[52] Although the eyes of the city fathers were on him, Thompson, the menial, apparently eluded them. In 1784 he was listed by Excise among the licensed tea dealers. Clearly these are *grocers* of a very different status than those who feature in the directories or the 1797 survey.

Of the various types of unfree tradesmen, the most numerous were the alesellers. Twenty-two were selling "ale by retail." But as they had paid the annual licence fee and were "in general of low circumstances," the committee felt they should not be pressed to purchase their freedom until the time came for renewal or decline of their licenses.[53] But in addition to those "selling ale by retail," the committee listed twenty-nine who are identified as "ale-drapers." We do not know what in the eyes of the committee distinguished an aledraper from an aleseller. Income alone was certainly not the criterion. True, eighteen aledrapers were able to pay the twenty-five pounds for their freedom but eleven were in circumstances similar to the alesellers. Did the aledraper keep a small shop from which he sold ale and other sundries, like Mary Smith of Flixton? The names of at least three of the aledrapers appeared in an excise survey of licensed tea dealers in 1784.

However aledrapers are identified, the committee report lists a great variety of small shops, the proprietors of which could claim neither patrimony nor apprenticeship to obtain their freedom. For these petty tradesmen, purchasing their freedom was an enormous step up the ladder – a step impossible for many to make. The committee report lists 164 in the distributive trade. Of these, only 55 were able to purchase their freedom. Many fell by the wayside and either left the city or promised to give over the business. Forty-seven were in such a deplorable state that the comittee recommended they be indulged and allowed to pay a small acknowledgment for the privilege of continuing their trade. For such people the act (3 Geo. 3, c. 8), allowing a man who had served in the army or navy or his children to set up trade in any place in the country without prejudice, was a boon. The committee recognized the right of 9 to so do. They included, among other trades, 3 aledrapers, 1 pot shop, and the fruiterer. The widows, however, do not appear to have been covered by the law. The right of Elizabeth Hawksworth, an aledraper on Peter Lane, whose husband had served in the army, was not acknowledged.

Most of the shopkeepers who feature in the committee's report had escaped not only the vigilant eyes of the hungry city fathers, but also the enumerators of the commercial directories and the 1797 survey. Nor do they appear in the bankruptcy records. When misfortune hit, they moved away or were thrown into prison, as Mr Bowen was. Like their counterparts in Exeter, they were petty retailers whose front rooms were converted into shops and whose business, confined to the poor in the immediate neighbourhood, yielded "an income barely sufficient for the means of subsistence."54 Many of the shops listed by the committee were in fact located in the poorer districts across the Ouse and east of the Foss and in the parishes that had few or no principal shopkeepers. Too poor to contribute to the rates or pay the assessments on windows and shops, they held a very precarious position in the business world, often slipping down to swell the ranks of the assisted poor. Indeed, such a possibility (or threat) was very much in the minds of the committee when it suggested the acceptance of small acknowledgments. But the shops lived on; new hopefuls entered the list of those struggling to climb the slippery ladder.

The London and York records clearly demonstrate the presence of petty shops in these two cities. Petty shops formed a very large proportion of all shops in London, over 50 percent; possibly less in a city such as York. However small the trade of an individual shop, the total amount of business handled by petty shopkeepers was no trifling affair. Based on the incomes of the assessed classes in London, some 40 percent of the revenue derived from the retail shop trade went to small shopkeepers. And as shall be demonstrated, London and York were not exceptions.

CHAPTER SIX

Number and Proportion of "Principal" and "Petty" Shopkeepers

In order to assess the wealth and importance of the shopkeeping sector of the economy, particularly for the end of the eighteenth century, two tasks must be tackled: the proximate number of shops in the country and the proportion of petty shops yielding incomes below £100. No figures, comparable to those for midcentury, are available on the total number of shops at the end of the century. To secure the required information, we have pursued a number of different sources. Definitive answers to the questions raised cannot be obtained from a single source, but the cumulative information drawn from several provides sufficient evidence to support a thesis affirming the existence of a large number of petty back-street shops long before the nineteenth century, not only in London but also in the provinces.

According to Gregory King's estimate of 1688, there were 40,000 shopkeepers and tradesmen in England and Wales with an average annual income of £45.[1] The shopkeeping population represented 2.9 percent of all families or 7.8 percent of families increasing the wealth of the kingdom. Their share of the national income was 4.13 percent compared to the 6.9 percent allocated to the 10,000 merchants and traders by sea. How King arrived at the £45 average income is not known, but it was very close to the net profit made by William Stout during his first year of business (1688–9). Stout calculated that he gained that year about £50 besides shop rent and boarding; profits for later years were, however, considerably more. In 1697 his net worth was £1,117. As he commenced trade with £119 10s. in cash, his average yearly net profit for the nine years must have been over £100.[2] However abstemious he may have been, shop rent, travelling expenses, clothing, housing, charitable donations, etc. would have eaten into his gross profits. With all due allowance to William Stout's business acumen, if he could earn over £100 a year in Lancaster, perhaps it would not be rash to presume that those in the more prosperous centres of the kingdom were well above that mark. If Gregory King's estimated annual income is a judicious average and bears some correspondence to reality, his 40,000 shopkeepers would appear to include a relatively large group whose annual income fell well below £45.

Almost a century later Adam Smith reckoned that "a little grocer" in a "small seaport town" might make £30 to £40 a year on a "stock" of £100, while the grocer's stock in the capital might amount to as much as £10,000, but his profit would be no more than 8 or 10 percent.[3] Neither figure is necessarily accurate. One doubts that many grocers in Edinburgh in 1776 were in the upper bracket. In London, on the other hand, those with a "stock of ten thousand pounds" would not be at the top of their trade. On 24 June 1776, the firm of Davison, Newman and Company, "grocers, tea dealers and confectioners", wholesale and retail, drew up a partnership agreement covering five partners. Davison and Newman supplied a capital of £80,000. In 1793 with the death and retirement of some of the partners, a stock of £127,969 was divided and a new agreement drawn up.[4] This was a very well capitalized City firm and certainly can be ranked among the major grocers, although it was by no means unique. The firm of David Lloyd Pigott and Company, wholesale and retail tea dealers and grocers, was founded in 1760 by David Pugh. With what capital is not said. But upon his death, forty-seven years later, he bequeathed to his grandnephew £100,000.[5] Francis Garratt, another wholesale-retail tea dealer, accrued a similar fortune.[6] The point is not to illustrate the wealth of individual dealers but rather to show the wide gap that existed between the top and bottom of the scale. Whether or not Adam Smith's estimates reflect reality, he was at the least aware of the existence of small shopkeepers. Was Colquhoun equally cognizant of them?

The estimated average annual income of Colquhoun's 74,500 shopkeepers is £150, a figure very close to that of the 176 shopkeepers in York whose average income was £163. But the latter included only those paying assessed taxes of £2 or more, and they comprised a small proportion of all shopkeepers, probably no more than 36 percent. In 1785, 486 retail shops in York were subject to the shop tax. It would appear that at least 64 percent of the total number of shopkeepers were paying assessed taxes under £2 or were excused from paying. Their average income was undoubtedly considerably less than £163. Of the shops recorded in the 1797 London survey, 35.4 percent fell below the £2 assessment. The percentage for the

Tower Division was 54.9. In view of the very high rental in London compared to the provinces, it would not be unreasonable to assume a similar proportion of provincial shopkeepers as that for the Tower Division. As houses renting below £15 would rarely be assessed at £2 or over, the 1785 account of shops in provincial towns offers corrobative evidence. Of the total number subject to the shop tax, 62.9 percent had an assessed rental value between £5 and under £15. Indeed, 66.9 percent of all persons paying the assessed taxes in England and Wales fell below the £2 assessment.[7] It is likely that at least one-half, if not more, of all shopkeepers in the provinces were assessed under £2 and a considerable portion had their taxes abated. Certainly, there were many petty shopkeepers in the provinces. Of course, there was no one-to-one relationship between income and the assessed tax. But surely one can assume a rough correspondence between the two.[8] The tax office seems to have thought so.

This can be illustrated by an interesting table among the Pitt Papers. It arranges persons paying assessed taxes by occupation, profession, or social status, the amount of assessed taxes, the number in each category, and the "supposed annual expenditure" or income of each class of inhabitants.[9] Six major classes of persons are distinguished. Each class is further divided into tax categories. In all, thirty tax categories are listed, ranging from the first group of inhabitants paying an assessed tax of 3s. or less to the last paying £200 to £400. The total number of inhabitants for all classes is 800,212, sharing a revenue (or expenditure) of approximately £148,265,200 or an annual average of £185.[10] The document provides significant information on various types of shopkeepers at the end of the century.

The information is summarized in table 25. Whoever compiled the account showed a fine sense of social and economic distinction along with an astute awareness of appropriate income levels. Income or "expenditure" did not necessarily increase with every rise in assessed taxes, nor, as far as can be discerned, did it follow any set formula. The table appears to have been constructed and based on rather substantial evidence. Certainly, the tax office had at its disposal numerous assessment returns with detailed accounts of occupations and incomes, similar to the one remitted from York.[11] We have calculated the average income of the groups that coincide with those of the York shopkeepers, namely the £1 15s. to £8 assessment categories, ranging in income from £70 to £400. It includes some of the "shopkeepers" in Class II and "tradesmen" in Class III. The average income for the sample was £175, very close to that of the York shopkeepers.[12] The sample forms 34.7 percent of all inhab-

itants paying assessments ranging from 3s. to £8, very similar to the
proportion of London shopkeepers in the two upper-assessment
classes. It may not be safe to conclude that the proportion of major
shopkeepers in the kingdom was similar, but the proportion is perhaps not too widely off the mark.

Class I contains the "journeymen mechaniks and small shopkeepers" with incomes of £40 or £50. Although there is no way to determine the number of shopkeepers within this class, it is evident
that to some contemporaries the "small shopkeepers" had no higher
status or income than "journeymen mechaniks." The range of income for shopkeepers in Class II is much wider, from £50 to £180.
No shopkeepers as such are listed in Classes III and IV, they now
appear as "tradesmen" or "capital tradesmen." The change of no-
menclature of shopkeepers is interesting and reflects contemporary
views: mere "shopkeepers" were relegated to the lower or middling
class of persons. The more important members of the business community, with higher incomes, retained the older, more prestigious
term, "tradesmen" – the Newmans, Pigotts, and Garratts of London
and the large provincial cities. For the last two classes, if tradesmen
qualified by income, they were now identified with "the richest class
of commons" and coupled with the nobility-merchant-financiers,
perhaps on the order of Francis Baring.

The number of inhabitants who paid assessed taxes under £2 was
535,192, or 66.9 percent of all inhabitants listed. Their average annual "expenditure" was £50 10s. In this group were the "small shopkeepers" in Class I and those "shopkeepers" in Class II whose
incomes ranged from £50 to £80. These are the shopkeepers who
do not appear in the York survey and whose existence Colquhoun
seemed barely cognizant of. Neither his number of shopkeepers, nor
his estimated annual income allowed for a considerable portion
whose income equalled the journeymen-mechaniks and artisans.
York may have been a backwater with respect to industrial development, but it was renowned for its shopping facilities. If its principal
shopkeepers averaged only £163, the income of those in smaller
market towns would have been much less.

Two other documents from the Pitt Papers shed further light on
the number of shopkeepers in the higher and lower income brackets
at the end of the century. Ca. 1798–9, Pitt drew up six differently
organized "estimates of the national income" of which two are particularly pertinent.[13] The first was entitled "estimated income of the
several families and classes of the kingdom having £200 a year upwards." Among others included in the list were: 50,000 "shopkeepers" in the kingdom with "average incomes" of £200; and 40,000

Table 25
Amount of Assessed Taxes, Annual Expenditure, and Persons Inhabiting Assessed
Houses, 1797 (arranged by tax categories)

Class or Description of Persons Inhabiting Assessed Houses	Amount of Assessed Taxes	Annual Expenditure or Income (in £)	Number of Inhabitants
I Journeymen mechanicks and	0-3s.	40	190,122
small shopkeepers	6-10s.	50	129,563
II Higher class of artisans, small farmers, shopkeepers, merchants and traders clerks, inferior	10s.-£2[1]	50-80	215,507
government officers, persons of small independent fortune	£2-£4[2]	50-180 (av. £87 10s.)	116,293
III Large farmers, tradesmen, merchants, manufacturers, beneficed clergymen, persons of middling independent fortune, higher officers of government (7 categories)	£4-£10	200-400	102,764
IV Capital tradesmen, merchants and manufacturers, persons of good independent fortunes (7 categories)	£10-£20	600-1,500 (av. £829)	29,126
V Noblemen and gentlemen of large estates or incomes	£200-£400	2,000-4,000	16,768
VI Highest order of nobility and richest class of commons	£200-£400	12,000	69

Source: PRO, 30/8/281, fol. 125.

Notes: [1]6 categories.
[2]6 categories.

"artisans, such as jewellers, silversmiths, copper[?] makers, ironmongers, potters and persons at the head of the woolen and cotton
trade" with "average incomes" of £500. The total estimated income
of all groups was £91,757,000, with the 50,000 shopkeepers contributing £10,000,000 or 10.9 percent of the total, and the artisans,
£20,000,000.[14]

That the first estimate was not intended to include all shopkeepers
is clear from Pitt's second attempt (see appendix 3) to arrive at the
wealth of the nation – "Estimates of the National Income deduced
from the several sources of land rents, interest of capital, public
dividends, profits of commerce, manufacturers, professions, etc."[15]
It is worth reproducing in full both for its intrinsic interest and as
a means of demonstrating the proportion of shopkeepers Pitt
thought fell below an income of £100. The figures in the first column

of appendix 3 differ considerably from those the Reverend H. Beeke reproduced as Pitt's estimates of assessable income, particularly for "home trade."[16] Pitt's estimate for home trade was £62 million from which he deducted one-half for those whose income was "less than £100."[17] "Home trade" included the two groups listed in his first estimate: the 50,000 "shopkeepers" with a total income of £10 million; and the 40,000 "artisans" or manufacturers with a total income of £20 million. Presumably, these are the two groups identified in appendix 3 as having incomes over £100. However, Pitt's second estimate allows for an additional number, those whose income was under £100. If they shared an income of £31 million, the estimated number of shopkeepers, artisans, or manufacturers in England and Wales must have been over 300,000. Pitt and his advisors apparently thought there were over three times as many shopkeepers and artisans with incomes below £100 as there were above £100.[18] In the light of the evidence from the table on assessed inhabitants, can it not be presumed that the proportion of small to principal shopkeepers approximates the ratio – 3:1 – for the whole group?

These are, of course , estimates. They were, however, made by a person who took pride in mastering the details which formed the basis for his financial measures. Pitt never worked in a vacuum; he sought advice and information from those in a position to know, and he cast his net widely. In the field of finances, Pitt was a professional who thoroughly enjoyed resolving the intricacies of a problem; but he retained a keen ear for the politically possible. On an issue as important as the income tax, Pitt would leave no source of information untapped, at the same time bringing his own considerable abilities to bear on the subject at hand.[19] His conclusions cannot be dismissed lightly.

Moreover, Pitt's judgment on the proportion of principal shopkeepers is strikingly similar to Joseph Massie's. Table 26 is based on Massie's figures. It lists the number of tradesmen and alesellers by income categories. It is, in some respects, a rather stereotyped classification – for each decline in income for the first four groups, Massie merely doubled the number of families. Nevertheless, his estimates reveal several noteable features. The income range for tradesmen coincides with that of the 1797 assessed tax table (table 25) and his first four categories, with the incomes of the principal shopkeepers of York. A large number, almost 77 percent, were allocated to the lowest income group – those with an income of forty pounds a year – the same income he assigned to the lowest category of artisans (the "journeymen-mechaniks" of table 25 perhaps). The ratio of Massie's petty to principal tradesmen is 3.3:1, almost the

Table 26
Number of Tradesmen and Alesellers in Great Britain, 1760

Rank	Number of Families	Income or Expenses per Family (£ per Annum)	Total Income (£m)	% in Each Rank
Principal Tradesmen	2,500	400	1.0	
	5,000	200	1.0	
	10,000	100	1.0	
	20,000	70	1.4	
Subtotal	37,500		4.4	23.1
Petty Tradesmen	125,000	40	5.0	76.9
Total	162,500		9.4	

Average income of principal tradesmen: £117　6s.8d.
Average income of all tradesmen: 　£　57　17s.0d.

Innkeepers, Alesellers	2,000	100	.2	4.8
Alesellers, Cottagers	20,000	40	.8	47.6
	20,000	20	.4	47.6
Total	42,000		1.4	

Average income of alesellers, cottagers: £30 0s. 0d.
Average income of all alesellers: 　£33 6s. 8d.

Source: Mathias, "Social Structure," table 1.

same ratio as that calculated from the national income accounts. The number of principal shopkeepers is only one-quarter less than Pitt's estimate of 50,000 – an increase of some 25 percent during the intervening forty years would not be at all impossible.[20] The average income of the principal shopkeepers is, however, considerably less (41.3 percent) than Pitt estimated. Massie may well have underestimated the number of shopkeepers in his two top categories, although an increase both in number and income might be expected. When Pitt and his advisors were attempting to calculate the average assessable income on the basis of Gregory King's estimate for England and Wales in 1688, they concluded "that in the present period it may be reasonable to multiply those incomes at least by three."[21]

Massie's figures for "ale-sellers" are equally impressive. He was the only contemporary calculator to recognize the existence of very lowly "ale-sellers, cottagers," 20,000 were assigned an income of £20. It will be recalled that Mary Smith of Flixton was an aleseller and chandler. Whatever income group she belonged to, she was obviously not one of the more affluent publicans if the term is at all applicable to her. Lowly "ale-sellers, cottagers," as we have seen, certainly formed a not inconsiderable proportion of those receiving the coveted licences. Among Colquhoun's 50,000 "innkeepers and publicans," a relatively accurate figure, there were undoubtedly a number of alesellers with incomes very much below his estimated average of £100. The close correspondence between the number of shopkeepers listed by Massie and those enumerated by Excise was noted earlier. Massie is no less accurate in his estimate of alesellers. According to an excise account, in 1759–60 there were 40,166 victuallers and 1,116 common brewers.[22]

Massie was familiar with King's calculations and adopted a similar classification of social and economic groups. His figures can, therefore, be used to demonstrate the changes that one contemporary thought had occurred in the distributive system. The wealth of the mercantile community is increased only slightly. King estimated the number of merchants as 10,000 with a total annual income of £2.4 million; Massie, 13,000 and £3.4 million respectively or 5.6 percent of the national income. But Massie obviously believed there had been an enormous increase in the number of tradesmen, particularly petty tradesmen with an annual income of £40. King assigned shopkeepers and tradesmen an annual income of £45. The average annual income for all tradesmen listed by Massie is £57 17s., an increase of only 28.6 percent. But, as noted earlier, it is most unlikely that petty shopkeepers were included in King's figures – if indeed they existed in 1688. His shopkeepers and tradesmen should, therefore, be compared with Massie's principal tradesmen, and the comparison reveals an enormous difference. The average income of Massie's 37,500 principal tradesmen is £117 6s. 8d., or 160.7 percent greater than the average income of King's 40,000 shopkeepers. Massie's tradesmen represent 11 percent of all families and 13.9 percent if alesellers are included, compared to King's 2.9 percent. The income of Massie's tradesmen is 15.4 percent of the national total. These are very high figures, indeed, but they compare favourably with Pitt's estimates. If the ratio of principal and small shopkeepers implied in Pitt's estimate is accepted, the total income for all shopkeepers is approximately £26 million, roughly 14.4 percent of the national income (50,000 principal shopkeepers with total income of £10 million and 165,000 petty shopkeepers with total income approximately £16 million). Principal tradesmen were allocated 7.2 percent of the national income in Massie's account; principal shopkeepers represented 5.5 percent in Pitt's estimate. But among Pitt's 40,000 artisans with average income of £500, some were probably shopkeeping artisans: the jewellers, silversmiths, and ironmongers, for example. Moreover, Pitt's figures do not include Scotland; Massie's presumably do. Despite these differences, there is, at least, no grave discrepancy between the estimates of Pitt and Massie.

As Professor Mathias has suggested, Massie probably had access to government papers and perhaps to the original compilations long since destroyed. His classification of alesellers, for example, might have been drawn from excise reports on the number of barrels of small and strong beer charged to each individual trader – information available at the time. An ingenious, indefatigable, and methodical calculator, qualities Massie seems to have possessed,[23] could have extracted from the excise riders' vouchers or the supervisors' abstracts, which listed the total amount of commodities charged to every trade, sufficient information to produce a very respectable classification. Indeed, given other corroborative evidence, one is persuaded to accept Massie's classification of tradesmen as a rough approximation of the contemporary scene. It does not follow that his figures for the agricultural sector are equally reliable. There was far less information in the London tax offices on this sector of the economy. But as an observer of the commercial population, Massie should be ranked above Colquhoun.[24]

Colquhoun's figures for shopkeepers and tradesmen raise a number of knotty questions. He estimated the number of "shopkeepers and tradesmen dealing in goods" as 74,500 with an annual average income of £150. A further 25,000 are identified as "persons employing capital as tailors, mantua-makers, milliners, etc. in the manufacture of stuffs into wearing apparel and dresses, including army clothiers." Their estimated average income is also £150.[25] It is very difficult to believe that for every three "shopkeepers of all description" there was a bespoke-tailor, mantuamaker, or milliner.[26] It is equally difficult to believe that their average income was £150. In fashionable York, Pitt's correspondent listed sixteen milliners, staymakers, tailors, and breechesmakers or one for every ten *principal* shops. The average income of the group was £120. But the shopkeepers listed in the York survey included only those paying an assessment of £2 or more. The number of petty shopkeepers not included in the survey may well have equalled or surpassed those enumerated. It is difficult to believe there were many tailors, milliners, and breechmakers among the petty shopkeepers, or that their average income was £150. One can only conclude that Colquhoun has either inflated the figures for milliners, and others or grossly underestimated the number of shops or both.

Colquhoun certainly underestimated the number of shops. During the excise year ending 5 July 1803, the number of tea licences issued in England and Wales was 58,343.[27] As no licence was issued except to proprietors of "entered shops," those licences represent the minimum number of shops selling tea.[28] It is simply inconceivable that 78.3 percent of the shopkeepers listed by Colquhoun were entered tea dealers. However widespread the sale of tea may have been, the cities and large towns in the kingdom contained many specialized shops the proprietors of which would have disdained mingling tea with their more select articles. Nor would all shopkeepers have been prepared to add to their other concerns the vexatious excise regulations on the sale of tea.

Probably, Colquhoun's 74,500 shopkeepers were those established on the market streets up and down the country, those who paid the shop tax willingly or unwillingly. The figure is suspiciously close to what can be estimated from the shop tax assessments. In 1787, the total assessment for the country was £59,000; that for Middlesex £42,710, leaving £16,290 for the rest of England, Wales, and Scotland. If one assumes that the proportion of shops in various rental caterories in the provinces is similar to that of Northamptonshire and Suffolk, a not very rash assumption, the average tax per shop would be 61d., which gives a total of roughly 64,000 shops. Deducting 15 percent for Scotland leaves some 54,400 paying the assessment in the English and Welsh counties outside Middlesex. If the shops assessed in Westminster and the City are added, the total is 66,800, leaving some 8,000 shops for the rest of Middlesex. These are of course very rough estimates. It is highly probable that Colquhoun had access to the county reports (now missing), which would have given him the number actually assessed in each county. Unfortunately, unlike the excise survey of 1759, the probable source for Massie's figures, the shop tax was confined to a relatively small range of shops, particularly after the 1786 amendment, and is thus a poor source for estimating the total number of all shops.

Colquhoun's average annual income for shopkeepers is equally suspect. The £150 appears to be an average based on the principal shopkeepers, whose who, in 1787, paid the shop tax and whose assessed taxes in 1797 were over £2. In 1797, the average income for the 23,771 shopkeepers in London works out to be only £115. As the wealth and opulence of London's principal shopkeepers exceeded by far that of their counterparts in provincial towns, the income for all shopkeepers throughout the country must be far lower.[29]

Colquhoun's figures raise another problem. His shopkeepers formed only 3.9 percent of all families compared to King's 2.9 percent, surely a very small proportionate increase during a period when enormous changes were taking place in the economy. The total income of Colquhoun's shopkeepers was £11,175,000, only 5 percent of his estimated national income. Presumably, that income was derived from the mark-up on goods sold. It is possible, therefore, to estimate roughly what the total value of goods sold would be in order to produce an income of £11,175 million. On an average, the mark-up cannot have been much below 20 percent, particularly if one considers that before most of the goods reached the final seller they had passed through the hands of one or more shopkeepers.[30] For shopkeepers to earn an income of £11 million with an average mark-up of 20 percent, the total value of the goods sold would have been only £55,875,000.[31] That amount seems far below the actual value of goods sold over the counter.

It is possible to roughly estimate the value of some articles stocked by shopkeepers. Most of the figures are based on cost value and thus will understate the costs to the shopkeepers. Table 27 lists the value of some goods stocked by grocers. Of the items listed, only the value for tea is a fairly accurate measure of the first cost to the buyers at the East India Company's auctions. There is no way to determine the value added to the import cost of sugar, tobacco, etc. Presumably, the prices paid by grocers for such products were higher. Moreover, there is one very important omission from the list – flour or bread. It has been estimated that a little over 20 million quarters of corn were consumed in England and Wales in 1800.[32] At the price for a quarter of wheat in 1803, the value was almost £60 million. Some of that wheat, in the form of flour or bread, found its way into grocery and bakery shops. What proportion was sold in the market one cannot say. But, if only one-sixth was distributed through shops, at least £10 million would be added to the trade of grocers and bakers, or a total of £28,5 million for the articles listed. And what was the value of cheese sold by shops, and pepper, salt, spices, Italian oil, dried fruits, nuts, and all the other goods generally stocked by grocers?

The value of the drapers trade was equally high or even higher. The estimated value to the manufacturers of goods in wool, cotton, linen, and silk consumed in Great Britain ca. 1803 was £30.6 million.[33] Not too much reliance can be placed on the figures but they probably indicate the approximate magnitude of the textile industry. The value of the textiles sold by drapers cannot be ascertained. But

Table 27
Value of Goods Stocked by Grocers, ca. 1802

	£ m.	Comments
Tea	6.7	First cost to the buyers at East India Company auctions
Sugar	4.6	Import value of quantities retained for home consumption
Coffee	.9	" "
Tobacco	.4	" "
Wine, Rum, & Brandy	1.5	" "
Candles	2.8	Approximate value of quantities charged with duties
Soap	1.7	" "
Total	18.5	

Sources: Tea: Calculated from Tea Sold by East India Company, 46(191), *PP1845*; Sugar, coffee, tobacco, wine, rum, and brandy: Schumpeter, *English Overseas Trade Statistics*, 59, table 17; 61-2, table 18; Candles, Soap: Mitchell and Deane, *British Historical Statistics*, 262, 265.

even for the few articles noted, the value of the goods sold by shopkeepers is above that calculated from Colquhoun's estimate of income. No reliable figures are available for the value of the stock of haberdashers – hats, gloves, stockings, ribbons, handkerchiefs, and other small wares, or ready-made wear such as breeches, waistcoats, petticoats, and capes – but it was certainly not small. And the ironmongery trade must have been quite extensive. There still remain the drysalters, apothecaries, bookshops, furniture and upholstery shops, dealers in chinaware, jewellers, and watchmakers. In all, one may suggest that the total value of goods distributed over the counter would seem to be much greater than what can be calculated from Colquhoun's income figures for shopkeepers. Their contribution to the national income was considerably greater than Colquhoun's estimate.

Colquhoun's figures for hawkers also raise doubts. His estimated number of "hawkers and pedlers, duffers, and others, with and without licences" is 2,500 with a yearly income of forty pounds.[34] But in 1783–4, the number of licensed hawkers alone was 1,313. By 1799–1800, they numbered at least 1,868; in 1809–10, 3,728. By 1819, they numbered 5,030.[35] That is, in 1799–1800, at least 1,868 of Colquhoun's hawkers were licensed, leaving only 632 unlicensed pedlars. There were, undoubtedly, many more unlicensed pedlars in London alone. One may also note the singular absence of carriers, an important commercial group without whose services commerce would have ground to a halt.

No precise figures can be given on the total number of shopkeepers at the end of the century. But the various estimates suggest that many small shopkeepers escaped Colquhoun's enumeration and have eluded the historian's mesh. Pitt estimated the number of principal shopkeepers with average income of £200 as 50,000. But many shopkeepers had incomes below £100. If the ratio of 3:1 approximates reality, the total number of all shopkeepers would be over 150,000. Whatever may have been the average annual income of the small shopkeepers, their contribution to the national income was not negligible. Certainly, no history of retail trade can afford to ignore them. The next several chapters will attempt to capture these very elusive retailers.

CHAPTER SEVEN

Role of Village and "Back Street" Shops in the Household Economy of the Workers

Historians of shopkeeping have frequently overlooked or denied the presence of small village or town shops in the eighteenth century. Such major changes in the retail trade as the rise of back-street shops are reserved for the stirring nineteenth century. It is a view based on the more easily available evidence for that century. Shop records of petty chandlers are very sparse, if not nonexistent. To appreciate the role of the small shop and its importance in the commercial life of eighteenth-century society, it is necessary to draw on less tangible evidence, such as contemporary observations and comments, and on knowledge of the general economic and social life of the workers. Fortunately, objective evidence of their presence can be extracted from excise accounts of licensed tea dealers. Information gleaned from these various sources leaves little doubt that the petty shop was not only a thriving institution in the eighteenth century, but also a necessary concomitant of the many changes occurring in the social and economic life of the country. Indeed, one may well wonder if the enormous increase in the consumption of such articles as tea and sugar would have been possible without the presence of these petty shopkeepers who were an integral part of a retail network that made available the new exotic imports to a wider range of people. They were as necessary to the trade of the principal shops as they were to the comfort of the people they served.

Judging from the comments of some contemporaries, the small village shop had been creeping into existence as early as the seventeenth century.[1] One irate observer noted: "petty shopkeepers living in country villages ... doth greatly increase and add to the number of shopkeepers ... which was never wont to be formerly; for now in every country village where is (it may be) not above ten houses, there is a shopkeeper, and one that never served any apprenticeship to any shopkeeping trade whatsoever."[2] He thought hawkers had made it possible for such persons to set up shop. Like most critics, he may well have exaggerated the extent of shopkeeping in country villages, but the existence of the small petty shop, and not only in the villages, cannot be denied. Surely the shop on Cheaney Lane that William Stout set up for Elin Godsalve in 1711 with "about £10 value of grocery goods and other small ware" was none other than a back-street shop. And one may presume that similar shops existed in Lancaster. According to Stout, "she had quickly good custom ... and sould by retail as much as any shop in the town."[3] He was obviously not comparing her trade with his or that of the other shopkeepers on Market Street. Shops like that of Elin Godsalve, catering for a clientele very different from the more exclusive shops of the market streets, multiplied during the course of the eighteenth century both in towns and in country villages. These were the shops that were "devouring markets," a charge levelled at them well before Cobbett.[4]

In 1775, the Reverend John Clayton admonished the poor of Manchester for their "shameful extravagance" and indulgence in gin and tea. By buying "on credit from shopkeepers instead of in the open market, their money," he claimed, "is generally spent before it is received." According to the reverend, "retail shopkeeping in milk, butter, coals and so forth was unknown to this town till very lately."[5] He was, of course, referring not to the establishments on market street but to the small back-street shops. By the 1770s critics assumed the widespread existence of village shops. One writer in a long letter to the *Leeds Mercury*, having berated the farmers for reducing wages and increasing the price of grain and the millers and bakers for various frauds, turned finally to

the petty shopkeepers ... the next class of oppressors. Far from a market, the poor are forced to buy all their necessaries at these petty chandlers, who never fail to set their prices high enough, at least one shilling in eight above what the same may be bought for at retail shops in market towns and often one shilling in six. But a still greater evil is their false weights or scales; the scale in which they weigh their goods being considerably heavier than the other, to hide which they never exchange weights without putting in one weight before they take out the other.[6]

Such statements bear eloquent testimony to the acceptance of, and necessity for, village shops. The writer did not propose to eliminate them. Rather he urged the justices of the peace to conduct systematic and continuous inspection of weights and scales. It may also be noted that the writer compared the prices of necessaries at petty chandlers with those at retail shops in market towns and not with market prices. Presumably, he did not expect the poor to buy their necessaries at the market.

The emergence of small village and town shops in the eighteenth century was a response to changes in the economic structure and in consumer demand. As the century advanced, an ever-increasing proportion of the population became dependent almost entirely on the market economy. This was true for both the agricultural and industrial sectors or, perhaps one should say, the agricultural/industrial sector as the two continued to be intertwined. And it was almost as true for the agricultural as the industrial labourers, particularly in the south. The viability of small shops in country villages and towns depended on the economic and social structure of an area and wide differences existed from one part of the country to another. Farm hands in the north continued to live in or to receive most of their wages in home-grown produce and small farmers had little disposable income, drawing much of their sustenance from the farm. But the general movement was towards a more extensive money economy. As a larger proportion of workers joined the wage-earning labouring force, patterns of consumption changed and more food and more clothes had to be purchased. Where did they shop? Certainly, not at the annual fair. By the eighteenth century, the retail functions of the fair were minimal, confined to trifling articles. Nor is there evidence that the weekly market was a buoyant, flourishing institution. Rather the picture is one of decline, at least for the retail trade, certainly not growth. Had the workers and other members of society used their increased purchasing power at the market, surely it would have generated a quickening in the retail activity of markets. On the other hand, there is evidence of growth in shopkeeping in terms of numbers, types of shops, and methods of distribution. That growth could not have occurred without an increased demand for the kind of services provided by shops, services that were as important to the workers as they were to the middling classes.

One of the most persistent myths in the history of retailing has centred on the shopping habits of the agricultural and urban labourers. The local markets, it is claimed, remained the major source for the workers' meagre supply of food until well into the nineteenth century. It has even been suggested that "newly urbanized ... country people ... accustomed to buying from market traders and pedlars" were totally unprepared to add "such a vital function as shopping" to the many "bewildering experiences" encountered in the industrial towns. "Rather than confront the city shopkeeper and his assistants," they turned to such familiar channels of distribution as market traders and pedlars.[7]

The myth has been tied to a related but somewhat different problem – the timing of changes in the structure and organization of the distributive trades, an association that may owe its origin to Clapham. Having stated that during the first half of the nineteenth century the commercial organization of "the trades in home-grown foodstuffs ... had changed less than those in clothing materials," he went on to note that "there had been little change in ... direct dealing of producer and consumer" in the markets.[8] But neither in this passage nor elsewhere was Clapham specifically concerned with the purchasing practices of the workers. It was J.B. Jefferys who established the myth of the workers shopping habits. He linked them firmly to a distributive system whose methods and techniques "still bore the marks of a pre-industrial economy", and in which no great transformation occurred until the second half of the nineteenth century. Within the system, Jefferys draws a rough distinction between the markets, fairs, and itinerant traders catering to the urban and agricultural workers, and the specialist shopkeepers servicing the more affluent.[9] Subsequent studies have focussed on the timing of changes in the distributive system, the crucial issue revolving around the displacement of the market by the small back-street shops from which the workers without fear or prejudice could obtain a full range of goods.[10]

Such an approach tends to obfuscate the issue. The small shop was not dependent upon changes in the "methods and techniques" of the distributive trades. It was able to function within the folds of the "pre-industrial economy." Nor does an increase in their number necessarily involve a transformation in the distributive system. On the other hand, the fully-developed multiple shop system does mark a departure from traditional methods of distribution, but only in the scale of its organization. Many of the methods had been emerging for almost a century. The extension of the multiple shop system throughout the country may have truly effected changes in the distributive system. But what did such shops replace? Certainly not the markets.

It would be more fruitful to tackle the problem of where the worker spent his money by determining the contents of his shopping basket, where such items could be purchased, and what his purchasing power was. The latter is, of course, an important consideration. It is obvious that as rates of pay increased during the nineteenth century, and more and more people joined the ranks of wage-earners, there would be more money to spend on consumer goods. Most studies of retail trade have rightly emphasized this aspect. But in addition to wage rates (and prices), the effective purchasing power of the workers from week to week would be determined by how, when, and where they were paid. As we know, in the "pre-industrial economy," methods of payment differed widely from one group of workers to another: some received cash; others, partpayment in goods; still others were given notes drawn on shopkeepers or truck shops owned by the employers; some picked up their pay at the alehouse, or what remained of it. For all, "long pay" was the norm. Few workers were paid on a regular weekly basis, for many, the day of reckoning varied from weeks to months.[11] It is, therefore, hardly surprising that many workers were, as even their most sympathetic critics sadly noted, improvident; that, rather than buy good wholesome food more cheaply for "ready money" at the market, they became indebted to small shopkeepers for such extravagances as tea and sugar. One may question the wisdom of critics whose model for the workers was their own well-ordered household with its exemplary budgeting, but one should not ignore the critics' observations. If they failed to understand the springs of human behaviour, they were genuinely concerned about the conditions of the poor.

The detailed reports on the wages and expenses of the poor compiled by Sir Frederic Eden and Rev. David Davies leave little doubt that at the end of the eighteenth century the "ordinary Englishman," to quote Ashton, "was a granivorous and not a carnivorous animal ... meat was for him a luxury" and, we might add, for the ordinary Englishwoman an even greater luxury.[12] And he was decidedly not a vegetarian. Vegetables, with the exception of potatoes, which were used rather extensively in Lancashire and some of the northern counties, were resorted to only as an extreme measure to eke out a slender diet. If potatoes were creeping into the workers' diet south of the Trent, it was due to lack of money, certainly not to preference. In his disdain for the root, Cobbett spoke for his countrymen. But "however abstemious the ordinary Englishman may have been in respect to meat" and vegetables, without his small beer he would have felt utterly deprived.[13] To his wife and children, tea or any of its loathsome substitutes had become an equal necessity, much to the disgust of Cobbett.

What do the reports of Eden and Davies reveal about the household economy of the poor at the end of the century? First, that food, including candles and soap, absorbed somewhere in the neighbourhood of 65 to 70 percent of the income, a figure remarkably similar to the workers' budget in the midnineteenth century.[14] Rent bore little relationship to size of family, varying even within the same community from £1 7s. to £2 10s. per annum.[15] Together with fuel, the rent could run as high as 20 percent of income or as little as 10 percent. With 75 to 90 percent of wages devoted to food and shelter, little was left for clothes and other incidentals, even among some skilled workers. A spectacle framemaker in Wolverhampton whose family earned £49 9s. 4d., claimed he spent only £4 10s. for clothing during the year.[16] Visits to drapery shops were undoubtedly infrequent. Much of the allotment for clothes would in any case go to the shoemaker, although foreign observers rarely failed to comment, possibly with some exaggeration, on how well-dressed, even fashionably clothed, the "ordinary Englishman" was. But however little individual workers purchased in the way of clothes, their total purchases formed a *mass* market for the clothing industry, a fact that manufacturers were only too well aware of when prices of wheat soared. Frugal north country families might still spin the yarn and weave the cloth for their own use, but even there the practice was declining among those less well off.[17] It had long since declined in the Midlands and southern counties. Most, if not all, of their clothes, first-or second-hand, were purchased from the shopkeeper.[18]

Shops also supplied most of the articles in the food basket. Indeed, for workers south of the Trent, the market may well have been a far more important source for food in the late nineteenth century when their consumption of meat and vegetables increased.[19] South of the Trent, the staple diet of agricultural labourers was bread, tea, sugar, cheese, butter, small beer, occasionally milk and potatoes, and butcher's meat or bacon. How much meat such a family purchased largely depended upon the price of bread. When the quartern loaf cost ten pence, those earning less than forty pounds a year, or a little over fifteen shillings a week, would have very little to expend on meat. As the sample budget in table 28 shows, at the end of the eighteenth century, rent, fuel, and the most essential food items would cost over thirty-five pounds for a family of five.

With the exception of bread, it is a very modest budget, less than the quantities allowed in the workhouses and not representative of better-paid workers.[20] Two pounds of cheese and one-half pound of butter a week would not go far among five people. Double the quantity and the cost would be £38 7s. If the quantity of meat were also doubled, the cost would exceed their income. To many eighteenth-century critics, it was a dry, monotonous fare which surely required some liquid to wash it down. But it was the standard fare for many agricultural labourers in the southern and eastern counties. If a joint of meat could be purchased once a week, they were,

Table 28
Annual Budget for a Family of Five, South of the Trent, 1795-6

Items	Cost £	s.	Explanation
Rent and Fuel	3	—	
Bread	19	10	9 quartern loaves per week @ 10d., allowing 1 lb. per person per day
Tea	1	9	2 oz. per week @ 4s. 6d. per lb.
Sugar and Treacle	1	3	½ lb. per week @ 7d. per lb. for sugar ½ lb. @ 3.5d. per lb. for treacle
Butter	1	2	½ lb. per week @ 10d. per lb.
Cheese	2	3	2 lbs. per week @ 5d. per lb. (a little under one ounce per person per day)
Candles, Soap & Salt	2	—	very rough estimate
Small Beer & Ale	2	12	estimate 1s. a week
Bacon or Meat	2	3	1¼ lb. of bacon @ 8d. per lb. or 2½ lbs. of butcher's meat @ 4d. per lb.
Total	£35	2s.	

Sources: Bread: Assize price in London, average for 1795-6. Mitchell & Deane, *British Historical Statistics*, 498, table 14. The average price for the two years was in fact 10.48d. for a quartern loaf weighing 4 lbs. 5½ oz; Beer: average of small beer and ale. All other items based upon prices charged at William Wood's shop at Didsbury in 1786; Quantities: Based on various budgets: Davies, *Case of the Labourers*, 178; Eden, *State of the Poor*; Arthur Young; William Marshal; and surveys of agricultural labourers.

Note: We have, however, used some discretion in allocating the various quantities. David Davies compiled budgets for three Lancashire families, two using two pounds of salt per week and one, one pound. This seems an extraordinary amount given the other items in the budget. The same applies to the quantities for soap, starch, and blue. Starch and blue were, in fact, used infrequently by labourers. Beer, on the other hand, is suspiciously understated in most of the budgets – a subject about which informants were probably shy.

in their own eyes and those of the less fortunate, in very comfortable circumstances.

Among the items, only butcher's meat would have required a trip to the market, and even that might have been available at the local shop. Wood of Didsbury supplied some of his customers with meat, perhaps by prior arrangement. One of Eden's correspondents reported that the shopkeepers in Hothfield, Kent, "readily take orders for any article that may be wanted."[21] Bacon was certainly sold in the markets, but it was also just as certainly available in small village shops. Bacon was the most convenient meat product, it required little cooking, kept well and was easily apportioned. The housewife could, moreover, purchase it in small quantities at the shop. Wood's customers sometimes purchased as little as a penny and one-half worth of bacon, enough, perhaps, for a meal.

Table 29
London Assize Price of Bread and Cost of Flour in Didsbury, 1786-8

Year	Flour		Household Bread
	in pence per 1 lb.[1]	in pence per 3 lbs.[2]	in pence per 4 lbs.[3]
1786	1.66	5.0	5.5
1787	1.75	5.3	5.7
1788	1.75[4]	5.3	6.4

Notes: [1]Based on numerous entries in Wood's Customer' Ledger. The prices did not vary from customer to customer. Prices were for the best bluestone flour.

[2]According to Dr Charles Irving, 3½ pounds of old flour required 2 pounds of water to make the dough and lost 10 ounces in the baking. New flour required less water. Three pounds of flour might yield a loaf slightly heavier than 4 pounds. Quoted in Eden, State of the Poor, 1:544. Report to the Committee of the House of Commons, 1774, ordered to be printed November 1795, p. 72.

[3]Mitchell and Deane, British Historical Statistics, 498.

[4]Prices are for the months of February and March; the following harvest year, prices of wheat jumped from forty-eight shillings to sixty-two shillings per quarter. See Ashton, Economic History, 239, appendix, table 1, "Prices of Wheat Per Quarter at Michaelmas."

The above account of purchases does not provide for flour, and the cereal allotment has been confined to bread. Admittedly, some families continued to bake their own bread, but those critics who constantly bewailed the extravagance of the workers for purchasing bread were apparently thinking in terms of days long since gone – days when agricultural workers could purchase wheat and have it ground by the miller. To the worker's wife at the end of the eighteenth century, the saving might have seemed negligible. Table 29 compares the London Assize price for a quartern loaf of household bread with the cost of the equivalent amount of flour at Wood's shop in Didsbury. Three pounds of flour cost only slightly less than the price of four pounds of household bread. In Preston in 1795, the price quoted for 3 and one-half pounds of wheat flour was one shilling; 4 pounds of household bread was also one shilling.[22] Nor does the table include the cost of salt, yeast, or baking. Wood's customers generally paid one and one-half pennies for "berm", but he never indicates the quantity. And how convenient was it for cottagers to bake? Unless the dough was carried to a nearby baker to proof and bake, fires would have to be lit. But warm, cozy cottages were not the norm for lower paid workers at the end of the century. They were fortunate if they had sufficient fuel to cook a hot dish once or twice a week. Moreover, if the housewife were not an expert breadmaker, the whole exercise could result in a ruinous mess of undigestable bread.

The Norwich Court of Guardians for the workhouses discovered it was cheaper to purchase bread from the baker than to have it made at the workhouse. The Guardians found it "extraordinary" that the bakers were able to sell it cheaper and accounted for it by the fact that bakers were able "from a more perfect knowledge of the art, to produce a larger quantity of dough, from a given quantity of flour, than those who were employed to do this business at the workhouse." Due to the ignorance of the latter, "a great waste of flour had been made, an extravagant quantity of yeast had been used, and the dough so improperly compounded, and so imperfectly fermented, as not to admit of the due increase."[23] Did the ordinary housewife of a labourer possess superior culinary skills? But even if a housewife could bake excellent bread, she had no need to go to market to buy the flour. It was readily available in the shops and not necessarily at a greatly enhanced price compared to market prices. At Mongewell, Oxfordshire, the Society for Bettering the Conditions of the Poor reported an overall saving of 21 percent to its customers on items sold in its shop "at prime cost and for ready-money."[24] A mark-up of some 20 percent on "prime cost" with credit allowed can hardly be considered excessive. Provision merchants in the markets were certainly not retailing at prime cost.

By the end of the eighteenth century, the earlier regulations prohibiting bakers from selling bread in their shops had long since fallen into desuetude – not only did they sell from their shops, they also supplied other shops with bread. At the same time, bakers often branched out and added other small items to the goods available to their customers. Freshly baked bread might still be sold from baskets on market day, but it is doubtful if the housewife was dependent upon the markets for her supply of bread.

Sugar and tea were never, as fas as can be ascertained, sold in the markets. In fact, the laws regulating the sale of tea precluded such a possibility. Tea could only be sold from "entered places," the usual place of abode of the proprietor. A market stall would hardly fulfill the requirement; nor would a stallholder sell sufficient tea to cover the licence fee. Candles may have been sold in the market, but they were the stock-in-trade of the small chandler's shop. Butter and cheese were certainly available in the markets, but so were they in shops, and had been for many years. As early as 1691, William Stout was selling cheese he had purchased at the Garston and Preston fairs.[25] Wood sold a lot of cheese; butter, somewhat less. Wood's customers may have bought some butter along with butcher's meat at the market. However, such purchases hardly support the contention that until some time in the nineteenth century the local market was the major source for the workingman's food.

Indeed, the kingpin of the weekly market was the butcher. On the periphery were the market women selling homegrown fruits and vegetables, bread, butter, and fresh eggs, few of which appeared on the workingman's table. Eggs did not become a common breakfast food for workers until the nineteenth century. In addition, there were usually some provision dealers, along with the potmen, tinkers, and hucksters, offering a varied selection of oddments. With the exception of butcher's meat, few items sold in the market could not be purchased more expeditiously in small quantities as needed at the chandler's shop. If the housewife paid a little more for the convenience, she could also expect short-term credit in a place where she was well known. Wood was certainly extending credit to his local customers, some of whom could have featured in Eden's survey of the poor.

Contemporary observers leave little doubt that for the labouring poor in the villages in southern England the petty shop was largely replacing the open market as a major source of supply for their meagre diet. However wasteful and reprehensible such behaviour might appear in the eyes of concerned observers, the local shop was both a convenience and a necessity. At a shop, the housewife could purchase, on credit, small quantities of daily necessaries such as candles, cheese, bread, butter, sugar, tea, soap, and salt, and even flour if she had fuel to bake. Market buying required ready money. Budgeting for weekly cash purchases at the open market was not a habit easily acquired by lower-paid workers, even had they been able to extricate themselves from the treadmill of credit.[26] To do so required some control of family resources and a far greater sense of stability and security than persons at this level could achieve. One suspects that the major buyers at the market in the eighteenth century were the middling orders whose consumption of meat, fruit, and vegetables was much greater than that of the labourers. In 1795, the annual household account for food of Rev. Laurie of Newburn, Fifeshire, amounted to £59 13s. of which 29.6 percent was for meat, fish, and fowl and 2.1 percent, for fruit.[27] Not until well into the nineteenth century were the workers able to expend that proportion of their income on meat. In fact, the great rebuilding of town markets for retail trade took place not in the eighteenth but in the nineteenth century.

The situation north of the Trent was somewhat different. In the first place, there was much less reliance on bread as the staple food.

The customary breakfast consisted of oatmeal or barley, with or without milk. Stews of all types that required little meat and could be stretched or watered endlessly formed the major meal. In Lancashire, the potato had early found a place at the workingmen's table and not only among Irish workers. With such a diet, one might expect greater recourse to the market. It is interesting that Wood sold little barley, oats, or potatoes. The inhabitants of Didsbury either had adopted the southern diet or were purchasing such items at the market. But if agricultural labourers in the more remote northern counties clung to the traditional diet, much of which was supplied by their employers, those in industry were acquiring a taste for shop-bought goods. With some exceptions, tea was the standard fare for women, and along with tea went the more monotonous diet of the southerners, especially among town dwellers. In Wales and the northern countries, shops certainly played a minor role in the domestic economy of agricultural workers, but these remote corners of the kingdom were the exceptions. Cobbett was essentially correct about shops replacing markets, although the change was distasteful to him. The past he lamented was in many respects a figment of nostalgia for what rural England should be.

The myth that the market was *the* important source for the workers' food is associated with an assumption that the only alternative to the market was the high-class grocery shop. If that were true, one would be forced to accept the myth. In fact, at no time were true-born grocers very numerous. Neither the bankruptcy reports nor the directories for the eighteenth and early nineteenth centuries record a large proportion of these specialized shops. The traditional trade of the grocer consisted almost entirely of foreign produce – dried fruits and nuts; spices, oils, sauces, and vinegar; tea, coffee, and chocolate; and, of course, sugar. Outside of London and the large provincial towns, few shopkeepers could afford to confine their sales to groceries, which formed an infinitesimal portion of the household expenses for even the wealthy. Indeed, among traditional grocery wares, sugar and tea probably accounted for half the value of the true-born grocer's turnover; sugar, because of the large quantities used, and tea because of its high per unit price.[28] However high the mark-up on spices and dried fruits, etc. the total amount expended for such items was small compared to other household needs. Thus, to maintain a viable financial position, the traditional grocer required a large clientele, which was in truth, drawn primarily from the upper echelons of society. One is hardly surprised that the percentage of grocers in the bankruptcy lists is low. On the other hand, if the *grocer* maintained a high-class shop with all its appurtenances, not all the commodities he handled were restricted to the affluent.[29]

Table 28 illustrates the household economy of the lowest paid workers, particularly agricultural labourers in southern England, who were, admittedly, suffering as prices rose at the end of the century. Nonetheless, even these lowly agricultural labourers depended upon shops for many of the articles in their food basket. Those who benefitted from rising wages and whose incomes were well above the subsistence level could, of course, spend more money at the shops. And the latter represented a sizeable and growing proportion of the workers during the eighteenth century. No one doubts that by mideighteenth century the use of sugar and treacle had penetrated the most humble homes. And what of pepper, cloves, mustard, and other spices – did such condiments never enter the poacher's pot? Was salt a luxury? Where did the poor buy their supply? At Didsbury they could get one pound for three-half pence at Mr Wood's village shop – for credit too. If the labouring poor rarely tasted an almond or sugar plum except at the annual entertainments provided by the squires and lords for their tenants, surely currants and raisins found their way into the puddings of all but the most deprived.[30] Did this submerged portion of the population hoard their few coins for the day when purchases could be made at a high-class grocery shop in some town near or distant? Or were these necessary *luxuries* obtainable closer to home? The latter has been suggested. While such activities of the *menu peuple* have left few traces, there is firm evidence that some groceries found their way into shops not remotely resembling the Market Street grocers. By the mideighteenth century, the trade in tea, legal and illicit, was brisk; and its consumption had moved down the social scale, penetrating the homes of even the Manchester poor. Rev. Clayton may have exaggerated, but when the Commutation Act was passed in 1784 an extensive demand had grown up for this "deleterious" beverage. The sale of tea was confined by law to "entered" shops, and the trade closely supervised by Excise. Not surprisingly, excise records have proved a fruitful source of information on the number and types of shops selling tea. It can be safely assumed that where tea was sold, so too was sugar, its almost necessary accompaniment, and other small household articles. The following two chapters will demonstrate that the sale of tea was not confined to high-class grocers. Nor was its consumption restricted to the affluent members of society.

CHAPTER EIGHT

Tea Dealers: Grocers vs "Back Street" Shops

In 1752, Mary Smith, chandler of Flixton, had available for her customers "108 pounds of run tea." Probably her shop had not been entered at the nearest excise office. Until the demise of the illicit trade in the early 1790s, she and countless others escaped the excise records on tea dealers. But for the years following, the parliamentary account prepared by Excise of the annual number of licensed dealers in Great Britain can be accepted as a relatively accurate record.[1] Unfortunately, the licence regulation did not commence until 1780. Moreover, the parliamentary account lists only the total number of licences for England and Wales, for Scotland, and for Ireland from 1815. However, some scattered accounts are available on the number and disposition of tea dealers in various parts of the kingdom and one record of the number of *entered* dealers before 1780. As scanty as the evidence is, it casts substantial light on eighteenth-century shopkeepers, at least those selling tea.

The Seven Years' War occasioned a slight abatement of the illicit trade in tea. At the end of hostilities, the trade, much enlarged by new continental entrants, returned to its old channels with renewed vigour. Faced with this unholy competition, many fair-trade dealers either joined ranks with the illicit traders or gave up their tea business completely.[2] Francis Garratt, a London tea dealer and an active member of an association formed to combat the illicit trade, and his fellow dealers found it "almost impossible to do any business within thirty miles of the sea coast."[3] In 1767 the government, responding to the pleas of the legal trade, instituted a rescue operation by removing the one shilling duty on certain teas – not however, before making its own inquiries on the state of the trade. On 2 January 1767, Treasury requested the excise commissioners in London to submit an account of the number of tea dealers in the whole kingdom. They replied that "the number of entered dealers in tea in England and Wales" for the excise year 1764–5 was 32,234, but no account of the number in Scotland was available at the London office.[4] Given the flourishing state of the illicit trade, over 32,000 *legally*-entered dealers in England and Wales constitute no small number, approximately 210 persons per dealer.[5] Some twenty years later, the number of licensed dealers just prior to the Commutation Act of 1784, when smuggling again flourished, was very little more – 32,754 or roughly a ratio of 234 persons per dealer.

The tremendous increase in the number of licensed dealers with the decline in smuggling after 1784 gives some indication of the possible underenumeration of the persons from whom tea could have been purchased previously. By 1793 the number of licences issued for England and Wales was 52,292, an increase of 60 percent. Such a sudden entry of new dealers into the trade suggests that some at least had merely shifted from illicit to licit sales. The situation in Scotland is even more revealing. Prior to the Commutation Act, very little legal tea was available in Scotland.[6] It is therefore not surprising that in 1782 only 893 licences were issued; a decade later, 3,874 – an increase of 334 percent. It seems incredible that some 3,000 shopkeepers decided quite suddenly to add tea to the line of goods available to their customers or that there had been a precipitate increase in the number of grocery shops. Surely, it can be presumed that in 1765 many tea dealers were also not recorded by Excise. At the very least, the 32,234 entered dealers represent the minimum number of shopkeepers selling tea.

Does this mean that there were over 32,000 true-blue grocers in 1765, representing some 23 percent of the total number of shop-keepers recorded in 1759? That the percentage of those identified as grocers in the bankruptcy records for England and Wales – 7.6 percent for the years 1768–70 – is wholly unrepresentative? The answer to both questions is no. In mideighteenth century, England and Wales had no more than 800 market towns, some of which hardly qualify as sizeable villages.[7] There were also a number of relatively populous towns without market rights. Such towns, to-gether with those provided with markets, were the natural habitat of grocers. Outside such places, only the small general store could survive. However many grocers, large towns such as Bristol, Nor-wich, Liverpool, Leeds, and York, to name a few, could support, in the smaller market towns, no more than one true-born grocer could survive, and in some, not even one. However the figures are juggled, one cannot escape the conclusion that tea was not confined to the grocery shop or even to large general shops such as Abraham Dent's.

Excise figures for 1784 present an even more revealing picture of the geographical distribution of licensed tea dealers. Pitt's decision to reduce the duty on tea to a nominal rate of 12.5 percent *ad valorem* met with the full approval of the fair-trade dealers, but there were a number of problems. One was the date when the new duties should commence. Pitt, warned of the large quantities of tea expected on the continent for the 1784 season, was eager to reap the benefits of the new duties as early as possible. But the dealers, faced with the possibility of having on hand large quantities of tea for which they had paid heavy duties, wanted sufficient time to sell their high-priced tea first. To resolve the problem, Pitt sought advice and information from various sources among which were the excise officials.[8] They provided Pitt with data on the number of dealers and quantity of legal tea on hand for roughly one-third of the excise collections.[9] In addition, the officials submitted a complete account for the city of York, listing the name of each dealer and the quantity of green and black tea on hand.[10] Also submitted was a truncated account for London that lists the names of the principal dealers and the quantity of each kind of tea they had in stock, as well as a summary account of the number of tea dealers in the remaining districts within the Bills of Mortality and St Marylebone.[11] In all, this series of excise reports forms a valuable source of information on shopkeepers in urban areas and a glimpse at their dispersal in the countryside.

In response to Pitt's request, the officers of Excise made a detailed survey of a group of collections. The sample then served as a basis to calculate the total quantity of legal tea on hand. In choosing the collections for the sample, Excise displayed considerable acumen. For example, no collection north of the Trent was included in the survey. This was an area inundated with illicit tea. Large quantities were smuggled on the east coast via Yorkshire and all along the west coast facing Ireland. The north English counties were also supplied with illicit tea from Scotland. Such an area was not one that would reflect the general state of the legal trade in the rest of the country.[12] However, Excise did not ignore the effects of smuggling on the number of dealers and the quantity of legal tea on hand. The area covered by the sample was fairly representative. It included inland collections least disturbed by the illicit trade to coastal collections notorious for smuggling. It is therefore essential in assessing the figures for the principal towns to identify the type of collection in which the town is located. Those inundated with illicit tea will have far fewer legally entered tea dealers. An account on smuggling observed: "In some collections the greater part, and in most of them, many of the fair traders ... have been obliged to discontinue their business."[13] In 1778 Excise, reporting to Treasury on the increase in quantities of goods smuggled, noted that in the collection of Barnstaple, which comprised only a small part of Devonshire, "many public tea shops had closed, the number dwindling from 177 in 1773 to 70 at present and even these are going to close as they sell only two or three pounds in several months."[14] In 1796 the collection of Barnstaple had 850 licensed tea dealers!

Table 30 lists the collections in the order they appear in the excise account. Column six gives the percentage increase in the number of licensed tea dealers between 1784 and 1795–6 for each of the collections. A brief glance will show that the number of shopkeepers who had "discontinued their business" must have been unusually high for the five collections from Sarum down to Rochester. For these five collections, the average increase of licensed tea dealers is 207 percent; for all seventeen collections, 62 percent.[15] The five collections were in three counties – Kent, Sussex, and Hampshire – particularly notorious for the large quantities of tea illicitly landed on their coasts. The average increase for the top twelve collections is 36 percent. Of these, four – Suffolk, Gloucester, Bristol, and Bath – have a higher percentage increase. They were all in areas well known as haunts for smugglers.[16] No particular significance should, therefore, be attached to the figures for the principal towns in the bottom five collections, except as evidence of the sorry state of the fair trade. In Chichester the average quantity of tea on hand among the thirty-eight dealers was only seven pounds; the same was true for the forty-six dealers in Rochester and Chatham. The population for the sixteen parishes "in the City and suburbs of Canterbury" was estimated in 1770 as approximately 9,000.[17] The twenty-two licensed tea dealers should have had brisk business. In fact, they had in stock on the average only nineteen pounds of tea each and even that may have been lying heavy on their hands.[18] Given the sixfold increase in the number of licensed dealers in the collection after the Commutation Act, those twenty-two, probably true-born grocers, must have been very quickly swamped by a host of now-legal sellers of tea. The figures certainly tell us little about the extent or number of small shopkeepers in Canterbury able and willing to sell legal tea when it became as profitable a commodity as smuggled tea had been.

The figures for the towns from Colchester to Reading provide far more reliable evidence on the number of tea dealers. True, those for Ipswich, Gloucester, Bristol, and Bath are probably registering the effects of smuggling, but far less than the figures for the bottom five towns. What is particularly striking is the large number of shopkeepers – even at the height of smuggling – who had paid an annual

Table 30
Number of Tea Dealers: Seventeen Collections and Their Principal Towns, 1784

Principal Towns in Each Collection	Number of Tea Dealers 1784	Collection	Number of Tea Dealers		% Increase
			1784	1795-6	
Colchester	179	Essex	830	930	12.0
Ipswich	100	Suffolk	693	1,194	72.3
Norwich	142	Norwich	704	938	33.2
Cambridge	174	Cambridge	754	1,036	37.4
Oxford	94	Oxford	776	964	24.2
Leicester Coventry	230	Coventry	735	867	18.0
Birmingham	342	Lichfield	675	861	27.6
Worcester	120	Worcester	621	817	31.6
Gloucester	70	Gloucester	685	1,084	58.2
Bristol	472	Bristol	472	740	56.8
Bath	200	Bath	644	980	52.2
Reading	140	Reading	761	944	24,0
Salisbury Southampton	100	Sarum	277	941	239.7
Winton Portsmouth	140	Hants	441	883	100.2
Chichester	38	Sussex	190	957	403.7
Canterbury	22	Canterbury	104	749	620.2
Rochester Chatham	46	Rochester	486	1,066	119.3
Total	2,609		9,848	15,951	62.0

Sources: 1784 Report submitted by Excise 2 August 1784, "An Account of the Quantity of Tea in the Hands of Several Dealers in that Article at the Undermentioned Towns on the Excise Officers' Last Survey," 30/8/293, fol. 74, PRO; 1795-6: PRO, 30/8/288, fol. 56.

licence fee of 5s. 6d. to legalize their sales of tea. The figures are indisputable evidence of the existence of the small back-street shop in large towns and cities in mideighteenth century. The number of licensed dealers in England and Wales in 1783 was merely 520 more than the *entered* dealers recorded by Excise for 1764–5. Surely it can be assumed that their geographical distribution was not drastically different. Indeed, with the increase in population, some 15 percent by 1784, the ratio of population to "public tea shops" in the principal towns was probably lower in 1765.

The 1801 census provides relatively accurate population figures. It is, therefore, possible to estimate the approximate ratio of persons to licensed tea dealers in the principal towns. The census and excise boundaries for towns may not always have coincided. However, the very detailed account for the city of York, and the various comments of the excise officials seem to indicate that Excise followed fairly closely what was considered the limits of the towns surveyed. Moreover, the excise organization was somewhat different in large towns than in small communities and rural areas. Large towns were divided into divisions – York, for example, had eight divisions – not rides.[19] As officers covering divisions did not keep horses, one can presume that the geographical area was at least confined to what was easily surveyed on foot. The organization by divisions and rides also explains why Excise chose to provide Pitt with very specific information on the principal towns in the collections. It would have been relatively easy for them to do so. Such considerations do not preclude the possibility that the suburbs of some towns have been included in the enumeration. Were the surrounding hamlets of Colchester, the liberties, considered part of the town? But then town limits are a besetting problem for anyone attempting to determine population density over time. Between 1784 and 1801, the population of England and Wales increased on the average some 15 to 20 percent. In the light of this increase, even if some excise officers surveyed beyond the town boundaries, a doubtful supposition, a ratio based on population figures for 1801 can hardly be far off the mark.

The average ratio of persons to tea dealers for all the towns listed is 151; from Colchester to Reading, 136; from Salisbury to Chatham, 245. The latter towns were in collections that had the highest percentage increase of licensed tea dealers between 1784 and 1795–6. Their high ratio in 1784 is therefore hardly surprising. What is surprising is that the ratio for the towns from Colchester to Reading is well below the national average – 226 for an estimated population of 7.7 million. Was their ratio lower because it was more difficult to sell illicit tea from unentered places in these large towns, or because the urban setting was particularly congenial to the small chandler's shops? Probably both. There is, however, a considerable spread in the ratios for the towns in each division. For the thirteen towns in the upper division, ratios range from a low of 58 in Cambridge to 259 in Norwich. The ratio for Cambridge is almost unbelievably low. And yet is it so unbelievable? In the 1759 excise survey, the ratio of persons to shops for the Cambridge collection was equally low. Did the Sturbridge Fair leave as its legacy to Cambridge a disproportionate number of shopkeepers? Had the decline of the fair converted into settled shopkeepers those who no longer "keep the fair" but sold at their shops "on the same terms as at Stirbitch Fair *all the year round*"?[20] As the Sturbridge Fair, even after it had lost many of its former functions, still attracted large numbers of people, drawing into the town potential customers for the shopkeepers, it is perhaps not so surprising to find a particularly low ratio in Cambridge. And the trade of undergraduates was undoubtedly not insignificant to shopkeepers, even if the students were not always the most creditworthy customers. Oxford without a famous fair to boost its shop trades had a ratio of 124. Three other towns had ratios below 100 – Colchester, 64; Worcester, 95; and Reading, 70 – all manufacturing towns whose workers had reputedly a strong yen for that deleterious beverage, tea. If ratios were an adequate gauge of tea-drinking habits, one would have to conclude that the people in the eight towns in the lower division satisfied their thirst otherwise. Ratios range from 125 in the small town of Chichester to 409 in Canterbury. The ratio for Rochester and Chatham is 377, and for Winchester and Portsmouth, 271. But, as noted above, the figures reflect the extent of smuggling rather than the shopkeeping propensities of the population.

One striking feature in the figures for the upper thirteen towns, is the tendency for the ratio to be higher in very populous centres. The ratio for Norwich with a population of almost 37,000 is 259; that for Birmingham, the largest city in the list, (population over 73,000) is 215. Even Bath (population 32,200) conforms to the pattern – its ratio is 161. The figure for Bath may be registering the effects of smuggling. The increase of licensed tea dealers in the collection was higher than the average for the upper division. However, this does not apply to the other two cities.[21] Are we already witnessing the effects of a higher density of population and therefore a higher ratio of customers per shop? Not unlikely. For the years for which figures are available, the ratio of persons to licensed dealers in London was consistently higher than the average for the country.[22] In 1801 the ratio for the London Bills was approximately 212; for the rest of country (England and Wales), 156. In 1821 the number of licensed dealers in London was 6,004 or an approximate ratio of 200; for England and Wales, 171.[23] The rise in the average ratio for the country at large is also significant. By 1831 it had reached 185; and in 1841, well after the abolition of the East India Company's monopoly, the ratio for England and Wales was 193 despite the fact that the *per capita* consumption of tea had been increasing.[24] These were, of course, years when a much larger proportion of the population was living in densely packed cities. By 1841 over one-third of the population of England and Wales was concentrated in towns with more than 20,000 inhabitants.[25]

In short, two conflicting forces were at work affecting the number of persons per shops. The ratio will at first tend to decline as a greater number of people live in nucleated settlements. But with increasing density of population in the larger towns, the ratio will rise and so, one suspects, will the amount of business conducted by such shops.

Tea dealers were not, however, concentrated in large towns. If Bristol, which is co-extensive with the collection, is omitted, the proportion of tea dealers in the principal towns of the other twelve collections is 22.8 percent. And what was true for the sample was apparently true for the rest of the country. In comparing the overall ratio of tea dealers in the principal and "other large towns" to those in country districts, Excise thought it "reasonable to take it as 3:14."[26] In the excise year 1783–4, the London Bills of Mortality had a little over 3,000 licensed tea dealers; the rest of England and Wales almost 31,000.[27] If Excise was correct in its judgment, of the 31,000 licensed tea dealers in the provinces, over 24,000 were carrying on business in small towns and villages. The labouring poor would not need to travel far to get their ounce or two of legal tea and the sugar that all but the most deprived considered a necessary accompaniment.

The excise accounts also reveal how inadequate eighteenth-century commercial directories and even Pigot's more famous series for the nineteenth century are as a means of determining the total number of shops in individual towns. It is our contention that Pigot, no less than Bailey, confined his listing of shop trades in 1822–3 primarily to major shopkeepers. As a result, many small shops retailing a restricted line of groceries have not been included. How large a group has been excluded can be roughly gauged by comparing the number of licensed tea dealers in the principal towns with the number of grocers and other likely sellers of tea listed in the directories. The shop trades of four of the towns for which we have excise figures – London, Bristol, Norwich, and York – have been analysed in tables 7 and 22.

Compared to the principal towns in the upper division, Norwich had a particularly high ratio of person to tea dealers. In 1784, the town had 142 licensed tea dealers. But what do the directories show? Bailey (1784) listed 53 grocers and tea dealers, 4 confectioners and fruiterers, and 1 provision dealer or a total of fifty-eight shops retailing food. The picture depicted by Pigot some forty years later is not drastically different, even though the population of Norwich had increased by 38.9 percent since 1801.[28] Pigot listed 56 grocers and tea dealers, 1 cheesemonger, 29 confectioners and fruiterers, 4 of whom were identified as fruiterers only and therefore not likely sellers of tea. In addition there were 5 "corn chandlers" who may in fact have been dealers and not shopkeepers at all. But even if they are included along with the 4 fruiterers, only ninety-one shops can be classed as retailers of groceries.[29] If Pigot's figures are accepted, the number of tea dealers had declined during the intervening forty years. Actually, there had been an enormous increase. By 1822–3 the number of licensed tea dealers in England and Wales was 72,502, an increase of 113 percent since 1784. It is simply inconceivable that Norwich had departed so radically from the national trend, however depressed the city may have been.

The situation in York is similar. In 1784, York had seventy-three licensed tea dealers. Bailey identified only nine grocers and tea dealers, four confectioners, and four cheesemongers; the 1797 survey, twenty-six grocers and tea dealers, three petty grocers, five cheesemongers, seven confectioners and fruiterers, and seven specialty bakers. But, this survey covered only shops paying an assessment of two pounds or more. Twenty-five years later Pigot listed seventy-three grocers and tea dealers, fifteen cheesemongers, and twenty-two confectioners and fruiterers, or an increase of 50 percent over the number of tea dealers in 1784. And, prior to the Commutation Act, Yorkshire, like some of the southern counties, received large quantities of smuggled tea. One would expect, therefore, an increase greater than the national average.

As the excise figures for Bristol included dealers in the surrounding hamlets, the comparison is less certain. But can those hamlets possibly account for the differences in the figures? In 1784, Excise reported 472 licensed dealers. Bailey identified 37 grocers, 5 retailers of sundries, 5 cheesemongers, and 5 confectioners and fruiterers. Pigot listed 132 grocers and tea dealers, 76 "grocers and sundry retail dealers in flour, bacon, etc.," 19 cheesemongers, and 32 confectioners and fruiterers or a total of 261. If those 261 shops were the only ones retailing tea, Bristol had a ratio of over 326 compared to the national average of 173.[30]

A comparison of the figures for that monstrous city London is far simpler. Excise accounts give the number of licensed tea dealers in the Bills of Mortality for both 1784 and 1822–3. The total number of grocers and tea dealers, retail and wholesale, general retailers of flour and sundries, cheesemongers, Italian oil dealers, and confectioners listed by Bailey was 500; by Pigot for 1822–3, 2,277. The number of licensed tea dealers in the London Bills of Mortality and

St Marylebone was 3,079 in 1784; 6,251 in 1822–3, almost three times the number of shops recorded by Pigot.

One can agree that an enumeration of all tradesmen in London is an Herculean task, well beyond the compass of even a James Pigot. Indeed, were the directories intended to be inclusive? They were designed primarily for the use of tradesmen. One suspects that the business of petty-parlour shopkeepers who purchased their wares at the market or from larger shops nearby was too trifling for those seeking new accounts. And petty shopkeepers would hardly form a body of customers for Pigot's 1822–3 directories. For whatever reason, Pigot's 1822–3 surveys have largely ignored the small shopkeeper.

In 1834, Pigot broadened his coverage of the shopkeeping trades by adding a new category – mere "shopkeepers." Their inclusion was a distinct departure from his former practice – not merely a reclassification. Had no such category been introduced, very few of those listed as "shopkeepers" would have found a place among the more specialized trades. Why the change of policy remains a question to ponder. Could it be that the amount of business handled by such shops was increasing and they were therefore becoming more important trade customers? Certainly mere "shopkeepers" did not suddenly appear on the commercial horizon in 1834. That such shops existed in 1822 (as they undoubtedly did in 1784 and earlier years) but were omitted from the directories is demonstrated in table 31. It compares the average ratio of population to tea licences in England and Wales with what appears to be their ratios in a selected sample of towns.[31] In calculating the ratios it has been assumed that in addition to the wholesale and retail grocers and tea dealers listed by Pigot, all those classed as "shopkeepers" had obtained a licence. No "shopkeepers" are listed for Liverpool in 1846, but in addition to the 53 "provision merchants," there is an entry for "provision dealers," who number 510. These were presumably the missing "shopkeepers." A few other towns have entries for provision dealers, rarely very numerous, and they too have been included.

As table 31 shows, for every town on the list, the ratios of population to grocers and tea dealers in 1822 bears no comparison to the ratio of population to tea licences. It is obvious that the grocers and tea dealers listed by Pigot comprised a small percentage of the shops licensed to sell tea. In the London Bills, the ratio for tea licences in 1822 was approximately 200; [32] for Pigot's grocers and tea dealers, 1,400. For the excise year 1822–3 the average ratio of population to tea licences for the rest of England and Wales was 166. But what

Table 31
Ratios of Urban Inhabitants to Grocers, Tea Dealers, and Shopkeepers in London
and Selected Towns Compared with the Average Ratio of Population to Tea
Licences in England and Wales

Place & Date	Number				Ratio		
	Grocers & Tea Dealers	Shopkeepers	Provision Dealers	For All Shops	Grocers & Tea Dealers	For All Shops	Tea Licences in England & Wales
London							
1822	1,093			1,093	1,400	1,400	173
1834	2,050	2,192		4,242	900	435	185
Bolton							
1822	23			23	1,435	1,435	173
1834	33	145		178	1,364	253	185
Leeds							
1822	92		10	102	957	863	173
1834	96	313	41	450	1,375	293	185
1841	104	362	43	509	1,462	299	194
1848	104	620	38	762	1,596	218	180
Leicester							
1822	60			60	458		173
1835	85	176		261	541	176	184
1841	72	81		153	736	346	194
Liverpool[1]							
1822	163		35	198	883	735	173
1834	233	571	80	884	978	258	185
1846	273		510	783	1,213	423	184
Manchester							
1822	115		11	126	1,148	1,048	173
1834	154	723	49	926	1,286	214	185
1841	211	1,037		1,248	1,114	188	194
Norwich							
1822	55			55	927		173
1839	81	133		214	759	462	187
Nottingham							
1822	91			91	450		173
1835	94	343	7	444	537	114	184
1841	108	292	5	405	482	129	194

Table 31 (continued)

Place & Date	Number				Ratio		
	Grocers & Tea Dealers	Shopkeepers	Provision Dealers	For All Shops	Grocers & Tea Dealers	For All Shops	Tea Licences in England & Wales
York							
1822	72			72	311		173
1834	68	88		156	397	173	185
1841	67	123		190	433	153	194

Source: Calculated from the compilations in Alexander, *Retailing*, 239-55 appendix 1; see also note 31 below.

Notes: Tea may have been sold by other shop traders, particularly cheesemongers and confectioners. However, with the exception of London, there were very few in most towns and some had none. In 1822-3 Liverpool had: ten cheesemongers and forty-seven confectioners; Manchester: eleven cheesemongers, twenty-seven confectioners; Leeds: twenty-five confectioners; Norwich: nine confectioners; Leicester: nine cheesemongers, seven confectioners; Nottingham: five cheesemongers, twelve confectioners. The figures for other years are similar. The inclusion of cheesemongers and confectioners would not have changed the ratios appreciably, certainly not for 1822. Less obvious sellers may also have stocked tea. A few milliners and some of the smaller drapery and apothecary shops sold tea. No attempt has been made to assess their number. As they have been omitted for all the years surveyed, for the purpose at hand the margin of error may be considered constant. In fact, between 1822 and 1834 the percentage increase of clothing shops was considerably greater than the increase for grocers and tea dealers. In Liverpool, for example, the number of grocers and tea dealers increased by 42.9 percent; the clothing group, 106 percent; in Manchester, 33.9 percent versus an increase of 182 percent for drapers, milliners, haberdashers, and other small ware dealers. If tea were being sold by a large proportion of such shops, the effect of their omission from the calculated ratios should be greater in 1834 and subsequent years than in 1822. As the table shows, that was very far from the case.

[1]No "shopkeepers" are listed for Liverpool in 1846, but in addition to 53 "provision merchants," 510 "provision dealers" are listed. Presumably these are the missing "shopkeepers."

do we find in Pigot's directories? The ratio in Manchester is 1,148; in Liverpool, 883; Bolton, 1,435, and so on. In only three towns, Leicester, Nottingham, and York, it is less than 500, still a long way from the national average. And it will be remembered that in 1784 most of the towns surveyed by Excise had ratios well below the national average. Figures of this magnitude are inexplicable unless many shops selling tea were omitted from the directories. This is strikingly illustrated by the precipitate drop in the ratios when Pigot included "shopkeepers" in his 1834–5 directories. For example, the ratio for London in 1822 was 1,400; with the addition of "shopkeepers" in 1834, 435. Although a number of small shops probably continued to elude Pigot's enumerators, the ratio for grocers, tea dealers, *and* "shopkeepers" is far closer to that of tea licences. Indeed for Leicester, Nottingham, and York, it is below the average for the

country (see table 31). But the decline in the ratio is due almost
entirely to the inclusion of "shopkeepers." The ratios for grocers
and tea dealers have changed only slightly. In fact, in a number of
instances the ratio in 1834 is higher than 1822. For example, in
1822, the ratio of population to grocers and tea dealers in Leeds was
957; in 1834, 1,375, but the ratio "for all shops" had declined from
863 in 1822 to 293 in 1834.

One is forced to conclude that until 1834 Pigot's directories are a
totally inadequate guide to the number of shops where tea was available, and with tea went other small articles in daily use. The directories are, therefore, equally unreliable as a means of determining
changes in the number of shops retailing groceries between 1822
and 1834, or even for later years. Only in 1851 does the ratio for
most towns approximate the national average. The number of small
"shopkeepers" may well have increased in the period from 1822 to
1834–5, but the extent of that increase cannot be ascertained from
Pigot's directories.[33]

In 1834 mere "shopkeepers" outnumbered grocers and tea dealers
by a considerable margin. Of the total number of grocers, tea dealers,
and "shopkeepers" in each of the provincial towns, the proportion
for "shopkeepers" ranged from a low of 56.4 percent in York to 81.2
percent in Bolton. For the years 1834–5, the average proportion of
"shopkeepers" for the provincial towns was 76.9 percent. These are
the shops that have eluded not only Pigot's enumerators but also the
historians of the retail trade – the back-street shops from which
urban workers had been purchasing their daily necessaries since the
eighteenth century.

CHAPTER NINE

Tea Dealers of London and York: Their Number and Shop Trades

LONDON TEA DEALERS

There is much firmer evidence of the existence of petty tea dealers for the cities of London and York. From two detailed excise reports submitted to Pitt, it is possible to draw a relatively complete picture of the types of shops retailing tea in 1784, one, moreover, that confirms the conclusions drawn in the last chapter on the proportion of small back-street shops in large towns.

Excise prepared two accounts for the London Bills. The first was a detailed account of the "stock of tea in the possession of the large dealers."[1] Each dealer was listed by Christian and surname along with the quantity of black and green tea on hand in his shop. There were 432 large dealers and they had in stock on the day of survey a total of 263,199 pounds of tea or an average of 609 pounds each. The quantities entered refer only to the tea currently in the shops and warehouses of the dealers, not to the far larger quantities lodged in their names in the East India Company's warehouses. It was customary for the principal London tea dealers to clear their tea from the company's warehouses only as needed and in 1784 they were particularly slow clearing their stock in anticipation of the Commutation Act. The company had agreed to receive back at cost price all the tea not delivered out of its warehouses before the first sale in September. The tea amounted to 2.6 million pounds most of which was in the names of London dealers. Clearly there were very substantial tradesmen among the licensed tea dealers.

By means of the London directories for 1783 and 1784 it has been possible to identify the shop or other trades of 359 of those listed and to depict their geographical distribution, a task made easier by the excise format. The names of the dealers in each small area surveyed have been alphabetized, making it possible to trace the steps of the officers. For example, the first 20 names, from William Arnold, a small grocer with fifty-one pounds of black and thirty-four pounds of green tea on hand, located on Old Gravel Lane, Radcliffe, to John and Samuel Waddington, well-known grocers on St Katherine's, cover the area around Radcliffe Highway, Shadwell, Wapping, East Smithfield down to Little Tower Hill and form the eastern limits of the survey. The officers then moved west to Fenchurch, Leadenhall, and Bishopsgate Within – so it went for the whole survey. The western limit was Grosvenor Square, the north-eastern, Clerkenwell, Spitalfield, and White Chapel. Across the river most shops identified were on Borough High or Tooley Street with a few scattered on neighbouring streets.

Certain areas stand out as above or below the average in the number of principal tea dealers and the quantity of tea on hand. The most densely populated area was within the City – bounded on the north by the Wall, on the west by St Martin's-le-Grand, on the south by Cannon Street, and on the east by the triangle formed by Houndsditch and Fenchurch. In addition to serving as the business and financial hub of the country, this area contained the source of all legal tea – the East India Company on Leadenhall. Shops and warehouses of 85 principal dealers were located here. They had on hand a total of 114,625.5 pounds of tea or an average of 1,348.5 pounds each. East of the City there were only 35 principal dealers holding an average of 305 pounds of tea; and across the river in the Borough there were 30, with an average of 377 pounds. Almost three-quarters (267) of those identified were concentrated in an area some two and one-half miles long, from Regent Street to Leadenhall and Fenchurch, and less than a mile wide, running roughly from Holborn to the river.

Not all shops were located on fashionable streets. Besides those on Radcliffe Highway and Wapping Wall, at least one shop, the proprietor of which identified himself as a "tea dealer," was situated on foulsome Butcher Row. He had 119 pounds of tea in stock. Several shops were in the vicinity of Clare Market and five, on White Cross Street. There was even one on Rosemary Lane (Rag Fair). Quite a few were in the Clerkenwell and Spitalfield area, but Bethnal Green had apparently no large dealer.

The geographical distribution of the 73 dealers not listed in the directories was similar to those identified, although there was some clustering.[2] A slightly greater proportion were in areas such as Tottenham Court Road or Bishopsgate Without or near the river. Judging by the quantity of tea in stock, most were not sufficiently important or "credit-worthy" to be listed in the directories. The total quantity of tea they had in stock was 6,489 pounds or an average of 89 pounds each, the average for the remaining 359 dealers was 715 pounds.

The quantity in a dealer's shop on the day of survey may not correspond exactly to the extent of his trade, but seems a sufficiently adequate guide to distinguish principal dealers from the less important sellers of tea. In table 32 the dealers are classified according to the quantity of tea on hand. Quite obviously those with less than 100 pounds of tea in stock lived in a different business community than the dealers in the two upper classes with over 500 pounds. Among the latter were some of the wealthiest and most influential dealers in the country. These were the people who dominated the domestic trade in tea, whose bidding at the East India Company's auctions determined the market price, and who formed the numerous committees that sprang into action to negotiate with the government or the East India Company on matters important to the trade. Many were firms with two or three partners. Of the fifty-six dealers in the upper class, at least forty were old established firms. In the 1770s when smuggling was at its height, these London dealers formed themselves into a committee to combat the illicit trade. In 1776 they petitioned Treasury to reduce the duty and to enforce stricter regulations against smuggling. The petition was signed by seventy-seven London dealers, forty-two of whom gave their firm names.[3] Almost all appear in the excise list with over 500 pounds of tea. These are the capital tradesmen who held large quantities of tea in the East India Company's warehouses and who were pressing Pitt to make some provision for that tea before reducing the duties, a request that led to the survey.[4]

No classification can nicely distinguish the minute variations in the wealth of the tradesmen listed by Excise. But in terms of importance in the tea trade and status within the business world, most of the dealers with 100 to 500 pounds of tea fall within the middling group of moderately well-to-do tradesmen, merging at the lower end with the bottom class. Many probably purchased their tea not at the East India Company's auctions, but from one of the larger dealers and in trade matters followed the lead of their suppliers, as they did in 1784–5. At that time there was a controversy between the East India Company and the Committee for the Tea Trade, chaired by Richard Twining. A number of dealers in the middling group jumped into the breach as supporters of the committee and there ensued a veritable battle of advertisements. Thus, Samuel Yockney, grocer and tea dealer on Bedford Street, with 330 pounds

Table 32
Principal Tea Dealers in London and Quantity of Tea in Stock, July 1784

Stock on Hand (lbs.)	Total Number of Dealers	Number of Dealers not Identified
Under 100	98	54
100-500	190	19
501-1,000	88	—
Over 1,000	56	—
Total	432	73

Source: PRO, 30/8/293, fols. 59-66.

of tea on hand vowed to sell his high quality tea cheaper than any newly established warehouse supported by a friend of the East India Company. Mundy and Walker, tea dealers on Old Broad Street, followed suit. Thomas Newland, tea dealer and grocer on Cheapside, proclaimed his "New Tea Warehouse." Theomartyr Crane, grocer on Great Trinity Lane, had only 211 pounds of tea on hand but vowed it was pure and unadulterated. Thomas Delafield, grocer on Bishopsgate Within, sarcastically commented on the proprietors of "tea warehouses" for whom a "shop" was not good enough.[5] And others followed, some perhaps taking advantage of the situation to advertise their shops and increase their trade.

Unfortunately, such advertisements, along with the bankruptcy records, the directories, and the meagre information garnered from excise surveys are almost the sole sources for information on these middling tradesmen. Few have left records of their business activities. In terms of rent and income they probably fall within the assessment Class 4 (£5–£10) and were probably not first buyers at the East India Company's auctions. Any grocer worth the name would have to carry a wide selection of teas as well as different qualities. The 1784–5 advertisers listed the price for as many as twenty-five sorts. To buy such a stock at the company auctions would require the purchase of dozens of chests of different qualities and types of tea, and a capital outlay which few in this class could command.

The shop trades of 359 "large dealers" can be more readily identified. Whatever variations existed in turnover and style of shop, most were grocers. Table 33 gives the number of dealers for each shop trade. A few mistaken identities may have crept into the list. Was the John Rea who had 262 pounds of tea on hand the John Rea, "gunmaker," at ninety-one Minories? The address fits the group alphabetized by the surveyor. Perhaps John Rea was both gunmaker

Table 33
Shop Trades of the Principal London Tea Dealers, 1784

Trades		Number in Each Trade
I Food and Drinks		
Grocers and Tea Dealers		257
Tea Dealers		59
Confectioners		2
Cheesemongers		3
Italian Oil Dealers		2
Fruiterers		2
Wine and Brandy Dealers		5
	Subtotal	330
II Other Shop Trades		
Chemists		8
China and Teamen		5
Upholsterer		1
Mercer		1
Army Clothier		1
Slopseller		1
	Subtotal	17
III Other Trades		
Merchants		9
Corn Factors		2
Gunmakers		1
	Subtotal	12
IV Not Identified		73
	Total	432

Sources: *Bailey's Western Directory, 1783*; *Bailey's Eastern Directory, 1784*; *Kent's Directory, 1784(?)*; *Lowndes London Directory, 1784.*

Note: All available London directories for 1783 and 1784 have been used to identify the dealers. As a consequence, the total number of grocers is greater than the number entered in *Bailey's Western Directory* (1783). Some appeared in Kent's directory, which was particularly good for shopkeepers in Southwark; others were listed in *Bailey's Eastern Directory* for 1784 and even Lowndes yielded a few names.

and shopkeeper. The army clothier looks even more suspicious. In this instance, Excise gave the firm name, John Hetherington and Company, exactly as it was entered in the directory. The address, however, does not fit the group. Were the army clothiers on Buckingham Street, the Strand, also proprietors of a shop in the Eastcheap-Lower Thames area that was not listed in the directories? Perhaps. But there are only a few whose trade is doubtful.

Very few, if any, "grocers" or "grocers and tea dealers" listed in the directories failed to appear in the excise survey. The analysis in table 33 shows that in London very few major shopkeepers in trades other than groceries were in the tea business, not even shopkeepers retailing other types of food. Of the 197 cheesemongers listed by Bailey in 1783, only three appear in the excise survey; only 2 of the 23 confectioners and 2 of the 34 Italian oil dealers. Of the 110 chemists listed by Bailey, only 8 had added tea to their other drugs. And yet, in the early eighteenth century, tea was often sold in apothecary shops, in part because it was originally thought of as a drug and was available, like many other drugs, at the East India Company sales. When tea became a popular beverage, it moved into the grocers' province. By the latter part of the century, very few apothecary shops even in the provincial towns continued to handle tea.

The selling of tea by dealers in china and glass was also a common practice in the early eighteenth century, probably because much of the china sold in their shops came, like tea, in the East India ships from China and both were purchased in the first instance at the company's auctions. Thus, the major dealers, in addition to stocking the fine china teapots and dishes, were able to provide their customers with a selection of teas. With the rise in demand for British-produced wares, dealers no longer needed to repair to the East India Company for their supply of chinaware. It thus became less convenient for them to purchase tea. In any case, tea was a costly item and involved dealers in onerous excise regulations. In 1784 only five of the eighty-three dealers in chinaware had retained the linkage and none carried a large stock of tea. Of the five, three were listed in the directories as "Chinamen"; a fourth, with eighty-nine pounds on hand, listed himself as a "China, Glass and Teaman."[6]

A few wine and brandy merchants dealt in tea. As for the other merchants, with the exception of Etcher whose stock comprised prize tea, their names have not surfaced in the records of the East India Company, although one might expect buyers of the company's textiles to have taken an occasional venture in tea. On the other hand, if they were acting as merchants, there would have been no need to remove the tea from the company's warehouses and incur all the bothersome excise regulations. It could have been shipped directly from the company's warehouses, a very common practice among the larger tea dealers. But, as noted earlier, the title merchant often masked other activities.

With respect to the upholsterer and mercer, both may be cases of mistaken identity.[7] As for the two corn factors, were they perhaps just provision dealers who had inflated their importance in the directories? The slopseller, on the other hand, was not an unlikely seller of tea. He had in stock 105 pounds and may well have been dabbling in tea and old clothes, both items popular with his customers.

In selecting the 432 "large dealers," Excise appears to have included a considerable number who barely qualify. Of the 98 with less than 100 pounds, the names of 54 could not be traced. The average quantity they had on hand was 39.6 pounds compared to the 52.9 pounds for the remaining 44. But even these, the smallest of the *large dealers*, rank well above those not listed in the first excise account. Probably the excise selection was based not solely on the quantity in stock in July 1784 but also on the amount of legal tea sold during the year.

The second excise report to Pitt is an account of the quantity of tea held by the remaining dealers in the London Bills. This account lists by district the total number of small tea dealers and the quantity of black and green tea they had in stock.[8] There is no way of determining the particular areas included in each district, but, as table 34 shows, there is little to distinguish one from another. The total quantity of tea held by the 2,647 dealers was 30,164.25 pounds or an average of 11.4 pounds each, 6.2 pounds of green and 5.2 pounds of black. Not even the 842 licensed dealers in District 3, with an average quantity on hand of 15.4 pounds, approached the quantity held by the 98 listed in the account of large dealers. Had Excise supplied the names of the dealers, it is very doubtful their shop trades could have been identified. However the 30,000 pounds of tea were distributed, few dealers in this group would seem to qualify as full-fledged grocers. We can only presume that here are the petty chandlers whose names never appear in the directories and whose activities have not been fully appreciated. These are the shopkeepers whose customers purchased their tea by the ounce. One small bit of information concerning the taste of their customers can be deduced. The customers of the large dealers appear to have preferred black tea which represented 63 percent of the total quantity on hand, compared with the 45 percent of the petty dealers. In every district green tea predominated. Presumably it was preferred.

The total number of dealers in the Bills of Mortality was 3,079. They had in their shops 293,283.5 pounds of tea of which only 10.3 percent was in the hands of the small dealers on the day of survey (see table 34). This does not mean that the trade of small dealers during the year represented only 10 percent of the total quantity of tea sold to retail customers. Given the fact that such petty chandlers had little cash and even less credit in the business community, their stock had to be purchased in small quantities, at frequent intervals, from the large dealers. During the course of the year, a petty chan-

Table 34
Small Tea Dealers: Quantity of Tea on Hand, London, 1784

		Quantity of Tea						Average
District	Number of Dealers	Green		Black		Total		Quantity per Dealer (lbs.)
		lbs.	oz.	lbs.	oz.	lbs.	oz.	
1	272	1,448	5	1,399	2	2,847	7	10.5
2	382	2,175	7	1,508	12	3,684	3	9.6
3	842	7,066	3	5,908	13	12.975	—	15.4
4	706	3,458	8	2,952	12	6,411	4	9.1
5	445	2,323	1	1,923	5	4,246	6	9.5
Total	2,647	16,471	8	13,692	12	30,164	4	11.4

Source: PRO, 30/8/293, fol. 69.

dler may have sold over 100 pounds of tea. In view of the large number of such dealers, their trade was not insignificant. In 1784 they formed 86 percent of all the dealers in the London Bills, a figure remarkably similar to that of 1822. In that year, there were 6,251 licensed tea dealers in the London Bills. The number of grocers and tea dealers sufficiently important to be listed by Pigot was only 1,093 or 17.7 percent of the total number licensed to sell tea.

Judging from the figures for tea dealers, the widespread consumption of tea had enabled a particularly high proportion of petty shopkeepers to enter the retail food trade. In 1797, principal shops accounted for 31 percent of all shops assessed in London, but only 14 percent of all tea dealers qualified as principal shopkeepers in 1784. London, with its large industrial wage-earning population, may have offered greater opportunity to such petty dealers, but it was not unique. In most industrial centres, the number of petty chandlers was large. As table 31 shows, in 1834–5 grocers and tea dealers represented a small proportion of all food shops in the industrial cities. For such centres as Bolton, Leeds, Liverpool, Manchester, and Nottingham, the proportion of grocers and tea dealers ranged from a low of 16.6 percent in Manchester to a high of 26.4 percent in Liverpool. Only in York was the proportion of grocers and tea dealers particularly high, 43.6 percent – not very different, as we shall see, from the figures for licensed tea dealers in 1784. Clearly, the sale of tea (and sugar) served as a significant engine of change in the shopkeeping sector of the economy well before the industrial revolution "took off."

TEA DEALERS OF YORK

The survey of York lists the names and the stock on hand of all licensed tea dealers "Within the City of York on the last week of July 1784."[9] There were seventy-three dealers with a stock of 16,206.5 pounds of tea or an average of 222 pounds per dealer, a far larger quantity than the other principal towns listed by Excise. In these towns, the average quantity per dealer ranged from 7 pounds in Chichester to 80 pounds in Norwich. Even in London, the average per dealer was only 95 pounds. Indeed, York dealers appear to have generally kept a large stock on hand. In December 1783 the dealers had in stock 14,937.5 pounds.[10] Moreover, the ratio of population to dealer – 223 – is also higher than most of the principal towns surveyed by Excise.[11] York was in an area where the illicit trade flourished. Well-armed smuggling boats landed large quantities of illicit tea on the Yorkshire coast. But the high ratio is in part due to the type of shops in York. It had far fewer petty shops than industrial towns. As can be calculated from table 35, the proportion of petty tea dealers was considerably less than in London.[12] Tea dealers with less than 25 pounds on hand formed only 46.6 percent of licensed tea dealers in York, compared to 86 percent in London. Even as late as 1834, mere "shopkeepers" formed only 56.4 percent of all food shops in York (see table 31). It is, therefore, hardly surprising that the quantity of tea per dealer is on the high side.

Table 35 lists the shop or other trades of those licensed tea dealers who could be identified. Of these, the family names (sometimes with the same Christian name) of at least fifteen appear in the 1797 assessment survey – almost all were principal tea dealers and grocers. However, many dealers remain mere names with no other identification than that supplied by the excise report. In the table, dealers are grouped according to the quantity of tea in stock. The major tea dealers are the four in Class I. Indeed, the quantity of tea they had in stock is comparable to principal London dealers. But unlike their counterparts in London, they probably had on hand all the tea purchased at the last East India Sale. The supervisor of the district thought it would "be at least three months before the principal tea dealers in York can dispose of their present stocks of tea."[13] Thus they had on hand sufficient tea until the next East India Sale. Of the four principal dealers, three were old established firms. Henry Raper, Esq., of Henry Raper and Company was the son of John Raper, Esq., alderman, and admitted to his freedom in 1749–50. In 1784 he was listed in the directory as "Henry Raper, Esq., tea dealer" on Ouzegate. The honorific title is an indication of the upward

Table 35
Shop Trades of Licensed Tea Dealers in York, 1784

Class	Average Quantity on Hand (lbs.)	Number of Tea Dealers	Shop and Other Trades
I	2,506	4	All "tea dealers"
II	652	3	1 – "tea dealer" 1 – grocer 1 – merchant (?)
III	195	15	2 – "tea dealers" 6 – grocers 3 – confectioners 3 – merchants (?) 1 – not identified
IV	76	9	1 – dealer in wines, spirits, and tea 4 – grocers 1 – grocer and apothecary 1 – confectioner (?) 1 – tallow-chandler 1 – not identified
V	34.7	8	7 – grocers 1 – not identified
VI	18.5	12	2 – grocers 1 – "shopkeeper" 1 – aledraper 1 – soap dealer 7 – not identified
VII	4.7	22	1 – "shopkeeper" 2 – aledrapers 1 – linen-draper (?) 1 – butter-factor 1 – hardwareman 1 – dealer and chapman 1 – bridler 1 – bricklayer 1 – carpenter 12 – not identified

Sources: Licensed tea dealers PRO, 30/8/293, fols. 67-8; Identification: Freemen's Roll, 1743-1811, D. 4, York City Archives; Report on Unfree Tradesmen, House Book, 44: 385-411. York Corporation Records; Commercial directories for York, 1781 & 1784; *York Courant*; *Leeds Mercury*.

Note:

Class I	1,000 pounds and over	V	25 to 49 pounds
II	500 to 999 pounds	VI	10 to 24 pounds
III	100 to 499 pounds	VII	under 10 pounds
IV	50 to 99 pounds		

mobility of the Raper family who were in the process of becoming bankers. By 1797 the Rapers had apparently discontinued the tea business. Thomas Smithson of Smithson and Company was apprenticed to Henry Raper and later opened shop on High Ouzegate. He was still in the tea business in 1797 with an estimated income of £300. The firm of William Tuke and Son was established by Maria Tewk in 1725. "William Tuke, grocer" was admitted freeman in 1753. In 1782 when his son "Henry Tuke, tea dealer," was admitted, William Tuke was entitled "merchant," although he was listed in the directories as tea dealer. By then the Tukes were an esteemed family and, like the Rapers, moving up the ladder. The only puzzling entry is Robert Wright with 3,410 pounds of tea in stock. The directory listed him as "teaman" on Nessgate, but his name was not among the freemen. Excise also listed a John Wright and Company with a stock of 167 pounds of tea. John Wright, "grocer, late apprentice to Seth Agar, grocer and confectioner" was admitted in 1768. If Robert Wright was related to John, a son perhaps, and claimed partnership with him, he would have been exempt from the obligation to become free.

Whether the four confined their shop trade to tea, coffee, and chocolate cannot be ascertained; but at least one, William Tuke and Son, claimed to have. The firm had, according to family tradition, specialized from the beginning in the tea business, wholesale and retail.[14] Presumably, none relied solely upon retail customers to dispose of their stock. Together with the three dealers in Class II they formed a source of supply for the grocers and shopkeepers in York and the surrounding villages and even further afield. The trading area of the Tukes included all the northern counties, and by the end of the century the firm had business connections in Edinburgh and had penetrated the Birmingham and Bristol markets.[15] Despite the absence of conclusive evidence, there is reason to believe the four principal dealers were purchasing most of their tea, not from London dealers, but through brokers at the East India Company auctions. The Tukes were certainly doing so later in the century. In 1784 the average price, duty included, of 2,500 pounds of tea at the East India Company's auctions, allowing 1 percent commission to the brokers, would have been approximately £800, an investment not beyond the reach of the Tukes and Rapers. Provincial wholesale dealers were in effect competing for the same customers as the London dealers who toured the country seeking good business accounts. By purchasing from their counterparts in London, the York dealers would have placed themselves in a competitively disadvantageous position. With a capital outlay of several thousand pounds sterling for a year's supply of tea, it is difficult to believe that firms as experienced in the tea business as the Tukes or the Rapers would not have sought the cheapest source. On the other hand, the scale of business of the three dealers in Class II would not have allowed them to purchase their tea at first hand. The East India Company normally put up its tea in lots consisting of several chests of one kind and quality of tea. And the company required buyers to pay one month after purchase. As each dealer kept a stock of both green and black tea, at the very least two lots would have to be purchased. And that does not take into consideration the need to have a variety of qualities and sorts of tea. The latter would have required the purchase of many lots of tea, an amount exceeding the needs of these buyers. Very likely they purchased their tea from the principal London dealers from whom they could receive credit. Had they been buying from dealers in York, there would have been no need to stock the large quantities they had on hand.

The dealers in Class II clearly demonstrate the ambiguity of the title merchant. Each is listed in the 1784 directory as "merchant." But Richard Sutcliffe, with 690 pounds in stock, admitted as freeman in 1758 and listed in the directory as a merchant on Spurriergate, advertised in the *Leeds Mercury* in 1781 his "wholesale and retail tea warehouse in Spurriergate, York."[16] Thomas Smith, "grocer, son of Thomas Smith, grocer" was admitted as a freeman in 1758 and trained several of the grocers in the list. His title in the directory seems no more accurate than Sutcliffe's. The third "merchant'," William Wallis, is more problematic. Apparently he had evaded the freemen regulations and was admitted "by order" in 1774 as a "merchant." If merchant he were, his mercantile enterprise, with only 361 pounds of black and 237 pounds of green tea on hand, was reduced to selling by the pound.

Among the fifteen licensed dealers in Class III, only one had over 400 pounds in stock; five had 200 to 400, and nine under 200 pounds. Most were old established grocers and tea dealers. The family names of twelve were listed in the 1797 survey of York as tea dealers or grocers with incomes ranging from £80 to £250.[17] James Maude, teaman on High Ouzegate, had 441 pounds on hand. He was admitted in 1782 as the son of John Maude, teaman. The latter, the son of William Maude, teaman, was admitted in 1777. The Agar family had been grocers and confectioners since midcentury and were still in the business in 1797.[18] William Agar, who had 287 pounds of tea in 1784, had an estimated income of £200 in 1797; Seth Agar, grocer, £250. Again in this group a few listed themselves in the directories as merchants, although they were clearly grocers or confectioners. John Grave, for example, appears in the 1784 directory as a merchant, but the city fathers considered him a grocer as the following entry shows. In 1780 "Robert Baxter, grocer, late apprentice to Seth Agar, grocer, and afterwards assigned to William Agar and then to John Grave, grocer" was admitted to his freedom. [19] Francis Clubley was also listed in the directory as a merchant but he was apprenticed to John Atkinson, confectioner, and admitted as such in 1773. In 1797, Magdalene Clubley, the widow of Francis perhaps, was identified as a confectioner with an estimated income of £150. Wilfred Pyemont, with 107 pounds of tea on hand, son of a butcher, and admitted in 1783, was also identified in the directory as merchant but appears in the 1797 survey as grocer with an estimated income of £250. It will be recalled that during the 1785 controversy over the shop tax, it was the Merchants Company which called the meeting in York to protest the tax. Probably those listed in the directories were identified as mechants by virtue of membership in the Merchants Company.

But with the exception of these rather dubious merchants and Ann Sponear who cannot be identified, dealers in Class III were the typical high-class grocers and tea dealers whose shops graced the main streets. In the chain of distribution they too served the dual role of wholesale-retail dealers with greater emphasis on the latter. It would be surprising and uncharacteristic if some were not a source of supply for the smaller shops in York or even those in the nearby villages. Indeed, well-trained grocers performed important and necessary functions in the redistribution of tea. In the eighteenth century, a chest of tea as imported weighed anywhere from 35 to 40 pounds for a small chest of very fine hyson to 250 to 320 pounds for a large chest of low-quality bohea. Moreover, except for inferior bohea, little tea was sold to the retail customer as imported from China. Taste, tradition, and perhaps business profits required the blending of different varieties and qualities of tea, a highly valued art that could only be acquired by training with a master in the trade. There was, in addition, the basic distinction of black and green tea; each had its devotees. It is an interesting commentary on the response to consumer demand that only four of the seventy-three licensed dealers in York lacked a stock of both and each of these had under 10 pounds of tea. Given the various marketing problems, small shopkeepers, often selling as little as an ounce or less at a time, had to rely on the experienced grocer for his stock of blended tea. In fact some, if not all, of the fifteen grocers may have purchased a variety of already blended tea from William Tuke and Son or from its London competitors. Certainly they were in no position to purchase at the East India Company auctions. The links in the chain of distribution from importer to final consumer were many and varied and nowhere more so than among the wholesale-retail middlemen in the tea trade. The Tuke firm may itself have purchased some varieties little used in its market area from tea dealers in Hull or London. Abraham Dent purchased some of his groceries from Kendal grocers who probably acquired much of their stock from grocers in the larger towns – Newcastle, for example. Dent may then have supplied some of the smaller shops in his vicinity.[20] It is a pattern which continues well into the nineteenth century, making the distinction between the wholesale and retail shopkeeper meaningless.[21]

Except for the scale of their trade, little distinguishes dealers in Classes IV and V from their brethren in Class III, and some were moving up the business ladder. In 1784, Simeon Gray, grocer, had 29 pounds of tea on hand, but in 1797 his estimated income was £350, the highest income for grocers.[22] Some had crept into shopkeeping from other trades. Samuel Cowling, "worsted man," was admitted "by order" in 1773. In 1781 he was listed as a grocer in Goodramgate. By 1797 his estimated income was £250. Two entered the grocery business via apprenticeship as wine coopers. Mathers Todd, for example, was admitted in 1777. He does not appear in the directories but in 1787 he was advertising as a dealer in tea, wines, spirits, and groceries.[23] In 1797 he was identified as a grocer with an estimated income of £200. Coltan Birdsall, apprenticed to a wine cooper, was admitted in 1779 as a "grocer" and appears as such in the directory, although he had on hand only 27.5 pounds of tea. One dealer was admitted as grocer and apothecary in 1786, the only apothecary dealing in tea. The tallow-chandler, admitted in 1758, was the son of a tallow-chandler. The directory identified him as "tallow chandler and merchant"; tallow-chandler and grocer, a common combination, would seem a more fitting title. He had 72 pounds of tea. The questionable confectioner is Esther Birkett. Invariably women are difficult to identify. Edward Birkett, confectioner, is listed in the 1781 directory. Of the two who cannot be identified in Classes IV and V, one was a woman with 33.5 pounds of tea; the other, possibly a cabinetmaker.[24]

All the major dealers in tea are included in the first five classes. If Jane Benson with thirty-three pounds of tea is excluded, they number thirty-eight or 52 percent of the licensed tea dealers in York, a very high proportion of all dealers. With the exception of the rather dubious *merchants*, almost all were tea dealers, grocers, or confectioners. One combined groceries with drugs and another, with candles. No other major shop trade is represented. Even the milliners were, it seems, eschewing the trade in tea. But perhaps more important the number of grocers and tea dealers in 1784 is almost identical to the number in 1797 who were paying an assessment of two pounds or more. Apparently the reduction of tea duties in 1784 had not effected any noticeable change in the number of principal grocers in York. The great increase in licensed dealers occurred lower down the scale.

Tea dealers in Classes VI and VII inhabited a different shop-keeping world. Of the thirty-four dealers in these classes, only one had served an apprenticeship, Aaron Price, grocer, with 19.5 pounds of tea. He had been apprenticed first to John Owlam and later assigned to John Grave, grocer. In 1789 he was admitted a grocer by order. He was not listed in the directories. The other grocer in Class VI is George Thompson, the menial, who was accused in 1775 of keeping an inner room to sell groceries. The "shopkeeper" is John Playforth who was ordered to pay £25 in 1776. He had 14 pounds of tea. It is difficult to believe that any were true-born *grocers*. None, of course, appear in the directories. The soap dealer is Eleanor Fardinando who in 1775 had a "doubtful" claim of exemption as a distiller's widow. She had a stock of 13 pounds. In 1775, John Dawson, aledraper on Jubbergate, promised to give over the business, but Excise records he had on hand 20 pounds of tea. What kind of shop the other seven dealers in Class VI had remains obscure, but a shop it must have been as tea could be sold legally only from "entered places." From the beginning the hawking of tea was strictly forbidden. By 1779, every dealer in tea was required to have "painted in large, legible characters over the door of every shop" or "in some conspicuous part of such shop" the sign "dealer in ... tea" (19 Geo. 3, c. 69, secs. 18 & 22). A very heavy fine of £200 was imposed on violators. How strictly the law was enforced is difficult to say, but one presumes that a licensed dealer, however small his trade made some attempt to comply with it by giving physical evidence of selling tea from his shop. The same requirement obtained for those who pompously entitled themselves merchants.

Among the twenty-two dealers in Class VII, only one was identified as "shopkeeper." He is John Jackson on Micklegate who was admitted by order in 1776. He had on hand four pounds of black and one and three-quarter pounds of green tea. The two aledrapers were John Ould on Skeldergate and Mary Elles on Thursday Market. Thomas Doeg, a linen-draper on Walmgate had promised to give over the business in 1775 but in 1784 he had two and three-quarter pounds of tea on hand. His was certainly no high-class drapery shop.

Thomas England was listed in the directory as a butter-factor on Micklegate, an address that conforms to the other dealers in the group listed by Excise; but this may be a mistaken identity. On the surface the other five appear to be unlikely sellers of tea. Why, for example, would a hardwareman stock tea? He is, in fact, the one who in 1775 was too poor to purchase his freedom; possibly he was little more than a chandler with a few pots. As to the bricklayer, carpenter, and bridler, they were doing what seems by no means unusual – augmenting their income by running a little parlour shop. Needless to say, the names of these petty dealers are not listed in the directories.

It is perhaps not without significance that ten of the fifteen dealers identified in Classes VI and VII were keeping shop in poor areas south of the Ouze and east of the Foss (see map 4). Of equal significance is the proportion of women in these two classes. Dealers in Classes I and II were all males. Classes III, IV, and V each included one woman shopkeeper. But of the twelve in Class VI, five were women, and in the under ten pound group, nine. Were they widows, as those in the higher classes most probably were? Or were they, like the wives of London tradesmen, supplementing the family income by keeping a little shop? Widowed or not, the large number of women in the two bottom classes supplies corroborative evidence that the dealers in these classes were petty shopkeepers. The percentage of women is in marked contrast not only to the evidence from York for 1797 but also to the information derived from the sampling of bankruptcy records. The latter include very few women. The total for London for all bankruptcies was 16, of which 6 were identified as "shopkeepers." The figures for the provinces are 21 of which 14 were in shopkeeping trades. The total number of bankruptcies was 1,821 with about, 2 percent women or 3 percent for just shopkeepers. Some of the women were clearly identified as "widows," and some of the occupations hardly seem appropriate for women – for example, Elizabeth Hanbury, ironmonger. Was Marie Theresa Winnarvan of St. Clement Danes really a merchant or was the bankruptcy the result of the demise of her husband? The bankruptcy records are confined to the upper reaches of the economic ladder. The humble women running petty shops escaped that particular degradation, although they may not have escaped the criminal law or the eagle eyes of the officers of Excise.

The average quantity of tea held by the thirty-four dealers in the two bottom classes was 9.5 pounds, very little less than that held by the small dealers in London. And yet these dealers had paid the annual licence fee of 5s. 6d. to legalize their sale of tea. How much tea would they have to sell and at what mark-up to pay for the licence? Were they perhaps replacing their stock on a weekly basis? The records for York are silent on these petty transactions. But were they collectively petty? These petty dealers formed 48 percent of the licensed tea dealers in York.[25] True, it is a much smaller proportion than obtained in London. But even in 1834 the proportion of "shopkeepers" in York was only 56.4 percent of all grocers and shopkeepers compared to an average of 76.9 percent for the provincial towns. Indeed, the remarkable similarity in the figures for York a half century after the Commutation Act is itself instructive. Without an industrial population, the city was not able to support a large number of petty shops. Of equal or greater significance is the fact that in 1784, when smuggling was at its height, 48 percent of the licensed tea dealers in a city such as York were little more than chandlers. Moreover, there is no reason to suppose that the proportion of such shops was less in 1765 when the number of licensed tea dealers in the country was only several hundred below that of 1783.

Perhaps the warning given to William Pitt by Francis Baring with respect to proposed new shipping regulations should be heeded. Having noted that the new regulations would prove advantageous to the rich merchant but injurious to those with little capital, Baring observed that "the bulk of the trade of this country is carried on by persons with small capital, and that such trade is upon the whole more beneficial to the country than that part which is carried on by large capital."[26] He was, of course, referring to foreign trade and the "persons with small capital" were wealthy compared to the elusive shopkeepers with less than twenty-five pounds of tea in stock. But in the context of the inland trade, they too were beneficial to the country. Would the consumption of tea and sugar – two important staples in the foreign trade – have increased so phenomenally without these petty retailers?[27] It is doubtful.

In 1837 Excise suggested that the licence fee be graduated according to the quantity of tea sold annually by the dealers. It was believed that of the total number of dealers in England, Scotland, and Ireland only 11.3 percent sold over 400 pounds annually, a further 23.6 percent were selling 200 to 400 pounds, and some 65 percent were below the 200 pound mark.[28] While the figures were rough estimates from a total of over 100,000 dealers, they were not idle guesses. Excise continued to receive full accounts of the quantities of tea entered and sold by every dealer in the kingdom. It can, therefore, be presumed that the figures represent a reasonable assessment of the trade. They are, moreover, remarkably similar to the figures derived from Pigot's directories of the ratio of "shop-keepers" to grocers and also to the figures for 1784. However restricted the tea sales of these small shopkeepers may have been, the total effect on the trade of the country was enormous. Some 50 to 70 percent of the strictly retail sale of tea was in their hands, a percentage very little less in 1784 or for that matter in 1759. To ignore such shopkeepers is to ignore a large part of the inland trade in groceries.

Geographical Distribution of Tea Dealers in Great Britain at the End of the Eighteenth Century

An analysis of the geographical distribution of licensed tea dealers casts some light on the general level of retail shopkeeping in various parts of the country at the end of the eighteenth century. Although no record exists of the total number of shops for the period, there are reliable excise accounts of licensed tea dealers in Great Britain for 1795–6.[1] In addition to providing information on one shop trade, the figures in the account can serve as a basis for estimating the approximate number of shops in the country, and for assessing the changes that had transpired since the 1759 survey. To arrive at a reasonable estimate, it is first necessary to examine the proportion of shopkeepers who sold tea.

Shops licensed to sell tea formed a significant proportion of all shops in the country, although the precise figures are far more difficult to ascertain. In 1765, when smuggling was increasing, entered tea dealers represented almost one-quarter of the total number of shops enumerated in the 1759 excise account. The proportion may have been less in 1784. In the seventeen excise collections surveyed in 1784, the proportion of licensed tea dealers was 20 percent of the number of retail shops in those collections in 1759. The 1785 shop tax account (chapter 4, above) provides more specific figures. A few towns in that account are also in the 1784 excise survey of tea dealers. Table 36 lists these towns along with the number of tea dealers and assessed shops. The towns have been arranged according to the extent of the illicit tea trade. Those in the lower division were in areas subject to extensive smuggling. The very low proportion of tea dealers to shopkeepers in this division – 14.7 percent – is due primarily to the small number of licensed tea dealers. The figure is not typical of the country at large. London, as in so many respects, remains an exception. In 1797 the proportion of shops licensed to

Table 36
Tea Dealers and Shopkeepers in Selected Towns, 1784

Towns	No. of Tea Dealers 1784	Persons per Dealer	No. of Shopkeepers, 1785	Persons per Shopkeeper	Percentage of Shopkeepers with Tea Licences
Birmingham	342	215	780	94	43.8
Bristol & Bath	672	132	1,769	50	38.0
Ipswich	100	112	179	58	55.9
Oxford	94	124	286	41	32.9
Worcester	120	95	602	19	19.9
Subtotal	1,328		3,616		36.7
Canterbury	22	409	223	44	9.9
Chichester	38	125	197	24	19.3
Salisbury & Southampton	100	156	683	24	14.6
York	73	233	486	35	15.0
Subtotal	233		1,589		14.7
Total	1,561		5,205		30.0

Sources: Number of Tea Dealers: table 30, chapter 8. Persons per Dealer and Persons per Shopkeeper: population taken from Census 1801. Number of Shopkeepers: PRO, HO 42/7.

sell tea in London was probably no more than 16 percent of all shops.[2]

The proportions of tea dealers for towns in the upper division vary considerably, ranging from 19.9 percent at Worcester to almost 56 percent at Ipswich. It is perhaps not without significance that high proportions tend to occur where the ratios of persons to assessed shops are high. Birmingham, for example, has high ratios for both in contrast to Worcester, with low ratios. In the two towns with high ratios for shopkeepers – Birmingham and Ipswich – there may have been a large number of shops which escaped the shop tax. The average proportion of tea dealers to shopkeepers for the towns in the upper division is 36.7 percent, for both divisions, 30 percent.

In a recent survey based on Pigot's directories for nine urban centres ca. 1848–51, grocers, provision dealers, and shopkeepers accounted for anywhere from 24 percent in Leicester to 44 percent in Bolton of all shops.[3] The range for 1834–5 was similar: 24.5 percent in Norwich to 41.5 percent in Bolton. Unfortunately, the proportions can serve only as a rough guide for the country as a whole, or even for the nine cities. The dubious inclusions and ex-

clusions of various shop trades, in addition to the doubtful compre-
hensiveness of the coverage in the directories, do not inspire
confidence in the figures. For example, all greengrocers, fruiterers,
fishmongers, and butchers have been excluded as shop trades in
calculating the percentages; but some of each of these trades certainly had shops outside the market in the midnineteenth century.
And if the markets were open for sale six days a week, as many
covered markets were in the nineteenth century, is there any basic
difference between a "shop" in the market and one situated on market street? Shoemakers, on the other hand, appear a doubtful entry
as a shop trade, although there were certainly shops retailing ready-
made shoes. And yet, of the nine cities, only Manchester has an entry
for "shoe warehouses." Indeed, the figures in the directories for
shoemakers, as well as tailors, milliners, and bakers are suspiciously
erratic from year to year. There is, moreover, an important shop
trade that has been overlooked: the upholsterers and cabinetmakers.
They formed no small proportion of shops in large cities. Nor have
dealers in wines and brandy been included as a shop trade.

On the basis of available evidence, shops licensed to sell tea formed
no small part of all shops in the 1780s – probably 30 percent or even
higher in industrial cities. If the estimate bears any relation to reality,
the proportion of shops retailing groceries remained relatively constant for two centuries. In 1950, grocery, delicatessen, and other
general food shops represented 27.9 percent of all retail establishments.[4] Whatever the precise proportional relationship between tea
dealers and shopkeepers in general may have been, the excise accounts provide a useful gauge of retail shopkeeping.

The excise account for England and Wales lists the number of tea
dealers in each of the fifty-five collections in 1795–6; the account
for Scotland, the number in each of the sixteen collections from
1800–1 to 1802–3. Together they form a comprehensive and accurate survey of an important sector of the shopkeeping world in
Great Britain.[5] Since the 1759 survey (see chap. 2), the number of
collections has increased by five and their disposition conforms to
changes in the structure of the economy (see map 5). Lancashire,
for example, has three new collections: Liverpool, Manchester, and
Preston, the last formed sometime after 1784.[6]

In appendix IV the counties and collections are grouped by region
following the pattern for 1759 (see appendix I). One exception has
been introduced. Cheshire has proved a most awkward county. The
Manchester collection includes parts of Cheshire, but the collection
of Chester (30) in addition to covering "a greater part of Cheshire"

Map 5
Excise Collections of England and Wales, 1796

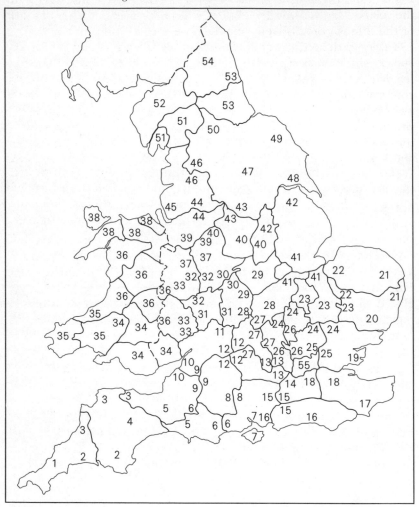

Note: Numbers indicate the approximate location of each collection.
Collections are identified in appendix 4.

also includes "part of Staffordshire." Cheshire is, therefore, grouped with Staffordshire, Herefordshire, and Shopshire.

The county population figures are more reliable than the estimated population used for the 1759 survey, but they are for 1801, not 1795–6. The calculated ratio of population to tea dealers has therefore an upward bias. Based on an estimated population of 8.56 million in 1795–6, the average ratio for England and Wales is 163 in contrast to the 173 shown in the table. In the faster-growing regions the difference would be greater. But the overall effect on the relative ratios for individual regions or for areas north and south of the line is not sufficient to invalidate the results.

Table 37 demonstrates a number of significant changes have occurred since the 1759 survey. Although the ratio of population to tea dealers in counties north of the line still lags behind the southern counties, the gap between the two has been considerably narrowed however the difference is measured. In 1759, 63.5 percent of the provincial shops were in counties south of the line, 33.1 percent in the north, and 3.4 percent in Wales. The corresponding figures for tea dealers in 1795–6 are: south, 52 percent; north, 43.3 percent; Wales, 4.7 percent.[7] The difference in the ration of population to shops is even more striking. In 1759 the average ratio for counties north of the line was 63.9 percent higher than that of the south; in Wales, 205.6 percent. In 1795–6 the average ratio north of the line was only 14.9 percent higher; in Wales, 70.7 percent. Devon and Cornwall had a low ratio in 1795–6 in contrast to its high ratio in 1759. The two counties have therefore tended to lower the average ratio in 1795–6 for the area north of the line. However, if they are placed south of the line for both periods, the northern counties still register a considerable improvement. Calculated on the new arrangement, the ratio in 1759 would be 47.4 percent higher; in 1795–6, 16.1 percent.

It has been suggested that the area south of the line had achieved its substantial growth in shopkeeping during the decades preceding the 1759 survey. Indeed, for many counties, the ratio of population to shops was so low that future growth would necessarily depend upon an increase in population. Unless the ratio of tea dealers to all shops is unbelievably erratic, the 1795–6 survey indicates that many counties north of the line experienced their phenomenal increase in shopkeeping during the latter half of the century. If 30 percent of the retail shops in the five English regions north of the line were licensed tea dealers, the total number of shops in the area would be almost 71,000, an increase of 78.4 percent over the number of shops in 1759. No comparable increase occurred in the area south of the line. The number of shops in that area, excluding London, would be 85,183, an increase of only 11.7 percent. The area north of the line had not yet reached parity with the southern counties, and Durham and Northumberland lagged well behind. But in closing the gap, the north had accomplished more than appears on the surface. Between 1751 and 1801, the increase in population of the southern counties was 54 percent compared to an increase of 60.6

.1 the north.[8] It would not perhaps be rash to presume that
,rowth in shopkeeping in the north was somewhat greater than
.1e increase in their population, that as the wheels of industry turned
faster, so too did the doors of the shopkeepers.

One catches a glimpse of this movement at Wilmslow, a small
Cheshire village only twelve miles south of Manchester and most
probably included in the Manchester collection. According to Samuel
Finney, ca. 1745, Wilmslow was an agricultural village with only a
small number, mainly women and children, employed as outworkers
in the making of mohair and silk buttons. The diet of the workers
consisted of "barley bread, potatoes, buttermilk, whey and sower
porridge." Shopkeeping was confined to a few petty shops that sold
"treacle, brown sugar, salt, tobacco, coarse linens and woolens and
other small necessaries." But in the course of the following forty
years, great changes occurred in the economy of Wilmslow. First
came the Jersey wheels with the Yorkshire clothiers who employed
many more outworkers at higher wages. Within a short time, there
were few families who were not spinning wool on the hand-turning
wheels. They were followed in the 1770s by the cotton manufacturers
with the jenny that attracted an even larger work force including
men. Finally in the early 1780s, Samuel Gregg arrived with his mill
at Styal, just a mile and one-half from Wilmslow. The quickening
of industry brought changes in diet and dress that led to a great
expansion in the retail trade. The workers, who continued faithful
to the potato, "have utterly forsaken all the rest and use fresh meat
and bacon ... wheat bread ... well buttered, and tea, forsooth, generally thrice a day." By 1785, the number of shopkeepers had "increased amazingly, some of whom dealt in a great variety of articles
... tea, coffee, loafe sugar, spices, printed cottons, calicoes, lawns,
fine linens, silks, velvets, silk waistcoat pieces, silk cloaks, hats, bon-
nets, shawls, laced caps and a variety of other things."[9] Wilmslow
was certainly not unique.

When one turns from the broad differences north and south of
the line to individual regions, two in particular appear to defy explanation. In 1759, Cornwall and Devonshire had a very high ratio
of population to shops, even if the population for Devonshire is
adjusted downward. But in 1795–6 the number of persons per tea
dealer matched that of other regions south of the line. And however
one allocates the collections and counties of Region II, which extends
from Sussex to Oxfordshire and Gloucestershire, the ratio is low
(see appendix 4 and table 37). No great industrial surge occurred
in either of these two regions to account for the large number of
tea dealers. On the contrary, compared to other parts of the country,

Table 37
Distribution of Tea Licences in England, Wales, and Scotland, 1795-6 (by regions)

		Number of Tea Licences	Population 1801	Population per Licence
London: Bills of Mortality, Marylebone, and parts of Paddington and St Pancras		3,982	864,645	217
Country Collections				
South of Line:				
Region II		9,924	1,468,199	148
Region III (minus London)		6,845	1,085,311	159
Region IV		2,992	499,243	167
Region V		1,036	130,965	127
Region VI		4,758	753,295	158
	Total	25,555	3,937,013	154
North of Line:				
Region I		3,468	548,226	158
Region VII		3,820	709,684	186
Region VIII		4,712	858,119	182
Region IX		7,676	1,305,025	170
Region X		1,578	327,594	208
	Total	21,254	3,748,648	177
Wales		2,308	605,867	263
England		50,791	8,550,306	169
England and Wales		53,099	9,156,173	173
Scotland		4,566	1,625,000	356

Source and explanations: See appendix 4.

decline or stagnation is the more common feature associated with these areas, except in the agricultural sector. And even here, the agricultural labourer fared less well with respect to wages than in the more pushing industrial counties in the north. What these two regions did have in common was a prolonged and extensive experience in handling illicit tea.[10] The widespread use of tea in Britain owed not a little to the trade practices of the traditional smugglers who brought the exotic beverage into areas far removed from the usual sources of distribution and within reach of the more humble folk.[11] The large number of dealers in these two regions may, therefore, reflect a demand created long before the Commutation Act of 1784 brought an end to the illicit trade. Certain it is that in the southern counties there was a great thirst for the deleterious beverage,

ecome a necessity for agricultural labourers no less
nners and weavers who were notorious consumers of
re, if anywhere, the standard diet of bread, cheese, and tea
evailed.

Wales had not remained stagnant but it was still a long way behind
England, although well ahead of Scotland, with respect to its shopping facilities. Of the four divisions in Wales (34, 35, 36, 38), the
eastern collection appears to have experienced a somewhat greater
growth, but it is only marginal.[12] It had, however, the lowest ratio
of population to tea dealers, somewhere in the neighbourhood of
210. The highest ratio was found in Wales-west, approximately 360
persons per tea dealer; that for Wales-middle, over 253.[13] The only
collection whose boundaries coincide with those of the counties is
Wales-north, covering Anglesey, Caernarvonshire, Denbigshire, and
Flintshire. The ratio for this area was 253 (see appendix 4).

The high ratio of population to tea dealers in Scotland requires
little explanation. Given its social and economic structure, one would
have been surprised, if not suspicious, had the ratio been low. In
fact, Scotland did not achieve parity with England until 1827–8, a
period when the ratio in England was rising due probably to the
increasing density of population: that year the ratio for England
and Wales was 179; for Scotland, 180. For the next several years
Scotland dropped below England. By 1830–1, the ratio in England
and Wales was 185; in Scotland, 175. After 1831, Scotland followed
the trend of England. The 1840–1 ratios were: England and Wales,
194; Scotland, 196.[14]

The Scottish excise account for the years 1800–1 to 1802–3 provides more specific information on the distribution of tea dealers in
Scotland. Although the boundaries of the collections are not described, a broad geographical division can be made between what
may loosely be called the lowlands and the highlands. And one can
be reasonably certain that the Edinburgh collection was restricted to
Edinburgh and Leith.[15] Table 38 gives the ratio of population to
tea dealer for the areas distinguished. As the table shows, the difference between the highlands and the lowlands is enormous. The
ratio of the former (474) is more than double that of the lowlands.
Even with Edinburgh excluded, the ratio for the remaining lowland
areas rises to 205. Indeed, the ratio for the lowland counties is not
very much above the average for the English counties north of the
line. And is this not what one would expect if, as suggested, the
figures for tea dealers are reflecting the general level of shopkeeping, a level which is itself a response to the social and economic
structure of an area?

Table 38
Distribution of Tea Licences in Scotland, 1800-1

Collection	Number of Tea Licences	City or County	Population 1801 (000)	Population per Licence
Lowlands				
Edinburgh	479	Edinburgh	83	174
Glasgow	553	Renfrewshire	79	
Teviotdale	400	Lanarkshire	148	
		Peeblesshire	9	
		Selkirkshire	5	
		Roxburghshire	34	
Linlithgow	429	Dunbartonshire	21	
		Stirlingshire	51	
		West Lothian	18	
Fife	707	Fifeshire	94	
		Kinross-shire	7	
		Clackmannanshire	11	
Haddington	482	Midlothianshire (minus Edinburgh)	40	
		East Lothianshire	30	
		Berwickshire	30	
Dumfries	395	Dumfriesshire	55	
		Kircudbrightshire	29	
Ayr	787	Ayrshire	84	
		Wigtownshire	23	
Total	4,232		851	201
Highlands				
Perth	684	Perthshire	126	
		Angusshire	99	
		Kincardineshire	26	
Argyll-South	46	Buteshire	12	
Argyll-North	58	Argyllshire	81	
Inverness	187	Inverness-shire	73	
Aberdeen	499	Aberdeenshire	121	
		Banffshire	37	
		Morayshire	28	
		Nairnshire	8	
Caithness	66	Caithness-shire	23	
		Sutherlandshire	23	
		Ross & Cromarty	56	
Orkney	41	Orkney	24	
Shetland	22	Shetland	22	
Total	1,603		759	474

Table 38 (continued)

Collection	Number of Tea Licences	City or County	Population 1801 (000)	Population per Licence
Scotland	5,835		1,610	276
England & Wales	56,249		9,061	161

Sources: No. of licences: Excise Revenue Accounts, XIV, SRO. Population: Mitchell and Deane, *British Historical Statistics*, 21.

In 1800–1 slightly over 62,000 shopkeepers were licensed tea dealers in Great Britain. If they represented as much as 35 percent of all shops, the total number of retail shops in the kingdom was over 177,000. Whatever the actual number may have been, there seems little doubt that shops were far more numerous than has commonly been supposed. In the retail sector of the economy a quiet revolution had been occurring, at least in terms of numbers, well before the explosive events of the industrial sector. The lines which converged to form the industrial revolution were intricate and many although no completely satisfactory answer has yet been accepted as to why it should have first and foremost emerged in Britain. The agricultural, commercial, and industrial forces that set it in motion we now know had a long period of gestation. Although the rise of shopkeeping may not have played a causative role, the extensive network of shops in place by midcentury contributed not a little to the smooth movement of goods from importers and manufacturers to final consumers. Shopkeeping was not the generating motor of change, but an essential "wheel whereon the inland trade" turned. The preceding chapters have explored the number and types of shops in the kingdom. The chapters to follow will trace the continuity and changes in the business practices of the shopkeepers.

CHAPTER ELEVEN

"Petty" Shopkeepers: Business Practices and Customers

It is not likely that many shop records of petty chandlers will be found, although even these small tradesmen, if they dealt in tea, would have been required to keep an account of their sales and purchases of tea in the books provided by Excise. Certainly, persons at this humble level were in no position to establish a "correspondence" with tradesmen "of established credit" in some distant town. For their stock, they were almost wholly dependent upon local suppliers who could control the type, quantity, and price of goods periodically purchased, as well as the form of payment. Indeed, information about these petty shopkeepers is drawn largely from the accounts of their suppliers. But meagre and scattered as the sources are, they show that such shops were able to function within the folds of the pre-industrial economy and often proved a useful adjunct to the trade of the more respectable shopkeepers.

In the mideighteenth century, Lancaster had not achieved parity with the southern counties in its shopping facilities. Early in the century, William Stout of Lancaster set up Elin Godsalve in a small shop fitted with "about £10 value of grocery goods." "She had," as he says, "quickly good custom by retail and diligently attended both day and night." And how was she supplied after the initial investment? Stout, it appears, "gave her liberty, as money came in, to buy in goods with ready money, without paying me till she easily could."[1]

Stout was a sharp observer of the foibles and weaknesses of his neighbours, even though somewhat pompous and self-righteous. He did not hesitate to confide in his personal memoir the burdensome responsibilities that he dutifully carried out. On the other hand, his autobiography supplies ample evidence of his business acumen. If some mercantile ventures ended in the red, the loss was quickly retrieved by profits from his highly successful grocery and iron-

mongery shop. Even his investments in property were carefully designed to secure with safety a return on the capital he accumulated.
He lived frugally and conducted his personal and business life with
probity. Professing to detest the "customary" practice "to ask more
for goods than the market price, or what they be afforded for," he
claimed to have "usually set" a fixed price, presumably one based
on what he considered to be a deserved profit.[2] At the same time,
he was not averse to exploring all avenues to reduce costs. In his
purchase of tobacco, for example, he took every possible advantage
of the custom allowances for ready money and especially for any
damage that could be claimed – as much as 100 pounds a hogshead
duty free if it could be proved that 20 pounds were damaged. And
the laxity of the outport custom officials was notorious.[3] In 1709
Stout "got half-penny allowed."[4]

While he righteously disclaimed charging undue prices, he was a
keen businessman who followed those practices he deemed appropriate for his calling in life. Tobacco was one of his "most profitable"
articles, in part because of the allowances by customs but also because
"by liquoring" it was "increased in weight about a penny in the
pound."[5] He estimated the cost to Henry Coward of a pound of
tobacco as 2d.; it was sold for 6d. a pound or 200 percent gross
profit.[6] Stout does not state what his profit on tobacco was. But as
he levelled no criticism at Coward's price, although he made some
ungenerous comments on the conviviality and social pretensions of
his old master, one presumes the profit accorded with his sense of
business ethics.

William Stout was a hardworking businessman, but among his
many virtues an innovative spirit was conspicuously absent. The
memoir records few changes in the general pattern of his personal
or business activities. True, in 1709 he established connections with
agents in London and Sheffield.[7] These were changes sufficiently
significant for him to record. In fact, they were not trifling but hardly
evidence of a bold venture into new territory. Throughout his career,
he paid in hard cash for most commodities. There is little indication
that he adopted the bill of exchange. In his account with Backbarrow
Iron Company, a local firm, he paid mainly in "ready cash"; only
three times were bills of exchange credited to his account.[8] Even in
his mercantile ventures, he was merely following the common practice of his fellow grocers and ironmongers. In sum, William Stout
may be taken as a prototype of the good old-fashioned tradesman
at the turn of the century – not for him any newfangled ideas or
projects.

Given Stout's character, it does not seem likely that the shop he set up for Elin Godsalve or the methods adopted to assure her a continuous supply of goods were novel. Nor was it a purely elee-mosynary gesture on his part. William Stout was a good-living Quaker, who performed his duty towards his fellow creatures but he was not suffused with warm-hearted charity. When money and business were involved, he was cautious to the extreme. Elin Godsalve was no novice in shopkeeping. Before her marriage she had run a millinery shop and later helped her husband in the grocery business prior to his bankruptcy. In effect, Stout advanced Elin an interest-free loan by stocking the shop. And she obtained new supplies for "ready money" (at ready-money prices?) as she sold the old stock, almost on a daily or weekly basis. For such a petty shop, not much capital or stock was necessary, nor any extensive knowledge of, or contact with, the business community outside Lancaster. Her com-petitors in the town, those who "sould by retail as much" as she, were probably supplied in a similar fashion – perhaps not at such fa-vourable prices. Contrary to the view expressed by the seventeenth-century critic,[9] the relationship between the small chandler's shop in the towns or country villages and the well-stocked market-street establishment was mutually beneficial. Henry Coward had at least two satellite shops in nearby villages, one of which he turned over to his former apprentice, John Lawson, and the other he sold to Roger Hynd, a shoemaker.[10] Undoubtedly both purchased most of their stock from Coward.

The precise transactions between Stout and Godsalve may be somewhat obscure. However, the records of an Edinburgh tea dealer and grocer a century later provide a more detailed description of petty shopkeepers. Andrew Melrose, tea dealer and grocer of Edin-burgh, opened his first shop in 1812 and within a few years had three shops and two warehouses in the city.[11] He stocked a wide variety of grocery goods, wines, and spirits; household wares, such as soaps, blue, starch, sand, candles, etc.; fruits, particularly oranges which were specially featured in Scotland for the making of mar-malade; butter, cheese, and ham; and macaroni, vermicelli, oils, rice, and barley. But there was no trace either in his purchases or sales of flour, oats, or tobacco, and no haberdashery, drapery goods, or ironmongery. Melrose was, as featured, a tea dealer and grocer.[12]

Melrose served both retail and trade customers, ranging from major grocers in Edinburgh and elsewhere to petty shopkeepers. His Day Book, 1818–34, is the most enlightening source of his trans-actions with petty shopkeepers. From the many customers recorded, three have been analysed as samples of the purchasing practices of small tradesmen: "Mrs. Taylor, Niddry," Edinburgh; "Mr. Alex[r] Grieve, Portobello"; and "James Calder, Edinburgh." The purchases and payments of the three have been tabulated for periods extending beyond the sample years (see tables 39 and 40) and are not appreciably different, except in one respect. In May 1819, Mrs Taylor began purchasing tea by the chest, presumably to take advantage of the discount allowed by Melrose.[13]

Mrs Taylor seems to have run a rather small shop. The account with Melrose for the year (22 January 1818 to 18 January 1819) amounted to £194 14s. 10.5d. or £3 15s. a week. Her purchases were confined to a narrow range of commodities: tea, coffee (very little), sugar, cheese (Dunlop and Gouda), salt butter, pepper, liquorice, candles, and yellow soap – no dried fruits, spices, vinegar, or other condiments, not even blue or starch to accompany the soap – just the bare essentials to stock a small neighbourhood shop. In her own small way Mrs Taylor was, however, a specialist. During the year she bought 244 pounds of tea at a cost of £73 13s. 6d. and approximately 15.25 hundred weight of sugar for £64 10s. Together they accounted for 71 percent of her purchases. She was selling about 7 pounds of sugar to every pound of tea. That year Andrew Melrose offered his customers "sugars .5d. cheaper ... to the proportion of six pounds of sugar to one pound of tea or coffee."[14] Taylor may have obtained the discount,[15] but it is unlikely that her customers could have taken advantage of such a favourable offer, even if she had held out similar inducements. Most working class families purchased their tea by the ounce as needed. If the proportion of 6 pounds of sugar to 1 pound of tea was the expected standard in the trade, the East India Company's tea trade acted as a considerable stimulant to that of the West Indian sugar planters and merchants who so frequently opposed the interests of the East India Company.

It was often stated that the workers avoided buying, whenever possible, the low quality teas, preferring a more expensive tea with greater strength, perhaps because more infusions could be produced from a given quantity.[16] Mrs Taylor's stock was designed to attract such customers. Her supplier, Andrew Melrose, always maintained a very wide assortment of teas, both black and green, although the latter was little used in Scotland. In 1818 his prices for black tea ranged from "5s. 2d. (or lower)" for plain "Congou," to 10s. a pound for "best Pekoe." He "particularly recommended to families for common use ... Congous at 6s. 4d. and 6s. 6d." He maintained they were "strong and well-tasted teas."[17] Indeed, the most popular teas purchased by Melrose's retail customers, among whom were some of the leading Edinburgh families, were "fine Congou" at 6s. to 6s. 6d. a pound and "finest," at 7s. And these were the teas selected by Mrs Taylor for her working-class trade. The vast majority of the population north or south of the border enjoyed a similar sort of tea. Those who purchased their tea by the ounce may have been more sparing in the quantity infused (not quite so profligate as Dr Johnson), and they undoubtedly paid more for their luxury. But tea, like beer, was a common beverage, at least for the women and children throughout the kingdom.

How much did the increasing popularity of legal and smuggled tea in the eighteenth century contribute to the rise of small shops such as Mary Smith's of Flixton or Sarah Swale's of York, or the many petty dealers in London and the urban centres in the provinces? Before the demise of smuggling, the considerable gains that could be expected on even a small stock of untaxed illicit tea must have attracted many hopefuls into the market. As consumption reached further down the social ladder, tea and the sugar that accompanied it, together with other small commodities in daily use, made the petty chandler's shop in the back streets of large towns a viable unit. After 1784, legal tea was a profitable item of trade for the well-established grocer. Demand increased slowly but steadily. The regular supply provided by the East India Company discouraged extensive speculation and maintained relatively stable prices, which rose gradually and predictably with the increase of the *ad valorem* duties. Unlike the coffee trade, there was no glut in the market and consequently no need to fear a sudden drop in prices. Tea was not a particularly bulky commodity. It was easily portable and did not deteriorate if kept in a dry place. In fact, black teas improved in taste and quality when stored properly. In short, it was a commodity that could hardly fail to yield a secure profit to large and small dealers.[18] For Taylor, as for Melrose, tea was certainly the feature article; it was also one for which she obtained special credit concessions.

One of the most striking features of Mrs Taylor's account with Melrose was the very small amount of capital necessary to set up and run such a shop – less, perhaps, than the ten pounds laid out by Stout. But with a modest mark-up of 25 percent, she could have grossed almost fifty pounds on the few items purchased from Melrose in 1818 – not an insignificant amount to add to the family exchequer. Such small shops were a refuge for working-class widows and redundant mechanics and a source of additional income for those slightly better off. In Lavenham, as noted earlier (p. 96), a number of workers combined shopkeeping with other trades. Indeed, it would be surprising if the slightly more ambitious workers who were able to read, write, and reckon had not seized the opportunity which was almost literally at their doorstep. Not much more was necessary than a scale, a front parlour, and a credit-worthy reputation with a nearby supplier.

Equally if not more impressive is that the business practices of Melrose and Taylor parallel those of William Stout and Elin Godsalve. Surely the hazards of survival have not preserved two documents wholly unrepresentative of business practices. The 1818 account indicates that Mrs Taylor replenished her stock a little under once a week, somewhat more frequently for the six months from May to October (thirty-four entries) than November to April (twenty-five), a pattern repeated in 1819. Interestingly, her purchases of sugar reveal a similar discrepancy – 8.75 hundredweight for the first period against 6.5 for the second. Are these signs of seasonal fluctuations in the purchasing power of workers due to heavier expenditure on fuel, candles, and clothing during the cold winter months? The average turnover for sugar was a little over a week.[19] The usual quantity of "fine raw sugar" purchased by Taylor was 28 pounds, less frequently, 56 pounds. Only once, 30 June, did she purchase a hundredweight.[20] Sales that week must have been exceptionally heavy because she returned on 7 July for her customary 28 pounds. With the exception of the hundredweight, most of her purchases were not particularly bulky or weighty and probably did not require special delivery.

Her stock of soap and cheese was renewed every few weeks; salt butter, usually bought by the cask, not quite so often. Judging from her account, she sold very few candles during the months of May to August. Coffee, liquorice, and pepper were only occasional items in the account.

In obtaining a stock of tea, Mrs Taylor displayed considerable discrimination. Her purchases were timed to coincide with Melrose's fresh supply from the East India Company's quarterly sale. She always selected two qualities. For example, on 23 January there is a debit for twenty pounds of "fine Congou" at 5s. 5d. a pound and twelve pounds of "finest Congou" at 6s. 6d. Apparently, she had received a trade discount – Melrose's retail customers were paying 6s. for "fine" at that time. The order was repeated in April, but in June she increased the quantity of "finest" to twenty pounds. Her next order was for thirty pounds of each, a sufficiently bulky and heavy load to require special packing and for which she was charged an additional 2s. Her weekly sales of tea averaged about four and one-half pounds of tea to 32.8 pounds of sugar. Had she purchased tea by the week, as she did sugar, the excise surveyor would rarely have found more than five pounds of black tea in stock.

William Stout gave Elin "liberty, as money came in, to buy in goods with ready money." Andrew Melrose did no less. Table 39 reproduces a typical segment of Taylor's debit and credit account. Surely few market-street grocers would not welcome, indeed encourage, such an account. Payment was prompt and to the half-penny; no new stock was purchased until after the debit for the old had been cleared. Even the payment for tea followed a similar pattern. As she had engaged to buy a larger quantity than could be disposed of within a week or two, Melrose allowed her to pay for it as it was sold, generally within two months of purchase. It was a convenient arrangement for both. From the beginning he had pushed the sale of tea. Mrs Taylor was a means of tapping potential customers who may have been unable or unwilling to buy at his shops, or whom he may not have been particularly desirous of serving. Only one entry appears in the Day Book of a customer buying as little as two ounces of tea, "Mrs Blackie, Canongate, upstairs" who was apparently well-known to Melrose. Small shopkeepers like Mrs Taylor relieved the large grocer of the annoyance and trouble involved in selling such tiny amounts as an ounce or two. Moreover, as neighbourhood shopkeepers they were in a better position to judge which of their customers could be allowed credit. Judging from Mrs Taylor's account with Melrose, her customers were paying as promptly as she – money and goods were turning over very quickly, almost on a "ready money" basis.

In the shopkeeping hierarchy, Alexander Grieve of Portobello was several degrees above Taylor. Her shop may never have appeared under any rubric in the classified trade directories. Grieve's shop, on the other hand, was clearly a small grocery shop in a seaport town, not unlike the shop described by Adam Smith. Tea and sugar were still the major articles purchased, followed by cheese and salt butter. But he also carried a small variety of spices and condiments: nutmeg, cloves, ginger, cassie, cayenne, and pepper. The latter two were purchased three times during the year, each of the other items only once. He kept a very meagre stock of dried fruits and nuts – one entry for currants, two, for raisins and nuts, very minor purchases. He even had one order of ham. In the sweet line there was liquorice – no more than Taylor – and a little "candy." Rice, East India and Carolina, was purchased three times; oranges and lemons appear twice in the account. The items from currants to lemons do not appear to have formed a regular part of the general stock on hand. Probably, they were bought only after receiving specific re-

Table 39
Mrs Taylor of Niddry: Account with Andrew Melrose, 1818

Debit		£	s.	d.	Credit		£	s.	d.
1818									
8 Aug.	sugar, soap	3	2	0	10 Aug.	cash	3	2	0
11 "	tea	18	7	6	17 Aug.	cash in part	5	2	0
	ball on goods		2	0		[tea]			
18 "	sugar, soap	3	2	6	26 "	cash	3	2	6
28 "	sugar	2	2	0	27 "	cash in part	3	7	6
	butter, candles		9	10½		[tea]			
2 Sept.	candles, butter, sugar	7	7	9	1 Sept.	cash	2	11	10½
5 "	liquorice		1	8	7 "	cash	7	9	5
7 "	cheese		14	10	10 "	cash	2	17	10
8 "	sugar, soap	2	3	0	23 "	cash in part	5	0	0
						[tea]			
24 "	sugar	2	2	0	28 "	cash	2	2	0
29 "	cheese, sugar	1	18	4					
					6 Oct.	cash	1	18	4
6 Oct.	butter	3	18	0		cash in full	5	0	0
						[tea]			
					13 "	cash	3	18	0

Source: Day Book, 1818-34, Andrew Melrose Archives.

quests from customers. In the same category were aquavita (one entry) and wine (two). "Best yellow soap," however, was a frequent and regular item in the account; pearl-ashes somewhat less frequent. Starch, blue, and common soda were apparently little used, each was purchased only once.

Alexander Grieve dealt in a wider range of goods than Taylor, but his staple commodities were no different. Without tea, sugar, cheese, butter, soap, and candles, his shop would not have been viable. These were the items in common demand. The few spices, condiments, and dried fruits that he occasionally bought and which entitled him to the name of *grocer* were decorative rather than remunerative. They gave his shop tone and marked him as a man with some ambition and pride. But his was decidedly a small shop. The total purchases for the year (24 October 1818 to 22 October 1819) amounted to £187 1s. 3.5d., a few pounds less than Mrs Taylor. During the same period he bought 171 pounds of tea at a cost of £54 17s. and 28 pounds of coffee for £3 15s. 6d. Together they account for 31.3 percent of all his purchases. Like Taylor, he replenished his stock about once a week (fifty debit entries) a little more frequently in June, July, and December. During the summer months his purchases of sugar were somewhat heavier than usual. In December, he was apparently preparing for the holiday trade. That month he was debited for aquavita and 10s. 6d. for raisins. Grieve generally kept a slightly larger supply of sugar on hand than Taylor, renewing his stock about once a fortnight (twenty-six entries).

But Grieve handled his tea business somewhat differently than Taylor. He renewed his stock of tea about twice a month. The usual quantity purchased was four to six pounds of "fine Congou" at 6s. a pound, and the same of "finest" at 6s. 6d. a pound.[21] It is difficult to determine whether or not his "fine Congou" was a slightly better quality than Taylor's, or because of the smaller quantity purchased he was not given the same trade discount.[22] But his pattern of purchases may well have been dictated by the excise regulations. No package of tea above six pounds could be removed from Melrose's shop or brought into Grieve's unless accompanied by a permit specifying the quantity and type of tea and the names and addresses of the seller and buyer. Obtaining the permit from the nearest excise office could sometimes take the better part of a day. If Grieve himself came into Edinburgh perhaps he thought it more expedient not to risk the chance of delaying his return trip to Portobello. In any case, he never exceeded the six-pound limit for any one kind of tea and thus kept within the letter of the law.

Grieve's credit account is different to Taylor's. He paid regularly but not as frequently, and the amounts credited were in round figures.[23] There is only one instance of a sixpence; even shillings are rare unless he was credited for "empty kitts" [kits]. Perhaps small change was less available in Portobello than in Edinburgh; Mrs Taylor never seems to have had any difficulty. Grieve, like William Wood of Didsbury in the 1780s, was probably paid in round figures by his customers. Grieve settled his account with Melrose by "cash" not bills. Presumably, his customers rarely if ever paid by bills of exchange. But however Grieve was paid, he discharged his account with Melrose promptly as table 40 shows. It appears that he paid for his previous order on the day he came to replenish his stock. In every segment of the account, credits approximate debits. It is also apparent that without tea and sugar, Grieve's trips to Edinburgh would have been infrequent.

James Calder of 75 Cannongate was listed in the 1824–5 *Edinburgh Post Office Directory* as a mason. His account in Melrose's Day Book commenced in April 1825. That month he purchased a cask of sugar,

Table 40
Alexander Grieve of Portobello: Account with Andrew Melrose, 1818

Debit						Credit				
1818		£	*s.*	*d*				£	*s.*	*d.*
3 July	tea	1	19	0		3 July	Cash	2	0	0
9 "	candy, mustard, pepper, cheese, coffee, sugar, butter, liquorice	4	18	6		9 "	Cash in part	6	0	0
20 "	rice, nutmeg, soap, sugar	7	9	8½		20 "	Cash in part	8	0	0
24 "	tea, sugar	2	19	6		24 "	Cash	3	0	0
30 "	sugar, pepper	5	6	2½						
2 Aug.	sugar	4	16	9		2 Aug.	Cash in part	4	0	0
21 "	soap, sugar, tea, coffee	6	8	0		21 "	Cash	8	0	0
26 "	sugar, tea, blue, currants	6	9	5¾		26 "	Cash	5	0	0
31 "	tea, sugar	3	2	8		31 "	Cash	5	0	0
16 Sept.	cheese, coffee	2	3	7		16 Sept.	Cash & kits	4	5	0
	Total	45	13	4¾				45	5	0

Source: Day Book, 1818-34, Andrew Melrose Archives.

a chest of tea, soap, and cheese and during the next several months fairly large quantities of malt and grain aquavita, rum, gin, brandy, porter, and ale. James Calder had changed trades. In the 1825–6 *Directory* he was listed as a spirit dealer and continued as such until at least 1832–3.[24] Except for the spirits, the items debited to his account are similar to those of Taylor: tea, sugar, soap, cheese, butter, coffee, candy, pepper, candles, one entry each for raisins and nutmeg, and vinegar occasionally. The total purchases for the year (14 April 1825 to 14 April 1826) amounted to £259 13s. 10.5d. His major expenditure was for sugar, roughly £85; tea, £74 14s.; spirits, porter and ale, approximately £60. Together they represent almost 85 percent of the debit account. His shop was very close to one of Melrose's, which probably accounts for the frequent debit entries, rarely less than twice a week. Nine or ten times a month was the norm. He paid regularly, generally twice a month, and to the half-penny. Thus, on 18 July 1825 he was debited £10 16s. 4d. for aquavita and soap; on 1 August the account was credited for the exact amount. Again on 15 August there is a debit of £11 17s. 10d.

credited "cash in full" 29 August. The only exception was in his tea transactions for which he, like Taylor, was allowed more extended credit. The first chest of tea (eighty-four pounds at 6s. a pound) was purchased on 22 April; he completed payment on 18 July and bought a second chest, 30 August, and so on. James Calder's shop was a Scottish version of a chandler's shop in London – both carried the national beverages, tea and alcohol, along with a few necessary household goods.[25]

Despite the absence of similar accounts for the petty tea dealers in York and elsewhere, they were undoubtedly supplied in a manner similar to Andrew Melrose's trade customers and to Elin Godsalve in the early eighteenth century. Perhaps not all small shopkeepers paid as promptly, but a grocer stood to lose very little on such transactions if he insisted on receiving payment before further purchases were allowed. And with such petty tradesmen, a grocer could easily afford to do so. He faced greater financial hazards with the larger shops whose business he might court and who demanded credit in exchange for their trade. At the same time, the number of back-street shops had been increasing throughout the eighteenth century. Indeed, it would be surprising if they had not. Such shops required little capital and few commercial or technical skills. Nor was apprenticeship necessary. The goods Mrs Taylor bought were processed and ready to be weighed off to her customers. What was necessary was an effective demand of which there was no lack as increasing numbers of the labouring poor joined the ranks of wage workers. The tea, sugar, cheese, butter, soap, and candles that feature in the accounts of Melrose's small tradesmen were staple items in the worker's shopping basket. Of these items, the two most important commodities for the small urban back-street shopkeeper were tea and sugar.

The Melrose Day Book delineates the business relations and practices of a principal tradesman to petty shopkeepers. The account book of William Wood of Didsbury, on the other hand, displays a petty grocer's dealings with customers. While there is no record of how Wood settled accounts with his suppliers or how frequently he renewed stock, the ledger does record the daily purchases of credit customers along with the time and form of payment.[26] Most accounts open with a debit balance in 1785 and run to 1789. A few "sundry odd debtors" dating back to 1763 are listed as well as various other accounts for the inn or for ploughing. During the early years each item purchased by a customer is listed; but by 1788–9, as Wood was reaching the end of his life, only the total daily amount is entered, "bill out of shop" or "goods out of window."

Wood had at least thirty credit customers whose monthly purchases for shop goods ranged from 5s. to £1 10s. His annual sales
totalled roughly £300.[27] At least seven of his shop customers also
bought coal. In 1786 he was charging 7s. for twelve "loads" of coal
and 7s. for "drawing" plus a few pennies for the men's ale. Wood's
shop does not seem to have attracted the leading families of Didsbury. For example, "John Broome, Esq.," "James Broome, Esq.," and
"William Broom, Esq." bought their coal from Wood, ran up bills at
the inn for ale, brandy, wine, and other liquors, and had some
ploughing done; but no shop goods were charged to their accounts.
The same is true for "Mr. William Boardman," "Mr. Lawrence
Walker," and "Mr. Garnet." Wood's shop customers were drawn
from the more humble village folks. "Ould William Chase" was a
regular customer with an average monthly bill of 15s. and "William
Chase, young man" continued the family tradition. The Bancrofts,
William and Ann, both had regular accounts. Ann paid off part of
her bill by "spreading mole hills" at 1s. 2d. a day. Robert Blomily's
monthly account ran as high as £1 10s. but he or his namesake was
not above working in Wood's garden for 1s. 6d. a day. The same
was true of George Fletcher. Joshua Barlow's account was credited
for day work done by his son. Thomas and William Birch were both
shoemakers, the latter less well established. His daughter and wife
hayed to pay off their debt to Wood. Three members of the Cash
family had accounts with Wood; none appeared particularly affluent. The monthly bill for William Cash, "auld man," averaged 10s.;
purchases never rose to the level of meat or other delicacies. James
Walker was identified as a gardiner. Betty Walker was the mother-
in-law of James Mason, another of Wood's customers. In 1793 Betty
was working as menial servant for the son of William, Thomas Wood,
who ran the Ring O'Bello Inn after his father's death. One may
conclude that Wood's shop customers formed a cross-section of the
village population, ranging from Thomas Birch, an enterprising
shoemaker, to common labourers.

The small village shop of Didsbury would have received the approval of Adam Smith. Wood's customers did purchase their "subsistence from day to day or even from hour to hour."[28] They were
in the shop three or four times a week, sometimes more frequently
and occasionally twice a day. The shop was open seven days a week
– apparently there were no Sabbatarian restrictions. The wife was
the major shopper, but the husband and other members of the family
or even a neighbour were also sent for provisions, their names or
relationship carefully recorded by Wood. Most items were purchased
in small quantities, sufficient to last a few days. Thus, on 3 January

1787, "Matha," the wife of "ould William Chase," bought one pound of treacle. Later in the day she returned for currants and a clove pepper, three pennies worth. On the fourth she bought treacle, flour, berm, and paid for baking. The next day she had a manchet (a small loaf of wheaten bread)[29]; the following day her "son fetched" a manchet and she came in later for tea and sugar, 5.5 pennies worth. On the seventh, "Matha bought sugar, coffee, and bread for 8d. On the ninth, she had treacle and sugar, 7d., and later bought salt and a manchet. Two days later she was buying flour and treacle again. The following day she made a major purchase – almost 6 pounds of cheese for 2s. 4d. But the very next day William was back in the shop for 1.5 pounds of treacle. It is a typical segment of the account. Cheese was the one item purchased in large quantities. "Matha" bought anywhere from 3 to 11.5 pounds at a time, roughly a little under once a month. Most of the customers did the same, although Ann Bancroft even bought her cheese in small quantities at more frequent intervals. She was apparently a spinster or widow.

The items featured most prominently in the accounts were flour, meal, manchets, cheese, candles, treacle, sugar, salt, and soap. Coffee rarely appears. Almost all the customers purchased a little tea occasionally, but in very small quantities – an ounce or half an ounce at a time. Only two customers bought it regularly, usually a quarter of a pound at a time. Tea was not, apparently, a daily part of the diet of most of Wood's customers in the 1780s. Of the two sweeteners, treacle was somewhat more popular than sugar, particularly among the older inhabitants, although both were consumed in large quantities. For example, during the week of 17 February 1786, the account of "William Cash, auld man," was debited for 6 pounds of treacle and 1 pound of sugar. The quantities are not unusual. If tea was purchased, it was usually accompanied by sugar – a typical combination was an ounce or one-half an ounce of tea and one-half a pound of sugar. Large quantities of cereals were used by families that baked. In the winter, the family of Thomas Birch appears to have relied primarily on meal. From 15 January to 13 April 1786, the account was debited for 160 pounds of meal but only 42 pounds of flour.[30] In the summer, the family switched to flour. During the months of June, July, August there were no debits for meal but 81 pounds of blue-stone flour and 66 pounds of barley flour were purchased. By mid-October, meal reappears in the account. Manchets and bread were bought only occasionally by the Birch family, but Wood sold a considerable quantity of both during the course of a week. Customers bought substantial amounts of salt, and constantly replenished their supply – one wonders at the large quantities. As purchases were not seasonal, the salt could not have been used primarily for preserving. And their diet, as indicated by the accounts, would not seem to require the use of salt to any great extent. Most families purchased their candles in small quantities at frequent intervals; soap, less frequently, two to four times a month. Very little starch or blue was used but sand was a regular item. Potatoes, peas, plums, and apples were purchased rarely. Only a few customers bought an occasional egg. Wood did sell a little ale and spiritous liquours to almost all the customers but hardly sufficient to have been a regular source of supply.

Only three families bought fresh meat from Wood, and the amounts were not insignificant. During the month of July, the account of Robert Blomily was debited for 12.3 pounds of veal and 7 pounds of lamb; in August, 16 pounds of beef and 3 pounds of lamb. Wood certainly did not keep a stock of meat on hand for such few customers. Perhaps he received specific orders before getting the meat from the butcher. In several of the customers' accounts, Wood has entered: "paid boucher for beef," or "paid for beef." Whether or not he made a slight profit on the transaction is impossible to determine. It is not improbable that he was providing a cost-free service to good customers. During the summer of 1787 he was charging 4d. a pound for veal, 4.5d. for pork and beef, and 5d. for lamb. Wood sold bacon, however, to many customers, generally in small quantities, rarely a pound at a time. The small quantities purchased by Wood's customers seem to indicate that his shop was not their major source of supply.

Over half the customers purchased butter. Either they used far less than is commonly supposed, or they were getting a regular supply elsewhere, perhaps from the shoemaker. Wood obtained at least part of his supply of butter from Thomas Birch, the shoemaker. During the months of August, September, and October 1786, Birch's account was credited for seventy-three pounds of butter. The cost to Wood ranged from 9.5d. to 10d. per pound in September and October.

One of the major criticisms levelled at village shops was the high prices they charged. In his butter transactions, Wood was certainly not guilty of this charge. Indeed, unless he was obtaining a much cheaper supply elsewhere, Wood was not covering his overhead costs. On 12 September 1786, the wife of William Chase, young man, bought one-half pound of butter for 5d., the same price credited to Thomas Birch's account at that date. Other entries reveal a similar correspondence, with prices rising in the winter months. By 1788 Wood was charging only 8d. a pound. Nor can Wood be accused of varying his prices from customer to customer. Apparently, haggling was not common in his shop. His accounts do, however, reveal market changes. His prices for cereals and sugar have been tabulated from November 1785 to December 1788. Until the latter part of October 1786, raw sugar was 6d. a pound; it then rose to 7d. and remained at that level.[31] During the early period he charged 8d. for three pounds of treacle, but 2.75d. for one pound. By November 1786 treacle had gone up to 10d. and 3.5d. respectively, dropping to 8.5d. and 3d. in October 1787. Cereal prices reveal a somewhat similar pattern. Until the latter part of October 1787, he charged his customers 1.66d. per pound for "blue stone flour." It then rose to 1.75d. a pound. Meal was 1.45d. a pound, rising slithtly to 1.5d. in February 1788. There are too few entries for barley flour after February 1787 to note changes – until that time it was 1.25d. a pound. Treacle appears to be the only item for which Wood allowed a discount for quantity.

In settling their accounts almost all customers left a debit balance, and paid in round figures. For example, on 1 April 1786, Ann Hadkinson had a debit balance of £1 8s. 6.5d. On that day a credit for £1 1s. was entered in her account. By 5 May she had run up a bill of £1 7s. 4d., that was reduced by payment of £1 1s. On 30 May, she was again credited for £1 1s., leaving a debit balance of 11d., and so it continued until 2 September, when she paid Wood 16s. 6d. Indeed, the guinea payment was a very common occurrence, followed by 10s. 6d. It was very rare for a customer to pay the odd pennies, half-pennies, and farthings, or even odd shillings. Wood usually received the money from the wife. Payments varied from once every several weeks to once in several months, rarely longer. If a large debit balance was accumulating, purchases tended to decline. Perhaps Wood restricted the amount of credit extended. For example, on 12 February 1787 the debit balance of James Cash was £3 2s. 1.5d.; on that day Wood "received of Peggy" £1 1s. By 13 March the debit balance had crept up to £3 4s. 10.5d. From then until 15 May, goods purchased amounted to only 12s. 1.25d. for a total debit of £3 16s. 11.75d. Wood then received in payment £2 12s. 6d. On 17 June "Peggy" having bought a few articles, made another payment of £1 1s. bringing the debit balance down to 7s. 3.75d. Although Wood was rather careless and irregular in totalling the accounts, often waiting until a payment was made, he apparently kept a weather eye on customers whose credit was shaky. Indeed, when the accounts were settled after Wood's death, very few bad debts were found.

Given the shortage of coins in the eighteenth century, one may well wonder if either customers or shopkeepers could have settled daily accounts in cash. For example, debits to John Hampson were as follows: 5 March 1786, sugar, manchets, treacle – 9.5d.; 7 March, soap, starch, and sugar – 6.75d.; 8 March, sugar, manchets – 8.5d.; 13 March, soap, salt, pepper – 6.75d.; 17 March, candles, soap – 4.75d. This is not an exceptional account. From 21 June to 29 June 1787, the account of "William Cash junior" was charged with 5.5d., 2d., 1s. 6.75d., 1s. 5.5d., 4.5d., 2d., and 5.5d. Even if Cash had been able to lay down sixpence or a shilling on the day of purchase, it is doubtful that Wood would have had sufficient copper coins to have given the proper change. He was certainly not receiving any from his credit customers. Few eighteenth-century village shops would have been viable had credit not been extended to customers. "Ready-money" purchases had to await a greater abundance of circulating coins and prompt payment of the labourers' weekly wages.

Although William Wood's spelling and writing were so poor that it is often difficult to decipher, his arithmetic was good. There are very few errors in extension or addition, and what appear as such may well be due to the illegible figures. For most customers, Wood merely kept a running account of purchases and payments. He was, however, aware of more formal methods. Thomas Birch was given a debit and credit or "contra" account. In fact, Wood was usually indebted to Birch when reckoning time came.

Wood stocked a fairly extensive range of groceries and in that respect his ship was several rungs above that of Mrs Taylor; but it was basically a small neighbourhood shop. He carried no drapery or haberdashery, or ironmongery, not even pots, or patent medicines and drysaltery. The commodities most prominently featured in the accounts were flour, meal, treacle, sugar, cheese, candles, manchets, bread, butter, salt, and soap, roughly in that order. It was, in short, a village grocery shop catering almost exclusively to the labourers. Without a regular demand from the agricultural or urban workers for the above items, such shops could not have functioned. They did not attract the custom of the more important members of the community. In places where such groceries were not in general use by the common folk, only the general shop could survive. This is most clearly demonstrated by the trade of "Roberts" at Penmorfa.

Penmorfa was a tiny village on the slope of the hills above Tremadoc in Caernarvonshire. The nearest market towns were Pwllheli and Caernarvon, about fifteen to twenty miles away. Robert's shop was in truth a general shop and carried a very wide range of goods – all sorts of ironmongery, drysaltery, draperies, haberdashery, medicines, as well as groceries. The index of the ledger lists over 200 customers who came from places as far away as Ffestiniog, Garn, Glynnog, Nantcall, and Wern, to name a few which are easily deciphered.[32] One or two entries date from 1788 but most accounts commence in 1792, carrying balances from previous ledgers, and were transferred to Ledger D at the end of the century. The shop, one may assume, had been in Penmorfa several decades. Entries were sometimes posted from daybooks or from a "scrap of paper." Roberts also served as collector of the "round" tax and medium of exchange for bills, charging usually 1.5d. and occasionally 2.5d. There is no indication that any of his customers paid by bills.

The shop was no corner store, even fortnightly shopping was rare. During the heart of winter, few people seem to have made their way to Penmorfa. Most of the goods purchased were semidurable, such as, breeches, waistcoats, petticoats, hats, handkerchiefs, and worsted, cottons, dawlas, fustians, silks, and ribbons among wearing apparel; or nails, screws, hinges, locks, hoops, and vessels; or materials for industrial or agricultural purposes, such as, indigo, logwood, redwood, copperas, sumach, pitch, oil, sulphur, alum, and various drugs for ailing "beasts." All these articles formed the solid base of Robert's trade, and were essential to the people who crossed the hills to his shop. Groceries, on the other hand, appear to have been a luxury in Caernarvonshire and Merionthshire in the late eighteenth century, at least among his customers. In fact, he carried a very meagre stock that moved slowly — tea, coffee, sugar, spanish juice, pepper, mustard, cloves, ginger, raisins, and currants, along with soap, starch, blue, and candles. Not surprisingly, he sold no flour, meal, cheese, or butter. More surprising is the absence of treacle and salt, although he did sell a little medicinal "salts." Hardly any candles and very little soap were charged to the accounts. Tea and sugar were only slightly more frequent. During 1793, some twenty-odd customers were charged for tea. Of these, only three or four were regular tea drinkers. Mrs Anwyl, given the honorific title of "Mrs." was quite exceptional. From May to September, she bought a little less than three pounds of tea of a cost of 14s. and two pounds of sugar. Her closest rivals were "Owen Thomas Candllyn" and "Jane late Wern."Owen Thomas's expenditure for tea was not heavy but regular. The amount debited was always 9d. for green tea, a practice continued in 1794. From September through December 1793, he spent a total of 3s. 9d. for ten ounces. Jane bought bohea, usually an ounce or two at a time, although on 18 March 1793 she got four ounces. Her bill from March to August for nine ounces was 2s. 6.5d., but she spent only 4.5d. for sugar, no more than half a pound. Another regular purchaser was Margaret Pritchard. From 4 October 1792 to 7 October 1793, she spent 5s. 3d. for tea and 1s. 8.5d. for sugar, that is, a little over one pound of tea and two pounds of sugar during the year. Her total bill that year was £1 8s. 1.5d. Margaret was a rather unusual customer who shopped frequently, often once a week. Perhaps she lived nearby. Nonetheless, she bought no candles and soap only three times. On 4 October 1792, the account was debited 5d. for soap; in July 1793, 2.5d. and 2d.

Women were apparently the major purchasers and imbibers of tea. Of the small number of accounts in the name of women, almost all are charged with tea. More revealing is the element of deception that appears in the accounts for both tea and sugar. For example, the account of "Owen Thomas Cyfmach ucha" was charged for alum, indigo, logwood, linen, and thread, but the cost of the sugar was not extended to the debit column and the shopkeeper appended a special note – "sugar nor to tell 2.5d." Elias Griffiths, no mean spender, ran up a bill of 13s. 1d. from 27 October to 27 November 1792. Among the various items listed were "goods nor to tell 13.5d.," "unp[aid] for sugar 1.5d.," "Bohea nor to tell 7d.," and "unp[aid] for sugar 1.5d." On 4 May 1793, an entry for "tea 1s. 3d. nor to tell" is not extended and later crossed out. Presumably Mrs Griffiths came in and paid for it. Many other accounts have similar entries, with the shopkeeper noting only "unp" 1.5d. or 3.5d. "Evan Jones Tymawr" may even have objected to buying soap. From 6 August to 15 December he ran up a bill of £1 6s. 10d. for hops, hinges, screws, nails, handles, "drugs for beasts," tobacco, buckram, buttons, thread, linseed oil, and other such goods. However, a note is entered on 12 November, "unp for soap ... 1d." No other charge was made for soap in the account. Was Mrs Jones buying soap surreptitiously and trying to hide the fact from her husband? Wives, and sometimes husbands, also disguised the cost of such highly desirable articles as handkerchiefs and hats. For example, in the account of "Harry Evans Tyddyesfelis" is an entry "handkerchief wife nor to tell." It cost 1s. 2d. but was later crossed out and not included in the bill. Later, 13 November 1792, the shopkeeper noted "hat if not down before ... 4s." Next year in March a hat for 7s. 6d. was entered but not extended to the debit account. On 25 September, we find "paid for hat per wife 7s. 6d." Mrs "William Evans Wern" also appears to have deceived her husband. On 15 August 1793, the shopkeeper entered "hat 11s. 6d. to tell 8s.," which was, in fact, the amount extended. Later that year there is a note "hat due 3s. 6d. unp nor to tell ... paid per Mary."[33] The 3s. 6d. was never included in the bill presented to William Evans.

It is, therefore, possible that the accounts for tea and sugar understate the actual quantities purchased. But they reveal something more important: in the rural areas of North Wales in the late eigh-

teenth century, some men objected not only to their wi͟
tea, but also to using sugar. The former aversion is w͟
Cobbett, as so often, was spokesman for his fellow c͟
There is, however, little evidence on the attitude tow͟
Perhaps the farmers of Caernarvonshire and Merionthsnire were
unusual. But typical or not of isolated rural areas, such attitudes
would certainly have acted as a deterrent to the sale of tea. They
also help explain the particularly low density of shops in Wales.
There, only the general shop could have functioned; and it required
a fairly heavy capital investment compared to back-street shops in
the towns and cities, or petty grocery shops in the villages. The
general shop not only had to carry a more extensive range of goods
and therefore a larger stock, but the rhythm of its trade was also
sluggish. Melrose's small shopkeepers renewed their stock weekly;
the daily shopping habits of Wood's customers would have enabled
him to do the same. He was, moreover, receiving a return on his
capital far quicker than Roberts. At Penmorfa, customers generally
paid at the most twice a year, usually in the fall and spring. Rarely
were the bills fully settled. Much of Robert's stock moved no faster.
It is, therefore, not surprising that the excise collection of North
Wales in 1795 had a high ratio – 253 – of people to tea licences. But
in the late eighteenth century, such areas were the exception, the
backwaters of the shopkeeping world. Elsewhere the rhythm of trade
had not only quickened but also given rise to many innovative practices.

Although petty shops have left few records, they served an important function in the distributive trade, particularly in areas with
a sizeable wage-earning population. In addition to providing a source
of income for the more enterprising worker or his wife, such shops
complemented the services performed by the principal grocers. Both
were necessary in easing the movement of goods to the final consumers. To the grocer fell the task of acquiring the goods. Melrose's
suppliers included importers, wholesalers, producers, manufacturers, agents, and grocers. They were scattered all over the kingdom
and beyond and numbered over sixty for the years 1815–20. Only
a well-trained grocer who knew the sources of supply and had already established a widespread correspondence during his years of
apprenticeship could successfully organize an undertaking that required knowledge, capital, and a creditworthy reputation in the business community.[34] And to prepare the goods for sale, considerable
skill was necessary in processing, sorting, and blending. All these
were tasks the petty shopkeeper was not trained to undertake. He
could only act through the grocer. His role was, nevertheless, an

essential adjunct to the grocer's. By carting the bulky goods from the centre to the byways and outskirts of the town or to nearby villages, he made groceries easily available to the humble folk – to those who purchased their "subsistence from day to day or even from hour to hour."[35] These were the people whose custom was not particularly welcomed in the elegant shop of a high-class grocer nor for that matter easily handled by those accustomed to serving more affluent customers. But an enterprising grocer was eager to extend his sales. The Taylors and Grieves were the means by which he could indirectly supply an ever-widening circle of customers. Their trade was no mean addition to a grocer's business. Together, Taylor and Grieve annually purchased almost £400 worth of groceries almost on a ready-money basis. They, in turn, supplied the daily needs of customers who may well have found it both inconvenient and arduous to have made their way to a principal grocer for half an ounce of tea or a quarter pound of sugar.

While the general pattern of business relations between principal grocers and petty shopkeepers may have changed little during the eighteenth century, the number of such relationships and the quantity of goods moved thereby undoubtedly increased. But change there was in other sectors of the retail trade. How shopkeepers adapted to changes in their economic environment will be explored in the following chapters.

CHAPTER TWELVE

Changes in Marketing and Sales Techniques

Marketing and sales techniques of shopkeepers are dependent upon the technological, economic, and social milieu. The large plate glass windows and brilliant gas lighting so frequently offered as evidence of the new entrepreneurial attitudes and skills of midnineteenth-century shopkeepers were, of course, not available to their predecessors. But the absence of these attractions hardly warrants the assumption that eighteenth-century shops "existed solely to fulfill customers wants" and were not "designed and planned to attract customers and create wants."[1] Defoe would have been delighted to learn that shopkeepers had taken his advice and discontinued a practice he condemned as unnecessarily expensive. He strongly objected to the new tendency of attracting customers by expending large sums to decorate shops with fine glass windows. His particular dislike was that these highly decorated shops were catering to new luxury tastes. He spoke disdainfully of the proprietors and their shops: the periwig makers, cane chairmakers, guilders of leather, braziers, toy shops, looking-glass shops, china shops, coffee houses, and so forth. After describing the decorations of a pastry cook's shop, with its brilliantly lighted interior, he concluded that such extravagant expenditure "will hardly be believed in ages to come, when our posterity shall be grown wiser ... at our expense."[2] He was apparently right – it has not been believed – but he was wrong about posterity. Defoe estimated the cost of fitting out a brazier's shop as over £500; the pastry cook's £300. Little reliance can be placed on the figures. They do, however, indicate what Defoe considered extravagant expenditure. In the 1820s, two London confectioners situated in the West End valued their fixtures at £755 and £422 respectively.[3] Despite Defoe's stern warning, expenditure on displaying goods to attract customers continued. In 1728, a Frenchman found shop windows in London a most attractive sight. He observed: "What we do not on the whole have in France is glass like this, generally very fine and very clear. The shops were surrounded with it and usually the merchandise is arranged behind it, which keeps the dust off, while still displaying the goods to passers-by, presenting a fine sight from every direction." In the mideighteenth century, the London cabinetmakers shop might be "so richly set out that it looked like a palace."[4]

Defoe, given to hyperbole, was contrasting the new-fangled decorations with the old-fashioned furnishing that gave the shop an appearance of a warehouse rather than a place to set out goods for display. In his day, the highly decorated shop was probably confined to London, and only later copied by shops in major provincial centres. Nor should it be forgotten that shopkeepers were very particular about the site of their shops. One has only to observe how shops followed in the wake of the westward movement of the more exclusive residential areas in London, suggestive of modern ecological developments in urban areas.

The business correspondence and records of eighteenth-century shopkeepers are unfortunately very scarce and provide little information on sales techniques. Nonetheless, available sources still provide firm evidence on parts of the subject. On methods adopted to promote sales, newspaper advertisements are almost the only available source. But the use of newspaper advertisements also creates several problems. The first is the sheer magnitude of the task. It would require a host of searchers to cover all the newspapers published, often ephemerally, in various parts of the country. And would the resulting information justify expending so much time and energy? But if reliance is placed on a few, can they be accepted as representative of the country at large? It is doubtful. There were certainly regional differences. Places distant from the major areas of commercial and industrial activity, places where shops were thin on the ground, would cling to the old and trusted traditional methods, particularly as their market was restricted. Moreover, it is precisely such areas that are least represented by newspapers and, therefore, least subject to the winds of change. Newspapers, then as now, depended largely on advertising revenue. It was, one might say, a vicious circle which could be broken only by the rise of industrial and commercial activities. And there is a more crucial question. How reliable are advertisements? At the least, they indicate how the shopkeeper tried to attract custom, even if he did not always fulfill his announced intention. Whether he should be cast out of the group of "established" shopkeepers because his behaviour does not accord with received opinion must be left to the judgment of the reader.

The practice of haggling over price, it has been said, was common in practically all retail sales. "Very few retailers ever clearly and openly marked the price of their goods or expected the customer to pay promptly and without question the price first demanded."[5] Such a statement projects an air of unreality: it ignores how some of the so-called established shopkeepers conducted their trade and assumes all sales to have been on a face-to-face basis over the counter. In fact, a considerable portion of the trade, particularly groceries, liquor, and other daily household goods, was transacted by correspondence or servants, as household accounts show. Among the Stowe Papers are many bills remitted by London grocers and other tradesmen for goods shipped to the various houses maintained by the Marquis of Buckingham. For example, William Winter, a grocer at 148 Borough High Street, regularly supplied Wotton House with groceries for the account of the "Most Noble Marquis of Buckingham." The bills are particularly interesting as they give evidence of the types of goods handled. William Winter was a high-class grocer, but he carried a wide variety of household goods in addition to the usual teas, coffees, sugar, spices, and dried fruits. Besides groceries, he sent to Wotton ham, chine, cheese, wine, French brandy, rum, tobacco, pipes, candles, Fullers Earth, soap, blue, "sash line," mops, kitchen scouring paper, black lead, "flannal," silver sand, "Harts Horn Shaving," pack thread, lamp oil, yarn, and once "12 Seets Nitin Needles."[6] Haggling certainly did not enter into the transactions of the Noble Lord with William Winter.

The records of the Dunham estate near Altingham, the seat of the Earl of Stamford, do not include bills. But many of the groceries and other articles undoubtedly came from London. The housekeeping book records that from 1808 their tea came from the Twinings. They were good customers – in the 1790s their annual purchase of tea ranged from eighty-five to ninety-five pounds.[7] The Twining records show that the firm sent tea to many country homes – and, the prices were known. In 1739 Francis Cust, a student at King's College, Cambridge, wrote to his brother: "Concerning that I at present labour under a scarcity of tea, and that it is bought much cheaper and better at London than here, I make recourse to you and would be obliged to you if you would send me a pound of Green and half a pound of Bohea, bought of Mr. Twining at 16s. a pound, which I will repay."[8]

Ordering by post became a common custom. The bishop of Exeter appended a note to a friendly letter to the Twinings: "P.S. Mrs.

Fisher wishes to be supplied with tea. Is it your custom to send out – or must we send for it from time to time? She wishes two pounds of 8s. green tea in a canister and a proportionable quantity or perhaps smaller of coffee."[9] Indeed, such country orders formed a very considerable portion of the trade of the principal London shopkeepers. London was a lodestar that attracted the fashionable world at the expense of provincial shopkeepers. David Pugh and Company, "Grocers and Tea Dealers" of London, shipped to Scotland for Sir Robert Menzies a large order including tea, dried fruit, nuts, spices, and hops amounting to over £65. They informed him:

Agreeable to your favour at 16 Inst., we have sent the goods as per annexed invoice ... ; they are charged at ready money prices and we make no doubt that you will send us a remittance for amount in a short time.

Hops are an article not in our line; but we have bought them at one of the most respectable houses in the City, and we trust they will turn out to your satisfaction.

The *dessert* Raisins we have on hand at this time are not so fine as we could wish, therefore, we have sent but half the quantity ordered.[10]

The firm took care of the shipping and also, as can be seen, shopped for him. One wonders if this was a customary practice. The goods were sent to Hawleys Wharf for *Lord Duncan Alex Ross* per Perth and addressed "to the care of Mr. T.R. Robertson Perth." The cartage, wharfage, and shipping cost four shillings. The parcel was no light bundle. In addition to sixty-six pounds of tea, it included four hundredweight of sugar, fourteen loaves, and over a hundredweight of hops, besides the dried fruits, nuts, spices, and rice. Davison Newman and Company received orders by letter even from London residents.[11]

The same practice occurred lower down the social scale. Charlotte Sheyd wrote to Walthal Fenton informing him that "Mr. W. Sheyd means to have both the waistcoats that was wrote for, but as he has no pattern to send, he leaves it to Mr. Fenton to order a light Hone colour and as it must be done as soon as possible does not think it worth while to send for patterns." She wrote later: "Mr. Sheyd desires Mr. Fenton will send for two pair of breeches ye same as the pattern, to come by the coach. If Mr. Fenton sends for six pair, Mr. Sheyd is sure they will not lay long on hand. Mr. Fenton is desired to send tonight."[12] Did Miss Sheyd haggle over price? One doubts it. Fenton may have had to wait some time, as did Winter, for his subsequent bill to be settled; but it was probably all handled in the most gentlemanly manner.

Rev. Thomas Laurie of Newburn, Fifeshire, puchased a few groceries from nearby Largo and Colinsburg, but his major supply came from Edinburgh and Leith.[13] The small country shop could rarely attract the carriage trade – one of its perennial problems. Few of Wood's credit customers were drawn from the more substantial residents. They probably got their supplies from Manchester or even from London. Indeed, Rev. Laurie may himself have tried the London shops. There is one rather mysterious entry – "Mrs Dewar of Gilston for tea commissioned by her from Catheral and Butcher at 92 Pall Mall, £5 8s." As he purchased very little elsewhere that year, it would appear that Mrs Dewar ordered it for him from the well-known London grocers and tea dealers, Catheral and Butcher.[14] The firm also supplied the Marquis of Buckingham.

Advertisements by provincial and London shops show that retail customers as well as shopkeepers were encouraged to order by post or carrier. A typical advertisement reads: "All orders from Gentlemen and tradesmen in the country will be punctually observed."[15] Haggling by post or carrier for goods received and billed is rather inconceivable, although complaints were undoubtedly made about quality. Moreover, there is indirect evidence that in the sale of tea, at least, grocers kept on their shelves canisters with prices well known to their customers. Shopkeepers ordered from their suppliers tea for their six-shilling, eight-shilling, or ten-shilling canisters. And, as in the case of Mr Mills of Colchester, customers chose their tea by quality and price.

"Open advertisement," it has been claimed, "was frowned upon by all established tradesmen," and not adopted until the midnineteenth century. Even handbills were not allowed; they had to await the "late Victorian period."[16] Josiah Wedgwood, it appears, need not have feared that the use of handbills in 1772 would have placed his showroom on the same footing as "common shopkeepers." Indeed, trade cards, the forerunners of the more detailed handbills, were used extensively by shopkeepers throughout the eighteenth century. Often decorated by an elaborate engraving depicting the particular trade, they gave the name and address of the tradesman and the goods he dealt in, sometimes in great detail. Even early in the century many claimed to sell "at ye lowest prices," or "at reasonable rates." Ca. 1760, Samuel Forsaith informed "noblemen, gentlemen and others" that they "may depend on being dealt with for a very moderate profit and the lowest prices fixed without abatement and the goods warranted as neat and substantial as any in London."[17] Surely, trade cards should be considered a form of advertising, a means of reaching a wider range of customers than was possible by word-of-mouth. Large-scale advertisements, it is true, had to wait for a more extensive publication and distribution of newspapers than were available in the early part of the century. But, as will be shown, shopkeepers were not slow in using those available, despite the heavy tax imposed on newspaper advertisements.

Moreover, trade cards, handbills, and newspaper notices are not the only method of calling the attention of the public to one's shop. That was done most elegantly in the eighteenth century by the use of beautifully gilded and painted signs, for which the artists were well paid. Thomas Twining, founder of the tea firm, chose a Golden Lyon as the sign of his coffeehouse. Engraved Golden Lyons in various postures subsequently appeared on bill heads and decorative wrappers. A wrapper dating back to the 1730s featured a lion rampant. Under this was printed in Roman lettering: "Thomas & Daniel Twining, At the Golden Lyon in Devereux-Court, near the Temple, sell all sorts of fine Teas, Coffee, Chocolate, Cocoa-nuts, Sago, and Snuff: Also true German Spaw, Pyrmont, Bath and Bristol Waters, Arrack, Brandy, &c." A billhead of 1737, printed in Gothic and cursive type, featured a more graceful lion.[18] An intriguing note was printed on a 1757 billhead informing customers: "A more Commodious Way is opened from the Strand through Palfgrave's head Court."[19]

The billheads, wrappers, and circulars were designed to make the name of Twining at the Golden Lyon known to a wide circle. That the firm also aimed to associate the name with high quality goods and good service is axiomatic. The life-blood of any business depends to a large extent upon its "reputation and skill." To describe the eighteenth- and early nineteenth-century shopkeeper as one who "relied upon his reputation and skill to attract his custom" is to beg the question.[20] What we want to know is how he went about acquiring that reputation. Skill must be known to yield rewards, as Josiah Wedgwood well understood. "Fashion," he wrote, "is infinitely superior to merit in many respects." To establish his name as first potter, he assiduously sought the patronage of the leaders of fashion: "the monarchy, the nobility and the art connoisseurs."[21] He did so by accepting uneconomical commissions for special individual sets of china, by cultivating the friendship and sponsorship of important persons through flattery and other subtle means, and by establishing in London an elegant showroom to display his china. Above all, he advertised: his wares, his showroom, his royal patronage, his aristocratic support, his agents, his trademark.[22] His was indeed a wide-ranging sales campaign and in its entirety was hardly matched by any one retailer. But the various techniques he adopted were not novel. Was not the Golden Lyon of Tom Twining but the trademark of his tea shop? Did he not advertise that mark on his wrapping paper, on his billheads, and correspondence? Even notices of his coffeehouse appeared in newspapers.[23] Did he not cultivate in his coffeehouse the friendship and sponsorship of the great, probably in the same fashion as the famed Josiah – by flattery, by special service, and by allowing long credit to his noble patrons? And when he established the family residence in 1720, he chose an area fitting to his position as purveyor to the great – Twickenham. In 1695 Princess Ann had lived in a mansion opposite his house; in 1715 Pope purchased a house there.[24]

It is highly unlikely that Tom Twining advertised his wares in the newspapers but that is hardly surprising. In the early eighteenth century, advertising in newspapers would have borne little fruit. A notice, however, may have appeared announcing the opening of the coffeehouse and later the tea shop. In 1756, one of Daniel Twining's former employees placed the following notice in the *Whitehall Evening Post*: "Thomas Fletcher, upwards of Twenty six years shopman to the late and present Mr. Twining, begs leave to acquaint his friends and the Public, that he has open'd his shop, The Grasshopper, near Essex Street, Temple Bar, sells all sorts of fine Teas, Coffee, Chocolate, etc., at the most reasonable prices."[25] Mr Fletcher apparently anticipated some reflected glory from having served as shopman to the Twinings, as did Mr Mills who a decade later announced: "John Mills, Tea Dealer, from Messrs. Twining's in London, proposed to open next week a Tea Warehouse at the Golden Lion, opposite the Exchange in the High Street, Colchester, where those who will favour him with their custom may depend on being served with tea, coffee and chocolate as good and upon as reasonable terms as in London."[26] Mr Mills, a relative by marriage, even borrowed the Twining trademark. He purchased his stock, as we have seen, from the Twinings so it was "as good" as that of London dealers. Whether prices were "as reasonable," we cannot know. What is clear is that the Twinings of the Golden Lyon were by then well known, and the name had advertising value for aspiring shopkeepers. One wonders if the "Misses B" and the firm's other trade customers featured Twining's teas.

In 1784, Richard Twining served as spirited defender of the reputation of fair-trade tea dealers and in rapid succession authored three books.[27] It is not suggested that he did it as an advertising ploy. He and other principal dealers were genuinely disturbed by the aspersions cast on their fair names and responded quickly and vociferously with books, pamphlets, unsolicited articles, and letters to the newspapers as well as with "open" advertisements.[28] Mr Bourdillon at "No. 10 Piccadilly" headed a long advertisement proudly displaying his royal patronage: "Grocer to His Majesty and Teaman."[29] An advertising campaign of this order would not have been feasible in the early eighteenth century; both the means and the demand were inadequate. As long as consumption is confined largely to the upper reaches of society, sales techniques tend to reflect the genteel character of the trade. More aggressive methods require a larger and broader range of customers. This can be seen in the much neglected trade of proprietory or patent medicines, the sale and distribution of which matches any of the lauded methods attributed to the Victorians.

The proprietors of patent medicine advertised their products in the London and provincial newspapers. They stated the prices of the products; they packaged and branded their wares; they listed the names of the shopkeepers from whom the medicine could be purchased, where they resided, and often their particular shop trade. They supplied shops with elaborately designed handbills featuring the name and address of the shopkeeper, the various virtues of the medicine, and sanctified the product and the trademark with the "King's Royal Patent." For example, the broadsheet of "Jackson and Co's Great Original Wholesale Daffy's ELIXIR Warehouse" noted it had just sent "a FRESH PARCEL ... to be sold by" their appointed agent "Mr. Ashburnar, Bookseller and Stationer in Kendal, Wholesale and Retail, and by no other Person in this Town." After numerous affidavits, often naming the shop from which it was purchased, seventeen other preparations sold by Jackson were listed, "Dr. Anderson's ... True Scots Pills ... Hungary and Lavender Water ... Bathing Spirits ... Jackson's only true British Powder for the TEETH and GUMS." "All" it was stated, "under Sanction of the King's Royal Patent, under the Great Seal of Great Britain." Daffy's Elixir was a popular item with Abraham Dent's customers.[30] Such products had an extensive market both geographically and among all social goups, one that enabled the producers to evolve novel methods of distribution and to engage in widespread advertising specifically designed for particular areas. An advertisement for Dr Daffy's Elixir appearing in the *Leeds Mercury* in 1751 was apparently aimed at the Yorkshire trade. Of the twenty towns listed as selling the elixir, eighteen were in Yorkshire; the other two, across the border in Lancashire: Rochdale and Rosendale. The towns were scattered over a wide area, extending from Scarborough and Richmond in the north to Hull and Beverley in the southeast, Doncaster and Sheffield in the south and on up to Rosendale in the west.[31] Not all places were large towns; a few, such as Penniston, Brighouse, and Elland, did not even have a market. Several trades were represented – booksellers, Mr Lord of Wakefield, for example, a "Postmaster," a number identified simply as shopkeepers, and a merchant, Mr Bland of Scarborough. Even "high class" grocers, it would seem, were not averse to allowing their names to be featured. "Askwith and Seaton" of Pontefract were identified as "grocers." Was the list of names genuine? Where the full name and trade is given one suspects it is. But what of "Mrs. B, shopkeeper" of Otley? (She was, we may add, listed in other advertisements.) Puffing was, of course, common in the eighteenth, and in earlier and later, centuries. And some places named may represent only the dreams and expectations of Jackson and Co. of Fleet Market, London. Presumably those named were appointed agents, like Mr Ashburner of Kendal who sold "wholesale and retail" and acted as redistributors to nearby shops. Whatever doubts one may have on the medicinal value of the products, the advertisements surely reveal a very well-organized system of distribution. Those appointed or willing to serve as wholesalers probably found it a not unprofitable addition to their trade.

In January 1751, James Lister of the Printing Office on New Street, Leeds, had just received a new supply "where it may be had both by wholesale and retail, paying ready money." It is, one may note, one of the early advertisements featuring "ready money" sales. Given the nature of the product, perhaps James Lister had discovered extending credit inadvisable.[32] James Lister was printer of the *Leeds Mercury*. Faced with the heavy tax on newspapers and other expenses, publishers valued the income from patent medicine advertisements and often worked to promote its sale. "Dr. Benjamin Godfrey's Cordiall" was, it was claimed, "sold in most Cities, Boroughs and Market Towns throughout Great Britain." But the country trade was not to be ignored. The readers of the *Leeds Mercury* were informed that "for the convenience of those who live in the country, [the Cordiall] will be brought by the men who deliver the News to any place within the reach of this paper."[33]

If one accepts the advertisements as evidence, Boulton and Wedgwood were not the earliest to seek foreign connections by providing customers with circulars in their own language. The proprietor of "Steel's specific cake for Rheumatism" appointed a special agent at Lincoln's-Inn Fields "where merchants, captains of ships ... will have good allowance to sell again." The proprietor also claimed to have available "bills in any language." His boasting was perhaps excessive, but it is not impossible that he did have some foreign-language handbills. The proprietors had close relations with publishers and booksellers. As early as 1730, William Dicey, printer of the *Northampton Mercury*, and Robert Raikes, printer of the *Gloucester Journal*, formed a partnership with Thomas Cobb and Benjamin Okell to market "Dr. Bateman's Pectoral Drops." John Newberry, who commenced his highly successful publishing career at the *Reading Mercury*, had a quarter-share in "Dr. Hooper's Female Pills" and in 1746 obtained the exclusive right to market "Dr. James Fever Powders" both in England and America. Proprietory medicines had, in fact, an extensive sale in the colonies.[34]

Various herb tobaccos and teas competed with the elixirs. "Rowley's Herb Tobacco and snuff" claimed to be "sponsored by Her Grace Charlotte, Duchess Dowager of Somerset." The advertisements for "The Swedes Tea" are rather intriguing. Illicit tea from Sweden had long had a reputation for good quality and may account for the adoption of the trade name. "Swedes Tea" had, among other virtues, the ability to strengthen the nerves and counteract "the ill effects of tea."[35]

With a few exceptions, (for example, Robert James and his fever pills), the proprietors of these various concoctions are shadowy creatures. Their products, however, remained on the market for long periods of time. One can discount or ignore their contributions to the retail trade on the plea that these products were not handled by "established tradesmen." But Mr Ashburnar, bookseller and stationer in Kendal, was an eminently respectable shopkeeper, and so was Abraham Dent who, in the 1760s, was selling Daffy's Elixir as well as Dr Anderson's True Scots Pills. However disdainful one may feel about the products and the huffing and puffing, the marketing and sales techniques employed in their distribution were openly and vigorously aggressive. Among the revolutionary changes attributed to the late Victorians are "the branding of goods, their advertisement by the producers, and the determination of the retail selling prices under systems of resale price maintenance.[36] But surely these were precisely the same techniques that had been used for well over a century by the producers and vendors of patent medicines. One can also dismiss the trade as too petty or insignificant to consider. Unfortunately, too little is known to even guess at the total annual sales. One suspects they were not small. Fortunes, as we know, were made in the nineteenth century, the most famous of which accrued to the Beecham family. Were Victorians more gullible than their ancestors? The labourers admittedly had more money in their pockets in the nineteenth century but the cost of these nostrums in the eighteenth century was small. Dr Benjamin Godfrey's Cordiall cost only six pence for above "3 ounces in a glass." Dr Anderson's True Scot

Pills were priced at one shilling a box, but customers at Abraham Dent's shop could purchase as little as threepenny worth.[37] Such prices were within reach of the labouring people. Moreover, as the advertisements never failed to point out, the cost was infinitely less than that incurred by an expensive treatment from a medical doctor. And who is to say which did less harm?

A far more respectable trade, one with distinctly modern overtones, was the trade in books. The dealers advertised widely, issued printed catalogues listing the books and their prices, and sold for "ready money." John Hildyard of York informed the public in 1751 that he had lately purchased "several libraries and parcels of books, about 30,000 volumes" to be "sold cheap, for ready money only" at his place in York. "The lowest price is printed in the catalogue, and marked on the first leaf of every book."[38] Joseph Lord of Wakefield had more extensive connections. He too had just published a catalogue with "the lowest prices printed" and "marked" on the first leaf. His catalogues were obtainable at his place in Wakefield and at "Mr. J. & J. Revington, London; Mr. Merril, Cambridge; Mr. Fletcher, Oxford; Messrs. Stabler and Barstow, York; Mr. Newton, Manchester; Mr. Scolfield, Rochdale; Messrs. Binns & Edwards, Halifax; Mr. Lister, Leeds and by most booksellers in the country."[39] Mr Lord must have been a busy and enterprising dealer. In addition to his shop at Wakefield, he had two other shops, one at Barnsley and the other at Pontefract.[40] Similar advertisements continued throughout the eighteenth century. James Lackington was only one of many when he opened in 1780 a highly successful shop in London, "The Temple of the Muses," and it was devoted entirely to books. He was only following the traditions of the trade when he marked "in every book the lowest price" and sold for "ready money."[41] J. Milner of Halifax and John Binns of Leeds were doing the same.[42]

The trade in stationery and books increased enormously during the eighteenth century, and so did the number of booksellers and stationers. But they were only the tip of the iceberg. Books, almanacs, magazines, maps, pictures, and all kinds of stationery were sold by a great variety of shops. In 1751, "John Berry, Grocer, at the new Tea-Warehouse, next door to the Long-room in Manchester" informed the public that he had available the famed *Map of Manchester* which "any shopkeeper may have to sell again, with good allowance."[43] Daniel Peck of "St. Helen Square, York," a bookseller, featured his "maps, prints, painting in glass, etc." and offered them to "gentlemen for furniture and shopkeepers to sell again ... at the most reasonable prices."[44] Abraham Dent did a thriving trade in books, magazines, and stationery, some of which he got in Kendal from the Ashburnars. But he also sought suppliers as far afield as Newcastle where he dealt with William Charnley, a bookseller and publisher. Almanacs and books not sold were sometimes returned to the suppliers. It is highly possible, as Willan suggests, that "the Dents worked on a sale or return basis."[45] Certainly booksellers pushed their wares by every conceivable means. Many of the almanacs, spelling books, readers, and magazines had standard retail prices. Did shopkeepers receive standard discounts from the major suppliers? Dent retailed *Old Moore* for nine pence; for those he returned he received eight pence, which implies a rather modest mark-up. But if he was allowed to return unsold books, the trade involved little trouble or heavy capital outlay and offered a very sure profit.[46] Given the extensive advertising by producers and major suppliers and the increasing popularity of all types of books and stationery, it is not surprising that many different types of shops found them a useful and profitable addition to their stock. The same is true for patent medicines that often came from the same supplier.

Inventions or new ideas do not spring out of the void, but from an already existing body of knowledge. By denying change in eighteenth-century retailing, historians have overlooked the influence on the retail trade of the innovative practices of the sellers of medicine and books. The marketing and sales methods they devised formed a stock of ideas others could adopt when warranted by their trade. The list was formidable, including national advertising by the producers, price ticketing, and even ready-money sales. Ambitious and aggressive producers or shopkeepers, like the Wedgwoods and Boultons or the drapers and tea dealers, had easily available tried and proven methods that could be revised and extended for their particular purpose. The shopkeeping world was a well-integrated system, and ideas as well as goods circulated freely and often by the same carriers. As more shopkeepers acquired access to the methods, the tempo of change accelerated. Newspaper advertisements are the most visible evidence of the process.

Although it is not possible to date precisely the first adoption by a particular shop trade of more aggressive sales techniques, the advertisements do reveal when, where, and by which shop trades various sales methods were publicly announced. The advertisements show clearly that books and patent medicines were not the only articles whose prices were openly stated. Contrary to what is generally conceded, there was far more open display of prices, a practice that gathered momentum during the latter half of the century. As early as 1751, "John Davenport & Co., at their warehouse in Walmgate, York," advertised its wallpaper "as good and as cheap by retail as is sold in London by wholesale; such as is sold by the upholsterer, etc. for 3d. or 3.5d. per yard, we sell for 2.5d. and all other sorts in proportion. The price is printed at the end of each piece without abatement and sold for ready money."[47] That may have been a special offer similar to the one by S. Cole and Company of London who informed "the public they have now on sale of their own manufacture" at their shop at the Peacock corner of Bedford Street, "a large and elegant assortment of silks ... which they propose to sell retail on the same terms as to wholesale dealers. The lowest price at a word and no pattern cut."[48]

James Donaldson was a grocer and teaman near the Cross, Leeds. He was no ephemeral grocer. On the contrary, he was a well-established tradesman who continued to advertise his prices well into the 1790s. In 1774, Christopher Routh, Jr., who had just opened shop as grocer and tea dealer, saw fit to note he was the "late apprentice of James Donaldson."[49] At least as early as 1769, Donaldson placed advertisements in the *Leeds Mercury* for several weeks after the East India Company auctions informing the public that he had "just got in a large assortment" of tea "which he sells on as low terms, and as good in quality, as the teamen in London." The prices were clearly stated, for example: "Good Bohea, 3s. 10d.; Fine Bohea, 4s.; Good Congou, 5s.; Fine Congou, 6s.; Finest Congou, 8s." and so on for twelve different kinds. The highest price was "Finest Hyson, 16s." Donaldson featured "Churchman's Patent Chocolate" at 6s. per pound and "best Turkey Coffee freshly roasted" that came "from London by wagon weekly." He sold "all kinds of groceries, of the best quality and at the lowest prices, wholesale and retail." And as a further inducement, "tret will be allowed with quantities."[50] In 1773 he featured "Sir Hans Sloane's Milk Chocolate" as well as "Churchman's Patent Chocolate." Prices for tea had gone up – "Good Bohea" was now 4s. 2d. a pound.[51] John Tennant, "Tea-Dealer, Within Boar Lane, Leeds," offered some competition. "Congou Bohea" he priced at 4s. 1d. His price for "Fine Congou Leaf" was, however, the same as Donaldson's 4s. 4d. to 4s. 8d. A week later he saw fit to note an error in the earlier advertisement: Common Green priced at 6s. 11d., should have been 5s. 10d. Donaldson was selling his lowest quality green tea at 6s. per pound. Tennant sold Churchman's Patent Chocolate at 6s. per pound, but he also had available Crown Chocolate.[52] These various patented chocolates were apparently well known to the public. R. Sutcliffe was also a reputable tradesman. At his "Wholesale and Retail Tea Warehouse in Spurriergate," York, the public could still buy bohea for 4s. 2d.; his "Good Common Green," however, cost 6s. 11d.[53] Not all listed their prices, but most assured the public they sold on "the very lowest terms" or "as reasonable as London."[54]

Grocers were not the only shopkeepers to publish prices, although they appeared to have adopted the practice fairly early in the century. Far more significant is the price listing by drapers and mercers, reputedly the most notorious hagglers. There were, of course, those who offered the public special bargains. Mr Francis Dixon in the Marketplace, Wakefield, who was "determined to leave off trade," was selling "all his stock of Linen-drapery at Prime Cost or under." His stated intentions may have been genuine. The shop was "to be let, being a large handsome square room, with one other room behind and adjoining said shop," not unlike William Stout's first shop.[55] Did Dixon, like Stout, use the "room behind" as his sleeping quarters? In 1769 Timothy and Mary Wilks, near the Cross, Leeds, had just "laid in a large assortment of Linen-Drapery and Haberdashery Goods" and promised the public a "good pennyworth and civil usage."[56] Numerous advertisements appear in 1774 by linen- and woollen-drapers, mercers, and haberdashers of Leeds. Among the advertisers were: Lancelot Iveson, silk-mercer and woolen-draper; T. Jackson, linen-draper; Bramley and Sturdy, mercers and woollendrapers; Edward Sanderson, mercer and woollen-draper; John Fearn, silk mercer and woollen-draper; Sherbrook and Willot, linendrapers and haberdashers; Wigglesworth and Tetley, mercers, linen- and woollen-drapers; Samuel Horsfall, linen-draper; Thomas Thompson, linen-draper and haberdasher.[57] Most were still advertising their wares in the 1780s. To the list can be added the hatters, four of whom inserted advertisements.[58] Even ironmongers entered the fray.

The flurry of advertisements suggests that some time in the 1770s, changes were occurring in the wearing apparel trade that encouraged more aggressive sales techniques. The public were becoming more eager to display the newest creations in fashionable clothes. This is evident from the successful publication of fashion magazines that incited and enhanced the taste for the newest fashion.[59] At the same time, the rising incomes of the middling orders enabled far more people to satisfy their tastes and to emulate those in higher social positions. As a consequence, demand for fashionable goods increased. The following advertisements illustrate that some shopkeepers responded to the improved economic climate. Innovative sales techniques were introduced and affected the practices of many retail trades. The sample is admittedly limited in time and space, but it includes retailers in many trades. No doubt, many established shopkeepers continued to view with scorn the use of newspaper advertisements to attract custom. But those who anticipated benefits ranged from numerous drapers to ironmongers and they were willing to incur charges for advertising. Indeed, when one notes that the circulation of provincial newspapers had only recently been extended, their use for the promotion of the shopkeepers' trade was in itself something of an innovation.[60] Nor were the advertisers petty ephemeral shopkeepers. Most were well-established retailers who supplied small shops in the outlying villages and advertised repeatedly over an extended period of time.[61]

Advertisements were generally couched in language to appeal to the aspiring middling orders who were eager to acquire fashionable clothes at reasonable prices. The favoured time of year for the announcement was the spring, particularly the month of May. In the early 1770s, London was especially featured by drapers and hatters as the source of their high-quality wearing apparel. They had "just returned" or "acquired" a large, fresh, most fashionable or elegant assortment. But three advertisers, in particular, made a stronger appeal in terms of prices. In 1774, Sherbrook and Willot announced they proposed to sell "on the lowest terms for ready money."[62] Thomas Thompson, who sold on terms as low as London, noted in special print that he had come "from the Cheap-Shop in Sheffield."[63] Joseph Wood, hatter, made a more telling point. He was able to "sell on very moderate terms" as low as either London or Manchester as he had "formed a connection with a very capital manufacturer."[64] All this advertising presaged a change in the manner of sales.

By the end of the decade, advertisements were longer and price competition more common. An increasing number of shopkeepers sought to attract custom by listing prices; ticketing their wares with no abatement; offering special bargains or particularly low prices for ready money. The evidence points to a quickening of trade and keener competition. Local shopkeepers vied with each other for custom and sought to match or outdo their competitors from major centres such as London or Manchester. Not surprisingly, the shopkeepers of Leeds were more active and aggressive newspaper advertisers than their fellow shopkeepers in the smaller and more elegant city of York. But they too used similar sales appeals. Mrs Jane Dixon, a lace dealer in Micklegate, who had just "returned from among her workers," had a large assortment of the newest patterns that she vouched to "sell on the lowest terms, wholesale and retail." She offered "edgings as low as 2d. per yard."[65] T. Jackson, a linen-draper, who also sold at the lowest prices, particularly noted his "low prices for ready money." He listed prices for various sorts of material, for example, "Neat Camblets, 19 in. at 8d. yard ... Superfine Camblets, 20–21 in., 10d."[66] At Mr Mill's mercery shop in Minster Yard, the "lowest price" was "fixed" to each article.[67]

The fabrics most frequently featured by drapers in Leeds were cotton, muslin, and linen, and particular emphasis was placed on their low competitive prices. Joseph Ross, an avid advertiser, had imported from Dublin, Manchester, and elsewhere a "great variety of printed linens, cottons and calicoes ... likewise muslins." Country shopkeepers could be supplied on "terms as good as at Chester or any other market." The prices of his dark cottons were as low as any that could be purchased at Manchester warehouses, and he had a "greater variety."[68] By 1782 he was listing his prices. In 1785, having just returned from Scotland, he quoted the prices of hankerchiefs, muslin, aprons, and table linens. He had also purchased from the East India Company a great variety of muslin, the prices of which were listed. In 1782, William Wigglesworth informed the public that he was selling off his woollens at prime cost to concentrate on linen draperies. At the same time, price ticketing became more common, even among mercers. In 1782, Mr Sanderson, silk mercer, specially noted that the "lowest price will be fixed on each article." He may, however, have been an exception. By 1785, he was selling the remainder of his silk and turning his attention to cottons. There is also an increasing emphasis on cheapness. Thomas Skegg, who had "the lowest price fixed," headed a long advertisement: "Cheap linen-drapery and silk mercery." W. Tatham featured in large letters "his CHEAP Warehouse" carrying every article in the linen-drapery and hosiery line 10 or 20 percent cheaper on which "the lowest prices fixed from which no abatement can be made." R. Hindley of York particularly noted his "great variety of very cheap plain satin."[69]

Provincial shopkeepers, particularly in the clothing line, had to share their market with other sellers. Those eager to promote their trade and not prepared to rely on word-of-mouth reputation had to be cognizant of their competitors. To counteract the efforts of major wholesalers and the principal London dealers, provincial shopkeepers emphasized prices as low as those in Manchester or London. But the most immediate and visible competitors were the transient sellers who arrived in town generally twice a year and loudly proclaimed their special bargains in large, striking advertisements. Customers were informed of the place of sale – the large room at the Sign of Talbot – and the date when the sale commenced and ended. The quantity and prices of many articles on sale were listed and customers advised that "every piece of goods has the lowest price marked on it from which no abatement can be made."[70] Having no fixed place of sale, transient sellers would almost by necessity need to announce either by handbills or newspaper advertisements their impending sale. In all, they undoubtedly acted as catalysts in the towns they visited. Certainly some fixed-shop retailers adopted similar methods of attracting custom.

Throughout the century the principal London dealers supplied the upper reaches of society with fashionable goods and sought trade customers in the provinces with circulars and riders. The increasing number and more extensive circulation of newspapers confronted provincial shopkeepers with a new form of competition – advertisements by London dealers offering attractive mail-order service to country buyers. The "ladies" of York could buy from Mr Lamon of Hanover Square the newest and most fashionable millinery "on terms uncommonly advantageous." He also sought trade customers. To remedy the inconvenience that country milliners frequently laboured under, he proposed to supply them with "the newest fashion as they regularly change, on terms very advantageous for ready money."[71] Smith and Company of Fleet Street listed by price a long assortment of cottons, linens, handkerchiefs, and "ready-made" millinery. All orders from the country accompanied by "money or good bills" would receive prompt attention.[72] The advertisements of Edward Archer of Covent Garden were couched in language to appeal to the fashionable world. He entitled himself "Tabbinet and Poplin Mercer to Her Majesty and His Royal Highness the Prince of Wales." In both London and Leeds papers he featured "Her Majesty's Rich Ribbed Tabbinets ... equal to the most expensive silk or velvet for gentlemen." Some of his advertisements were in French addressed to "La Noblesse et le Public." But he also emphasized low prices. As he sold "only for ready money," his prices did not allow "the expected abatement to Taylors," which accounted for his goods "not having their recommendation." But he was prepared to send patterns to those unable to see his Tabbinets in the piece – "the only way to judge of their manufacture." At his shop, all articles were "marked with the price for ready money and so low that no abatement is ever made." Archer also gave money-back guarantees. "For the satisfaction and convenience of Ladies who may send their orders from the country, he makes it a rule to exchange or return the money for any goods that should not in every respect be approved."[73] Wheatley and Thompson of New Bond Street offered the ladies fine quality poplin at 3s. 2d. a yard, and particularly noted their former connection with Archer.[74]

The drapers of Leeds responded to the competition by offering customers specially reduced prices. Richard Wardle, who "bought at the best market," listed by price a large assortment of draperies that he was selling "at reduced prices."[75] At William Wilson's "Manchester Warehouse," country shopkeepers could save by buying "for ready money" upon Manchester terms. He bought and sold on the best terms because his brother in Manchester was a manufacturer.[76]

Some woollen-drapers and mercers used aggressive sale techniques, but the momentum seems to have arisen with the more widespread use of cotton and, with some exception, the appeal was to the middling orders and below. This is most clearly demonstrated by the advertisements in London. Charles Rymer of Covent Garden was a woollen-draper and mercer who sold "the best clothing for ready money" and listed by price a large assortment of woollens and silks.[77] But the majority stressed their cheap cotton apparel. At Ham's Muslin and Linen Warehouse on the Strand one could buy "cheap ready-made fashionable dresses, ladies' great coats, petticoats," etc. Prices were, of course, listed. The Hanway Yard Cheap Warehouse offered customers "satins ... linen drapery ... morning caps and dresses and ready-made linen" remarkably "cheap for ready money." Middleton, Innes and Jolly appended a note to their list of prices: "It has been and shall be their invariable plan to fix the very lowest ready-money price on every article they sell." The Indian Muslin Warehouse of Fleet Street was stocked with a variety of muslins, aprons, gowns, and fine millinery priced cheap for ready money. The advertisement of R. Garratt was openly pitched to the working people. He had purchased a large variety of Irish linens that he warranted "wash and wear well ... and some exceeding good House-wife Cloth, of a remarkable stout fabric, for working people's use, common shirts, etc." He sold "cheaper than before ... for ready money." Lee, a tailor, placed a half-column advertisement in the paper listing the prices "for ready money only" of coats, great coats, breeches, and liveries of various materials. He had paid ready money for the goods, which "makes them 20 percent cheaper than any ever proposed before." Dyde and Scribe of Pall Mall had an elegant assortment of ready-made hats as "fashionable ... as the first private milliners."[78]

The above sample represents shopkeepers' advertisements in only one newspaper for half a year. Without doubt, many shops which did not advertise were also ticketing their wares and offering customers low prices for ready money. The London haberdasher for whom Robert Owen worked in the mid–1780s had acquired a small fortune on ready-money sales and customers flocked to his shop. It had a far different clientele than the shop of Mr McGuffog at Stamford, Lincoln, where Owen served his apprenticeship. Mr McGuffog conducted his trade on a personal basis and was keenly aware of the exalted status of his customers. Time was not an important consideration to McGuffog in effecting sales; it was to shopkeepers who served the multitude. Their profit was based on a quick turn-over and goods were priced to attract customers whose name and status were a matter of indifference to the proprietors. Ticketing and ready-money sales were a means of attracting custom and, equally important, of effecting easy and speedy transactions by harassed shopmen. The London haberdasher's shop was crowded from morning till night and little time was devoted to individual customers. There was no bargaining and no attempt to persuade the customer to buy.[79] The "monster shops," as they were called in the early nineteenth century, required a large market. It is perhaps not surprising that they made their appearance first in the wearing apparel trades, particularly among drapers and haberdashers. Demand for moderately priced wares was high and competition keen on all levels, from the manufacturer of cotton goods to the retailer. In addition, an increasing number of towns had a sufficiently large population to support shops of this order, if not necessarily as large as those in London. By 1801, fifteen provincial towns had populations ranging between 20,000 and 100,000.[80] Leeds with its 53,000 inhabitants provided enterprising drapers and haberdashers with a large potential market that could be effectively exploited by aggressive sales policies.

A great variety of ready-made wearing apparel was available in the eighteenth century. In addition to hats, coats, cloaks, gowns, breeches, riding habits, waistcoats, petticoats, and boys' and girls' clothing, some shops sold frocks ready-to-wear. Mary and Ann Hogarth, in a trade card designed by their brother, announced in the 1730s that they sold the "best and most Fashionable Ready Made Frocks, sutes of Fustian, Ticken and Holland ... blue and Canvas Frocks ... at reasonable rates."[81] By the last decade of the century, ready-made dresses were a regular part of the stock of shops not aspiring to sell to the higher levels of society. But hats were the earliest ready-made clothing and had a widespread sale. Early in the century, hatters in Lancashire "envied drapers" selling hats. By mid-century even small general shops stocked hats. There were certainly bespoke-hatters, as in fact there are today. But those who advertised were primarily shopkeepers. They invariably stated that they "had just received" or returned from London with a large assortment of the newest fashion.[82] The advertisements were simple announcements of the arrival of fresh stock. Ticketing and ready-money sales were not common among either hatters or milliners.[83] Joseph Wood was exceptional in stressing his low terms and connection with a manufacturer. A more aggressive salesman appeared in Leeds during the 1790s. In a long advertisement, James Daniel, a patent hat manufacturer, announced the opening of his warehouse where shopkeepers would receive terms as good as at his warehouse in Stockport, Cheshire, or his manufactory at Leawood, Derby. Patent hats were, he claimed, "lighter, more pleasant, will preserve their shape better and wear superior to those made by hand, independant of being much lower in price." He had, of course, the "newest, most approved fashions" as he served "many of the first houses in London." For the convenience of ladies and gentlemen a "commodious, elegant shop" was being established in Briggate.[84] It is not known how successful Daniel was in spreading the fame of his patent hats or whether he had other retail outlets. But it is evident that the practice was not a nineteenth-century innovation.

The demand for footwear exceeded any other single article of wearing apparel. Shoes wore out very quickly in the eighteenth century and had to be replaced or mended, even by the poor. Whether the British pride in their well-shod workers was true or not, the market for shoes was enormous. It was one shared by many different types of sellers. In addition to the village shoemaker and the translator, who dealt almost exclusively in second-hand shoes, a great variety of shops had a flourishing trade in ready-made shoes. Thomas Turner of East Hoathly, a small Sussex village, supplied his customers with pattens and clogs purchased from nearby tradesmen.[85] Indeed, as early as the sixteenth century, "newe shoes" were being shipped from London to the provinces.[86] The whole gamut of sellers could be found in London. But London had master shoemakers whose bespoke business was conducted almost on an assembly-line basis. After the customer was measured, the work was handed out to a series of journeymen, apprentices, and other outworkers, each tackling one aspect of the job until the shoes were completed and ready for fitting. In 1738, one London shoemaster employed 162 persons ranging in age from eight to seventy. One would hesitate to call him simply a shopkeeper, but neither was he an artisan.[87] Besides the master shoemakers, London had many shops which specialized in cheap ready-made shoes. They were well established by midcentury and did a thriving business. It is difficult to say when such shops first appeared in the larger provincial towns.[88] By the 1780s, R. Kendall informed the public that he had a large assortment "of the neatest and best articles in every branch of the business ...

on the lowest terms." It is a formidable list: boots, cork shoes, red, green, blue and black Spanish shoes, clogs and slippers for ladies, Lashing, Russell and Callimanco shoes."[89] He had not just opened shop, one presumes he had been doing business in Leeds for some years. He was soon to be outstripped in sales appeal by a newcomer. In 1791, a short but striking advertisement appeared:

CHEAP SHOES
AT LOXHAM'S SHOE-WAREHOUSE
Bottom of Call-lane, Leeds
ARE SOLD

Men's Calf shoes, good as can be manufactured at		5s. 6d. pr.
Women's Calf shoes,	ditto	3s. 6d.
Women's Stuff shoes,	ditto	3s. 6d.

And all other kinds proportionately low.[90]

His followup advertisement a month later reveals his style. "By this time the Public will be able to form some kind of an estimate of the Goodness of the Shoes sold at Loxham's." He doubted not "the purchasers ... will find them equal to any they ever bought at any price." This is followed by the same listing. However, he also notes that "several of his customers" have been "disappointed by his not having their size." He then informed the public "that he has just received a fresh assortment of several thousand pairs, out of which he hopes to fit any foot."[91] A month later, he observed: "In consequence of a Rise of Wages in the Manufacturing Counties, R. Loxham is under the disagreeable Necessity of raising the Price of Women's Stuff Shoes to 3s. 10d." As the price is "still so much lower than the same kind and quality ... at any other shop in town," he was sure "the public will give preference to his shop." All other prices remained the same.[92] Apparently, Kendall and Loxham were not the only shops retailing ready-made footwear. But at least some shoe shops had achieved a sufficiently large market to warrant the expense and trouble of advertising. It is also clear that price ticketing was becoming a common practice.

The advertisements show that some shopkeepers in the clothing line were attempting to attract custom by competitive prices. The reputation they sought was to provide a "good pennyworth." Their claims of backward linkages with manufacturers or other suppliers were in part devices for emphasizing their particularly low prices. And the customers they sought to attract were not His Noble Lord but those who, unlike Lord Macaulay, did not "expect some reserve, some decent pride in our hatter and our bootmaker."[93] How many others were competing through handbills, a cheaper form of advertising, we do not know.

Shopkeepers in the clothing line were not alone in the attempt to draw in custom through advertising. Ironmongery had been a shop trade for a long time. William Stout was no metal worker and had no foundry. He was strictly a shopkeeping ironmonger as his master before him had been. As early as 1773, Thomas Warham, one of the principal ironmongers of Leeds, was advertising.[94] He listed an extensive assortment of hardware from locks and shovels to mahogany tea boards and coffin furniture. He was "determined to sell everything in the hardware business upon the most reasonable terms" and did not offer a "few trifling articles at PRIME COST; *and from 10 to 20 and 30 percent under*, in order to more securely impose" on the public a "greater value" on other articles.[95] Mr Warham was apparently rather irritated by the sale devices of some of his fellow ironmongers. But here is a well-known and reputable shopkeeper who did not disdain advertising. He was also an aggressive and highly successful businessman. Of course, ironmongery had never been a trade confined to the fashionable classes. Perhaps ironmongers never developed the snobbery associated in the nineteenth century with "our hatter and our bootmaker." In 1774, John Fothergill was able to "serve his customers with nails and laths upon the best terms" as he had "entered into contract with William Lister of Staincross, Nail Master (who for many years served this market)." William Horsfall of Barnsley prominently featured his cast iron goods of Walker's Manufactory and offered a "great allowance" to shopkeepers on his Birmingham and Sheffield ware. William Sturdy of York also called attention to a nationally known article. He was selling his "fresh assortment of Wedgwood Ware from Etruria" upon terms as low as in London. In 1796, the Sheffield Repository for Plated Goods informed the public that "every article will have the lowest price fixed thereon" and observed that their stock had come directly from "the original manufacture." Two years later Warham adopted the practice: "prices will be fixed without abatement." Their stock had been "laid in from their warehouse in Birmingham." Thomas Marriott featured the portable patent washing machine of Thomas Todd. He lauded the virtues of the washer: it got clothes "whiter," could "wash as much in one hour as 3, 6, or 10 women," and the price "is soon clear by what it saves in soap, coals, manual labour, and the preservation of the linens." Prices were listed for three sizes, from £2 7s. to £4 4s.[96]

Similar types of advertisements appeared in London papers. There was one with a very striking appeal. A manufacturer on Cornhill offered a remarkable roasting machine that dressed "any number of joints, fowls, etc." retained the gravy, "cooked meat better," roasting "equally on all sides". Joints could be taken out and put back if not sufficiently cooked "as every joint will act separately." And to the housewife's (or servant's) delight, "nor will want cleaning for 20 years." Even more remarkable, should they fail in three months to give the utmost satisfaction, the purchase money, fixing and all expenses will be returned."[97] Money-back guarantees were apparently becoming common. A dealer in wax candles and "foreign unadulterated honey" assured the public "if not approved the money to be returned." Tipper and Company who dealt in coal and Hambro Wax candles offered the same assurance.[98]

Household furnishings had a buoyant market in the eighteenth century. To the disgust of critics and the amusement of satirists, fashion dictated the replacement of old, traditional furniture by new, stylish designs. It was, however, a market largely confined to the comfortable middling groups and above, although, as inventories show, the betteroff workers also aspired to the treasured clock and other amenities. Price competition had not fully penetrated this trade, rather the emphasis was on new, fashionable furnishings. Were upholsterers and cabinetmakers primarily craftsmen, who built most of the furniture sold in their shops, or were they shopkeepers? The question is made more complicated by a confusion over the use of the term cabinetmaker. Some cabinetmakers were indeed highly skilled craftsmen. They made, or undertook the making of, the furniture they sold to retail and trade customers. But dealers in ready-made furniture also called themselves cabinetmakers, perhaps to enhance their status in the eyes of the public. They were basically shopkeepers. In fact, there was an active trade in ready-made furniture and not merely chairs. The sale of the latter had been common even in the seventeenth century. In the eighteenth, the trade in all types of ready-made furnishings quickened. Possibly, many designated as cabinetmakers in the towns and cities were shopkeepers who merely bought and sold their stock. Certainly some turned to open advertisement to attract custom for their high-class goods. William Armitage of Leeds, an avid advertiser, called himself "upholder, appraiser and cabinetmaker." But like his fellow shopkeepers, he had "just returned from London" with a "fresh assortment of paper hangings, papier mâché ornaments, bed furniture, carpeting – Persia, Wiltshire, Kidderminster, Scotch and List, tables, chairs, chest of drawers and every other article in the upholstery and cabinet branch."[99] In 1774 he offered to wait upon "any Lady or Gentleman ... in any part of the country ... not exceeding one day's journey" with patterns. He continued to advertise until 1782 and certainly stocked a wide assortment of furniture including easy chairs and sofas. John Riley of Leeds was an upholsterer and cabinetmaker – he too had just returned from London with a new assortment. T. Bradford of Doncaster sold new furniture but also took in used household furniture at a commission of 5 percent. And at least one transient seller offered competition to fixed shop retailers in Leeds. In 1781, he advertised a large assortment of "new furniture" consisting of bed furniture, sofas, easy chairs, and many other items to be sold "at the lowest prices" in the large Assembly Room in Kirkgate.[100]

Large towns were able to support more specialized shops in household furnishing such as the blanket and carpet warehouses. Their proprietors, unlike the traditional dealers in china, were aggressive salesmen. Laidler's Turkey Carpet Warehouse of London claimed to have the "largest choice collection of Turkey carpets in England" and sought buyers through provincial newspapers. Country gentlemen could obtain a list giving the dimensions of each carpet and the "lowest price ... from which no abatement can be made. The whole business transacted for ready money."[101] The market for furniture can never match that for clothing, but even in this highly restricted trade, there are indications that some shopkeepers were openly seeking to promote their business.

The market for fine jewellery was confined to the upper echelons of society, but there was a very brisk and extensive market for trinkets and watches, most of which were produced by largescale manufacturers whose organization matched that of the famed pinmakers. As Adam Smith noted, one could now purchase for twenty shillings a better constructed watch that would have cost twenty pounds in the previous century.[102] And there was a ready market. Cheap watches, buckles, and other articles of adornment were purchased with as much avidity and pride by artisans and the better-paid labourers as by the more affluent members of society.[103] Such articles were sold by jewellers and watchmakers, toyshops, ironmongers, pawn shops, and many other petty shops. Abraham Dent of Kirkby Stephen sold watches purchased from London dealers. The distribution of Boulton's buckles was exceedingly well organized and aimed at the multitude. Competition was keen among the producers, but there is little evidence in the newspapers that shopkeepers in this area were adopting the more aggressive practices of other traders. One "Goldsmith Jeweller" of Sackville Street, Piccadilly, did announce his intention of declining all orders upon credit and of dealing in the future only for ready money. Some provincial jewellers and watchmakers also advertised, but they merely announced the arrival from London of a new, elegant assortment.[104]

Specialty dealers in drinks or foods were far more aggressive. As early as 1751 a London liquor dealer was seeking custom by offering the readers of the *Leeds Mercury* specially low prices on "Old Batavia Arrack" and "good Jamaica Rum." In 1778, the custom of York was being solicited by two sellers. The Genuine Rum Warehouse of David Evans and Company had been established in London with "the unanimous approbation" of West Indian merchants to better accomodate retail customers. The proprietor aimed to provide "individuals of all ranks an easy opportunity of obtaining genuine rum and brandy in small quantities." Ready-money prices were listed and private families could "rely on being honourably served." The Genuine Jamaica Rum Warehouse of Bishopsgate assured the public that their spirits were of the highest quality and "equal" to those 1s. 6d. to 2s. per gallon more. But as the house was opened "to accommodate the public with Genuine goods on much lower terms than usual, no credit can be given. Casks to be paid for and when returned the same money allowed." Dealers in York countered the competition with their special buys. Mathers Todd, tea dealer and grocer, informed his friends that he had purchased a stock of French brandy, rum, Geneva, spirits, and wine that he proposed "selling wholesale in any quantity at the most reduced prices."[105] Numerous advertisements in the *Times* listed ready-money prices, the goods to be delivered carriage free to any part of London.

A number of specialty food shops advertised their wares. Mary Whitaker of Leeds announced she was continuing the various branches of the business of her mother. "Successor to the late Mr. James Doughty," and particularly featured her hams and tongues.[106] George Saltman, who had a shop opposite the Red-Bear, was more aggressive. He headed his advertisement: "Cream Cheeses" sold "Cheap." He had agreed with Thomas Atley of Moorby near York to obtain the best York Cheeses and was, therefore, able "to retail them at a lower price than they had yet been sold for." His price, one shilling each, "is the same money they are sold for in York Market." He was prepared to dispatch them to "any part of the country with all possible expedition."[107] Elizabeth Thompson at her shop on Call-Lane informed her friends "they may be regularly supplied with all kinds of Poultry either in the feathers or ready for the the spit," soups, various potted meats, collard pig's head, sausages, and other delectables.[108]

One of the most intriguing advertisements is that of W.T. Trant. He announced that he had returned from London with an extensive assortment of condiments and other specialties, such as olives, anchovies, and truffles. He assured the public of "the same *scrupulous* and *rigid* attention to quality" as he had given to his business since its commencement twenty years ago, and he added: "the wish nearest my heart, however singular it may appear, is to give entire satisfaction to all persons who favour me with their order, so that the poorest person, as well as the most ignorant, may be equally certain of being well used as the richest and best informed."[109] One wonders how many poor and ignorant persons he was able to attract.

Price competition among retailers of food stuff was more common in London. Long's Warehouse at 73 Cheapside claimed to sell "on lower terms than any other shop in Town." He particularly featured "fine new Muscatel Raisins ... 9d. lb. ... ; new Jordain Almonds; fine French fruit ... 2s. 6d. lb.; ... Brandy fruit ... equally cheap; sweetmeats ... cordials ... sauces ... Soy ... Curry."[110] Young's Warehouse on New Bond Street displayed a long list of the delicacies available at his shop – Parmesan and Gruyère cheeses, Westphalia and other hams, tongues, wines, etc. But he "distinguished himself in selling foreign eatables of the first quality on the most reasonable terms for ready money."[111] Burgess's Italian Warehouse on the Strand was not to be overshadowed. He placed almost a full column advertisement in the *Times* particularly noting his orange, lemon, and lime trees and other exotic plants selling "on the lowest terms for Ready Money." He also reminded the public that "his specialty sauces" – for some he provided recipes – were sent "carriage free to any part of England" to prevent "imposition on the Public" by imitations. He had the "best Westmorland and Westphalia Hams ... Tongues ... also Rein Deer Tongues ... Hambro Beef in Ribs ... Sturgeon ... Sausage with or without garlic."[112] These were surely high-class shops, but they too featured by "open advertisement" their low prices for quality items, ready-money sales, and even carriage free delivery – all presumably to attract custom. To whom were these advertisements addressed? Not, one supposes, the Marquis of Buckingham but those in the middling ranks whose numbers and income were increasing and for whom price was an object. It is perhaps no idle fancy that each styles its shop a "warehouse," a term carrying the connotation of a place where one can get a good buy.

In the large cities were elaborately decorated confectionery shops whose proprietors took great pride in their homemade specialties purveyed to the wealthy and who would have disdained vulgar advertising. But there was also a brisk trade in ready-made confectionery and its sellers had no such aversion. Their advertisements did not, however, show much initiative. Frances Clifton, a confectioner in Leeds, simply advised the public that she had just received a new shipment of "wine sous" and a large assortment of various confectioneries. B. Tinsdal sold millinery and other sundries but also stocked all kinds of confections. Eleanor Dickson, confectioner, announced she had "just received from London ... her confectioneries."[113] Sweets, it would seem, were a popular article even in the eighteenth century. One also has a feeling that the shops of these ladies were not very different from those one sees today.

If not all "established" retailers in the eighteenth century engaged in newspaper advertising, an impressive number and variety of dealers did. Besides those mentioned above, a few oil and colourmen advertised, but merely to announce the arrival from London of their stock.[114] Even dealers in coal found the newspaper a convenient means of informing the public. For example, Sara Barwick and Son, who had apparently received complaints about charges for delivery, gave notice that in the future the cost would be "no more than one shilling per whole wagon" within a certain area. To the poor who were "much imposed upon both in measure and price," the company offered a special price for "clean-dressed coals and full measure."[115] As early as 1751, seedsmen were advising that they had on hand a "large parcel ... of Norfolk Turnip Seed."[116] With the increasing number and greater geographical spread of newspapers in the nineteenth century, it is not surprising that more shopkeepers turned to open advertising as a means of attracting customers from a wider area. But handbills, as Wedgwood's snobbish aversion to them shows, were also used extensively by shopkeepers in the eighteenth century. Given the restricted circulation of newspapers, surely the untaxed handbill was a more effective and cheaper means of reaching prospective retail customers. It served the same púrpose as the circulars of the wholesale-retail shopkeepers. The handbills distributed by Andrew Melrose of Edinburg in the early nineteenth century were well designed to appeal to a broad range of customers.[117] There is no reason to suppose that Robert Sheppard, his master, had not used them with equal effect in the eighteenth century – he was certainly an avid newspaper advertiser. One can only regret that so few handbills have survived.

It is difficult to reconcile the activities of the advertisers with the received view of the retail trade in the eighteenth century. By the latter part of the century, price ticketing, leading articles, ready-money sales, mail-order services, free delivery, cheap articles purchased at the first market and even money-back guarantees, had all become the stock-in-trade of at least some shopkeepers. Those engaged in these activities came from a wide range of shop trades with perhaps the sole exception of the chemists. In self-defence, the more traditionally oriented shopkeepers had to adopt some or all of the marketing and sales techniques of their more aggressive competitors. This process is aptly demonstrated by the retail trade of tea, the subject of the following chapter.

CHAPTER THIRTEEN

Forces of Competition in the Retailing of Tea

INTRODUCTION

The foregoing chapters have been primarily concerned with shop-keeping in general – the number and types of shops and the prevailing business practices. To appreciate the significance of the changes which occurred in the century, a more detailed examination of the development of entrepreneurial skills in a specific retail trade seems desirable. Such a study will show how the responses of shop-keepers to their economic and social milieu effected changes in the structure of the retail trade. The trade in tea has been chosen largely because it is better documented than others. It was, moreover, a highly respected trade with firmly rooted traditional practices. That it was nevertheless penetrated by sales and marketing techniques pioneered by the scorned trade in patent medicine demonstrates the health and vigour of the retail trades. The discussion will focus on two periods which marked a change in the rhythm of the trade: the decade following the Commutation Act of 1784 and the years immediately after the wars with France.

By a drastic reduction of duty on tea from over 119 to 12.5 percent *ad valorem*, the Commutation Act offered fair-trade dealers an opportunity to capture the market formerly supplied by smugglers and to increase demand as tea prices fell. Competition became intense and new methods of sale were introduced. The impetus generated by the expanding market for tea was interrupted by the wars with France, largely because of increased duties and general inflation of prices. Trade revived after the return of peace in 1815 and set in motion a renewed competition. In response to postwar price deflation, on the one hand, and to promises of new markets on the other, innovative practices were introduced. In the end, the traditional structure and methods were substantially modified, if not "torn to pieces," as one of the innovators claimed. But, almost all the "innovative practices" adopted by the tea trade had been developed in one or another of the retail trades during the course of the eighteenth century.

INFLUENCE OF THE COMMUTATION ACT

Tea was one of the major commodities handled by grocers, one on which a considerable part of their profit depended. Although large quantities of sugar were sold, it was not an item that yielded a high margin of profit. Indeed, it was often used as a leading article to attract custom for tea or coffee. As early as 1756, Thomas Fletcher, the Twinings's former shopman, appended a special note to his advertisement: "N.B. And to oblige those who are pleased to favour him with their commands for teas, will sell all sorts of Refined Sugars at Prime Cost, particularly superfine Bristol Loaves on the very lowest terms."[1] But, until the Commutation Act of 1784, the retailing of legal tea was bedevilled by the large quantities of illicit tea clandestinely landed all along the British coast. In the decade 1773–83, the quantity of tea smuggled into the country was, we would suggest, almost double the amount of legal tea available, or some seven to eight million pounds per annum. During these years the fair-trade dealer was sorely pressed. In order to maintain a share of the market, the principal London dealers lowered the bid-up prices at the East India Company's auctions and reduced their mark-up on the sorts favoured by the smugglers. The tax on legal tea was, however, far too high for the fair trader to compete on the level of prices. He could, however, provide a good quality tea of various sorts to suit the tastes of British consumers. At the same time, he could seek to retain the trade of highly respectable grocers in the provinces – those whose social position and sense of honour were such that they would eschew dealing in illicit tea. But it was a losing battle. As Richard Twining observed, the failure to compete against the more profitable illicit tea forced more and more shopkeepers to deal with the "free" trader secretly while condemning him publicly.[2]

In 1783 only 3 million pounds of tea were delivered out of the East India Company's warehouses for home consumption. No innovative practices could emerge within the legal trade under such conditions. On the other hand, the illicit trade showed no lack of enterprise, particularly the "free" traders in Scotland who regularly supplied shopkeepers with tax-free tea. One Edinburg dealer in the

Table 41
Tea Dealers in England, Wales, and Scotland, 1783, 1801, 1816, 1834

	England and Wales	Scotland
1783	32,754	1,034
1801	56,248	5,817
1816	60,262	7,826
1834	78,278	13,423

Source: "Tea and Coffee Dealers' Licences, 1781-1855," 83, *PP1857*.

illicit article claimed to have "opened shops for the retail" of tea upon his own account in Newcastle, Durham, Shields, and Leeds with great success.[3] Certainly the "free" traders extended the sale and consumption of tea, creating a demand which, after 1784, could be exploited by the fair-trade dealers. The average annual quantity of tea delivered out of the East India Company's warehouses for home consumption during the excise years 1781–3 was 4.9 million pounds, in 1800–1, 21 million. That year marked the end of the expansion. For the following fifteen years, deliveries remained around 21 million pounds. They then moved upwards. By 1834 over 30 million pounds of tea were delivered out of the company's warehouses. The number of licensed tea dealers followed a similar pattern.

The number of tea dealers in England and Wales increased 71.7 percent for the period 1783–1801, 7.1 percent, 1801–16, 34.5 percent, 1816–34. The figures for Scotland are 462.6 percent, 34.5 percent, and 71.5 percent respectively. There was little growth in the tea trade during the years 1801–16. The slight increase in the number of dealers may, in fact, have adversely affected the amount of business of individual dealers. The interruption in the expansion of the trade was basically the result of the French Revolutionary Wars. Tea once again became a major source of revenue for the government. In 1795, the duty was raised to a modest 20 percent, but by 1801 it had reached 50 percent on teas sold for 2s. 6d. or above at the East India Company's auctions – those selling below 2s. 6d. remained at 20 percent. Two years later the duty shot up to 95 percent and 65 percent respectively. By 1806 it was 96 percent on all teas. It was lucrative for the government.[4] For the dealers, however, it meant a far greater capital outlay. In 1794, the dealers purchased from the East India Company 19.1 million pounds of tea for £2,928,964; with tax the total cost was £3,266,977; in 1806, they purchased 22.8 million pounds of tea for £3,727,812. With duty, the total cost was over £7 million. It should also be remembered that purchases at the company's quarterly auctions required prompt payment of both the tax and the cost of the tea. It was, as the dealers never tired of saying, a trade that required in the first instance "an immense amount of capital." It is small wonder that the principal dealers also required their correspondents to pay equally promptly, and that the number of buyers at the East India Company's auctions was restricted to several hundred.

The result of the increase in taxes was a steep rise in the price of tea to the consumer. The average per pound cost, including taxes, at the East India Company's auctions was 41.3d. in 1794; 77.5d. in 1806, and rose slightly the following years, reaching 81.7d. in 1814; after that it began to fall. In 1820 it was 66.4d., although the duty had increased to 100 percent on teas sold above 24d. All indices show a general rise of prices during the war, but that of tea was somewhat greater. Most economic historians agree that the standard of living of the working classes declined during the French Wars and did not recover until ca. 1820. Of course, not all sectors of the population suffered; many in the middling groups had rising incomes and were well able to afford their 8s. or 10s. tea. Nonetheless, per capita consumption of tea in Britain declined after 1803 and, with some fluctuations, did not recover until 1820 when it began a slow and laborious rise. The short period 1784–93 witnessed many changes in the domestic tea trade. Further developments in the marketing of tea were, however, brought to a halt by the social and economic conditions of the country during the wars of 1793–1815. The tea trade marked time. After 1818, improved conditions encouraged a flurry of activity among tea dealers and the pace of change was accelerated. But marketing methods employed by the new entrepreneurs followed the path laid down after the Commutation Act.

The buyers at the East India Company's auctions were the source for all legal tea. Composed of the principal tea dealers and grocers of London and the provinces, they formed a small but powerful group whose bidding at the auctions largely determined the first cost of tea. Prior to the auction, all the tea declared for sale was exposed for inspection by the brokers and buyers. Under the sponsorship of the company, a catalogue was issued describing the quality of each break of tea. When the buyers went into the auction, they knew precisely the quantity, quality, and put-up price of each sort of tea, and the put-up prices at the following auction. The East India Company sold the tea in lots consisting of a varying number of chests ranging from one to six chests of one sort and quality. Licensed tea brokers, rarely exceeding twelve in number, bid for the lots under instructions from the buyers. The leading broker opened the bidding, setting the price for each sort and quality, and continued until he had completed purchases of that sort or another broker offered a higher price. A normal sale was conducted smoothly and quickly and for any one quality and sort the range of prices was usually no more than one or two pence and often merely a half-pence. Disruptions only occurred if the buyers were disatisfied with the quality, quantity, or price – a rare occurrence. One such disturbance occurred during the second sale after the Commutation Act when the East India Company put up some singlo whose quality did not meet the approval of the buyers. When the directors of the company refused to remove the singlo from the sale, the buyers authorized Richard Twining to act as sole bidder, with the result that it was bought in at a penny advance on the put-up price. It was an acrimonious affair and created a hubbub of accusations and countercharges, well illustrating the power the buyers could wield if they so chose.[5] One is tempted to say that if the company had the sole legal right to import tea, power to determine the course of the domestic trade lay with the buyers at the auctions, particularly the principal London dealers. It was through their hands that much of the tea destined eventually for petty grocers and chandlers first went. Some provincial dealers certainly bought at first hand and attended the auctions. But scattered as they were over the country they could not, as the Londoners often did, form well-organized committees to protect and promote trade in tea.

Much evidence has been adduced on the price-fixing proclivities of manufacturers and dealers.[6] Tea dealers have left no specific evidence, but their activities at the auctions suggest that there was an unwritten agreement to maintain a certain level of prices that varied little from auction to auction. These prices allowed the East India Company a considerable profit, at least until the 1820s when the traditional buyers were challenged by new entrants into the trade. For example, congou, which became the mainstay of the trade, was put up by the company at 27d. but the average price realized at the auctions for the decade 1793–1802 was 37d. (annual range 34d. to 38.9d.), despite the increases in duties. What is perhaps even more revealing is that when the duty was raised to 95 percent in 1803, the average bid-up price immediately dropped to 34.3d. Can one presume that the dealers acting in concert were attempting to offset the increase in tax? Once the initial shock was absorbed and dealers discovered that consumers were willing to pay the higher prices, the bid-up price increased. By 1807 it was up to 39.4d. and remained at that level until 1815 when it dropped to 35d. By 1819, it was down to 32.5d., took another drop to 28.5d. in 1826, and continued to decline, reaching 25.9d. in 1833, the last year of the East India Company's monopoly. But these were years when the traditional channels of distribution were once again being seriously challenged by practices, which had first emerged during the last two decades of the eighteenth century.

The major buyers at the auctions of the East India Company were a wealthy and distinguished group of men. In marketing the tea, they followed methods established early in the century when the trade was small and tea-drinking largely restricted to the more affluent members of society. Many of their trade practices were aimed at cultivating the taste of the public in order to increase consumption. Quality, not price, was their major consideration. Prior to 1784, few had adopted the more aggressive sales techniques appearing in other trades. Almost all were both retail and wholesale dealers. In neither channel of distribution was a chest of tea normally sent out as delivered from the East India Company's warehouses. At the buyers' shops and warehouses the chests were opened and the leaves carefully examined for colour, texture, smell, and even touch. Samples were brewed to ascertain the smell, taste, and colour. Sometimes a whole chest was turned out and sifted to remove the dust, leaving a cleaner, higher quality tea. The whole consignment was then sorted to correspond to the recognized qualities of the different sorts. The trade distinguished at least nine distinct qualities for each sort. Certain sorts were rarely if ever used alone. For example, gunpowder tea, a high-priced green sort, was considered too strong for the taste of most people. It was, however, very useful to improve a weak hyson, or alternatively its strength was diminished by adding an equal quantity of hyson. On the other hand, bloom tea, a fairly high quality singlo sort, was generally too weak to produce a satisfactory brew and was usually mixed with other sorts to improve their colour or taste. Pekoe, a superior quality black tea, was not agreeable to many palates. But if a very small quantity of pekoe was added to an inferior black tea, the flavour of the mixture was improved enormously. The trade referred to pekoe as the backbone of the teas. Bohea stood at the bottom of the scale of teas. Although large quantities were sold under the name of bohea prior to the Commutation Act, it quickly lost favour with the public as the prices for all teas declined. In later years, it was rarely sold to retail customers as bohea. When mixed with low quality congou it was known as congou kind.

To manage the business successfully, a tea dealer with an extensive trade needed to know the fine distinctions in quality and the prices which could be realized for each. And above all, he had to master the mystery of blending upon which much of his reputation would depend. In the early years of the eighteenth century, when the consumption of tea was confined to the upper reaches of society, blending was a very personal and elaborate process. Leaves from open chests were mixed and brewed in the presence of the customer until a blend was found pleasing to his palate. Although that particular practice had died out, traditional dealers continued to prize their ability to obtain standard, uniform blends suited to the tastes and demands of their trade and retail customers. All these skills required years of training and considerable experience in handling tea. Only highly experienced dealers with large capital could safely buy at the East India Company's auctions and the buyers were well aware of their crucial role as intermediaries between the company and the public.

The principal London tea dealers were a proud set of men and chary of their reputation. Honour and integrity were their watchwords and much of their business was conducted on the basis of trust. Custom was solicited through circulars or travellers, usually a member of the firm. They maintained long-term, almost personal, relations with correspondents. The shopkeeper, following customary practice, remitted to his dealer an order requesting certain quantities of particular teas at given prices for the shopkeeper's eight, ten, or twelve shilling canisters and so on. He trusted the supplier to provide a tea suited to his trade at a price which would yield a reasonable profit. On the whole, the system had proved satisfactory. Shopkeepers with only a modest acquaintance with the infinite varieties and qualities of teas were able to stock each of their canisters with a relatively uniform article and, at the same time, were assured of their usual profit margin. The system, however, discouraged price competition and allowed the principal dealers to set the level of prices within the domestic market. They were, therefore, vulnerable to accusations that their mark-up to trade customers was unreasonably high. Indeed, as new methods of marketing arose under the pressure of competition, the whole system was sorely tried, if not completely dismantled.[7]

Francis Garratt, one of the leading London tea dealers, credited the Commutation Act of 1784 as having effected a "perfect revolution in the tea trade."[8] But the dealers deserve some credit. The controversy engendered by the act gave widespread and protracted publicity to all aspects of the trade. The London newspapers gave the subject almost daily coverage, and provincial papers faithfully copied the reports. Articles and letters were written on prices to be expected after the act; on prices realized at the first and later East

India Company auctions; on the activities of the smugglers; on the conduct of the buyers at the auctions; on the prices and quality of the tea in the shops; on the management of the trade by the Court of Directors of the East India Company; on the value of the trade to the country or the great injustice of commuting the tax on tea to one on windows. The East India Company published and widely circulated two reports on the sale and prices of tea; and Richard Twining, in the name of the tea dealers, authored three books explaining the practices and problems faced by fair-trade dealers. For several months tea was a subject of perfect notoriety. No planned advertising campaign, such as that of Wedgwood or Boulton, could have been better designed to catch the attention of the public, discredit the illicit article, and further the sales of legal tea. And the London and provincial dealers lost no time in seizing the opportunity now open to them to attract custom to their shops. Not surprisingly, they adopted sales techniques which had proved successful in other retail trades.

From September 1784 to February 1785, a barrage of advertisements appeared in the London newspapers. A spot check yielded an impressive number of shopkeepers who repeatedly sought publicity through the papers. And they were no petty dealers. Of the thirty-two identified, twenty-seven were listed in the excise survey of principal London dealers. The quantity of tea they had on hand in July 1784 ranged from 171 pounds held by John Jerman at the Golden Canister on Leadenhall Street to 3,029 pounds belonging to the well-known firm of North, Hoare, Nansen and Simpson.[9] Almost all were old established firms whose names appeared in petitions to Excise or to the East India Company. For example, John Smith and Son, who had 2,147 pounds of tea on hand in July, claimed to have been in business "over forty years." Mr Bourdillon was "grocer to His Majesty." Thomas Rutton, Thomas Delafield, and George Blakiston and Company were well-known City firms who had been active in the committees set up to combat smuggling. Many were buyers at the East India Company's auctions and all were both retail and wholesale dealers. In short, as a group they represented some of the most influential tea dealers in the country. And yet, only Thomas Rutton clearly expressed disapproval of "open advertisement." Nevertheless, "unpleasant" as it was for him "to appear in the character of an advertiser," he, not unlike Wedgwood, found it expedient to publicly proclaim the purity of his tea and to justify his prices.[10]

True, the number seeking customers through the newspapers formed a small percentage of all principal dealers. Unfortunately, it is impossible to discover how many more proclaimed the virtues of their wares through handbills distributed locally. Given the flurry of activity in the newspapers, the number could not have been small. And the advertisements at least demonstrate that some established tradesmen were not averse to employing such methods and were no novices in the art. On the contrary, they were well able to design attractive appeals for custom. Competition was keen, each attempting to match or surpass the offers made by his fellow advertisers. There was in effect a price war that undoubtedly contributed not a little to an overall increase in the consumption of tea.

Various advertising techniques were employed to entice both retail customers and the trade. John Hodgson (861 pounds of tea on hand in July 1784) commenced his advertising campaign by advising "all families who used tea" to obtain at his shop "a new treatise on tea." It described the "various species of tea ... the Act of Parliament for taking duties off tea ... the present price of tea, coffee and chocolate" and the prices to be expected after the Commutation Act.[11] Following the first East India Company Sale after the act, he and many other dealers especially featured the new reduced prices compared to those prior to the act, listing as many as twenty-four different qualities and sorts of tea.[12] Advertisements in subsequent months featured the drop in prices at the East India Company's auctions and the consequent reduction in the dealer's prices.[13] "Cheap" teas were offered at "reduced prices." Mr Cameron was "determined to sell teas at such low prices ... as the public have a right to expect."[14] Samuel Yockney promised to sell "at profits only sufficient to defray expenses, wholesale and retail."[15] Competitive price listing was a common feature in the advertisements. James Maund, who had "been in business twenty-six years" claimed to "sell as cheap, or cheaper, than any warehouse in London" and invited his customers to "compare the difference."[16] According to George Pressey, "should any person offer teas for less than here stated, the public may be assured they are mixed with those old musty, moldy and decayed sorts" which have been in warehouses for years.[17] For packages "not less than one pound" John Hodgson was selling at prices "fully 25 percent cheaper" than the new warehouses.[18] Edward Eagleton, "for the benefit of the poor," was selling "at the reduced prices in small quantities not less than 2 ounces."[19] Specially reduced prices were offered to those purchasing large quantities of tea. George Pressey and John Shaw gave discounts for purchases over twenty pounds.[20] Attractive tie-in sales were held out to buyers, for example, sugar at cost or reduced prices, or tea, "unadulterated upon oath," with free lottery tickets.[21] A number of the advertisers featured reduced or low prices for "ready money" sales.[22]

Such advertising techniques were rather scorned by traditional dealers. George Blakiston sarcastically observed that "regular tradesmen must sometimes give convenient credit that these affidavit warehousemen have artfully avoided in a manner old dealers would have been ashamed of." Their prices, he stated, were "positively no lower, nor the teas any better than every reputable house."[23] He then listed his prices. The great variation in quality for any one sort of tea undoubtedly offered ample opportunity to advertise deceptively low prices. What is particularly intriguing about Blakiston's advertisement is that a dealer of his standing and reputation should have felt compelled to justify his prices. And he was by no means alone. John Smith stated that he "never asked unreasonable prices ... just a fair profit."[24] Thomas Rutton appended a special note to his twelve-shilling hyson: "This tea was purchased at the last private trade Sale and is allowed by the East India Company to be finer than any tea sold at their last publick Sale."[25] Others did the same.[26] Richard Twining addressed a two and one-half column letter to the *Morning Chronicle* justifying the prices charged by "old tea dealers." He asserted that since the Commutation Act, he had reduced his profits which "have not only been less than they ever were ... and less than the fair profit of trade ought to be, but I can with truth say that I have gained ... much less by my trade notwithstanding a very great increase in business."[27] The evidence clearly demonstrates that competition was effecting a downward pressure on prices as the dealers attempted to gain a share of the prospective increase in demand for legal tea.

The second major theme in all the advertisements, one closely associated with prices, concerned the quality of the tea. Advertisers employed various techniques to assure the public that the tea was pure, unadulterated, and of the highest quality. Some emphasized their long years of experience.[28] Almost all declared they had not bought or sold smuggled or adulterated teas. North, Hoare, Nansen, and Simpson even noted that they never bought "prize tea which ... has often been damaged and cured by persons employed by the trade" to make it merchantable.[29] A number went to the length of attaching to each parcel of tea sold an affidavit that it was legal, unadulterated "real" tea.[30] Thomas Delafield, critical of "old dealers ... pretending their shops are new or rather warehouses (for shop is now too mean a description)," made a telling point. He was quite willing, he said, to "swear an affidavit if the customer will pay expenses."[31] John Hodgson also hit out against "retailers of printed oaths." Nevertheless, the public were informed that he had just "cleared home a large stock of the purest Genuine Teas of the latest importations ... free from deceptions or adulterations." He added that "a great deal of Hyson tea of the last Sale had contracted a disagreeable, herby smell and taste, from being near some offensive drug as supposed," but he had "purchased none of that sort."[32]

To reassure the public on the quality or price of the tea, the *imprimatur* of the East India Company was prominently featured by a number of dealers. Some were even prepared to ship chests directly from the company's warehouses to their customers, an extraordinary measure, highly disapproved by traditional dealers. James Maund, for example, offered to sell "a large quantity of teas in the original packages, neat as imported, for the convenience of families or dealers that may like them in that state."[33] John Hodgson featured tea "at one penny a pound advance on the cost price" to buyers willing to have one or more chests delivered directly from the East India Company warehouses. He did so rather reluctantly, however, and warned that he could not "warrant them equal to what I have inspected at home."[34] "Mr Bourdillon, Grocer to His Majesty," having just purchased large quantities at the sales, "proposed to open at his house, an assortment ... in their original package, with the [East India] Company's warrants affixed to each package ... exhibiting the corroborating marks and numbers with their sale price" at the auctions and "to sell the same at 6d. per pound advance" of the prime cost.[35] Selling tea directly from the chest was, of course, not the usual practice. George Blakiston thought it extremely "silly ... to recommend teas to be purchased out of open chests. Everybody knows they improve after being canistered in large quantities in warm rooms at counting houses where continual fires are kept."[36] There was also the problem of blending, a subject about which the dealers were particularly sensitive. Undue profits, it had been said, lay behind the art of blending.[37] Such criticism was fiercely denied by Richard Twining. He maintained, quite rightly, that blending was standard practice in both the retail and wholesale trade, one used since the early eighteenth century. Mixing the various sorts and qualities, he claimed, not only improved the tea but also insured uniformity of taste.[38]

As an added assurance to the public, a few dealers gave money-back guarantees.[39] Perhaps the practice was more common than the advertisements indicate. Philip Constable admitted that his refusal to accept returned teas was "almost the only source of complaint." But, as he explained, he was "surrounded ... by enemies" and feared half his tea-papers would have been brought back ... filled with such miserable stuff ... as my competitors ... wished I had and which they could easily supply from their own canisters." In view of the special circumstances under which he intruded into the trade, he might have had some grounds for his fears.[40]

The Commutation Act had certainly generated exceptional activity among the principal London dealers who competed vigorously for the expected increase in the sale of legal tea. Cheap but pure teas at ready-money prices and even money-back guarantees were being offered to buyers by the more aggressive dealers. Although the survey of provincial newspapers was restricted to a few centres and extended over time, the evidence is overwhelming that the reduction in duties was indeed effecting a "revolution" in the course of the trade. The secret and unfair struggle for custom between the legal and illicit trade was now replaced by open and public competition among tea dealers. It was expressed on two levels. Shops vied with each other for the retail trade, but some provincial dealers also made strenuous efforts to outsell their London rivals. The latter were equally eager to regain their country trade, reduced to a trickle by the activities of the largescale smugglers who had dominated the trade in certain areas. It was, moreover, a period of exceptional surge in the economy. In short, the time was ripe for tea dealers to join their fellow shopkeepers in pursuing more vigorously the sale of tea.

Joseph Hall of St Mary, Port-Street, Bristol, competed against the London dealers by placing an advertisement in the *Morning Post*. His warehouse was to be enlarged in order to supply the "public at Bristol and the country in general with pure teas." An affidavit that he had never sold smuggled, or adulterated tea would be given with every pound of tea.[41] William Shackleton, grocer and teaman of Wakefield, Yorkshire, was selling fine quality tea on the same terms as London dealers.[42] On the Market Place, Ripon, Yorkshire, Mr Spence had just received "many chests direct from the East India Company warehouses." In a long advertisement headed "Pro Bono Publico," buyers were informed he dealt "in tea for Ready Money only, thereby avoiding bad debts, omission of putting down parcels, and the saving of interest on book debts." He was, therefore, "enabled and willing to sell lower than credit terms can possibly admit of. Ready Money and small profit is the prop on which he was embarked and relies ... for his further support."[43]

Competition was keen on all levels at Bristol and Bath. The Hulls, "former partners of Peter Paul," announced the opening of their new "Tea Warehouse" in Bristol for the express purpose of selling genuine teas. "Shopkeepers served on advantageous terms. Teas for exportation on same terms as London ... and warranted in their original package."[44] Peter Paul and Company of Bristol and Bath fired back immediately denying that William Hull and wife had been partners – only engaged as servants ... at £100 per annum" and dismissed last October. The public were assured that despite the "insinuations" of the Hulls, Peter Paul continued the same "laudable plan" and had on hand "prime fresh teas ... just received from the East India Company warehouses" to be sold at prices as low as London dealers. Country shopkeepers could be "supplied with whole lots or a single chest of any lot ... on most advantageous terms." In June, Peter Paul swore before the Council House that he never bought smuggled or adulterated teas.[45] The competition between the two was joined by the "Bath New Tea Warehouse" and later by the "London Tea Warehouse of Bath and Bristol." In long advertisements, both listed prices and noted in particular that their teas were "sent twice a week from the Company's warehouse in London" and therefore "guaranteed pure."[46] Peter Paul and Company accepted the challenge and assured buyers that its teas were not only cheaper but also of superior quality to the London Tea Warehouse. The price range, however, was identical to that of the other two firms – one shilling to ten shillings a pound. But Peter Paul gave additional security: a money-back guarantee if buyers were not fully satisfied.[47] In December, Evans and Shipway announced the opening of yet another "tea warehouse" in Bristol, the Turk and Tea Chest. Like the others, it served both the wholesale and retail trade and provided "genuine" teas warranted "unadulterated."[48]

The Bath and Bristol warehouses were competing not only against each other, but also against the London dealers. This area was one that prior to the Commutation Act was well supplied with smuggled tea. As the 1782 Memorials to Treasury show, Bristol was a major redistribution centre for the surrounding counties. Its dealers were not prepared to be displaced by London dealers and fought to retain their country custom. At least three firms operated shops in both Bristol and Bath and advertised in both places. Multiple shop retailing was not a nineteenth-century innovation.

But not only the newly styled warehouses openly advertised. In Bath, four grocers enticed buyers with special offers. John Coles, grocer and tea dealer at the Original Golden Canister, claimed to have purchased his teas at the East India Company sales and gave a warrant with every one-quarter pound or more to assure the public that the tea was free of adulteration. He was "determined to sell as cheap as any shop" in town.[49] William Daniel, grocer and wine merchant, an avid advertiser, appeared in every issue of the paper for months, but he appealed to the carriage trade. Customers could buy at his shop fine quality "teas of the best flavour and colour" in addition to a great variety of groceries and "foreign wines." "Cheap" teas were not mentioned.[50] John Kendall, "grocer and tea-man," added a special note to his description of teas – the only shop "selling Wheble's candles," presumably a prestigious article.[51] M. Tagg's "Grocery and Tea Warehouse" catered to the transient population of Bath. In addition to teas, coffees, cocoas, spices, and fruits, customers could obtain "plate, china, glass ... on hire." The four were obviously the usual market-street shopkeepers and, unlike the warehouses, competing primarily for retail customers. Several Bristol grocers and tea dealers advertised, but only one featured cheap teas and gave "good allowance for ready-money."[52]

At Leeds, James Donaldson's shop was converted to a "tea Warehouse." He featured "cheap teas" purchased at the East India Company sales "at reduced prices" and was "determined to serve country dealers" on London terms.[53] He was indeed facing competition. Philip Constable of London placed a long advertisement in the paper recommending his pure, unadulterated teas at reduced prices. He sold wholesale or retail for "ready money" only, and in quantities not lesss than one pound. Country orders "with good bills at short date ... duly attended" – every package accompanied by a sworn affidavit.[54] W. Sewell of Leeds not only claimed to sell at the "same price as wholesale dealers in London," but also gave 6.25 pounds for the price of 6 pounds, and "if not good" the customer could "return them." He had, of course, just received fresh teas from the East India Company.[55] There were in addition the usual short notices of grocers, "brandy merchants and tea dealers" and others.

But not only shopkeepers at Leeds sought publicity in the paper. Grocers from Bradford, Halifax, Knaresborough, Otley, Wakefield, and York advertised in the *Leeds Mercury*. William Tuke and Son of York, for example, announced the opening of their "Public Roasting-House for Coffee" where dealers were supplied "on as low terms as in London."[56] Such notices were designed to attract the trade of country shopkeepers and openly competed against the London dealers. James Rich of the "Bradford Original Wholesale and Retail Tea Warehouse" had attended the East India Company Sale and "bought largely ... the most approved lots of genuine useful teas." They were to be sold "on very low terms ... for ready money or bills of short date." The advertisement was particularly addressed to "country dealers" who were promised a "great saving." Chests of tea either from Bradford or "cleared from East India Company warehouses" would be shipped "to any part of the country at the lowest exchange prices."[57] To attract trade, James Rich was relying not on the art of specially blended quality teas, but rather on the demand for a "useful" and *cheap* article at ready-money prices. By so doing, he and others like him were undermining the trade relations of the traditional London dealers.

Prior to the Commutation Act, Scotland was the bailiwick of large-scale smugglers; and the principal dealers of Edinburgh and Glasgow experienced little if any competition from their London counterparts. Dealing almost exclusively in smuggled tea, they controlled its sale and distribution in Scotland. Traffic in the illicit article was well organized, and small shopkeepers were regularly supplied with a variety of teas at stated prices. All links in the chain from importers to small shopkeepers were closely tied by the cooperative need to evade customs and excise officers.[58] In 1784, the principal London dealers had few correspondents in Scotland. The Commutation Act opened up the trade in Scotland as elsewhere, and tea could flow through customary legal channels. But whatever expectations the London dealers may have had of obtaining a greater share of the Scottish market were soon quashed by the energetic actions of the principal dealers of Scotland. They quickly repaired to the East India auction room when illicit tea was no longer available. Moreover, the dealers could now openly pursue custom with a vigour and persistence that left little room for penetration by the Londoner. How much their success was due to national feeling or to the spirit engendered by the illicit trade is difficult to say. The smugglers were the great entrepreneurial *free traders* of the eighteenth century and found support in no less a personage then Adam Smith.

Scottish tea dealers certainly showed no reluctance to advertising. As advertisers, pride of place must be accorded the Edinburgh dealers. In 1791, at least twenty repeatedly proclaimed their commercial virtues in the *Edinburgh Advertiser*. And they were not trivial shopkeepers – among the group were some of the leading tradesmen of Edinburgh and Leith. Robert Sheppard was one of the most extensive grocers. By 1798 he was operating two shops in Edinburgh and one each in Leith and Aberdeen. At least four of his apprentices became important Scottish businessmen: Andrew Melrose in tea; James Richardson, a Glasgow and Edinburgh sugar merchant; William Law, who specialized in coffee and later held the post of Lord Provost; and John Christie, an eccentric but well-known Edinburgh grocer.[59] Other firms such as Alexander Forbes and Company, John Carnegie and Company, Robert Johnston and Sons, William Thorburn, and David Gray were influential in the business community of Edinburgh. Many were still advertising in 1798 and later.

Robert Sheppard and Company was the most frequent advertiser, having at least thirteen long notices in the paper, each repeated several times in later issues.[60] Not far behind were J. Carnegie and Company, Robert Johnston and Sons, and William Thorburn, each placing six long advertisements that ran for several successive issues in the newspaper. Advertisements appeared throughout the year – no month was without at least one notice. They were, however, far more numerous about a month after the East India Company's quarterly sale, time enough apparently for the fresh teas to have arrived from London. Tea was the major article featured and prices for the various kinds were listed. John Witchell, for example, sold seven different qualities of hyson ranging from six to twelve shillings per pound. But other foodstuffs were also mentioned. Robert Johnston and Sons gave prominent place to their ham, bacon, various cheeses, butter, meat, confectioneries, wines, spirits, fruits, and groceries. At James Thomson's "Grocery Warehouse" one could get China oranges and English apples. Wines and spirits were sold by most grocers. David Gray was a "tea, wine and spirit dealer." William Sutherland, who offered sugars at prime cost to buyers of tea, called himself a "tea and spirit dealer."

To promote sales, advertisers prominently featured the special quality of their tea or its low price. And they had no scruple in claiming to offer a better buy than their fellow shopkeepers. Competition was keen for both retail and trade customers and ingenious statements were made to attract buyers. For example, John Carnegie's souchong and pekoe were particularly "well-flavoured and strong" and cheap. The tea had been imported by captains and officers of East Indiamen, and was sold at lower prices than "teas of an inferior quality at the Public Sale."[61] He also announced the arrival – "the first from the Public Sale" – of a large quantity of black teas of "such fine quality at so reasonable price" as never before offered. An appended note cautioned customers to be sure the firm's "name and price always [appeared] on each package." Later in July he announced that he "had inspected the black teas himself before the sale and avoided the faint, weak and insipid teas that commonly come to this country."[62]

Indeed, the principal dealers placed particular emphasis on purchases at the East India Company Sale and announced the arrival in Edinburgh of the teas. While Alexander Forbes and Company assured the public that a member of the firm was "on the spot" to purchase tea, William Thorburn announced his return from the East India Sale. About the same time, Robert Sheppard noted the arrival of his teas "after a remarkably quick passage from the last India House Sale." And Robert Johnston and Sons had just received "a cargo of exceedingly high flavoured teas."[63] The arrival of the teas was the signal for a spurt of advertisements and many got into the act.

Edinburgh dealers employed various techniques to emphasize their particularly attractive prices. A common practice was to recommend medium-priced teas as particularly good buys. In January 1791, Sheppard's best buy was congou at 4s. and 4s. 6d. per pound. In February, Carnegie's "good pennyworth" was congou at 4s.; by July the "best for the money," "great bargain," or "very good bargains" were 3s. 6d., 3s. 8d., and 4s.[64] Some offered lower prices in general; some sold "cheaper and better goods"; or "equal in quality and price" to any shop. William Thorburn "sold for ready money much under the common prices."[65] Others, such as Forbes, Sheppard, and Carnegie, promised prices anywhere from 6d. to 1s. 6d. below those of other shops.[66]

The *Edinburgh Advertiser* published full details of the East India Company's quarterly auctions[67] and dealers were quick to capitalize on any fluctuations in prices. Carnegie, for example, noting the drop in prices for black teas at the March Sale, stated that never before had he been able to offer "such fine qualities" at such low prices. Sheppard and Thomas Spence followed suit.[68] Slight variations of the practice were adopted when prices were rising. In 1798, Thorburn regretted that "Bohea and Congou ... sold very much higher at the last ... Sale," and recommended "very good Souchong" at 4s. 6d. to 6s. and hyson green at 7s. to 9s., which sold "full as cheap as formerly. Teas under the above prices will be worse than they were."[69] Sheppard, on the other hand, had "cleared from the East India Company's Warehouses above five tons of fine green and black teas previous to the commencement of the present duty ... and is determined to sell ... at the following low prices."[70] Alexander Allison of Perth was fortunate – "tho the Teas in general sold much higher at Last March Sale, he had on hand a quantity of the December Sale ... at former low prices."[71]

As if to leave no stone unturned, some featured their peculiar advantages over other shopkeepers. David Gray at the Grassmarket claimed his teas were "cheaper than those on South Bridge as his shop rent is not one-third of theirs." The teas were, however, also sold for the same price "at the shop of D. Gray and Son, Frederick Street, New Town."[72] P. Maxton, at his Tea Warehouse, "first stair above entry to the Flesh Market," emphasized his favourable location – "the shop, being a few steps up, is free from any damp and consequently well adapted for keeping teas in great perfection ... [and] prices will be found low."[73] Alexander Thompson who sold at "common current prices for ready money" capitalized on the fact that he dealt "only in tea and coffee" and was therefore able to "exert himself to please customers."[74] William Sutherland, John Stirling and Company, and John Witchell attracted custom by offering "sugar at prime cost."[75]

The picture depicted by the advertisements of tea dealers in Edinburgh and elsewhere hardly conforms to the accepted view of eighteenth-century grocers. Apparently far more competition occurred than is generally supposed. Prices were openly displayed and not a few grocers sold only for ready money. Certainly they were not relying solely upon reputation and skill to attract custom and can hardly be accused of frowning on open advertisements or "puffery." And they were *established tradesmen*. Those advertising in the *Edinburgh Advertiser* were the leading grocers of the city. Their advertisements, however, were pitched not to the select few, the well-to-do who disdained puffery, but to the broad middling group who wanted value for their money. The emphasis was on good genuine articles at reasonable prices. Although the Edinburgh advertisers competed vigourously and vividly, they did not viciously attack each other. Advertising was accepted as part of normal commercial behaviour.

The old methods had not yet been discarded. Many principal dealers in London and the provinces continued to rely on travellers and circulars to draw in custom. Issued after each East India Quarterly Sale, the circular informed correspondents of the dealer's current prices and what changes had occurred in quality or price since the last sale. Certain teas might be recommended but no exaggerated claims were made. It was a formal business letter and expressed the style of the firm. Richard Twining sent out the following circular on 9 April 1785. The style is very characteristic of the man.

The Sale of teas being now over, we take the liberty of troubling you with a list of our prices...

Our teas in general are remarkably fresh and good and we cannot omit this opportunity of assuring our customers, that, in return for the many favors which they have conferred upon us ... they may depend upon every possible attention on our part to supply them with the best teas at the most reasonable prices.

Your most obliged Humble Servant.[76]

The Tukes of York were Quakers and their circular of 9 April 1785 is typically terse. Correspondents were informed:

The East-India Company's Tea Sale being ended, we advise the prices as under. Congous and Souchongs have sold higher than was expected; other sorts are very reasonable.

Thy Orders, as occasion offers, will be executed on good Terms, and oblige
W. Tuke and Son[77]

The announcement was followed by a list of teas, coffee, chocolate, and cocoa. But even in stating prices, the firm was very brief. The prices of congou, for example, were stated to be "3s. to 5s. 9d."; those of hyson, "6s. to 10s."[78] The circular of Brewster and Gillman, an old City firm, was far more explicit. Changes in the prices of each sort of tea were reported and suggestions made on the best buys. For example, "Congou Teas at 3s. 4d. and upwards are about 2d. a pound cheaper and are very good, those under 3s. 4d. are still the dearest in Proportion." They concluded the market report by observing that "the teas in general are good and at a safe price to buy. The favor of your orders will most oblige." In contrast to the Tukes, the London firm quoted an elaborate list of prices: nine for congou, ranging from 3s. 3d. to 5s. and "ord. lower"; nine for singlo, 3s. 3d. to 9s. 6d.; twelve for hyson, 5s. 3d. to 9s. 6d., and so on.[79]

Such circulars were remitted to correspondents to encourage further orders. But how did a firm acquire new accounts? A hired traveller, a rider, would be expected to bring in new business, but older, more traditional firms were rather disdainful of such an open, impersonal search for new customers. Circulars could also have been sent to grocers listed in the directories, but it seems highly unlikely that traditional dealers would have resorted to such a venturesome course. Davison Newman and Company, it will be recalled, were unwilling to accept a new account unless the shopkeeper was "well recommended" as a prompt payer. One suspects that for a traditional dealer, the building up of a clientele was a relatively slow, protracted affair with most new accounts being acquired by word-of-mouth. For example, an apprentice, after completing his training and opening his own shop, probably bought stock from the supplier of his former master. There is also some evidence that London dealers tended to concentrate their trade within certain areas where they would become well known over a period of time. John Waddington, London tea dealer, was particularly disturbed at the seizure by excise officers of 107 pounds of black tea sent, apparently without a permit, to Mr Gladhill, a grocer in Brighouse, Yorkshire. Waddington claimed to have been "near thirty years in business" and had never been "in the least suspected" of smuggling. Mr Gladhill, he explained, "lives in a part of Yorkshire where your Lordships' petitioner is very well known and does much business. The condemning of this tea will do much injury to his reputation which he has ever held sacred."[80] Perhaps John Waddington originated in Yorkshire or had family or friends there. David Pugh came from Wales and appears to have had a thriving trade in that country.[81]

Skill in the purchasing, blending, and pricing of tea and careful attention to the requirements of his customers were the basic, if not the only, means by which the fair-trade dealer expanded his trade. Although the market for legal tea had not been stagnant before 1784, it had grown very slowly. In the three decades, 1756–84, Excise deliveries of tea for home consumption had increased only 20 percent. The business philosophy and practices of the principal dealers in legal tea were formed by the market in which they acted, one in which demand increased almost imperceptibly. Indeed, fear of losing custom was more prevalent than a buoyant view of market possibilities. Demand, London dealers were convinced, could only be increased or even retained by providing a high quality tea pleasing to the palates of customers. It was a view that many traditional firms continued to hold and to act by long after the Commutation Act.[82] Their philosophy and practices were, however, to be seriously challenged by the new entrepreneurial spirit which emerged with the demise of smuggling.

One of the most interesting and earliest of the entrepreneurs was Edward Eagleton who introduced into the trade new methods of marketing. He was an old established London dealer with a shop at 9 Bishopsgate.[83] He was no petty dealer – in July 1784 he had in stock 2,359 pounds of tea. Eagleton did not, however, subscribe to the methods and practices of the traditional London dealers. In 1784 in a four-page letter to William Pitt, fulsomely praising the young minister, he described himself "as a considerable dealer and perhaps more so than any single trader ... who has no partner in London, having paid near £10,000 per annum duty on teas ... on my own account." In particular, his letter was critical of the traditional tea dealers. Eagleton, like Pitt, was one of the "new men of business." He suggested that Pitt open "all the ports of the kingdom to tea imports" in order to give the East India Company "a little competition."[84]

Edward Eagleton advertised extensively. In 1782 he featured in *Felix Farley's Bristol Journal* his "original Tea Warehouse, for the Cheapest, most curious and richest high flavored teas ... Eagleton, Tea-Man, at the Grasshopper. The Only Tea-Warehouse where the Nobility, Gentry, Wholesale Dealers, etc. do save from ten to twenty percent (particularly on fine tea). Many families are obliged to pay from 12s. to 21s. which I sell equally good from 10s. 6d. to 16s. and all lower teas cheap in proportion." He then gave a list of the prices of tea, coffee, cocoa, and the various chocolates. He observed that "the multiplicity of business which I do has induced several small dealers to advertise, therefore, request Ladies and Gentlemen, etc. coming or sending orders to be particular in not mistaking my Warehouse." But he was a ready-money dealer. "All goods must be paid for on or before delivery. Good bills at a short date inclosed with orders taken in payment. Orders wholesale or retail for Town or Country, by Post or otherwise sent to any part of London."[85] Similar advertisements, with some variation in prices, appeared in March, June, and July, and in the *Gloucester Journal* in 1784.

The Commutation Act gave him the opportunity to expand. In February 1785 he opened a second "tea warehouse at 42 Cheapside" for the stated purpose of reducing "the prices of genuine teas to the Public." The following year he advertised extensively in *Leeds Mercury*. On 7 November he placed a long half-column advertisement in the paper. As the following excerpt shows, he was launching a well-organized mail-order service designed to attract both retail customers and small shopkeepers.

NEW TEAS – Arrived by the Late Ships from China – The finest Imported by the East India Company, selling from £15 to £30 per cent *cheaper and better* in Quality than any ever before *offered* ... At the Real New Commutation and Original London and City TEA WAREHOUSES, the GRASSHOPPER ... *The First Places in London for Cheap New Teas* of the finest full flavour, warranted ... to be Genuine as Imported ... which are delivered with every parcel, the price marked on each and sold at such reduced prices as the Public have a right to expect, agreeable to the intention of the Commutation Act ...

The Nobility, Gentry, Families, Dealers ... and all consumers of tea ... in Town and Country, giving orders by Post or otherwise, for any quantity, small or large, sent agreeable to direction, to any Inn, Coach, Carrier, Wharf or Place in London, which, if on trial does not *exceed* any bought elsewhere at the same price, the *Money will be Returned*.

All goods must be paid for on or before delivery. *Good* country bills, inclosed with orders, *taken in payment*.

Ladies, Gentlemen, etc. honouring them with their Address, waited on, at their own time, in any part of the town with Samples and a list of their much reduced Prices or may be had or seen at either of their warehouses.[86]

Following this was a long list of teas with the current prices compared to the prices for the same quality before the Commutation Act. He also listed the prices of coffees and chocolates – "Sir Hans Sloane's Milk, Churchman's Patent and the Finest Vanilla Chocolate 4s. 6d. per lb."[87] Similar advertisements appeared in *Felix Farley's Bristol*

Journal in January 1787. In the London papers he claimed to be selling his teas one shilling cheaper than any other dealer and at least "four pence less than the reduced prices at which they were meant to be sold by the Commutation Act."[88]

Eagleton did not confine his attention to those who bought by the pound. Appended to the 7 November *Leeds Mercury* advertisement was a special note: "Town and Country Dealers served on Terms more eligible and cheaper than at any other House or Warehouse in London." What those terms were appeared in a long advertisement the following week. He was, in fact, proposing a radical departure from traditional methods. He offered to buy

LOTS or SINGLE CHESTS OF TEA ... for any Dealer at the rate of only one per cent Commission for our Trouble, either at the East India Company Sales, or at all Times, at the lowest Exchange Price, which are sent in the original package as imported from China.

The advantage to those who send us their Commissions, orders, etc. over other Dealers needs not any comment as they will have our judgment; their Teas bought at the same price as ours; and the benefit of the East India Company's weight, which will enable them to sell on the same Cheap Terms as we have always had the credit for with the Public.

Orders addressed to us ... mentioning the sorts, price and what it is wanted to sell for, shall meet our best attention.[89]

A chart of the various sorts of tea was presented in order that "every person can know at one view the exact deposit [at the East India Company Sale] ... nearly the net weight, amount of a lot or a single chest ... and the number of chests in each Lot."[90]

Eagleton then explained that the terms of sale at the East India Company's auction required the purchaser to buy in a whole lot and to pay the deposit immediately. Therefore, the amount of the deposit "must be sent with every order ... and the remainder of the money when the teas are taken away or punctually on or before the Prompt which is generally about two months after the beginning of their sales." If the East India Company's terms were not "strictly complied with," the buyer would forfeit the deposit and was henceforth forbidden to buy at the auctions. "Postage of letters, bills ... and every cost must be paid" by those ordering from him as his "terms will not admit of a Day's Credit or Open Accounts." And indeed he was correct. A 1 percent mark-up, which is what his terms amount to, is far below that charged by traditional London dealers. By acting as an agent and widely advertising his terms, Eagleton was making available to major shopkeepers all over the country a cheaper source of supply. Small shopkeepers, requiring a variety of teas, would not be able to buy so advantageously. They could, however, purchase their tea by the pound from him.[91] Eagleton was apparently successful in launching his agency business. By 1793 he had added to his establishment a third warehouse at "12 Rampant Horse Street, near the Market, Norwich."

Eagleton also introduced another novel method of marketing teas. He established retail outlets in various provincial towns. In 1793 Eagleton claimed to have outlets in twenty-seven towns and cities covering thirteen counties in England and two each in Wales and Scotland.[92] He sent down to these places small packets of tea priced and sealed with the sign of the Grasshopper. How much should be discounted as "puffing" is difficult to say. Besides a warehouse under his own management in Norwich, he had at least one retail outlet in Manchester. In 1795 Jonas Crossley informed the public that he had just received "fresh ... teas ... from Eagleton and Company ... London ... wholesale and retail ... selling from ten to twenty per cent cheaper than (are now) sold ... and carriage saved." The teas were "packed and marked with the sign of the Grasshopper" and the quality and price clearly indicated. He offered the same "money-back guarantee" and advised the public to "taste, try, compare and judge" the teas.[93] Lipton, the great nineteenth-century entrepreneur, was not the first to brand and market his teas through retail outlets. To emphasize the cheapness of his goods, Eagleton noted that those who keep travellers and give credits "must charge a profit" to cover the "great expenses" incurred and the "losses of bad debts. Therefore, as Eagleton and Company do not give credit, they can and will do business on much lower terms than any other house in London."[94]

Eagleton did not have the field to himself, although his competitor, G. Winter, does not appear to have operated on the same scale. Unlike Eagleton, he was not listed in the 1784 survey of principal London dealers. Winter had a tea warehouse on Newgate Street, London, and in 1795 he also was supplying shopkeepers with ready-packed goods. Samuel Satterwaite of Manchester had "Genuine Teas and Coffees, etc." from Winter's Tea Warehouse which he was "selling on commission." G. Winter informed the public that he "sends down a weekly supply of genuine Teas, Coffees, Chocolate, and Cocoa ready weighed up in pounds, half pounds, and quarters, each sealed with his seal and the price and quality wrote thereon (to prevent the imposition of adulteration so very much practiced by country dealers) ... to be sold by S. Satterwaite, Manchester." He sold at "London prices" and particularly noted that "teas, coffees, etc. above 4s. a pound are totally free from the additional duty." Perhaps, like some Edinburgh dealers, Winter still had on hand tea from the previous sale. Orders for his teas and coffees "delivered to Mr. Satterwaite will be forwarded with utmost dispatch either from London or Manchester."[95]

Eagleton was surely a pushing entrepreneur, trying various methods of marketing: selling by mail order; establishing retail outlets; prepacking teas in small quantities; sealing and branding each package with the quality, price, and the firm's emblem; serving at East India sales as a commission agent for country grocers; offering customers money-back guarantees; and making his name and his product widely known by extensive advertising. Many of these practices had been used earlier in the century in other retail trades, particularly patent medicine. But Eagleton brought together a formidable list of methods in the retailing of tea that could serve as a model for other practitioners. How many other London dealers were also adopting new methods or what inroads they may have made on the market of the traditional dealers is not known.[96] The French Revolutionary Wars and the subsequent rapid rise in tea duties brought a halt to the aggressive search for custom. Economic and social conditions favoured the more conservative approach of traditional dealers.

FROM CA. 1793

During the period of the French and Napoleonic Wars, the tea trade suffered from widespread inflation of prices and, in particular, from steady increases in tea duty. Quantities sold at the East India auctions were stable, but prices shot up and remained high. Such circumstances allowed for little expansion in the retailers' trade. They tended to favour the traditional dealers with large capital and the necessary skills to cater to those consumers to whom high prices were no object in the appeasement of their taste. It is not surprising that no pushing entrepreneur like Edward Eagleton or Robert Sheppard of Edinburgh appeared.

Trade increased at the return of peace, and business expectations were buoyant. In the last three years of the war (1810–12), the average annual quantities of tea delivered for home consumption was 20.5 million pounds; the following three years (1813–15), 25.0 million. Quantities declined to 21.3 million pounds during the difficult years of 1817–18, but returned to 23.8 million pounds (1822–4), and continued to rise. However, the heavy duty, 100 percent *ad valorem* by 1820, prevented a decline in price commensurate with that of other commodities. The dealers were thus squeezed between high initial costs and an increased demand for cheaper tea.

This was the situation behind the Edinburgh tea dealers' famous memorial of 1818, the major complaint of which was an inadequate supply of low-cost tea.[97] Some dealers even resorted to the sale of adulterated tea, a practice that was to have unforeseen consequences. All these pressures within the trade gave scope to new types of dealers to intrude into the arena. By adopting and revising marketing methods introduced in the 1780s, they competed more effectively against the old dealers than their forerunners and succeeded in acquiring a substantial portion of the domestic trade in tea. In the process, radical changes were effected in the relationships and practices of suppliers, dealers, and retail customers that, in turn, facilitated the adjustment of the trade to the abolition of the East India Company's exclusive privilege in 1833.

In 1818, a series of excise trials against manufacturers and sellers of counterfeit tea occasioned widespread publicity on the subject in London and provincial newspapers. Rumours abounded: ninetenths of the dealers were guilty of adulteration and Excise had agreed "to suppress the names of those found guilty." To dispell the atmosphere of public distrust and panic within the trade, the principal dealers of London responded to the threat by holding a general meeting. A special committee was appointed to inquire into the nature and extent of the offences and to seek the assistance of Excise and the East India Company. Shortly thereafter, statements signed by Richard Twining, Jr., chairman of the committee, were inserted in most London newspapers. Tea consumers were assured that "the most minute investigation" had revealed very few cases of adulteration. "The practice" was "extremely limited in extent and confined to a few unprincipled individuals" and the names of those found guilty would be published.[98] Excise agreed that such exposure was "absolutely necessary" in order to stop the practice of adulteration and to remove "the apprehensions ... of it being general amongst tea dealers." At the same time, the directors of the East India Company fully endorsed the proposal to seal and dispatch tea directly from the Company's warehouses to the dealers' customers.[99]

But before the upheaval subsided and trade returned to normal, Frederick Gye, a printer by trade, managed to intrude into the trade by exploiting the confusion and capitalizing on the rumours. Gye, who had been a principal in a City firm that printed lottery tickets as well as the posters of Tom Bish, a friend and business associate, acquired the capital for his venture by winning a lottery prize of £30,000. Although he had no previous experience or knowledge of the tea trade, Gye succeeded in establishing himself as one of the foremost dealers. He did so by: using skilfully drawn-up advertisements proclaiming the virtues of his establishment over all others;

using both London and provincial newspapers as well as handbills to attract custom; and adopting and revising practices that had sprung up after the Commutation Act.[100]

Gye opened his first shop, the London Genuine Tea Company, on 5 November 1818 with a great flourish of advertisements. The expressed purpose was to rescue the "Tea Trade from the opprobrium attached to it by the late disclosures of adulteration." To assure the public of a "genuine" article, unmixed with "inferior" teas, he engaged "to neither buy nor sell Bohea tea ... so commonly used to adulterate better sorts." By insinuating that the blending or mixing of teas was tantamount to adulterating, he tried to arouse suspicion of a hallowed practice in the trade and to asperse the honour and integrity of other dealers. Only he could be relied upon to provide "genuine" teas. To emphasize the point, he made a great display of always having at his shop twenty to fifty opened chests to enable purchasers to see their tea being "weighed from the Original Packages." Those desiring a whole chest could have it sent "direct from the East India Warehouses." Country customers were promised a genuine article, warranted "pure, unadulterated, without mixture of Bohea." Any quantity from one-quarter pound upwards would be sent in a lead package, "enclosed in an elevation of their warehouse," with the quality, price, and the company's seal firmly attached. Orders would be executed promptly and the tea sent "free of carriage within 10 miles of London." All transactions, however, were on a ready-money basis.[101]

Gye also adopted methods pioneered by Edward Eagleton. From the beginning he placed particular emphasis on his "agents" who were to be "appointed in every principal town in England." And he sought them aggressively. By February 1819, less than four months after opening his first shop in London, he claimed to have "one hundred agents and more appointed daily"; by October he was boasting of 500 agents. To facilitate sales in London and to establish his credentials, Gye opened two additional shops, one in Oxford Street, the other at Charing Cross. And he spared no expenses; his principal "warehouse" on Ludgate Hill was elaborately furnished and "decorated with impressive Chinese views."[102] From his initial announcement, Gye proved to be a formidable competitor and opponent of the principal London dealers, and succeeded in a remarkably short time in acquiring a considerable portion of the country trade. His impact on the trade was greater than Eagleton's although their methods were basically similar.

Gye owed his success, in part, to having commenced his business when economic and social conditions were more favourable for such a venture – an increasing demand for tea by consumers who had less refined tastes and whose purchases were not confined to high-class grocers. But another element figures in his rapid rise. Gye, unlike Eagleton, aroused the active opposition of many London dealers who resented the accusations levelled at the trade by an inexperienced newcomer. It was, as one highly respectable dealer stated, necessary "to repel the base attack on their character and most illiberal attempt to divert the trade out of its accustomed and regular channels." A general meeting of the trade was held on 3 November to counter the adverse comments in Gye's circulars and public advertisements. The meeting was followed by a flood of letters, advertisements, and editorials in the newspapers: the quality and stated prices of Gye's tea were questioned; his lack of experience was emphasized – mere "merchant-adventurers or lottery-office keepers"; his "puffing" and "scurrilous attack" on dealers was exposed as the "grossest deception" of an "empiric in commerce." Even Eagleton entered the fray, declining to use in future the term "genuine ... so frequently misapplied by unprincipled dealers."[103] Whatever truth lay behind the charges, Gye reaped the benefit of having the London Genuine Tea Company kept in the limelight and turned this to his advantage. The "opposition of the London tea dealers," he said, proved without doubt the "merits" of his undertaking over all others.[104]

In addition to the newspaper campaign, two dealers in particular – Henry Long and Frederick Sparrow – adopted measures destined to have far-reaching effects. They copied in every detail the practices of Gye. Sparrow went to the length of opening two additional shops on the same streets as Gye.[105] By the early part of 1819, the three were advertising extensively in provincial newspapers. In the course of their protracted competition, the use of retail outlets, or agencies as they were called, to distribute prepacked tea, sealed, labelled, and priced, was extended far beyond what Eagleton and Winter had accomplished. Within a few years it became a regular and accepted practice. The lack of business records precludes a detailed examination of the components of growth; the advertisements, however, reveal the means employed to attract custom.

Gye commenced his venture with a well-formulated plan and the capital from the lottery prize enabled him to carry it out. It included the sale of packaged tea, the appointing of agents, and widespread advertising. Within a month he was attacking London dealers in "Chelmsford, Cambridge and other journals."[106] His announcements were eye-catching, often a half-column or longer, with an engraving of his warehouse. He particularly emphasized the novelty,

superiority, and popularity of his undertaking. "Whilst others" incurred the expenses of "sending travellers ... to solicit orders, applications to sell the Company's teas are constantly arriving."[107] And
he continually featured the purity of his tea, never mixed with
"Bohea which trash is so constantly used to lower those teas sent
into the country." Moreover, he was able to retail at the "lowest price"
due to his large purchases and small returns."[108] Of the three, Gye
was the most artful and persistent advertiser, although neither Sparrow nor Long were far behind. Sparrow also had an engraving of
his "Original London Genuine Tea Warehouse" and warned the
public against imposters.[109] Long claimed to be the first to "expose
the use of Bohea" to lower the quality of tea.[110] Rather interestingly,
he took exception to the practice of packing "in that poisonous lead"
– it was something he never did.[111] Advertisements were spaced to
appear for several weeks following the quarterly sales of the East
India Company and generally featured a particular tea or its specially
attractive price.[112] At least until 1823, the three continued to vie
against each other and cautioned customers against imposters.[113]

But the most significant aspect of their advertising campaign was
the way they popularized packaged tea and its sale by agents. Both
Gye and Long played on the fears of the public. To assure consumers
of pure, unadulterated tea, unmixed with bohea, the teas were enclosed in the companies' wrappers, sealed, and labelled with the
quality and price.[114] Sparrow, on the other hand, specifically featured its quality, "the strongest and best full flavoured teas," and
emphasized the price of his teas – on "terms not before offered to
the public," Customers were warned, however, to be sure his "name
and address with price per pound is printed upon each packet."[115]
In short, customers were being urged to forsake the traditional grocer and purchase prepacked tea. At the same time, the appointment
of agents served as a means of bypassing high-class grocers who
would resist selling packaged tea.

Agents were actively recruited through newspaper advertisements
and other means. Applications from prospective agents were particularly requested for towns where no agent had yet been appointed.
Moreover, the appointed agent was assured of support from the
principal. Advertisements listed the names and places of abode of
agents, and notices were placed in newspapers with a circulation
radius that included the towns named. Gye listed thirty-seven towns
in the *Leeds Mercury*. With the exception of two in Durham, Stockton-
on-Tees, and Barnard Castle, all were in Yorkshire. The towns listed
in the *Manchester Herald*, on the other hand, included nineteen in
Lancashire, fifteen in Cheshire, and seven in Derbyshire.[116] Equally,

if not more, important, the product the agent was to sell was widely advertised, easily identifiable, and required no particular knowledge or skill to handle. As one London agency firm stated, "the established sale of these teas is a very valuable addition to any respectable business, being a handsome income produced by a quick return without the least possible risk, trouble or expense."[117] Agents may even have had the option of returning teas not suited to their trade.[118] Nor was an agent subject to excessive competition. In large towns, such as Manchester and Leeds, two or three agents were appointed, but it appears to have been a general practice to appoint only one in the smaller places.

The advertisements give no explicit information concerning financial arrangements with agents. Winter's agent in Manchester in 1793 sold "on commission" and the practice undoubtedly persisted. In 1825, one agency firm allowed "a commission of £5 per cent," which it asserted was "only one-third of what is allowed in similar cases." However, as the advertisement was directed at retail customers and designed to emphasize the cheapness of the firm's tea, no confidence can be placed on the stated rate of commission.[119] More pertinent, were transactions of agents with the principal on a strictly ready-money basis? There is some evidence they were. One firm was willing to ship tea to "any respectable person" who "wishes to sell," as an agent if "an order ... with remittance" was received.[120] An intriguing account in the ledger of Andrew Melrose of Edinburgh indicates he was acting as an intermediary by regularly transmitting money from one of his own trade customers to Gye.[121] The account records one way by which a small village retailer satisfied the requirement for cash payment. If the agency firms did, in fact, require cash transactions, they were indeed shortening the lines of credit and reducing their overhead expenses.

Although no specific or verified figures on the extent of Gye's effect on the traditional network of distribution are available, his promotional activities sent shock waves throughout the tea trade. Bohea tea was the first victim – both the price and the quantity sold at the East India Company's auctions declined immediately. The average bid-up price in 1817 was 29.6 d.; in 1818, 29.9 d.; it dropped to 22.0 d. in 1819.[122] And Gye's personal success is unquestionable. The London Genuine Tea Company was a profitable concern. At the end of 1821, Gye launched the London Wine Company, and planned to run it on similar principles. At the same time, he and a partner bought Vauxhall Gardens for £28,000. In 1823, he became member of Parliament for Chippenham and held the seat until 1832.[123] The extent of his trade is less easy to verify. By the end of

1819, he claimed to be selling 2,500 pounds of tea per day or 782,500 pounds per annum, "independent of teas sold in large parcels."[124] In a letter to Treasury in 1821, he stated that within three years he had established "the most extensive tea trade" in the kingdom, that during the last twelve months he had paid duties amounting to £100,000.[125] As the figures could have been easily checked by Excise, to whom the letter would be referred, they were probably not greatly exaggerated. With an average duty of 2s. 6d. per pound, Gye's annual turnover would have been about 800,000 pounds, undoubtedly an extensive trade for a single firm, particularly for one in business less than three years. His own statements on the number of agents employed show an equally rapid increase – within a year he claimed to have 500 agents. The number increased more slowly later: 800 in June 1821 and upwards of 1,200 in 1826.[126] Whatever the precise figures may have been, Excise was aware of his widespread connections. In disallowing Gye's application for the return of some tea to London from an agent in Edinburgh, Excise stated that it was not necessary as his company could send the tea to "their customers in any other part of Great Britain."[127]

In addition to personal success, Gye set in motion even more radical changes. The use of agents and "the branding of goods, their advertisement by the producers, and the determination of the retail prices,"[128] became far more widespread. Gye, Sparrow, and Long were soon followed by other firms supplying agents with packaged tea. At least five have been identified.[129] In the process of diverting a portion of the trade "out of its accustomed and regular channels," agency firms also disrupted customary practices within the trade. Trade customers were sought not by travellers, the personal representative of the principal, but by a nationally advertised campaign for agents that obviated the element of trust normally linking suppliers and retailers. The knowledge and skill of grocers in blending and pricing tea to suit the tastes and pockets of their customers were being made superfluous. The relationship between buyer and seller was being changed from one of confidence in a particular grocer to a reliance on a widely advertised and priced product. The close personal relations that normally obtained between supplier, retailer, and consumer were being replaced by the printed word. Competition was intensified, not only on the local level but also on the national level. The Twinings, Garrats, and Newmans would find it difficult to support their grocers against the encroachments of the agent. Provincial grocers would have to devise their own means of combatting the artful insinuations and seductive appeals of the national advertiser.

When Frederick Gye lauched his attack on the principal London dealers, their correspondents in the country, particularly in the manufacturing districts, were experiencing competition from a new type of seller – the itinerant vender. The grocers stated their grievances in a series of well-coordinated memorials to Treasury.[130] On the whole, the complaints were similar. The sale of tea by the memorialists had been seriously diminished despite a general improvement in employment after the recent depressed state of trade. The grocers claimed that the reduction was not due to any decline in the consumption of tea, but to the vending of that article by itinerant dealers. The usual arguments against hawkers – obscure locations, cheap rent, evasion of taxes, and possibility of smuggled and spurious goods – were recited.[131] Above all, the hawking of tea was prohibited by law. Hence, itinerant dealers should be suppressed, the memorialists claimed, as they inveigled customers away from country shopkeepers, apparently by selling tea at lower prices.

However, after careful examination, neither the Hawking Coach Office nor Excise found the practices of itinerant venders contrary to law.[132] Those licensed to sell tea had legally entered rooms at each town where they did business. Tea could thus be removed to such places by regular excise permits. Orders were solicited at houses in the surrounding area after which the tea, broken up into suitably small packages in the entered place, was delivered to customers. Payment was usually made on delivery, although some dealers preferred payment on another day to avoid accusations of hawking. Indeed, the itinerant venders were behaving no differently from wholesale dealers who solicited orders, or Eagleton who proposed to show samples of tea at the residence of customers.[133] In fact, Excise explained that the use of warehouses had required a somewhat liberal interpretation of an "entered place," and saw no reason why those selling by retail should not be similarly accommodated. Moreover, there were "grounds for believing the sale of tea has been greatly extended" by itinerant venders and "many ... very respectable dealers" who supplied these venders "have complained that their fair trade" would be obstructed by disallowing the practice.

In the end, the commissioners of Excise established the meaning of hawking by instructing the collectors to apprehend as hawkers all those who "expose tea to chance customers" outside their entered rooms or who "supply customers with tea not previously ordered." But licensed dealers were not to be molested from delivering tea previously ordered.[134] How much tea was so delivered, in what form, or at what price are questions available evidence does not answer. However, as the procedure was now clearly defined, the sale of tea by itinerant venders continued and became an accepted practice.

The emergence of this new form of retailing tea was a challenge, like the agency business, to traditional grocers. In 1818, the practice was confined to a few provincial counties and concentrated in the manufacturing districts. However, it soon became far more widespread and affected the trade not only of provincial grocers but also of their London suppliers. In a memorial to Treasury in 1821, two well-established London tea firms claimed to have evidence that the "evil ... complained of" by the Manchester grocers and tea dealers in 1818 "has been rapidly increasing ever since and has now extended over a very large part of the kingdom, which was not at that period affected by it." Their correspondents in the country have been complaining "for several years ... of the serious losses they are suffering by itinerant venders of tea."[135] The two London firms were presumably also suffering "serious losses" by the "unfair competition." The question is who were the suppliers of itinerant venders? It is highly unlikely they were the traditional wholesale-retail London dealers whose major trade customers were grocers. Clearly, prepacked tea was more suitable for itinerant selling than that provided by traditional London dealers. One may suggest that itinerant vending was abetted, if not initiated, by the agency business and that the tea trade was indeed being diverted "out of its accustomed and regular channels."

When Frederick Gye commenced his activities in 1818, the marketing of tea was undergoing strains not unlike those of 1784 and for somewhat similar reasons. The upsurge of adulteration, the rise of itinerant venders, and the sale of prepacked tea were responses to the increasing demand for cheap tea, one not easily satisfied by traditional methods of sale and distribution. Some unprincipled dealers sought to meet the demand by selling spurious or adulterated tea; others offered a *cheap* congou liberally mixed with lower cost bohea. Such deceptive practices became more feasible and widespread as consumption moved down the social scale to those who had not developed a cultivated taste for fine distinctions. Price rather than intrinsic quality was becoming the major determinant of purchase. As one informed contemporary observed, if one shopkeeper sells "tea at 4s. 8d. and Mr. P. at 4s. 6d.," to a buyer unable to judge quality, "Mr. P's tea is 2d. per pound cheaper."[136] He thought the competition engendered by the demand for cheap tea bore particularly heavily on fair-trade grocers whose customers were also being inveigled away by itinerant venders and agents of prepacked tea. The shopkeepers were under ever greater pressure to reduce the cost of their supply, and, as a consequence, all the more ready to embrace John Nicholson's innovation. By publicizing the cost of tea at first source, Nicholson promoted his service as purchasing agent to the country dealers. In the process, information concerning a product became the key to the market.

John Nicholson was not trained in the mysteries of tea. He, like Gye, used the talents acquired in the publishing world, in particular, the compiling of prices current to compete against what he termed "the old system of the tea trade."[137] On 22 December 1823, his first "proclamation" was issued, consisting of a *Tea Book* and a *Sale List*. As the *Tea Book* was a duplicate of the East India Company's *Sale Catalogue*, published and circulated among the buyers before each auction, a brief description of its composition would seem desirable. All the tea to be sold was arranged in the *Catalogue* by kind and break. A break, part of a chop, consisted of tea which had been manufactured at the same time and was therefore relatively uniform in quality. The breaks were further subdivided into lots, the varying number of chests in each lot specified. The publication of the *Catalogue* was subsidized by the company, but it was compiled by the brokers who had examined and sampled the tea individually. After consultation, they affixed a general character (quality) to each break. To each chest was then added a special symbol to indicate the variations or deviations – for example, "d" for dust, "OS" for odd smell. Altogether some twenty symbols were used. Besides this information, the *Catalogue* included for each break the name of the ship it was imported in, the date of arrival, the total number of chests in the break, the tare allowed, and the put-up price.[138] Nicholson printed this *Catalogue* in his *Tea Book* and added a *Sale List* giving the average bid-up price for each break. A reader could now know the quality of each break of tea as well as its cost price at the auction. The former comprised information always provided by the company's *Catalogue* and the latter was public knowledge to those who attended the auction. Nicholson's innovation consisted in making the information available to a far wider public.

To profit from the diffusion of the information, Nicholson distributed the books gratis to provincial grocers, the major target of his campaign. He then offered to serve as their purchasing agent on very attractive terms. For an individual chest, he charged a penny per pound on all teas except bohea, on which the charge was only a half-penny. Like Eagleton, his commission for a whole lot was 1 percent. All transactions were on a strictly ready-money basis. But, unlike Eagleton, he promoted sales by a virulent attack on the London wholesale tea dealers whose country correspondents he was attempting to attract. He accused the London wholesalers of forming

a "deputy monopoly that held the country dealers in ... bondage."
The trade, he told his readers, was "confined to a few dozen individuals or firms who employed an immense capital" to buy up the
whole of the tea. These "Hong merchants" then sent travellers all
over the kingdom to sell tea at enormous profit. "We proved," he
proclaimed, that this system "cost the country dealers more than a
million a year ... uselessly paid to the London dealers in supporting
their immense establishment, in maintaining their travellers with ...
splendid equipages, in paying their bad debts ... and [in] giving them
princely fortunes for the simple honour of being called upon by a
Traveller." The latter was Nicholson's *bête noir*. He further claimed
to have evidence that the "average profit charged ... was from £4 to
£6 per chest," in contrast to his fee of about seven shillings on a chest
of eighty-six pounds, the standard weight. Nor could the country
dealer purchase his tea at the public auction. "The London wholesale
dealers being the employers of the brokers made them ... enter into
a bond not to purchase tea at the Sale" for the country dealer. And
if he should be so bold as to attempt to attend the sale, these "few
dozen ... firms ... entered into a combination" to run up the price.[139]
The accusations were not wholly true. Principal dealers in the country certainly bought tea through brokers at the auctions – Andrew
Melrose of Edinburg often attended the sales. But they were telling,
especially to those provincial dealers who had depended hitherto on
their London suppliers.

Nicholson admitted that his scheme did not achieve immediate
success. "Our proclamation ... was in general received with sullen
contempt and thousands never deigned to read it and tore it up."[140]
But within a year and a half reverberations were rumbling in the
London tea market. Indeed, it would have been surprising had Nicholson failed. His offer answered well the current demand for
lower-priced tea and his fee of a penny per pound was certainly
attractive. Few London wholesalers could have afforded to meet his
prices. In 1824 the average per pound cost of congou at the auctions
was thirty-two or sixty-four pence with duty. At a penny a pound,
Nicholson's commission averaged only 1.56 percent, well below the
wholesaler's usual mark-up, which was probably not far below 10
percent.[141] A grocer buying through Nicholson also gained the
overweight and extra tare allowed by the East India Company,
generally about two to three pounds per chest, and the tea chests
were not opened after leaving India House.

As to his own firm, Nicholson claimed that he kept no stock on
hand and had therefore no heavy overhead expenses. As purchasing
agent, he acted almost as a broker to the country dealer. Moreover,

he allowed no credit – all orders had to be postpaid and the remittance received prior to the auction in order to obtain tea at the
sale price. His capital was provided by country dealers and he incurred neither interest on credit nor the loss of bad debts. Of course,
the country dealer was not supplied with a variety of teas blended
to suit his trade. Indeed, Nicholson severely denounced "the practice
of mixing tea." A grocer might safely depend on the characters
(qualities) printed in the *Tea Book* – blending was a "mere excuse to
gain a greater profit."[142] Perhaps an even more important key to
Nicholson's success was the publishing of the *Sale List.* By so doing,
he laid open the "secrets" of the trade and set in motion an almost
ruinous competition. At least one of Nicholson's contemporaries
observed: Nicholson "placed in the hands of all the country grocers
the means of knowing the cost price, weight and tare" of a chest of
tea and "compelled those who were not moderate in their profits
before to be so now." Although the writer acknowledged the existence of a "monopoly, or something very like one" within the wholesale tea trade, he condemned Nicholson's attacks. He did not believe
that "a more honourable and respectable body of men exist than the
wholesale tea dealers."[143]

But honour and respect aside, the wholesale dealers were hard-
pressed for a counter measure. A mere denial of Nicholson's accusations was useless, unless the accounts were opened and the
"secrets" exposed.[144] And there was an element of truth in Nicholson's assertion that country dealers paid for the "immense expenses"
incurred by London wholesale dealers. However honourable they
were in calculating the necessary profit-margin, they could not compete with Nicholson's simple and cost-efficient system. Some of his
more flamboyant statements were challenged in court and he was
found guilty of libel. But even that incident he turned to advantage
by reporting the proceedings in his own paper, *Nicholson's Commercial
Gazette*, with his usual comments.[145] Faced with a foe who wielded
a mighty pen in a newspaper that provided country dealers with
important trade information, the principal London dealers and brokers acted precipitantly and provided Nicholson with more fuel.

In April 1825, a committee of tea brokers together with a "considerable part of the tea trade" informed the East India Court of
Directors of a resolution to discontinue the publication of the characters of the breaks of tea in the *Sale Catalogue.* It was apparent that
without the specifications, the quality of the tea could no longer be
identified and the wholesaler's "secrets" regarding price would be
safeguarded. But being jealous of the reputation of their tea, the
directors were "much disappointed." Keenly aware of their "duty to

the public and the East India Company," they were determined that "the public shall continue to receive the usual and full information of the qualities or characters of the teas."[146] When the brokers persisted, the Court of Directors authorized its own publication of the *Sale Catalogue* with the customary comments on the teas.[147] Henceforth, the East India Company published its own tea books before each quarterly auction and defeated the brokers' move. The brief incident lent support to the judgment of a contemporary that the wholesalers' "battle had not been well fought."[148] They had failed to prevent Nicholson from obtaining the necessary information for his *Tea Book* and had exposed themselves to further charges of combination, a subject gleefully reported by Nicholson.

In one area, however, the London wholesalers acted with greater wisdom. One of the charges levelled at them by Nicholson was that the dealers, on the pretext of there being insufficient "means of cording and directing teas" at the East India Company's warehouses, took the chests to their shops "for the purpose of mixing them and repacking them with inferior teas."[149] The matter was readily and effectively remedied by the company's agreement to "cord and seal" the chests destined for the country.[150] The tea trade's delegates to the Court of Directors hotly denied they themselves resorted to such "dishonourable practices" but admitted the possible guilt of some who bought at the East India Company's auctions. Some dealers were indeed guilty of repacking and even extracting a few pounds weight from each chest, as Excise records show.[151] Under the pressure of intense competition, the integrity of the trade was being sorely tried.

One immediate effect of Nicholson's campaign was the rise of imitators. No record of their number, methods, or the extent of their trade has survived, but the vehemence in Nicholson's denunciation of them would seem revealing. He contended it was impossible to sell on the terms they offered. They were committing "monstrous frauds" by promising charges below the brokers' standard commission of one-half percent and by carefully concealing the identity of their tea through withholding information on the break and the particular auction.[152] In short, having excited competition, Nicholson was now feeling its effects which, if his accusations were accurate, could have involved further dishonour.

The system instituted by Nicholson had a substantial impact on the trade in tea and was beginning to spread to other articles in the grocers' trade.[153] The effects on the traditional structure and methods of the tea trade were striking. Armed with the *Tea Book* and the *Sale List*, Nicholson offered the country dealers reduced cost on their tea and, in turn, lower prices to consumers. The device exerted downward pressure on prices. The enhanced competition thus engendered is shown in the chorus of laments from various London dealers in the 1830s.[154] One observed that Nicholson was "as ignorant of the qualities of tea as I may be of precious stones."[155] Another complained that a dealer's "judgment or capital is not of much advantage to him" as "he is almost compelled to sell" according to the prices published in the *Sale List*.[156] The behaviour of the country trader was vividly reported by a traveller. The dealer would now request teas from specific breaks. "He then, instead of your fixing the price, says, it cost so much at the Company's Sale and I will give you so much for it."[157] Even the editorial writer of the *Times* chimed in by referring sarcastically to "the small monopolists ... who call themselves the tea trade." The accusation provoked an angry reply from a member of the Committee of Tea Dealers. "In no trade," said he, "is there so little monopoly or such contending interest. There is no town, and scarcely a village, where tea is not ticketed at 1d. or 2d. per pound advance only upon the sale cost and in many cases decidedly below it. For in no trade, whether wholesale or retail, is there more 'cutting' and opposition."[158] It would seem as if control of the tea trade had been transferred to the country dealers, with the role of the traditional London wholesalers now confined within the limits set by Nicholson's publications.

Nonetheless, "cutting" brought in its wake the frauds and deceptions which frequently accompany excessive competition and, in the process, the quality of the tea and the taste for it deteriorated.[159] One dealer thought "the public taste in tea had been perfectly vitiated from what it was ten years ago when any person would detect gradations of tea or even the quality." "By puff and advertisements, professing to sell tea at a lower price than we buy it at the Company's Sale," the intruders had managed to sell large quantities of inferior tea and to "destroy the public taste." He predicted that in "ten years the quantity of tea will be lessened one half of the present consumption."[160] Indeed, many traditional dealers firmly believed that the opening of the China trade would admit many free-trade merchants who could not be expected to exercise the same careful choice and selection of teas as the East India Company.

John Nicholson represented the new business mentality that was sweeping aside the old constraints. The government was being converted to the principles of *laissez-faire* and *caveat emptor*. The old restrictions, which in addition to guarding the revenue had protected the consumer, were being cast aside. It was a view clearly expressed by the Royal Commissioners investigating excise regulations before the introduction of free trade in tea. Having noted the need for public revenue from tea, the commissioners accepted the necessity for imposing a customs duty:

But, the condition required of the importer, namely, the payment of the duty, being once fulfilled, it appears to us that there is no further necessity for imposing any other restrictions on his *absolute right* of dominion over the article imported. If in the exercise of this right he should be led to injure the quality of his article by adulteration, with the fraudulent view of imposing upon a purchaser a deteriorated for a genuine article, the injury thus inflicted is one to which purchasers of all articles requiring the exercise of skill or judgement in their selection, are equally liable, and it is one against which they should be left to seek for protection on their own resources ... Any attempt to substitute protection by penalties on adulteration ... must have the effect of diminishing that reliance on themselves which individuals should exercise for their own security.[161]

When the ports were opened in 1834 to free-trade tea, there was a network of dealers prepared to adopt the aggressive policies of the new men of business. Changes in the sale and distribution of tea first emerged in the 1780s and were reinvigorated by the actions of Gye and Nicholson. The new methods were responses to changes in the demand for tea, changes the old established houses were least able to accommodate to. Neither their business philosophy nor their practices suited the needs of the new market. The increasing demand for cheap tea opened the trade to the forces of competition. This market emphasized not quality and taste, but price. The old wealthy London houses continued to maintain a commanding position in the trade, particularly among the more traditionally minded provincial grocers who catered for a special clientele. But even such grocers had to adapt to the new spirit. More and more country correspondents requested their tea be sent directly from the East India Company's warehouses.[162] In 1833, of the 400,000-odd chests sold annually by the company, 60,000 were corded and sealed and an untold number merely corded. All were sent directly to the country dealers.[163] Teas sent directly from the company's warehouses had black excise permits which many country dealers were "desirous of having ... to show in their windows" so that "their customers may see that the tea had come from the India House."[164] The black permit served two purposes for the country dealers: in addition to assuring his customers that the tea was genuine, it signalled a lower price. "Puffing," advertising, and ticketing had penetrated all levels of the trade.

During the fifty years following the Commutation Act, the structure of the retail trade in tea had undergone many changes – new methods of wholesale and retail organization had been developed and new techniques of selling had been adopted. Whether these should be considered revolutionary, as Nicholson claimed, is a moot point. But they surely do not support a view that little or no change occurred in the distributive trades until the midnineteenth century. Shopkeepers displayed marked initiative in responding to the changing nature of the market they serviced. By so doing, they enlarged that market. If the wholesale and retail trades still bore some of the marks of the pre-industrial system, so did many manufacturing concerns. The changes occurring in the distributive trades did not lag behind those taking place in other parts of the economic and social structure of the country. On the contrary, they served as a remarkably well-articulated conduit for the increasing supplies of manufactured articles and for imported goods and local products. The history of the tea trade illustrates and specifies these tendencies.

CHAPTER FOURTEEN

Conclusion

Britain in the eighteenth century was a buoyant, expanding society experiencing changes in its economic and social structure, the consequences of which were far-reaching and are still unfolding. Agricultural and industrial production increased; inland navigation, coastal port facilities, and road transport were improved; and overseas trade expanded. It has been estimated that total real output grew two and one-half times during the century. At the same time, population was increasing – by the end of the century it was 66 percent higher than the estimate for 1701 and a larger proportion of the people were living in urban centres. Until the last decade, there was a gain in real wages for artisans and labourers, particularly north of the Trent where wages had been low at the beginning of the century. England was distinctly a hierarchical society, but, unlike the continent, it had a substantial middling group whose numbers and income increased during the century. And the incomes of those in the upper strata of the hierarchy, the large landed proprietors, rose even more rapidly. All groups with the exception of the most deprived emulated the styles of their "betters." The pawned watches of artisans were redeemed as soon as money jingled in their pockets. In short, the market for consumer goods and services expanded, especially as the prevailing mood was one of optimism, of confidence in the growing strength and glory of the country. The function of supplying that market rested largely on the shopkeepers of the kingdom and they, like other groups in the society, responded to the challenge. The movement of goods to consumers was facilitated by a quickening in the lines of communication and by an increase in the number and variety of shops. And a substantial portion of shopkeepers actively sought to increase demand for their goods and services. In the process, some major changes were introduced in the methods of supplying shops and retail customers.

The shopkeeping world followed the social hierarchy of the society of which it was a part. At the head were those shopkeepers who prided themselves on their aristocratic clientele and who looked with disdain on vulgar advertising. They were the purveyors of high-quality goods and guarded zealously traditional methods of retailing. At the foot were the small village shopkeepers and petty chandlers, like Mary Smith of Flixton or Sara Swale of York, who had on hand in July 1784 three-quarters of a pound of green tea. The customers of petty shops were the journeymen-artisans and labourers who were dependent on wages for their subsistence, and as the century advanced their numbers increased, particularly in the agricultural sector. By the end of the century, few agricultural labourers south of the Trent were farm servants boarded by the farmer. It has been argued that the higher density of shops south of the Trent at mid-century was due in part to the large number of petty shops that had sprung up in the villages and on the back streets of urban centres to meet the needs of the workers. The growth of petty shopkeeping north of the Trent occurred during the second half of the century with the expansion of industrial activity. The proprietors of such shops ranged from poor widows and ambitious workers, whose status and income were little different from that of the customers they served, to experienced tradesmen like William Wood of Didsbury. Lowly as they were, these petty shops provided increasingly important services as society became more and more urbanized and industrialized. They enabled workers to purchase their "subsistence from day to day, or even hour to hour" and by so doing speeded the flow of goods from suppliers to consumers.

The midrange of the hierarchy included a great variety of shops which graced the market streets and clustered in the fashionable centres of large towns. Their customers were drawn primarily from the middling group whose members and incomes were increasing. They formed a substantial and expanding market for good, solid consumer goods and responded to reduction in prices by increasing demand. These were the customers to whom most of the advertisements were directed and for whose trade the shopkeepers vied with each other. The market was one that encouraged, if it did not generate, price competition, particularly for goods such as groceries, draperies, and a wide range of household furnishings and articles of personal adornment. The expectation of a steadily increasing demand also encouraged innovative practices in marketing and sales techniques. It was shopkeepers in this range who pioneered new methods of retailing – men like Eagleton who grasped the opportunity made possible by the lowering of tea duties in 1784. In the drapery and haberdashery trades, demand, especially for the ever-increasing output of the cotton manufacturers, led to open advertising, price ticketing, and ready-money sales.

When the century opened, the major shopkeepers of London dominated much of the trade in shop goods. With the exception of ironmongery and local produce such as cheese, provincial shopkeepers were largely dependent on the London wholesale-retail dealers for their stock. It gave the Londoner considerable power to determine prices. London continued to hold sway throughout the century, especially for highly fashionable goods, as many of the advertisements show. But London was challenged by the rise of colonial markets in the outports and by the more aggressive marketing methods of manufacturers. With the more widespread dissemination of commercial information on prices, opportunities were opened for provincial shopkeepers to purchase much of their stock at the cheapest source and to escape the domination of London. By the 1780s, drapers were featuring not only their fashionable goods from London but also their good buys at Manchester and Glasgow, and hatters and shoe shops were emphasizing their connections with manufacturers. Even ironmongers found it expedient to note they bought at the first source. During the last quarter of the century, provincial shopkeepers were actively competing not only against each other, but also against the Londoner for trade and retail customers. The provinces were, in fact, displaying a new-found pride in their accomplishments. The great Wen was no longer the sole source of wealth and power. Provincial shopkeepers had to be wooed with attractive offers by London dealers. Not all flung Nicholson's price lists at their suppliers but a growing number were alert to cost differentials. Price competition was even penetrating the small village shops. The great hue and cry by grocers in the manufacturing towns against itinerant venders of tea arose because grocers found their sales to "country shopkeepers" declining.

Identifying the source and nature of demand is always difficult. Price and income elasticities relate to economic man; but man is a social creature and his wants are largely a function of his position in the social-cultural world. Tea was not a valued object to the farmers of north Wales, although it may well have been so for their wives. In the eighteenth century, it was associated with the tea table of ladies and much of the demand for it first arose from a desire to emulate those in higher social positions. By the end of the century, the desire had percolated down to the wives of lowly workers for whom it had become a "necessity." Their critics accused them of wasting money on "luxuries." Such percolating down of patterns of consumption was a common feature of eighteenth century England.

Groups like the farmers of north Wales might still remain outside the main stream of cultural values, not yet a part of the new society that was forming, but such self-contained enclaves became increasingly rare. England, unlike much of the continent, was an open society. There were no rigid barriers to upward mobility and increasing incomes allowed those in lower status to adopt some of the practices of their "betters." But to do so, those practices had to be known if desire was to be generated and the commodities easily available if demand was to be satisfied. The extension of newspapers to the provinces, the publication of magazines showing the latest fashions, the relatively easy relations between persons of different social ranks, all enabled people from widely different groups to become familiar with the latest styles in dress, in household furnishings, and even in the foods served at the table. And shops, in addition to making the wares easily available, excited desires by advertising in newspapers and handbills the newest fashions and by displaying their wares. Jane Austen's characters enjoyed window shopping and were not infrequently enticed to enter the shop and buy.

It is frequently observed that one of the conditions that facilitated the industrial revolution was the absence of artificial barriers to the flow of goods within the country. But little has been said in positive terms about how and what enabled the goods to flow in increasing volume. The present study has aimed to offer an answer, even if a partial one, to these questions. As Excise and other records show, there had occurred in the first half of the century a considerable expansion in the number and variety of shops. By midcentury, an extensive network of retail establishments of various sizes and types was in existence. Shops ranged from the well-capitalized wholesale-retail specialist dealer to the small chandler whose stock, amounting perhaps to no more than ten pounds, consisted of a few sundries in daily use. There was, in short, no bottleneck in the retail sector and as the century advanced new methods and channels of distribution were developed to handle the expanding volume of manufactured and imported goods. The commercial travellers and circulars of the wholesale-retail dealers were later jostled by the mail-order agency business that distributed packaged goods, priced, labelled, and ready to be handed over to the retail customer. Principal dealers in provincial towns made attractive offers through newspapers and handbills to shopkeepers in the surrounding villages and supplied petty chandlers on their own terms. If the major purpose of all these activities by shopkeepers was to drum up business, by so doing they eased the flow of goods and at the same time helped to stimulate as well as satisfy an increasingly widespread demand, a demand that encouraged expansion in industry and overseas trade. It was not an unimportant contribution to the overall economic development of the country – industry, overseas trade, and inland distribution moved in tandem, each fructifying the other. Within the retail sector, the petty shopkeeper, so frequently ignored by contemporary social enumerators and later historians, was an important cog in this "wheel whereon the inland trade turns."

Appendices

Appendix 1
Geographical Distribution of Retail Shops in England and Wales, 1759

Region	Collection	Number of shops	County	Population	Ratio – Population /Shop
I	1 – Cornwall	1,544	Cornwall	131,901	
	2 – Barnstaple	850			
	3 – Tiverton	777	Devonshire	306,524	
	4 – Exon	2,866			
	Total	6,037		438,425	73
II	15 – Sussex	2,658	Sussex	94,315	
	7 – Isle of Wight	260	Hampshire	134,148	
	14 – Hants	3,253			
	6 Dorset	3,533	Dorset	88,318	
	5 – Taunton	2,271	Somersetshire	222,526	
	9 – Bristol	3,483			
	8 – Salisbury	2,126	Wiltshire	157,206	
	11 – Marlborough	2,672			
	12 – Reading[1]	1,964	Berkshire	85,977	
	26 – Oxon[1]	2,420	Oxfordshire	89,227	
	10 – Gloucester	2,824	Gloucester	203,000	
	Total	27,464		1,074,717	39
III	13 – Surrey	3,600	Surrey	133,427	
	16 – Canterbury	2,683	Kent	168,679	
	17 – Rochester	3,655			
	18 – Essex	3,735	Essex	180,465	
	23 – Bedford	3,911	Bedfordshire	55,407	
	24 – Hertford	2,447	Hertfordshire	76,457	
	25 – Bucks[1]	2,744	Buckinghamshire	81,723	
	50 – London Bills	21,603	Middlesex	590,165	
	Total	44,378		1,286,323	29
IV	19 – Suffolk[2]	3,135	Suffolk	159,577	
	20 – Norwich	2,195)	Norfolk	221,255	
	21 – Lynn	2,755)			
	Total	8,085		380,832	47
V	22 – Cambridge[2]	2,850	Cambridgeshire	72,674	
			Huntingdonshire	30,258	
	Total	2,850		102,932	36

Appendix 1 (continued)

Region	Collection	Number of shops	County	Population	Ratio – Population /Shop
VI	29 – Lichfield[3] – ½ of	1,726)			
		)			
	28 – Warwick	4,296)	Warwickshire	124,760	
		)			
		)	Leicestershire	91,649	
	30 – Worcester	2,426	Worcestershire	95,764	
	27 – Northampton	3,511	Northampton-shire	111,834	
	39 – Grantham[4]	3,154	Lincolnshire[5] – ½ of	76,635	
			Rutland	11,742	
	Total	15,113		512,384	34
VII	29 – Lichfield[3] – ½ of	1,727	Staffordshire	140,562	
	31 – Hereford	1,735	Herefordshire	70,426	
	35 – Salop	2,134	Shropshire	126,072	
	Total	5,596		337,060	60
VIII	37 – Chester	2,981	Cheshire	107,648	
	42 – Lancaster	3,522	Lancashire	317,740	
	46 – Westmorland	1,168	Westmorland	35,951	
	47 – Cumberland	1,065	Cumberland	81,060	
	Total	8,736		542,399	62
IX	40 – Lincoln[5]	1,048	Lincolnshire[5] – ½ of	76,635	
	38 – Derby	3,624	Derbyshire	100,734	
			Nottinghamshire	85,009	
	41 – Sheffield	2,873			
	43 – Leeds	2,815	Yorkshire		
	44 – York	3,647		484,248	
	45 – Richmond	2,070			
	Total	16,077		746,626	46
X	48 – Durham	1,909	Durham	130,091	
	49 – Northumber-land	1,366	Northumberland	139,011	
	Total	3,275		269,102	82

Appendix 1 (continued)

Region	Collection	Number of shops	County	Population	Ratio – Population /Shop
XI	32 – Wales – East	1,338	Monmouthshire	29,524	
	33 – Wales – West	693			
	34 – Wales – Middle	1,287	Wales	419,676	
	36 – Wales – North	771			
	Total	4,089		449,200	110
	Total for England	137,611	England	5,690,800	42
	Total for England and Wales	141,700	England and Wales	6,140,000	44

Sources: Number of shops: (1758–64), E/T 5: 16, HMCL; London Bills of Mortality, p. 14; provincial collections, pp. 19-20. A similar listing is in BM, Add. Ms. 33,039, fol. 253. Population: Deane and Cole, *British Economic Growth*, 103, table 24, estimates for 1751. Boundaries: Based on detailed description "An Account of the Gross Produce of each Duty in Each Collection and in London ... and Describing the Situation and Extent of such Collections ... The Number of Each Collection in the Map, for the Year Ending 5 July 1796," 30/8/288, fol. 56 PRO. See also "An Account of the Gross Produce of the Several Duties in Each Collection, 1741, Excise Documents, Ms. no. 525, fol. 52, Harrowby Trust. The number of collections and the names are similar to those in the 1759 account. Collections: The numbers on the accompanying map indicate the approximate area covered by the collections. Ratios: As the ratios are based on *estimates* of the population in *1751*, they should not be presumed factually correct, but rather a rough approximation of the number of persons per shop.

Notes:

[1] The collection of Reading and Oxon both included a small part of Buckinghamshire, probably not sufficient to change the ratios in either of the two regions.

[2] The collection of Cambridge covered a "small portion" of Suffolk. As the areas of Suffolk adjacent to Cambridgeshire were, for the most part, in the upland zone and not heavily populated with nucleated villages, it is unlikely that a large number of shops in the Cambridge collection should be allocated to Suffolk, particularly as the Cambridge collection is unusally large including not only the "greater portion of Cambridge", but also Huntingdonshire. If Regions IV and V are combined the ratio would be 44.

[3] The Lichfield collection straddled Staffordshire and Warwickshire. In 1784 Excise reported the number of tea licences issued in the collection as 675 of which the "principal town," Birmingham, had 342. We have, therefore, assumed that half the shops reported for Lichfield should be allocated to Warwick.

[4] As the collection of Grantham covered, besides the southern part of Lincolnshire, parts of Northamptonshire and Rutland (also a small portion of Cambridge), it has been included in this midland area although it is not the most appropriate arrangement.

[5] It has been assumed that one-half the population of Lincolnshire was covered by the collection of Grantham. This is surely a very rash assumption but in view of the high total population for the region the average number of persons per shop may not be too distorted. The other half of the population has been allocated to Region IX (also a populous area) along with the collection of Lincoln which covered the northern part of Lincolnshire and part of Nottinghamshire.

Appendix 2
Number of Shops by Rental Category in Provincial Towns and Population
per Assessed Shop, 1785

	Number of Assessed Shops					Highest Rent (in £)
Towns	£5-£15	£15-£25	£25 and up	Total	Ratio	
South of Line						
Aylesbury	39	4	—	43	74.1	15-20
Bath & Bristol	836	654	279	1,769	50.1	90-100
Birmingham	539	154	87	780	94.4	60-65
Bury St Edmunds	229	48	8	285	26.9	50-55
Canterbury	175	45	3	223	43.9	30
Chelmsford	45	30	4	79	47.5	30-35
Chichester	133	53	11	197	24.1	30-35
Coventry	126	37	18	181	88.6	35-40
Guildford	62	29	7	98	26.9	40
Hertford	77	11	3	91	36.9	35-40
Ipswich	134	30	15	179	58.1	30-35
Lewis	48	13	2	63	77.9	40
Oxford	236	37	13	286	40.9	35-40
Poole	66	37	6	109	43.7	40-45
Salisbury & Southampton	421	148	114	683	24.1	102
Stamford	127	15	—	142	28.3	15-20
Warwick	109	14	1	124	45.1	25-30
Worcester	277	235	90	602	18.8	100
Subtotal	3,679	1,594	661	5,934	46.6	
% in rental category	62.0	26.9	11.1			
North of Line						
Durham	79	19	11	109	71.3	20-30
Hereford	182	51	3	236	28.9	30-35
Liverpool	289	142	121	552	140.7	65-70
Ludlow	104	12	1	117	33.3	25
Newcastle	274	127	54	455	62.3	60-65
Nottingham	220	102	71	393	73.4	80-85
Pontefract	47	17	—	64	56.0	20
Scarborough	69	19	—	88	72.8	20-25
Shrewsbury	190	69	22	281	52.5	40-45
Tavistock	58	10	1	69	49.6	30
York	338	126	22	486	35.0	30-35
Subtotal	1,850	694	306	2,850	69.7	

Appendix 2 (continued)

Towns	Number of Assessed Shops			Total	Ratio	Highest Rent (in £)
	£5-£15	£15-£25	£25 and up			
% in rental category	64.9	24.4	10.7			
Total	5,529	2,288	967	8,784	54.8	
% in rental category	62.9	26.1	11.0			

Source: PRO, HO 42/7, fols. 3-11.

Appendix 3
Estimates of the National Income[1]

		Deduct for less than £100 income	Net income above £100
Land rents[2]	£41,315,000	£11,315,000	£30,000,000
Houses[3] – 50,000 at £40 to £200 a year (N. I omit all the other assessed houses 640,000)	4,800,000		4,800,000
Tithes	4,000,000	1,000,000	3,000,000
Mines and canals	3,000,000	1,000,000	2,000,000
Interest on Funds (after deducting million sinking Fund)	13,000,000	3,000,000	10,000,000
Private revenue (exclusive of trade from East and West Indies and from Ireland)	4,000,000		4,000,000
Foreign trade at 15 percent on 80 million	12,000,000	2,000,000	10,000,000
Home trade, shops, manufactures in iron, copper, linen, wool, cotton, silk, pottery, timber, building, etc.	62,000,000	31,000,000	31,000,000
Insurance offices & annuities; public compagnies; all the corporations & charities (?)	5,000,000	2,000,000	3,000,000
Scotland – the two last articles	6,000,000	3,000,000	3,000,000
Houses, cottages & other income belonging to the Poor not included above	26,685,000	26,685,00	—
	£181,800,000	£81,000,000	£100,800,000
	Deduct for any objectionable articles		10,800,000
			£ 90,000,000

Source: PRO, 30/8/302, fol. 266.

Notes: [1]Table and notes follow the format in PRO.

[2]Land rent – 40 million acres at 12s 6d – – –   £25,000,000
  add ¼ rent on 10 million of acres supposed to be in the hands of the owners   1,315,000
  add ¾ rent on 30 million of acres supposed to be in the hands of tenants
  add for ? , wastes, etc.   15,000,000

                                                          £41,315,000

[3]10,000 houses at £200 a year   £ 2,000,000
  10,000   at £100 a year   1,000,000
  10,000   at   80 a year   800,000
  20,000   at   50 a year   1,000,000

                                 £ 4,800,000

N. There are 51,000 houses assessed for 20 windows and upwards.

Appendix 4
Geographical Distribution of Tea Licences in England, Wales, and Scotland,
1795-6

Region	Collection	Number of Tea Licences	County	Population 1801	Population per Licence
I	1 – Cornwall	907	Cornwall	194,278	
	3 – Barnstaple[1]	660			
	2 – Plymouth	1,047	Devonshire	353,948	
	4 – Exon	854			
	Total	3,468		548,226	158
II	16 – Sussex	957	Sussex	164,396	
	15 – Hants[2] – ⅔ of	588	Hampshire	226,667	
	7 – Isle of Wight	407			
	6 – Dorset	857	Dorsetshire	119,000	
	5 – Somerset	880	Somersetshire	282,487	
	9 – Bath	980			
	10 – Bristol	740			
	11 – Gloucester	1,084	Gloucestershire	258,814	
	8 – Salisbury	941	Wiltshire	191,015	
	12 – Marlborough	1,059			
	13 – Reading[3] – ¾ of	708	Berkshire	112,701	
	27 – Oxon[3] – ¾ of	723	Oxfordshire	113,119	
	Total	9,924		1,468,199	148
III	55 – London Bills	3,982	Middlesex	844,240	
	14 – Surrey	793	Surrey	277,630	
	15 – Hants[2] – ⅓ of	295			
	17 – Canterbury	749	Kent	317,442	
	18 – Rochester	1,066			
	19 – Essex	930	Essex	233,664	
	24 – Bedford	916	Bedfordshire	65,416	
	25 – Hertford	857	Hertfordshire	100,691	
	26 – Uxbridge[3]	882			
	13 – Reading[3] – ¼ of	236	Buckinghamshire	110,873	
	27 – Oxon[3] – ⅛ of	121			
	Total	10,827		1,949,956	180
IV	20 – Suffolk[4]	1,194	Suffolk	217,147	
	21 – Norwich	938	Norfolk	282,096	
	22 – Lynn	860			
	Total	2,992		499,243	167

Appendix 4 (continued)

Region	Collection	Number of Tea Licences	County	Population 1801	Population per Licence
V	23 – Cambridge[4]	1,036	Cambridgeshire	92,198	
			Huntingdonshire	38,767	
	Total	1,036		130,965	127
VI	27 – Oxon[3] – ⅛ of	120	Northamptonshire	135,962	
	28 – Northampton	1,275			
	29 – Coventry	867	Leicestershire	134,233	
	30 – Lichfield[5] – ½ of	430	Warwickshire	214,835	
	31 – Worcester	817			
	32 – Wolverhampton[6] – ⅓ of	263	Worcestershire	143,780	
	41 – Grantham[7]	986	Lincolnshire[8] – ½ of	107,607	
			Rutland	16,878	
	Total	4,758		753,295	158
VII	33 – Hereford	736	Herefordshire	92,038	
	37 – Salop	872	Shropshire	172,989	
	32 – Wolverhampton[6] – ⅔ of	527	Staffordshire	246,786	
	30 – Lichfield[5] – ½ of	431			
	39 – Chester	1,254	Cheshire[9]	197,871	
	Total	3,820		709,684	186
VIII	44 – Manchester[9]	1,466			
	45 – Liverpool	721	Lancashire	694,202	
	46 – Preston[10] – ⅔ of	1,005			
	51 – Lancaster	567	Westmorland	42,945	
	52 – Cumberland	953	Cumberland	120,972	
	Total	4,712		858,119	182
IX	42 – Lincoln	903	Lincolnshire[8] – ½ of	107,606	
			Nottinghamshire	144,829	
	40 – Derby	963	Derbyshire	166,285	
	43 – Sheffield	1,068			
	46 – Preston[10] – ⅓ of	502			
	47 – Leeds	1,919	Yorkshire	886,305	
	48 – Hull	557			
	49 – Whitby	800			
	50 – York	964			
	Total	7,676		1,305,025	170

Appendix 4 (continued)

Region	Collection	Number of Tea Licences	County	Population 1801	Population per Licence
X	53 – Durham[11]	1,071	Durham	165,479	
	54 – Northumberland	507	Northumberland	162,115	
	Total	1,578		327,594	208
XI	34 – Wales – East	791	Monmouthshire	47,037	
	35 – Wales – West	354	Wales	558,830	
	36 – Wales – Middle	471			
	38 – Wales – North	692			
	Total	2,308		605,867	263
XII	Scotland[12] (16 collections)	4,566	Scotland[13]	1,625,000	356

Sources: No. of Licences: "An Account of the Gross Produce of each Duty in each Collection and in London," 30/8/288, fol. 56, PRO. The number of licences was reached by dividing the gross produce of the tea licence by 5s.6d., the annual fee in 1795/6, for each of the collections; Population: Deane and Cole, *British Economic Growth*, 103, table 24, county population for 1801. The London population in the summary is for the metropolis and from Rickman in "Municipal Corporations in England and Wales," 25(239):3, *PP1837*; Boundaries: Based on the detailed description in PRO, 30/8/288, fol. 56. Collections: The numbers on map 5 indicate the approximate area covered by a collection.

Comments: A discrepancy exists between the figures in PRO, 30/8/288, fol. 56 on the number of tea licences issued and those in "Tea and Coffee Dealers' Licences for England and Wales, Scotland and Ireland from 1781 to 1855," 83, *PP1857*.

The excise account submitted 13 September 1797, states the amount of "gross revenue" for the year 1795/6 as £14,601 18s., and the number of licences based on the annual fee of 5s. 6d. is a fraction short of 53,099. In the parliamentary account, however, the revenue is stated as £14,562 12s. 6d. and the number of licences as 52,955, exact to the penny in terms of revenue. The slight difference in these two accounts is not sufficient to distort the ratios for any of the regions. It does, however, raise questions about the accuracy of the parliamentary account. The lower figure for revenue reported in the latter account may be the net amount submitted to Treasury after deducting various expenses. That the amount of revenue is exactly divisible by the annuel fee is, in fact, suspicious. In very few instances was this true for the individual collections or even for the total amount of revenue in the excise account. The truth is that Excise did issue licences for a portion of the year, and from 1826 on, the parliamentary account gives the amount of the revenue derived by granting licences "for only a portion of the year." For the year 1825/6 the total amount of revenue stated was £39,388 15s., of which £6,828 2s. 3d. was the amount for a portion of the year. By that date, the annual licence fee was 11s. The total revenue divided by the licence fee gives exactly 72,525 licences, which is the figure stated in the account. Quite obviously more licences were issued than is stated if almost £7,000 was derived from licences for something less than 11s. If one accepts the figures in the parliamentary account the number of licences issued in 1825/6 for England and Wales was some 2,300 less than for the previous year. There was no actual decline in the number of tea dealers, but rather a larger number of licences issued for a portion of the year and in submitting its account to Treasury, Excise presented an arithmetically correct account. Treasury was, after all, only concerned that it receive what was due. In subsequent years, the amount of duty on licences granted for only a portion of the year fluctuated around £2,000 for England and Wales. Thus the new licences, which presumably they represent, granted one year would be offset by those granted the next. Nonetheless, it is clear that both the figures we have derived for 1795/6 from the excise account and those in the parliamentary account understate the actual number of licences issued to entered tea dealers. As the number of licences issued was generally on an ascending scale, the figure for the following year would more closely approximate the actual number of shops legally entered to sell tea.

Explanations: Since the 1759 survey (see chap. 2, table 2, p. 40), the number of collections increased by five. The boundaries of several collections have been redrawn. The decline of Tiverton and the rise of Plymouth are registered in the replacement of the old collection of Tiverton by that of Plymouth (2). The collection of Uxbridge (26) which straddles four counties – Middlesex, Buckinghamshire, Bedfordshire, and Hertfordshire – replaced the old collection of Bucks. Coventry (29) replaced the collection of Warwick, and Whitby (49) that of Richmond. Of the five new collections, only one is in the south, Bath (9), and the collection of Bristol (10) now covers only the city "and adjoining villages." A new collection appears in the Midlands – Wolverhampton (32) which straddles Worcestershire, Staffordshire, and Shropshire. Yorkshire has an additional collection at Hull (48) comprising the city and a "small part of the county of York near it." The old collection of Westmorland was dropped, the survey of that county now handled by the collections of Lancaster (51) and Cumberland (52).

Notes: [1]The Barnstaple collection included a "small portion" of the coast of Somersetshire.

[2]The collection of Hants covered parts of Sussex, Hampshire, and Surrey. As Excise gave no particular weight to any of the three counties, it has been presumed, probably rashly, that the proportion of licences should be allocated equally. But even if only one-half of the licences are allocated to Region II, the number of persons per licence would still be quite low, a little over 143 persons, with the ratio for Region III (minus London) dropping to 155.

[3]Both these collections included small portions of Buckinghamshire and Oxon, a small part of Northamptonshire.

[4]The Cambridge collection included a "small portion" of Suffolk in an area not heavily populated with nucleated villages. It does not seem likely that a considerable portion of the licences for Cambridge should be allocated to Suffolk. In 1784, there were 754 tea dealers in the Cambridge collection of which 174 were for the city of Cambridge alone (PRO, 30/8/293, fol. 74). Admittedly, the 167 persons per licence for Suffolk and Norfolk is too high and the ratio for Cambridgeshire too low. However, the average for the two regions – 157 – does not seem any more satisfactory.

[5]The Lichfield collection straddled Staffordshire and Warwickshire. In 1784, Excise reported the number of tea licences issued in the collection as 675, of which Birmingham had 342. We have, therefore, assumed that half the licences should be allocated to Warwickshire.

[6]The Wolverhampton collection covered "parts of Staffordshire, Shropshire and Worcestershire." The one-third in Region VI is a mere guess. If as many as one-half were allocated to Worcestershire, the ratio for Region VI would drop to 158 and that for Region VII rise to 193.

[7 & 8]As the collection of Grantham covered, besides the southern part of Lincolnshire, parts of Northamptonshire and Rutland (also a small portion of Cambridgeshire), it has been included in this midland area, not the most appropriate arrangement. It has also been assumed, rather rashly, that one-half the population of Lincolnshire was covered by the Grantham collection. The other half of the population has been allocated to Region IX along with the collection of Lincoln which included the northern part of Lincolnshire and part of Nottinghamshire.

[9]The Manchester collection included part of Cheshire. Given the very large population of Manchester, almost 40 per cent of the total population of Cheshire, it was impossible to hazard even a guess as to the proportion of licences that should be allocated to Cheshire. Obviously the ratio for Region VIII should be higher, but most probably not significantly so.

[10]According to Excise, the Preston collection included a "considerable portion of the inland parts of Lancashire with part of Yorkshire." In the *Leeds Mercury*, 6 December 1785, the collector for Preston advertised the date and time when he would attend the various market towns in his area. Among the towns listed were four in Yorkshire – Keighley, Sedbergh, Settle, and Skipton – which cover a fairly wide area compared to the boundaries in Lancashire. Nonetheless, it is an uncertain apportionment.

[11]The Collection of Durham included Newcastle and North Shields.

[12]The figure for Scotland is based on "Tea and Coffee Dealers' Licences," 83, *PP1857*, which lists the number of licences issued for England and Wales, Scotland, and Ireland from 1781 to 1855. The figure is for 1795/6.

[13]The population is from Mitchell and Deane, *British Historical Statistics*, 8, "Population and Vital Statistics 3" for 1801.

Notes

The following abbreviations or shortened references are used in the notes.

Add. Ms.	Additional Manuscripts
BM	British (Museum) Library
DNB	Dictionary of National Biography
HMCL	HM Customs Library
E/T	Excise and Treasury
H. of C.	House of Commons (British)
IO	India Office Records and Library
NCG	Nicholson's Commercial Gazette and Grocer's Register of Useful Knowledge (London)
PH	Cobbett's Parliamentary History
PP	Parliamentary Papers (British)
PR	Debrett, Parliamentary Register
PRO	Public Record Office (London)
SRO	Scottish Record Office
Times	Times (London)

INTRODUCTION

1 Westerfield, *Middlemen*.
2 Marshall, *William Stout*, and Willan, *Abraham Dent*. The recently published Vaisey, *Thomas Turner*, provides information on the social life of a midcentury shopkeeper in East Hoathly, Sussex. But it sheds little light on his shopkeeping activities.
3 Davis, *Fairs, Shops, and Supermarkets*, ix and chaps. 8–11.
4 Jefferys, *Retail Trading*.
5 Mathias, *Retailing Revolution*.

6 Blackman, "Food Supply of an Industrial Town," 83–97; "Development of the Retail Grocery Trade," 11–17; "Changing Marketing Methods and Food Consumption," 37. Also Alexander, *Retailing in England*.

7 Clapham, *Economic History*, 1: chap. 6 and Alexander, *Retailing in England*.

8 Adburgham, *Shops and Shopping*, is confined to changes in fashionable clothing shops for women and the methods adopted to attract custom. However, some evidence is available to show that many enterprising shopkeepers had commenced their business during the latter part of the eighteenth century. See also the fascinating studies of Heal, *Signboards* and *Tradesmen's Cards*.

9 Clapham, *Economic History*, 1:219.

10 Hoskins, *Industry, Trade and People*, 125–6.

11 Willan, *Abraham Dent*, 8. His earlier studies of coastal trade and inland navigation point in the same direction.

12 Ashton, *Economic History*, chap. 3 offers no specific comment on numbers of shopkeepers, the general burden of his summary is one of growth and change.

13 Mathias, *Brewing Industry*, 100–1 estimates the number of inns and public houses ca. 1780 as 50,000.

14 Davis, *Fairs, Shops, and Supermarkets*, 252.

15 McKendrick, Brewer, and Plumb, *Birth of a Consumer Society*, 5, 30.

16 Ibid., see esp. chap. 2, 34–99.

17 Carey, "Essay on the State of England," 323.

18 Smith, *Wealth of Nations*, 341–3.

19 See esp. Hartwell, "Neglected Variable," 201–25 and "Service Revolution," 358–96; also Minchinton, "Patterns of Demand," 77–186.

CHAPTER ONE

1 Marshall, *William Stout*, 89.

2 Ibid., 89.

3 One wonders if there is a correlation between the decline of highwaymen and the greater use of inland bills of exchange.

4 Marshall, *William Stout*, 160.

5 The importance of relations and personal acquaintances in business contacts deserves greater attention, as T.S. Willan has suggested.

6 Marshall, *William Stout*, 79.

7 Ibid., 119.

8 Stout claimed to have gained that year fifty pounds besides shop rent (five pounds) and board (five pounds). He had, however, restocked the shop. The fifty pounds may only represent the amount of money on hand.

9 Anyone who has lived on an island distant from the main avenues of traffic will appreciate the frustrations encountered when shops run out of particular items. One does learn to restrict desires and thereby save.

10 Marshall, *William Stout*, 90.

11 Ibid., 101.

12 Willan, *Coasting Trade*, xiv.

13 Marshall, *William Stout*, 94–5.

14 *Gentleman's Magazine*, 28 (September 1748): 409.

15 Willan, *Abraham Dent*, 41–2, 80, 91–3, 99. As Willan has observed, Dent "operated on a national market, which was probably freer from impediments in the movement of goods than elsewhere in Western Europe." The easy movement of goods must have contributed not only to "fostering the development of factory production" (110) but also to a more complex network of shops. See also Chartres, "Road Carrying," 73–94.

16 Eversley, "Home Market and Economic Growth," 257. For the earlier period see Coleman, *Economy of England*, 99–105, 117–18 and John, "Agricultural Productivity," 19–34.

17 Corfield, *Impact of English Towns*, 9. The information on urbanization is based on this carefully researched study of towns, esp. 6–15.

18 See the evidence of John Taylor and Samuel Garbett in *H. of C. Journal*, 28 (20 March 1759): 496. They were opposing the new licence fee for silver plating.

19 Duncomb Davies and Ingram, Birmingham, to Walthal Fenton, Add. Ms. 36,666, fol. 48, BM. Apparently the number of cards printed was limited as Fenton was kindly requested "to return the card by first opportunity."

20 Ibid.

21 Heal, *Tradesmen's Cards*, plate XXII.

22 Anon, *Chronicles of Cannon Street* 38–9. A firm history of Joseph Travers and Sons, Ltd., privately printed and circulated. The 1778 circular has a postscript, "P.S. – Our friends will please take Notice, We permit no Person whatever to take orders or transact any Business for us from Home, except by special Authority" (41). A facsimile of a March 1782 circular follows p. 48. The original records of the firm may have been destroyed when the firm changed hands.

23 BM, Add. Ms. 36,666, fols. 29, 41.

24 Mennel (Tuke) Archives. Mr Robert O. Mennell kindly permitted the writers to have reproductions of the firm's records. The earliest extant printed circular of the Tukes was 1782 but it is quite apparent that it had been in general use for some time.

25 See, for example, the advertisements in the *Leeds Mercury*, 5 March 1751 by John Hildyard of York and Joseph Lord of Wakefield.

26 *Bailey's Western and Midland Directory 1783*, 2.

27 Wadsworth and Mann, *Cotton Trade*, 85, 296–7.

28 J. Fothergill to Matthew Boulton, 7 May 1762, quoted in Robinson, "Matthew Boulton's Marketing Techniques," 42–3.

29 See Willan, *Abraham Dent*, 43–4. A number of Dent's suppliers or their travellers signed his ledger in receipt of payment – for example, John Pease of Darlington who supplied tea and groceries in 1763 (39).

30 Francis Garratt to Henry Dundas, 22 July 1800, Ms. 1063, fol. 173, National Library of Scotland.

31 BM, Add. Ms. 39,931, 39,932.

32 Anon's *Chronicles of Cannon Street*, 38. The circular was dated 14 March 1791.

33 The above is drawn from Jefferys, *Retail Trading*, esp. 159–165, 235–7. Jefferys dates the change from 1850; Alexander, 1830. Both stress the lack of innovation in the retail trade in previous decades.

34 For the sales techniques of the two, see the important articles by Robinson, "Matthew Boulton's Marketing Techniques," 39–60; McKendrick, "Josiah Wedgwood," 408–33.

35 McKendrick, "Josiah Wedgwood," 419.

36 Josiah Wedgwood to Thomas Bentley, 7 December 1772, quoted in McKendrick, "Josiah Wedgwood," 423.

37 Matthew Boulton to R. Chippendall, 9 August 1794, quoted in Robinson, "Matthew Boulton's Marketing Techniques," 59.

38 *Gentleman's Magazine*, 18 (September 1748): 408–9.

39 *Leeds Mercury*, 28 May 1751, 4.

40 For details see Mui, "Smuggling," 53–6.

41 E/T, Memorial to the Lords of Treasury from Bristol Tea Dealers, 1 January 1783, E/T, 21;5–7, HMCL.

42 Memorial to the Lords of Treasury from the Tea Dealers of Kingston-upon-Hull, 1 January 1783, ibid., 7–9. Signed by fifteen dealers.

43 "Board of Trade Minutes," present Pitt, Grenville, Jackson, Eliot, 4 March 1783, T.1/585, No. 410, PRO.

44 For a detailed picture of the provincial trade see Mui, "Smuggling," esp. 61–73.

45 Blackman, "Development of the Retail Grocery Trade," 110.

46 Willan, *Abraham Dent*, 28–41.

47 Ibid., 40–1. The firm apparently continued to supply shops directly. Nathaniel and F. Phillips were shipping to Dent "a wide variety of laces, superior striped, all cotton." (36).

48 M. Boulton and J. Fothergill to Wooley and Heming, 19 January 1771, quoted in Robinson, "Matthew Boulton's Marketing Techniques," 55.

49 Mui, "Smuggling," 69–70.

50 Henry Hargreaves acting for Lawson Rawlinson and Co. of Lancaster to Abraham Dent, quoted in Willan, *Abraham Dent*, 35.

51 Richard Twining to his son, Richard, 5 June 1802, Add. Ms. 39,931 fol. 64, BM.

52 Ibid., fol. 225b.

53 Richard Twining II to John Twining, 4 August 1804, ibid., fol. 162.

54 Richard Twining to his son, Richard, 8 September 1804, ibid., fol. 165.

55 Ibid., St. Faith's, 14 November 1807, fol. 202.

56 Ibid., 18 June 1802, fol. 68.

57 Ibid., 14 May 1804, fol. 151.

58 In 1793 John Mills opened a bank in Colchester. Twining, *Two Hundred and Twenty-Five Years*, 26.

59 Undated draft reply by A. Newman to a shopkeeper who wished to change grocers, his previous one not having treated him well. Davison Newman & Co. Papers, Ms. 8631/1, Guildhall Library. The context dates this reply to the early 1780s.

60 Anon, *Chronicles of Cannon Street*, 48.

61 Prior to 1784, duty was not paid until the tea was removed from the East India Company's warehouses. The buyers were, however, required to pay the company the sale value of the tea on prompt day. During periods of financial distress, the company generally extended prompt several weeks but usually charged interest at the rate of 5 percent for the extended period.

62 Wadsworth and Mann, *Cotton Trade*, 297.

63 Ashton, *Peter Stubs of Warrington*, 56–7 et passim.

64 Ibid., 58.

65 University of North Wales Library, Bangor Ms. 416. The ledger records the accounts of over sixty customers for the years 1784 to 1789. Some of the 1784 transactions may have been posted in an earlier ledger. It is possible that the ledger was for trade customers only as many whose trade was not identified were obviously firms, e.g., William and John Nichols, Chester; Lloyd and Evans; Raynor and Mounsey.

66 Willan, *Abraham Dent*, 37.

67 Davison Newman Papers, Ms. 8631/1, Guildhall Library.

68 R. Twining to son, Richard, 14 September 1802, Add. Ms. 39,931, fol. 76, BM. By 1803 the duty on tea sold at 2s. 6d. or above had gone up to 95 percent *ad valorem*.

69 Ibid., fol. 131b. Italics in original.

70 Ibid., 14 August 1805, fol. 171b.

71 Ibid., 12 November 1807, fols. 201b–202.

72 Fay, *English Economic History*, 16.

73 Owen, *Life of Robert Owen*, I: 12.

74 Samuel Finney, *An Historical Survey of the Parish of Wilsmslow*, quoted in Ashton, *Economic History*, 181.

75 Burley, "An Essex Clothier," 290–1, 299. Within six years, Griggs accumulated sufficient profits from the grocery business to establish himself as a yarnmaster.

76 For an excellent account of the retail trade in the seventeenth century, see Willan, *Inland Trade*, 76–100. His analysis of tokens issued by shopkeepers (83–9) shows that shops were scattered all over the countryside. Of the total number of places where shopkeepers had issued tokens, 330 to 400 "were not market towns."

CHAPTER TWO

1 Or 40,000, depending upon which of King's figures one accepts. The higher figure has been chosen as it is the one reproduced by Colquhoun in his table of King's estimates of national income.

2 See especially Mathias, "Social Structure," 32–4. For a general discussion of the subject, see Deane, "Early National Income Estimates."

3 Harrowby Trust, Ms. 285, 27.

4 Paine, *Case of the Officers of Excise*, 30, provides a description of the "strictness of the duty, the poverty of Salary," and the slowness of promotion. It was written originally to accompany an application to Parliament by excise officers for an increase in salary.

5 The following is drawn from Craig, *Excise Officer's Pocket Companion*; Huie, *Abridgement of All the Statutes*; Symons, *Excise Laws Abridged*; Anon, *Duties of Excise*; Harrowby Trust Ms. 525; HMCL, Excise and Treasury Series and Excise Letter Books provide information on daily practices.

6 For example, the collection of Marlborough (no. eleven in the records) covered parts of Berkshire, Gloucestershire, Oxfordshire, and Wiltshire.

7 "An Account of ... Duties ... in Each Collection," 5 July 1796, 30/8/288, fol. 56, PRO.

8 In addition to the problem of smuggled and counterfeit goods and surreptitious manufacture (e.g. candles, soap), some caution is necessary in interpreting the accounts. What legal allowances for industrial use or for wastage, for example, were made in the duty charged on soap and candles? How were various different but somewhat similar commodities distinguished? By necessity, the law, buttressed by custom, allowed some latitude in interpreting the general provisions. For a discussion of the allowances of weight and other discrepancies in the excise records for tea see Mui, "Trends," 28–43. Nonetheless, once

correctly interpreted, the accounts of tea delivered out of the East India Company's warehouses, to take one example, are as nearly perfect as any found in the more statistically minded twentieth century.

9 PRO, 30/8/293, fols. 73–4; ibid., 30/8/294, fol. 245.

10 BM, Add. Ms. 33,039, fols. 57–63. There is inscribed on the proposal "or shops," ca. 1757.

11 Ibid., fols. 95–6. The proposer was calculating the means to finance the required sums for the year 1758.

12 Ibid., fols. 161–162b. It was proposed that the licence law commence July 1759. A number of queries were raised on methods of rating and on those required to take out licences. For a later, somewhat similar proposal, see ibid., fols. 351–352b.

13 See Smith, *Wealth of Nations*, 804–5. Short of the reference in Adam Smith, the present writers have been unable to find any trace of a bill introduced in Parliament. See also Dowell, *History of Taxation*, 2:136.

14 HMCL, E/T, 5: 14.

15 Ibid., Excise to Treasury, 24 January 1759, 14; see also BM, Add. Ms., 33,039, fol. 253.

16 Excise to Treasury, 6 April 1759, E/T, 5, HMCL.

17 All quoted passages are from House Book, vol. 44, fols. 389–90, 395, York Corporation Records, York Public Library.

18 The wording of the new by-law that the city fathers of York saw fit to pass in 1775 may have been a recognition of such a distinction. It was made to apply to "any shop or other place whatsoever inward or outward for shew sale or putting to sale ... by retail." Ibid., fols. 408b–409.

19 See advertisements in the *Leeds Mercury*, esp. 5 June, 3 July 1770 by various tradesmen offering special goods to be sold on certain days at the inns or in rooms over a shop.

20 H. of C. *Journal*, 40: 1091, 1109, 1117–8.

21 Excise to Treasury, 6 April 1759, E/T, vol. 5, HMCL.

22 York Public Library, York Corporation Records, House Book, vol. 44, fol. 403.

23 It was stated in 1758 that there were in Manchester "16 common bakers, who bake for the inhabitants for hire, besides 88 hucksters who bake and sell flour, meal and bread in the market." Evidence of James Fletcher who had "known Manchester for 30 years and been overseer of turnpike roads for past 12 years." H. of C. *Journal*, 28 (9 June 1758): 297.

24 See George, *London Life*, 195–202 for a vivid description of the shoe trade in London.

25 Marshall, *William Stout*, 79.

26 See chap. 6 for an analysis of Colquhoun's estimate.

27 The Cambridge, Hereford, Reading, and Oxon collections are the most noted examples.

28 As a result, the areas distinguished differ considerably in size, and the particular regional pattern that has emerged is not ideal. However, the counties in one group were not particularly disparate in their economic activities.

29 County population figures derived from Deane and Cole, *British Economic Growth*, 103, table 24.

30 For a judicious discussion of the weaknesses of some of the county estimates, see ibid., 99–106.

31 With an estimated population of 6.5 million in 1759 the average ratio of persons per shop was 46.4; based on the population for 1751, 43.6.

32 For problems involved in estimates of population, see esp. Krause, "Population Change, 1690–1790," 187–205.

33 Deane and Cole, *British Economic Growth*, 102, note 1.

34 For a description of the settlement patterns of the various farming regions of England see Thirsk, *Agrarian History*, vol. 4: 1–112; for Wales, 147–52.

35 See ibid., chap. 8 by A. Everitt, esp. 467–80, 496–502.

36 These terms are of course vague references for the commodities they purportly designate. See Smith, *Wealth of Nations*, esp. 821–2; Eversley, "Home Market," 212.

37 Other instances could be cited: Durham (128 persons per square mile), Staffordshire (122), and Cheshire (106) had population densities higher than many counties in the south, e.g. Kent (111), Hampshire (82), to mention two.

38 Wadsworth and Mann, *Cotton Trade*, 311.

39 Ibid., 315–6.

40 Excise specifically stated "a small portion." Moreover, Huntingdonshire and Cambridgeshire formed a relatively large geographical area to be surveyed. If large portions of Suffolk were included it would be enormous. Given the fact that the number of officers allocated to Cambridge was less than the average – Cambridge, forty-six officers; Lynn, fifty-three; Norwich, sixty-two; Suffolk, fifty-eight (Harrowby Trust Ms. 285) – and the general level of its revenue, it is difficult to believe that the collection could possibly have included more than Excise stated.

41 Thirsk, *Agrarian History*, 46.

42 Ashton, *Peter Stubs of Warrington*, 38–9.

43 Based on an estimate of the population in 1759.

44 See chap. 5.

45 Deane and Cole, *British Economic Growth*, 7 and Corfield, *English Towns*, 9.

46 Jefferys, *Retail Trading*, 468–9, table 88. The total number of retail establishments including dealers in coal, pets, etc.; artisans providing services such as shoemakers, electrical repairmen, etc.; and places such as the gas and electricity authorities was 531,143. If such "shops" are excluded, the ratio would be 100, almost as high as that estimated by Gregory King.

47 Ibid.

48 See chap. 5 for the London collectors' estimates of the incomes and general conditions of the shopkeepers in their districts.

CHAPTER THREE

1 HMCL, E/T, 14: 322.

2 The population of Didsbury in 1801 was 619.

3 "Customers Ledger," F 942/73955/D32, Manchester Public Library, primarily for the years 1785–91 with a few entries from a book for 1780 and "sundry odd debtors" dating back to 1763.

4 Marshall, *William Stout*, 161.

5 "Order Book of W. Fenton, 1773–94," Add. Ms. 36, 666, esp. fols. 29–32, BM.

6 Willan, *Abraham Dent*, esp. chap. 2.

7 "Penmorfa Shop Ledger," ca., 1788–ca., 1798, Bangor Ms., 82, Bangor, University of North Wales Library.

8 A card was made out for each of the bankruptcies. Thus the count is based on the number of bankruptcies, not the number of bankrupts. In compiling the card index the reason for some of the discrepancies in the various published lists became apparent. Occasionally the same bankruptcy was entered in the summaries for several months. At other times, a bankruptcy involving partners residing in two or more different places would get double or triple entry, although that was rare. And a few bankruptcies were listed for New England, possibly because one of the partners was residing in England. They have been omitted. Three partners, "formerly of Montrose, Scotland, now in London" along with their London-based merchant partner, were listed but that was the only entry remotely concerned with Scotland. The listings in the *Gentleman's Magazine* were for bankruptcies under the English legal system and concerned only with England and Wales. The reference in Mitchell and Deane, *British Historical Statistics*, 246, to the possibility that the "discrepancies [in published lists] may result from the omission of the Scottish and Irish figures" is somewhat puzzling. The lists compiled by the *Gentleman's Magazine* are, of course, subject to all the human errors that creep into any compilation, com-

pounded by that proverbial devil reserved for the printers. We do not think such errors are of sufficient magnitude to invalidate the results.

9 George, *London Life*, 162.

10 See ibid., 173–6, for an excellent description of the watch and clock trade in London.

11 See, for example, Alexander, *Retailing*, 238–264, appendices I and II; Jefferys, *Retail Trading*, 468–9, table 88. Neither offer any explanation for the omission.

12 See "An Account of the Gross Produce of Exiseable Liquors Imported in the Outports at a Medium of Years, viz., 1738, 1739, 1740 & 1741," Excise Documents, Ms. 525, Harrowby Trust. Sixty-nine outports were listed, many of which had no legal imports during the four years. The gross produce for Bristol was £10,267 15s. 11.73d.; the next in rank was Liverpool with £1,841 3s. 1d.; and third, Ipswich, £1,524 8s. 6d.

13 The figures for other years are: 1748 and 1750, 54.5 percent of all bankruptcies and 52.2 percent for shopkeepers with Yorkshire contributing a hefty 40.9 percent; 1768 and 1770, 59.6 percent of all bankruptcies and 50 percent for shopkeepers evenly distributed between Yorkshire and Lancashire.

14 It should perhaps be noted that the years used in the sample, with the possible exception of 1770, were not exceptional for the number of bankruptcies.

15 Ashton, *Economic Fluctuations*, 114.

16 It should be noted that the figure for London hatters, hosiers, and glovers for the years 1768 and 1770 may be somewhat inflated. Hosiers usually comprised a very small number – an average of a little over one per annum – and were easily recognizable, e.g. "hatter and hosier," as shopkeepers. But in 1768 nine were listed simply as "hosiers." The fashionable addresses of a few would seem to indicate they were shopkeepers, but the others may have been manufacturers or agents. Nevertheless, even if all nine hosiers are omitted, the number of haberdashers, etc. would be twenty or, on the new total, representing 41.7 percent of the clothing group, with drapers and mercers comprising 31.3 percent.

17 The number of bankrupt carpenters in London also increased.

18 Ashton, *Economic Fluctuations*, 154–5.

19 *Bailey's Western and Midland Directory, 1783*, 2. He claimed to have "personally applied in each town for the requisite information and been particularly careful to make the list of names complete, with respect to such as are of established credit."

20 Pigot, James, *London and Provincial New Directory*.

21 Birmingham, whose population in 1801 was 71,000, lists only 94

shopkeepers, whereas Norwich, population 36,000, lists 245.

22 See chap. 8, pp. 167 ff. for more details.

23 York, a very different type of city and one for which we have far more information, is analysed in chap. 5, table 22.

24 *Bailey's Western and Midland Directory*, 2.

25 For details of this rivalry see Mui, "William Pitt," 457–8, and for further evidence of the rise of tea warehouses, see Mui, "Commutation Act," 250–1.

26 See Robinson, "Matthew Boulton's Marketing Techniques," esp. 50–4.

27 Some retailers of flour may have been identified in the bankruptcy records as corn dealers, a group not included in the list of bankrupt shopkeepers.

28 We have calculated the percentages for a number of other towns. While it is hazardous to generalize on such a small sample, it appears that the distribution of shop trades in towns that were small or were not fashionable centres approximated the bankruptcy figures for the provinces. Industrialization does not seem to have effected major changes. Although the listing for Birmingham seems quite inadequate, at the least it indicates who was considered a "principal inhabitant." Its shops were distributed thus: wearing apparel, 39.4 percent; food, 21.3 percent; drinks, 6.3 percent; sundries, 9.6 percent; household furnishings, 6.3 percent; hardware, 13.6 percent; special services, 3.5 percent. Fashionable Bath lists ninety-seven shops (three more than Birmingham!): wearing apparel, 34 percent; food, 16.5 percent; drinks, 10 percent; sundries, 8.3 percent – all but one were druggists; household furnishings, 8.3 percent; hardware, 7.2 percent; special services, 15.5 percent. Note that the distribution of shops is not very different from that of Bristol.

29 Fisher, "London Food Market", 1: 135–151.

30 See McKendrick, "Josiah Wedgwood," 408–33.

31 Mui, "Commutation Act," 249–51.

32 Cities, even within one area, differ in their socio-economic structure and the shop trades responded to these variations. The very high proportion of pawnbrokers and drysalters in Manchester, for example, is a response to a particular type of working population and to the needs of industry.

CHAPTER FOUR

1 *H. of C. Journal*, 40: 977–1001; *PH*, 25: 885–6.

2 See, *H. of C. Journal*, 42 (16 March 1787): 551. An account presented by Mr Brent on the number of shopkeepers assessed in "each county, city, borough or town corporate, each market town (not being a city)

and the highest sum assessed for any one such shop in such market town." We are tantalizingly informed it was "preserved among other papers of this session."

3 *PH*, 25: 554.

4 *PR*, 18: 354–8, 401–8.

5 *H. of C. Journal*, 40 (19 May 1785): 1000.

6 Ibid., 977.

7 Manchester, Liverpool, Bolton, Wigan.

8 Glasgow and Paisley.

9 One each from Kendal (Westmorland), Halifax, parish of Alstonfield (Staffordshire), and London.

10 *H. of C. Journal*, 40: 1017–18, 1020.

11 *PR*, 20: 214–24.

12 *H. of C. Journal*, 40: 1054–5.

13 Ibid., 1007–8, 1026.

14 The family of James Craig moved from Scotland to Shrewsbury in the late seventeenth century. In the eighteenth century, James Craig was identified as a draper. See Mui, *William Melrose*, lxxiii, note 3 and Shrewsbury directories.

15 *H. of C. Journal*, 40: 1017–8, 1020.

16 Ibid., 1037–8.

17 Ibid., 1062. According to the petition from Halifax, "their [hawkers'] trade consists chiefly of linen drapery, mercery and hosiery goods."

18 The organization of such a campaign may have owed something to the opposition to commercial union with Ireland set in motion by William Eden and Lord Sheffield and abetted by Josiah Wedgwood. See Ehrman, *Younger Pitt*, 205–11.

19 "Petition of Linen, Cotton and Silk Manufacturers and Calico Printers of Glasgow," *H. of C. Journal*, 40: 1039–40. Most of the petitioners expressed a similar sentiment. All commented on their industry and integrity. The London wholesalers described the hawkers as "honest, industrious and punctual" – the Londoners were the only group to note punctuality as a virtue, ibid.

20 Cornwall (six towns), Devonshire (one), Gloucestershire (two), Sussex (one), Kent (three), Suffolk (one), Yorkshire (three), Staffordshire (one), Lancashire (two), Westmorland (one), Cardiganshire (one), Carmarthenshire (one).

21 *H. of C. Journal*, 40: 1084, 1091, 1114, 1118, 1127–8.

22 Ibid., 1084, 1107.

23 Ibid., 1124.

24 Ibid., 1078, 1090.

25 Ibid., 1124.

26 *PH*, 25,: 562.

27 *Leeds Mercury*, 5 July 1785.

28 *H. of C. Journal*, 40: 1103, 1107.

29 Ibid., 41: 252–3, 283.

30 *PR*, 20: 77, 214, 224.

31 *H. of C. Journal*, 44: 295. The manufacturers of Manchester had even requested the repeal of that clause, claiming it would depress trade.

32 Ibid., esp. 331–2, 341, 351, 366, 378–9.

33 *York Courant*, 31 January 1786.

34 Ibid.

35 *PR*, 19: 285.

36 *H. of C. Journal*, 41: 156–7, 160. Petitions from shopkeepers of Southampton, Bath, and Liverpool.

37 See Pitt's brilliant refutation of the argument that the tax could not be passed on to the consumer, *PR*, 19: 273–9.

38 *H. of C. Journal*, 40: 1000.

39 Ibid., 41: 156, 158.

40 Ibid., 176–7.

41 Ibid., 176.

42 Ibid., 156–7, 219.

43 Ibid., 43: 306.

44 Ibid., 44: 244.

45 *PR*, 20: 214–34. He and other MPs from London were also urging the removal of the restrictive clauses in the hawkers' act.

46 Brentford, £57 10s.; Edgeware, £4 3s.; Enfield, £15 10s.; Staines, £14; Uxbridge, £84 3s.

47 "Shop Tax, County of Middlesex, Extract from the Shop Tax Account before Parliament with Explanation of the Same," 30/8/302, fols. 140–140b, PRO. This appears to be part of the account delivered by Mr Brent of the Tax Office "showing the assessments made on all shops ... for one year ending Lady Day 1787." Areas outside London included in the assessment schedule were: Chelsea, Fulham, Kensington, Hammersmith, and Chiswick assessed £495; Edmonton and Gore Hundred, £48; Hoxton, Hackney, Church and Liberty, Moorfields, and St Lukes, £961; Islington, Hornsey, Finchley, Fryern Barnett, Newington, £242.

48 *H. of C. Journal*, 43: 321; 44: 263, 276.

49 PRO, HO 42/7, fols. 247–253b. The number of shops in each of the towns is listed by rental intervals of £5, the rates of duty as suggested by Pitt, the average charge for each shop, and the total amount of tax for that category. In calculating the probable yield of the tax, it was reasoned that if thirty towns, containing 33,813 houses in which there were 8,784 shops, produce £10,843 11s. 3d., then the remaining ninety provincial towns containing 130,000 houses could be expected

to have 34,041 shops which would yield £43,372. To these figures
were added the exact amount of the revenue from London, Westminster, Southwark, and part of Middlesex, £59,947 15s. 3d. and an
estimate of £10,000 for other towns and villages in the rest of England and Scotland. The total estimated yield of the tax – £124,152 –
was indeed too optimistic, but primarily because it was calculated according to Pitt's original rates.

50 See note 2 above. As the format shows, they were definitely drawn up
after the 1786 amendments to the act. In the account for London and
Westminster, PRO, 30/8/281, fol. 141, the Tax Office summed up the
number of shops renting from five pounds to under thirty pounds. It
will be recalled that by the amendment only those shops renting for
thirty pounds or more paid two shillings in the pound; by the 1785
act, those renting at twenty-five pounds or more.

51 PRO, 30/8/281, fols. 141–146b. Each is numbered 53 on the outside.

52 For details see PRO, HO 42/7, fol. 247a. There were no shops in the
rental category £185 to £200.

53 Based on the 1801 census.

54 See Alexander, *Retailing*, 97, table 4:4. The figures were based on
shopkeepers listed in Pigot, *London and Provincial New Directory*.

55 The ratio for Norwich would be 181; that for Leeds, 244.

56 See below, chap. 8 for evidence on the inadequacy of Pigot's directory
for 1822–3. It could be argued that for some peculiar reason the major towns of Northamptonshire and Suffolk had very early achieved a
high density of shops. That, however, is difficult to believe.

57 The assessment for Clerkenwell was £585 16s. 10d. Based on the
number of shops paying assessed taxes in 1797, the shop tax assessment averages a little under 16s. per shop. See chap. 5 for an analysis
of the income of shopkeepers in these areas.

58 "An Account of the Number of Shops Showing their Rents in the
Towns and Parishes in the Following Counties: Northamptonshire,"
30/8/281, fol. 143, PRO.

59 For example, Needham, Debenham, Framlingham as well as smaller
market towns such as Blythburgh, Dunwick, and Woodbridge. These
may not have had taxable shops. The coastal towns of Orford and
Aldboro are, however, included, as well as Hadleigh, Sudbury, and
Bildeston. One suspects that the area omitted was under the collection
of Ipswich.

60 "An Account of ... Duties ... in each Collection," 5 July 1796, 30/8/288,
fol. 56, PRO.

61 *Universal British Directory 1799*. Lavenham was not unique. In Lowes-
toft, Suffolk, in addition to the usual shop trades, the directory lists

"grocer and twine spinner," "grocer and herring curer," "grocer, herring curer and tallow chandler," and "shopkeeper and tailor." In Fordingbridge, Hampshire, "shopkeepers" and "grocers" combined their shop trades with the manufacture "of ticks"; and in Glastonbury, Somersetshire, with "stocking making."

62 *H. of C. Journal*, 40: 1030–1, from Kendal, Westmorland.

63 The amending act also ordered the Tax Office to discontinue the customary discount for prompt payment, some 3.75 percent of the fee.

64 *H. of C. Journal*, 14: 498–521. Petitions from Beverley, Yorkshire; Hereford; Dorchester, and Shaftesbury, Dorset; East Grinstead, Sussex.

65 BM, Add. Ms. 33,039, fol. 179, ca. 1759.

66 "An Account of the Gross and Net Revenue, the Medium of Three Years to 1726," 30/8/81, fol. 35, PRO. "An Account of the Gross and Net Produce of the Duty on Licensing Hawkers and Pedlars for 10 Years Last Past," signed Office for Licensing Hawkers, 10 January 1759, Add. Ms. 33,039, fols. 177–8, BM.

67 "Hawkers and Pedlars: Number of Licenses Granted Annually for the Last Seven Years," 18 (2): 194, *PP 1824*; "Hawkers Licensed in 1800, 1810, 1820, 1830, 1840, and 1843," 22 (1): 123, *PP 1844*. Only the revenue is given for 1800 and 1810.

68 "An Account of the Gross and Net Produce of the Duties Arising from Hawkers and Pedlars licensed from Midsummer 1782 to Midsummer 1785 ...," submitted 31 October 1785, 30/8/290, fols. 43–7, PRO. This account gives the number of foot and horse licences for each county in England and the total for Wales for each year, signed by Mr Turner and Mr Beaumont. On 18 May 1785, Mr Beaumont, one of the commissioners for licensing hawkers and pedlars, presented to Parliament an "Account of the Hawkers and Pedlars Licensed ... with their Names and Places of Abode, so far as the same can be made up," *H. of C. Journal*, 40 (9 May 1785): 965. These undoubtedly formed the bases for the summary account by counties.

69 For a description of the methods of distributing smuggled tea see Mui, "Smuggling," 50–1, 58–60, 62–6.

CHAPTER FIVE

1 PRO, 30/8/280. Each report was signed by the collector of the district, ward, or precinct. Many include extensive comments on the residents. PRO, 30/8/281, fols. 1–16, provides a summary account, based on the individual reports in 280. But, in addition to a number of copying errors, the scribe has, in a few instances, repeated a district, making the

total number of shops in 281 over 300 greater than that calculated from the individual reports. The figures are, therefore, based on 280 as it appears to be the more reliable document.

2 The collectors have apparently adopted a practice similar to that of the excise surveyors in 1759 and the assessors of the shop tax and counted only one shop to a house. It should also be noted that the list comprises "retail shops" not artisans' *work* shops, nor for that matter, public houses. Cf. Schwarz, "Income distribution," 256–7. It will be recalled that the shop tax, for which the collectors of assessed taxes were responsible to collect, specifically excluded any building "employed ... for the purpose of ... carrying on any manufacture." Public houses were, as a rule, not subject to the tax on retail shops and it seems likely that most collectors of the 1797 survey did not consider them "retail shops." In the three instances where public houses have been included in the enumeration of shops, the collectors appended special notes indicating the number. More typical of the view of the tax commissioners is the following note submitted by the collector for St Paul, Shadwell: "Exclusive of shops [251] there is [*sic*] 85 public houses" (30/8/280, fols. 262–4, PRO). Many shops did retail alcoholic beverages – from the small chandler's shop to the high-class grocery shop. Moreover, the correspondence of the figures for the number of shops assessed in the City in 1797 and the number of shops actually paying the shop tax in 1787 is too close to leave any doubt on the matter. In 1787, 6,579 shops paid the shop tax; the number assessed in 1797 was 6,419. Their breakdown by rental and assessment categories is also similar. In 1787, 51.3 percent paid rents of five pounds to under thirty pounds; with such rents, assessments would range from one pound to five pounds. In 1797, 53.1 percent were in the one pound to five pound assessment categories.

3 Class 2, "£1 to under £2"; Class 3, "£2 to under £5"; Class 4, "£5 to under £10."

4 Thos. Law, Pudding Lane to Mr Hunter, Treasury, 16 December 1797, 30/8/280, fols. 19–20, PRO. Law was collector for the Upper Division of Billingsgate Ward and had attended "Mr Rose and other gentlemen at the Treasury on Thursday last."

5 As they are systematically tabulated in PRO, 30/8/281, fols. 1–16, we have used this source to calculate the percentage of shops letting lodgings.

6 PRO, 30/8/280, fol. 326.

7 See table 17 for a list of missing wards and parishes.

8 See page 111 and notes 19 and 20.

9 As the 1785 shop tax account ("Tax on Shops, 1785," HO 42/7, PRO) does not give the particular districts included in the survey, it is less

useful for comparative purposes. Of course, neither the 1785 nor the 1797 account included all shops, only those subject to the tax. Houses renting under five pounds did not pay the house or shop tax. The 1759 account includes all shops.

10 There is no such discrepancy for the City of London. See note 2.

11 Based on estimates for 1750 and the census returns of resident population in 1801. There are some discrepancies in the published figures. Cf. George, *London Life*, 329, note 5 and *PP 1837*, 25 (239): 3. See also Glass, "Gregory King's Estimate," 201, note 49.

12 No ratio has been calculated for the five parishes in Surrey – only scattered returns are available. The collector for Lambeth, for example, reported a total of 366 shops and houses. In fact, there were 2,789 houses in the parish. Is it possible that over 2,000 houses were not assessed? If so, rents in Lambeth must have been exceedingly low.

13 The Westminster ratio is based on the population in those parishes for which there are reliable figures. The ratio for the City is based on the total population and makes no allowance for the missing wards. Also included in the calculations for the City is the population of St Andrew, Holborn, Middlesex.

14 There is a considerable difference in the population figures for Southwark in the *London Summary* and the returns for Surrey. See George, *London Life*, 329–30, note 50. The ratio for Southwark is based on the Surrey figures for the five parishes. If Christchurch, Surrey, is excluded, the ratio is 21.2. However, if the much higher population figure, 98,700, reported in the *London Summary* is used, the ratio would be almost 32. As the population returns in 1811 reported only 75,000 people in the Borough, the lower figure derived from the Surrey returns is probably more accurate. The lower figure is, we may add, the one given by Rickman, see *PP 1837*, 25 (239): 3.

15 This judgment is based on PRO, 30/8/281, fols. 17–70. The document lists the amount of each assessed tax of the inhabitants in various areas in London and elsewhere.

16 See above, chap. 4.

17 By 1797 there were four separate house taxes: the inhabited house duty (old), old window tax, the Commutation Tax, and the new window tax, plus a 20 percent addition to the total assessment.

18 It should be borne in mind that income generalizations based on the London assessments are not necessarily applicable to other areas of the country, where rent and therefore assessment were on a lower level.

19 PRO, 30/8/281, fols. 17–70.

20 St Michael Street, Cornhill; Hanover Square, St George; St Giles-in-the-East, all missing from the London survey.

21 PRO, 30/8/280, fols. 33, 39, 156, 19, 212, 127.

22 Ibid., fols. 137–141, first, middle, and Pentonville districts. The collectors also described the low wages and lack of employment of the clock and watchmakers.

23 Ibid., fol. 228.

24 Ibid., fol. 247. The breakdown is as follows

Classes	Total Number of shops	Number in each Range of Income (in £)				
		Below 60	60-75	75-100	100-150	no comment
1	12	—	3	—	—	9
2	44	24	15	5	—	—
3	160	—	90	40	10	20

25 Ibid., fol. 326.

26 Pictet, *Voyage de trois Mois en Angleterre*, quoted in George, *London Life*, 92.

27 See George, *London Life*, 174–6.

28 The population of Clerkenwell in 1801 was 23,396. The number of houses was only 3,320, a little over seven persons per house.

29 Only 3.5 percent in St George and .8 percent in St John were in Class 5.

30 Classes 4 and 5: St Thomas, 33 percent; St Olave, 30 percent; St Saviours, 31 percent; Classes 1 and 2: 34 percent, 29 percent, and 30 percent respectively.

31 PRO, 30/8/280, fol. 326.

32 PRO, 30/8/281, fols. 72–82b. The name of the writer has been removed, but the envelope was addressed to Pitt. The covering letter was dated 2 December 1797.

33 Ibid., fol. 74. In the covering letter, the writer explained who had been included and made suggestions concerning the effects an increase in taxes would have on various groups.

34 "Tax on Shops, 1785," HO 42/7, PRO.

35 The following have not been included as shopkeepers, although some may have been: shoemakers (five), sadlers (four), curriers (four), and coal dealers (three). There were numerous retail dealers in coal in large cities. Many were recorded in the bankruptcy reports. In York in 1775, seven had not taken up their freedom but sold coal by retail.

36 Almost all the names listed in Bailey's directory appear in the 1797 survey, but the latter includes far more shopkeepers as can be seen in table 22.

37 Bailey's listing for Norwich and Bristol seems superior to his listing for York.

38 This may be merely a shift in emphasis of the leading articles sold. However, the term is itself indicative of the proprietors' view of market possibilities.

39 See map 4 for the approximate location of the parishes and table 23 for the number of major shops in each parish.

40 See *Victoria County History, The City of York*, 164, tables 3 and 4: "Hearth Tax, 1672"; also 213, table 2: "Baptisms and Burials in the City Parishes" for 1728–35 and 1770–6. In the seventeenth century, of the 124 enumerated households in St Mary, Castlegate, 47 or 37.9 percent were exempt from the hearth tax, 57, or almost one-half had only one hearth, only 27 or a little over 20 percent could be classed as comfortable, with four or more hearths. The situation does not seem to have improved during the eighteenth century. For the years 1728–35, burials exceeded baptisms by 24 percent for the twenty-three parishes recorded, but by 47 percent for St Mary, Castlegate. During the years 1770–6, baptisms exceeded burials by 4 percent, but in St Mary burials continued to outnumber baptisms by 32 percent.

41 See Blackman, "Retail Grocery Trade," 110.

42 The figure for London is based on the twenty shopkeepers in Class 3, in table 8. The sample is obviously too small to bear the weight of the comparison. On the other hand, the general comments by the London tax collectors certainly indicate that few shopkeepers in this class had comfortable incomes. Moreover, the sample is drawn from the more affluent districts.

43 See table 18. Based on the higher estimated income, the average income of the London shopkeepers in Class 4 was £185; on the lower estimated income, £168.

44 York Public Library, York Corporation Records, House Book, 44: 385–411.

45 Ibid., 395.

46 See chap. 2, p. 34–5.

47 York Public Library, York Corporation Records, House Book, 44: 395.

48 Of the 239 offenders, 87 purchased their freedom. Among this group, there are a few who were or later became substantial tradesmen. Ralph Dodsworth, merchant, was fined £30 for his freedom. In 1797, he and his brother William had an estimated income of £500. Robert Spence, bookseller, paid £25; his income in 1797 was £350. Richard Driffield, merchant, who purchased his freedom was sufficiently important to be listed in the 1784 directory. A few others appear in an excise list of tea dealers in 1784, but were obviously not major grocers. Two "shopkeepers," John Playforth and John Jackson, paid their £25, but judging from the excise figures were still very

small shopkeepers in 1784. The same was true for several aledrapers. They were not listed in the directories, or in the 1797 survey. In fact, there was a surprising continuity of family names among major tradesmen.

49 A seller in the market was not required to pay the twenty-five pound fee.

50 York Public Library, York Corporation Records, House Book, 44: 402.

51 Ibid., 387–8.

52 Ibid., 389–90, 395.

53 Ibid., 403.

54 Hoskins, *Industry, Trade and People*, 127.

CHAPTER SIX

1 King appears to have attempted to distinguish the more affluent in his journal, see Cooper, "Social Distribution," 439, appendix II. After noting the unfree merchants living in or within London, there is an entry "Tradesmen, Shopkeepers, and Vintners worth £300," numbering 10,000. This is followed by an entry "merchants, tradesmen or artificers living in a house of £30 p.a. in London or within 20 miles of London" who numbered 10,000, 500 of which were merchants and brokers.

2 Marshall, *William Stout*, 96, 119.

3 Smith, *Wealth of Nations*, 112. It is unclear what Smith meant by "stock," which he uses interchangeably with "capital." But his reference to the small grocer in the seaport whose gross income he estimates as thirty to forty pounds, is based on his making "forty or fifty percent upon a stock of a single hundred pounds." The reference seems to imply that the shopkeeper turned over his stock only once a year. It bears little relationship to reality in 1776 although in 1688 and later Stout purchased the major portion of his stock once a year.

4 The "Partnership Agreement, 1794," Ms. 8630, Guildhall Library, details the early history of the firm.

5 Jones, *Two Centuries*, 9. The title, "merchant," may have been accurate after the abolition of the East India Company's monopoly, but the firm was selling by retail before this time; see the invoices for private customers. The book is a firm-history.

6 "The Will of Francis Garratt" of the Old Swan near Thames St, London tea dealer, proved at London at the prerogative court of Canterbury, 13 January 1809, probated under £400,000, reveals a fortune well over £100,000. Garratt Papers, W.E. Taylor & Son, Ltd. Archives.

7 "A Table for Raising Ten Million by Way of Contribution," ca. 1798 30/8/281, fol. 125, PRO.

8 See, for example, the fairly strong correlation between income and assessed taxes among York shopkeepers in table 21.

9 PRO, 30/8/281, fol. 125.

10 Colquhoun's average, including paupers, vagrants, labourers, fishermen, etc. is £116 per "head of family." If those not likely to have paid assessed taxes are subtracted, the average for the remaining 822,819 is £197. Colquhoun, *Indigence*, 23; table exhibiting a "General View of Society."

11 PRO, 30/8/281 is replete with information on incomes and assessments of various occupations throughout the country. The documents were the source for Pitt's famous speech to the Commons on the introduction of the income tax.

12 It is not a perfect comparison; seven of the York shopkeepers had incomes of £60 and only one, £400 and two, £350.

13 "Estimates of the National Income: No. 1, From Personal Incomes; No. 2, From the Several Sources of Income; No. 3, From the Population and Prices of Labour and Provisions; No. 4, From the Add'l Assessed Taxes and Contributions; No. 5, From the National Income of 1688; No. 6, From Windows and Houses," 30/8/302, fols. 263–274, PRO, listed on fol. 263.

14 The total estimated income is shared among 168,378 persons. Pitt totalled 166,258, an error due probably to the fact that individual figures are very poorly aligned. The number of persons is almost identical to the number in the table based on assessments. Inhabitants with "expenditure" of £200 and above total 148,727. If those with an "expenditure" of £180 (income £200 ?) are included, they number 167,583.

15 PRO, 30/8/302, fol. 266, No. 2.

16 The figures in the first column of table 25 differ considerably from those Rev. H. Beeke reproduced as Pitt's estimates of assessable income, particularly for "home trade." Compare Deane, "Early National Income Estimates," 28, table 5.

17 Pitt was primarily interested in identifying and assessing the politically feasible taxable wealth of the nation. He may well have thought at the time that those below £100 were not likely contributors to the proposed income tax.

18 With an average income of £100 the number of shopkeepers and manufacturers would be 310,000 or a ratio of 3.4 to 1 (310,000 : 90,000). If the average income is reduced to £90 the ratio rises to 3.8 to 1.

19 For an excellent account of Pitt's handling of financial measures see

Ehrman, *Younger Pitt*, esp. chap. 10, 239–81.

20 There was certainly considerable entrepreneurial activity within the shopkeeping world in the last three decades of the century.

21 PRO, 30/8/302, fol. 272. Pitt calculated the total income for those "above £50 a year in 1688" as £34,500,000. This appears to be the total income for all those increasing the wealth of the nation, including those with incomes of £40. He refers to "Dr. Davenant as fully deserving of credit after a strict examination the scheme of income and expense ... calculated by Gregory King." Possibly, George Chalmers was one of Pitt's informants. See table "No. 5. Estimate of the National Income Deduced from the Increased Scale of the National Income, Prosperity and Population, as Compared with the Supposed Income of England in the Last Century."

22 "The number of Common Brewers and Victuallers in the Whole Kingdom [England and Wales] with the Amount in Barrels of x and *vj* Charged in the Respective years below, 1684–1762," fol. 27; for London, fol. 30 Ms. 285, Harrowby Trust. The separate listing of barrels x and *vj* was necessitated by the law (12 Car. c. 11, compare secs. 12–37 with 38–47 of c. 24), requiring common brewers to pay the duty on beer weekly; innkeepers, alehouse keepers, victuallers, or other retailers, paid monthly.

23 For a judicious assessment of Massie see Mathias, "Social Structure."

24 Massie combined the role of pamphleteer with that of businessman (not unlike Defoe, although less given to hyperbole). A diligent searcher for information, a practical man of affairs, his writing is an informative source on eighteenth-century economic matters. Colquhoun's magistracy, on the other hand, gave him a far more intimate knowledge of the indigent. His position may, however, have clouded his vision of those merely a rung above paupers.

25 Colquhoun, *Indigence*, 23, table exhibiting a "General View of Society." See also his "Summary Recapitulation of the Table, 1803." In the summary the 25,000 tailors, etc. were included in Category 6: "Manufacturers of all description." Category 7: "Inland traders and shopkeepers of all descriptions, trading on capitals" include the 74,500 shopkeepers, 500 "principal warehousemen, selling by wholesale" (average income £800) and 50,000 publicans.

26 Outside London there would be few army clothiers. One cannot suppose they ever formed a very numerous body. In 1822, a year of peace it is true, twelve army clothiers were listed in Pigot's directory for London; none were listed for the other towns checked, including Liverpool and Manchester. The enumeration does not include the manufacturers of hats who were listed among the general manufacturers with average incomes of £800.

27 "Tea and Coffee Dealers Licences for England & Wales, Scotland and Ireland from 1781 to 1855," 83, *PP 1857*. The number of licences issued in Scotland was 6,348 in 1803. A decade later (1812/13), the number of licences issued for England, Wales, and Scotland was 72,444. Cf. Colquhoun's figures for the United Kingdom for 1812.

28 In a partnership only one of the partners was required to obtain the licence but the licensee had to make entry of "every warehouse, room, shop or other places" from which tea was to be sold or where it was to be stored. Thus, one licence legalized the sale of tea of the licensee to any number of "places thereunto belonging." Multiple shops were not a nineteenth century innovation; they existed in the eighteenth century. See the "Tea Licence of David Bullock of Manchester," No. 362, issued September 1811, Manchester Public Library, and the laws governing the entry (10 Geo. 1, c. 10, sec. 10) and licensing of tea dealers (20 Geo. 3, c. 35, sec. 14–16).

29 Based on the average income for each assessed class in table 18.

30 Except for the principal shopkeepers in London and the major provincial towns, overhead costs were not particularly heavy in the retail trade. As a 20 percent mark-up is a conservative estimate, we ignore the problem of overhead costs. Moreover, until the separation of house and shop, so-called shop rent, rates, and taxes included household quarters often larger than the shop itself.

31 £11,175,000 = .2x; x = £55,875,000.

32 Deane and Cole, *British Economic Growth*, 65, table 17.

33 Ibid.: wool (ca. 1805), £14.5 million, 196, table 47; cotton (1805–7), £6.4 million, 185, table 42; linen (1803), £7.2 million, 203–4 and table 49; silk (ca. 1800), £2.5 million, 207–10 and table 51. The value of exports has been subtracted from the estimated value of each of the textiles.

34 Colquhoun, *Indigence*, 23.

35 All numbers for licensed hawkers are calculated from *PP 1824*, 18 (2), (194) and *PP 1844*, 22 (123).

CHAPTER SEVEN

1 See also the interesting evidence on seventeenth-century shop tokens in Willan, *Inland Trade*.

2 Anon., *Trade of England Revised*, 397.

3 Marshall, *William Stout*, 165.

4 See Anon., *Trade of England Revised*, 393, 397–8. The author accused both the hawkers and village shops of contributing to "the ruining of the cities and market towns"; see also Westerfield, *Middlemen*, 346, quoting R. Pococke, *Travels through England*.

5 Rev. John Clayton, *Friendly Advice to the Poor* (1755), quoted in Wadsworth and Mann, *Cotton Trade*, 388.

6 *Leeds Mercury*, 17 August 1773, 4, signed "Yorkshire Amicus Pauperis."

7 Alexander, *Retailing*, 61, 102–3, 234.

8 Clapham, *Economic History*, 1: 225.

9 Jefferys, *Retail Trading*, 3–5.

10 See introduction, p. 4 for the presumed emergence of backstreet shops in the nineteenth century. Cf. Scola, "The Relationship between Food Markets and Shops." Scola shows that in Manchester, at least, the small general shops were certainly present as early as the 1770s and in no small numbers – 125 in 1788. He notes that by the 1820s even the butchers were attempting to break away from the markets (11). The evidence on types of market traders certainly casts doubts on the presumed purchasing practices of the workers.

11 Ashton, *Economic History*, 206–9, 217–8, reminds us that "wage-earners have never been a homogeneous group." In the face of such diversity, sweeping generalizations are difficult to make with confidence.

12 Ashton, "The Standards of Life of the Workers," 30.

13 Ibid.

14 See John Burnett, *Plenty and Want*, 45–7 and Minchinton, "Patterns of Demand," 116–8.

15 Eden, *State of the Poor*, 3: ccxl, Cumberland. One family paid £3 6s., but their income was £30 per annum. The range for the other five families was £22 19s. to £26 17s. The former paid an annual rent of £2 10s., the latter, with eight in the family, £1 19s. 6d.

16 Ibid., 2: 661. Interestingly, he and his two sons had bread and milk for breakfast; his wife and two daughters, tea.

17 Ibid., 3: 753. According to the report from Kendal, "the labouring people do not manufacture their own clothing, as is done in other parts of the county; they generally purchase clothes at second-hand."

18 Ibid., 1: 554–5.

19 Minchinton, "Patterns of Demand," 121–2, table 14. Budget (1901) for a working family with an annual income of £78. The total for food was £32 3s. 6d. of which £14 1s. 8d. was for meat and fish and £3 4s. for green groceries: that is, 54 percent of the expenditure on food was spent on meat, fish, and vegetables, all of which might have been purchased at the market.

20 Eden, *State of the Poor*, 3: cclvi, appendix 15. Other sources show an even more generous allotment.

21 Ibid., 2: 286.

22 Ibid., 360.

23 Edward Rigby, "Reports of the Special Provision Committee, Appointed by the Court of Guardians, in the City of Norwich, with an Account of Savings ... ," Norwich, 1788, quoted in ibid., 2: 480–3.

24 Society for Bettering the Conditions, *Reports*, 1: 19–20.

25 Marshall, *William Stout*, 106.

26 The above is drawn from various contemporary sources. See Peter Kalm, *Visit to England*, especially his description of Hertfordshire and Essex in 1748, quoted in George, *English Social Life*, 82; Pococke, *Travels through England*, quoted in Westerfield, *Middlemen*, 346; *A Political Inquiry into the Consequence of Enclosing Wasteland* (1785), quoted in George, *English Social Life*, 44, where the writer refers to the harmful effects of enclosures on, among others, the "inferior shopkeepers." In *Labourers in Husbandry*, Davies found in his parish of Barkham, Berkshire, in 1787, "most families in debt to little shopkeepers" (6) and noted that the poor were "forced to buy dearly at the village shops instead of from the farmer or at Market," Even flour was bought not from the market, but from the shopkeepers, (33–4). Most of the agricultural surveys indicate that rural workers, especially south of the Trent, were dependent on the village shop. See, for example, Turner, *Agriculture in Gloucestershire*, and Eden, *State of the Poor*. Rev. H. Beeke in *Produce of the Income Tax* claimed that over half of the families of the kingdom had incomes below sixty pounds "derived from daily wages." Included among the group were "petty shopkeepers" who had some "small portions of productive capital" (121). Beeke estimated that at least two-thirds of internal trade was carried on by persons whose incomes were so low that few would have to pay the income tax (no more than one-seventeenth). He thought that not less than one-half of the amount and two-thirds of the profits of this trade was in articles of provisions (132). He thought it a fact "no one will dispute ... who also recollects the class of retailers among whom far the greater part is expended, of all the wages of daily labour; and indeed of all income below £100 a year" (132).

27 "Household Account Book of Rev. Laurie," Ms. 1934, National Library of Scotland. Bread, meal, barley, and pot rice accounted for 24 percent of his expenditure; cheese, butter, milk, and eggs, 5.5 percent; tea and sugar, 11.5 percent; candles, salt, pepper, mustard, soap, starch, and blue, 5.8 percent; beer, wine, and liquors, 21.6 percent. It may be noted that Rev. Laurie bought much of his cheese, butter, eggs, candles, wine, and other liquors from well-known grocers in Leith and Edinburgh. Even some of his fish and fowl came from shopkeepers. His total expenditure in 1795 was £119 17s.

28 The estimate is based on numerous household accounts for families in widely different social and economic positions. Some calculations have

also been made on the basis of the sales of shopkeepers. We have not taken into account the fact that grocers also sold flour, candles, soap, starch, blue, and other household articles, admittedly not their traditional stock.

29 Blackman, "Retail Grocery Trade," 110 refers to the grocer's "high-class luxury trade" and apparently assumes such wares were out of reach of workers.

30 Customers, some of whom were labourers, were certainly buying them at Wood's shop.

CHAPTER EIGHT

1 "Tea and Coffee Dealers' Licences," 83, *PP 1857*. It lists the number of licences issued for England and Wales and Scotland from 1781 to 1855; for Ireland, 1815–1855.

2 Mui, "Smuggling," 53–4.

3 Francis Garratt to Henry Dundas, 22 July 1800, Ms. 1063, fol. 173, National Library of Scotland. He was warning Dundas of the possible evil consequences of increasing the duty on tea by reminding him of the situation in the 1760s.

4 Treasury to Excise, 2 January 1767, E/T, 27: 270, HMCL and Excise to Treasury, 13 January 1767, ibid., 273. Scotland had its own establishment and reported directly to Treasury. We have not been able to locate the figures for Scotland. In the light of the number of dealers in 1781–3, one could hazard a guess that it hovered around 1,000.

5 Based on an estimated population of 6.8 million.

6 Mui, "Smuggling," 65.

7 Westerfield, *Middlemen*, 334, suggests 758 to 786 towns for the eighteenth century. A. Everitt (Thirsk, *Agrarian History*, 496) suggests 800 in the seventeenth century. Rather than an increase of market towns during the eighteenth century, the picture is one of decay in many small, out-of-the-way places. On the map drawn by Thomas Jefferys, "geographer to his Royal Highness, the Prince of Wales," which identifies, among other places, the market towns, a number named by Everitt are missing and no new ones appear.

8 See Mui, "William Pitt," 447–65 for some of the problems involved.

9 "An Account of the Quantity of Tea in the Hands of the Several Dealers in that Article at the Undermentioned Towns on the Excise Officers Last Survey," 2 August 1784, 30/8/293, fol. 74, PRO. The survey was made the last week of July.

10 "An Account of the Stock of Tea in Hand Within the City of York as it was Found on the Last Taking With the Date and Minute When Those Surveys Were Made," 1 August 1784. Edward Jackson, Super-

visor of Excise, 30/8/293, fols. 67–8, PRO. Surveys were made the last week of July.

11 "An Account of the Stock of Tea in the Possession of the Large Dealers under the Survey of the Brewery Generals," ibid., fols. 59–66. Surveys were made the last week of July. See also fol. 69, "An Account of the Number of Tea Dealers under our Inspection and the Quantity of Tea ... in Stock," 2 August 1784.

12 PRO, 30/8/293, fol. 74. The commissioners estimated that the quantity of legal tea among dealers in the remainder of the country (roughly two-thirds) was just about 50 percent more than the sample.

13 PRO, 30/8/283, fol. 187 [n.d.]. Internal evidence dates this ca. 1778–9 and suggests Excise as the source. It is addressed to "Your Lordships." Checked against a similar although not identical report to Treasury from Excise, 24 March 1778, E/T, 19: 359–67 HMCL.

14 Ibid.

15 The increase for the collections from Essex to Reading was 36 percent. The average increase for all collections in England and Wales from 1782/3 to 1795/6 was 61.7 percent which would seem to indicate that Excise knowingly or by chance had selected a fairly representative sample.

16 See an excise report which includes a chart of the quantities smuggled in various areas. PRO, 30/8/283, fol. 192.

17 *Gentleman's Magazine*, 15 November 1770: 565–6, written by J. Duncumbe.

18 It should perhaps be pointed out that the stock of tea on hand in July represented purchases made during the East India Company's March Sale generally held in late May or June. The next sale, called the September Sale, would normally have been scheduled for November/December.

19 "An Account of the Tea in the Stock of the Traders in the Town on the Survey Immediately Preceeding Xmas Day Last," York, 5 August 1784, 30/8/294, fol. 7, PRO.

20 *Cambridge Chronicle*, 25 September 1773. Advertisement by Mary Snow, china dealer, quoted in Clapham, *Economic History*, 1:222–3. Clapham notes that such notices "multiply" during the course of the century.

21 Bristol has been omitted as the excise figure for this city includes shops in the surrounding hamlets.

22 Excise Accounts, England: 1788–90; 1791–6, 1797–1803; 1816–28, E-600, HMCL. The account actually ends January 1826. These accounts distinguish the gross produce or the number of licences issued for London and for the rest of England and Wales.

23 Some intractable problems preclude a precise ratio for London. By

1801 the London collection included, in addition to the Bills, St Marylebone, and parts of both Paddington and St Pancras. The ratios
quoted for London and the rest of England and Wales are, therefore,
approximations, based on a reasonable judgment of the population of
London.

24 The ratio began to drop in the late 1840s just before the termination
of the licensing system, but still remained well above that for the late
eighteenth century.

25 Deane and Cole, *British Economic Growth*, 9.

26 PRO, 30/8/293, fol. 73.

27 The total number of licences issued for England and Wales during
the excise year 1783/4 was 34,076 of which 3,079 were issued in the
London Bills of Mortality. The number issued in 1782/3 was 32,754,
the figure used in comparing the percentage increase. The large increase in licences between 1782/3 and 1783/4 apparently registered
the proposed change in duty. By 1784/5 the licences issued jumped to
37,478. For that reason, the figure for 1782/3 was used in calculating
the increase.

28 36,000 in 1801; 50,000 in 1821. It has been suggested that the population of Norwich in 1786 had reached 40,051 and subsequently declined. See Chalkin, *Provincial Towns*, 33.

29 These figures are slightly different than those tabulated by Alexander, *Retailing*, appendix I, table A: 5. He appears to have overlooked six identified as "confectioners and fruiterers" and one grocer
listed at the end among the *errata*. We have also included among the
confectioners ten listed as "bakers (and confectioners)."

30 The ratio for Bristol is based on the census population for 1821
which was 85,000.

31 In calculating the number of shops the compilations in Alexander,
Retailing, 239–55 appendix I, have been used. The tables list the
number of shops in each of the various specialized trades for eleven
towns. Two towns have been omitted: Carlisle, because there are no
figures for 1822 and Merthyr Tydfil because the classification of its
shop trades is inadequate. Alexander also omits Merthyr Tydfil from
his analysis of "population per shop outlet" in appendix II, 256–65.
The towns chosen do not appear to be particularly unrepresentative.
A random check of other towns produced similar results.

32 This number is derived from excise account of tea licences for London, 1822.

33 Based on the evidence from Pigot, Alexander, *Retailing*, 234, concludes that "there was an enormous growth of shops between the
1820 and 1850s and much of this growth was dominated by the small
general shop," i.e., the "shopkeepers." See also, 91–9, on rates of
growth for various shop trades.

CHAPTER NINE

1 "An Account of the Stock of Tea in the Possession of the Large Dealers Under the Survey of the Brewery Generals," London, 1 August 1784, 30/8/293, fols. 59–66, PRO.

2 The judgment was based on the fact that their names appear in almost all the alphabetized surveys of areas.

3 HMCL, E/T, 19 (16 February 1776): 281–7.

4 They include, among others: Davison, Newman and Co. who had 6,150 pounds; Richard and John Twining, 4,344 pounds; David Lloyd Pugh and Co., 1,162 pounds; Cooper, Garratt and Taddy, 2,927 pounds. Charles Brewster and Co. who supplied Fenton with tea had 2,953 pounds. Only one person in the list, Richard Cadman Etcher, merchant, had a larger quantity, 33,123 pounds. He was, however, no tea dealer and his was prize tea. The quantity held in the East India Company warehouses by each of the dealers is not known.

5 For details of this controversy see Mui, "William Pitt," 454–9.

6 The amounts ranged from the 59 pounds held by Fogg and Co., Chinamen on New Bond Street to 372 pounds held by Henry Woods, Chinaman, 35 Poultry.

7 Whether Richard Asslin (or possibly Ashlin) who had 40 pounds of tea is in fact the Richard Ashlin, upholsterer, listed in the directory remains questionable, although the address does conform to his group. In the case of the draper, Excise gives the firm name, Hawkesworth and Co. As the company had on hand 873 pounds, one would expect to find it in the directories. There is an entry for Willan and Hawkesworth, mercers, Chandos Street which is within striking distance of the other addresses, Dean Street for example, but not sufficiently near for confident identification.

8 "An Account of the Number of Tea Dealers ... Under our Inspection," signed by H. Evans, M. Finley and Wm Bell, 2 August 1784, 30/8/293, fol. 69, PRO. The districts are distinguished by the name of the district supervisor.

9 "An Account of the Stock of Tea in Hand Within the City of York," 30/8/293, fols. 67–8, PRO.

10 An Account of the Tea in the Stocks ... Immediately Preceeding Xmas Day Last," York, 5 August 1784 30/8/294, fol. 4, PRO.

11 Based on the population for 1801, 17,000. Mitchell and Deane, *British Historical Statistics*, 26. Chalklin, *Provincial Towns*, 339, gives a lower figure, 16,145.

12 The ratio in Leicester (population 15,593) and Coventry (population 16,934) was 137.

13 PRO, 30/8/293, fol. 68. His opinion was based on "the usual consumption." To accommodate the country buyers, the East India Company

agreed in 1784 to receive back at cost price (tax included) any uno-
pened chest. Few provincial dealers took advantage of the offer.

14 Mennell, *Tea*, 41–2. Mennell was a descendent of Mary Tuke and a
partner in the London-based firm.

15 Ibid., 31–2.

16 *Leeds Mercury*, 27 February 1781. He listed the prices of his tea, coffee, and chocolate.

17 In 1797, Jane Watson was identified as a tea dealer with an income of
eighty pounds. Robert Watson, tea dealer, was admitted by order in
1784.

18 Both William and Seth Agar appear as masters. William, confectioner
and grocer on Stonegate in 1784, was the son of Thomas Agar and
admitted in 1758.

19 Robert Baxter was listed in the directory as grocer and had on hand
175 pounds of tea.

20 See Willan, *Abraham Dent*, chap. 3.

21 For a description of an early nineteenth-century wholesale-retail grocer see Mui, "Andrew Melrose," 30–48, Cf. Alexander, *Retailing*, 92,
table 4: 1, note 1.

22 He apprenticed to Stephen Brook, grocer, and was admitted in 1773.

23 *York Courant*, 23 October 1787. He claimed to have been in business
twenty years.

24 John Kibblewhite had fifty-six pounds of tea on hand. The Kibble-
whites, James, son of John, were listed as cabinetmakers in the freemen's roll.

25 Included in this group is Jane Benson with 33.5 pounds of tea.

26 PRO, 30/8/283, fol. 176. He specifically excluded the East and West
Indian trade from the generality. Baring's comments reveal this famed
financier as hardly conforming to the stereotype. He was certainly not
trying to feather his nest. On the contrary, he expressed a disinter-
ested and enlarged view on the economic wellbeing of the country.
Nor had he confined his attention to the higher reaches of interna-
tional finance. His marginal notes on each of the proposed regulations give evidence of a very practical mind and a thorough grasp of
the minutiae of trade.

27 For the years 1709–11 the average quantity of sugar retained for
home consumption was 40.9 million pounds; in 1759–60, 129 million;
tea increased from 122,600 pounds to 4.8 million respectively, without
considering the quantities smuggled.

28 "19th Report, R.C. on the Excise Establishment (Excise licences),"
30: 21, *PP 1837*. Their figures are based on the number of licences
issued in 1834–5, a total of 106,069. Ireland had only 12,400.
The excise estimates were: 12,000 selling over 400 pounds; 25,000
selling 200–400, and 69,069, less than 200 pounds.

CHAPTER TEN

1 PRO, 30/8/288, fol. 56.
2 This is a very tentative estimate based on the number of tea licences and the number of shops reported by the tax assessors for roughly comparable areas. But to equate the two entails some intractable problems. The excise collection of London in 1795–6 included the "Cities of London and Westminster and Borough of Southwark and the adjacent parishes within the Bills of Mortality with the parish of Marylebone and part of the parishes of Paddington and Pancras," 30/8/288, fol. 56, PRO. In calculating the percentage, all shops reported by the tax assessors for St Pancras were included (there are no figures for Paddington). Shops reported for parishes in Surrey as well as the four villages outside the Bills were excluded.
3 See Alexander, *Retailing*, 98, table 4: 5. If tailors, tailor-drapers, milliners, and shoemakers are excluded, the range is from 38 percent in Norwich to 59 percent in Bolton. The figures for Merthyr Tydfil are not included.
4 Jefferys, *Retail Trading*, 468–9, table 88. This table excludes 44,471 retail establishments. Among these are nurserymen and seedsmen, second-hand and antique dealers, off-licences, and shoemakers. If included, the proportion drops to 25.6 percent.
5 "An Account of the Gross Produce of Each Duty in Each Collection and in London," 30/8/288, fol. 56, PRO. The figures for Scotland are in Excise Revenue Accounts, 14, SRO. One account gives the amount of revenue for each collection for the years ending 5 July 1801, 1802, and 1803; the other lists the number of licences issued for the "country collections" and for "Edinburgh" from 1800 to 1827.
6 Cf. "An Account ... of the Gross Amount ... Charges of Management and Net Amount in Each Collection and in London," 1781/2 to 1783/4, 30/8/288, fol. 18, PRO. The great increase in printed goods undoubtedly made necessary the new collection of Preston. During the excise year 1783/4, 11.18 million yards of printed goods were charged with duty; in 1795/6, 30.06 million. That year the gross revenue from printed goods in the Manchester collection was £115,899; in the Preston collection, £171,106. Together they accounted for 58.3 percent of the revenue from printed goods. The collection of Surrey comes a poor third with £67,995.
7 The provincial population was distributed thus: 1751, southern counties, 49.3 percent; northern, 42.5 percent; Wales, 8.2 percent. In 1801, 47.5 percent of the population was south of the line; 45.2 percent, north; Wales, 7.3 percent.
8 If Cornwall and Devonshire are included in the southern counties, the corresponding figures are 42.6 percent and 68.9 percent.

9 Samuel Finney, *An Historical Survey of the Parish of Wilmslow*, MS written in 1785, quoted in Ashton, *Economic History of England*, 214–16. Samuel Finney was the brother of Peter Davenport Finney who set up as a confectioner in Manchester ca. 1755 and shortly afterwards established himself as a wholesale-retail grocer. He retired from the trade in 1768 with a substantial fortune. It seems that Samuel was no mean observer of the shopkeeping world.

10 As early as 1725, a Newcastle coal boat was carrying into Southampton 600 pounds of tea stored under the coal. Customs to the Court of Directors, October 1725, Miscellaneous Letter Received, XVI, No. 124, IO.

11 See Mui, "Smuggling," esp. 50–1, 60–1, 73.

12 In 1759, 32.7 percent of the shops were located in the eastern division; in 1795–6, 34.3 percent. The north and the middle collections accounted for 50.4 percent at both periods.

13 Each of these three collections includes parts of counties. Wales-west covers Pembrokeshire, "part of Cardiganshire," and a "great part of Carmarthenshire"; Wales-east, Glamorganshire, Brecknockshire, Monmouthshire, Merionethshire, Radnorshire, and "part of Cardiganshire, Herefordshire and Shropshire." This collection was allocated half the population of Cardiganshire but no allowance was made for the population in Herefordshire and Shropshire. Wales-middle was a particularly wideflung collection, including very small portions of Herefordshire and Shropshire, apparently to round off the collection. Nonetheless, the ratio for this collection is undoubtedly too low. Only one-quarter of the population of Carmarthenshire was included in Wales-east. But even if one-half is thrown into this collection, an unlikely possibility, given the excise description, the ratio would only be 230. The ratio for Wales-west may be inflated, but even if only one-half the population of Carmarthenshire and one-quarter of Cardiganshire are allocated to the collection, the ratio is 283.

14 The figures for Ireland reveal how far behind that country was in its shopping facilities. In 1814/15, the earliest date for which excise figures on tea dealers are available, the ratio was 1,385 and remained above 1,000 until 1825, when it dropped to 839. It continued to decline, reaching 632 in 1837/8. But the following year the ratio rose to 904 and fluctuated around that figure until 1845 when it dropped to 680. By 1854/5, the last year of the excise account, it was down to 360, the level Scotland had achieved in the 1790s.

15 Edinburgh was the head office for the Scottish Excise, and like its English counterpart, the accounts distinguish the "Edinburgh collection" from what is termed the "country collections." Presumably Edinburgh, like the London Bills, was under the supervision of the head office.

CHAPTER ELEVEN

1   Marshall, *William Stout*, 165.
2   Ibid., 90.
3   "The Causes of the Decay of Trade especially at London," *Gentleman's Magazine*, 18 (September 1748): 408–12. The writer noted, among other disadvantages faced by the Londoner, the ease of smuggling at the outports and the connivance of custom officers, while the imposition of the high duties was strictly enforced in London.
4   Marshall, *William Stout*, 165.
5   Ibid., 106. He noted that by watering "we usually got 8 or 10 pounds back in roule more than the leaf sent in to spin, all of which was an addition to the profit of it," 161.
6   Ibid., 80.
7   Ibid., 160, 166, and chap. 1 above.
8   Ibid., 296.
9   See above, chap. 7, pp. 148–9. He thought the rise of village shops was detrimental to the trade of the shops in market towns.
10 Marshall, *William Stout*, 79.
11 For a description of Andrew Melrose's business practices see Mui, "Andrew Melrose," 30–48.
12 The wide variety of goods carried in his shop should serve as a caution in confining the trade of the grocer to that of "high-class luxury" items. The ancient trade of the grocer, yes; but not the grocery shop in the eighteenth and nineteenth centuries. And this was as true south of the border as in Scotland.
13 None of the three tradesmen appears in the one remaining "Customers' Ledger" for this period. But while the daybook entails tedious tabulation and the possibility that entries may have been overlooked, it is frequently the only source for detailed descriptions of daily transactions. Andrew Melrose's Day Book was a model of its kind. Each of the items purchased is listed: by quality, e.g., yellow soap, finest congou, raw sugar, Dunlop cheese, Stockton cheese, etc.; quantity and per unit price; by methods of payment – "cash in full," "cash and empty kit," – and a rather delightful entry to Mrs Taylor, "cash returned not current."
14 *Edinburgh Advertiser*, 15 May 1818.
15 Because of the different qualities and prices of sugar, it is difficult to be certain. She was paying nine pence per pound for "fine raw sugar."
16 See long discussion on the subject in "Report, S.C. on Tea Duties," 17 (518): 28–63, *PP 1834*.
17 *Edinburgh Advertiser*, 15 May and 4 August 1818.
18 With the introduction of new methods of distribution in the third

decade of the nineteenth century, mark-ups probably declined. However, only a particularly incompetent shopkeeper would lose money on transactions in tea.

19 From May to October, twenty-four entries; November to April, nineteen.

20 1/4 cwt., twenty-seven entries; 1/2 cwt., fifteen; plus the cwt.

21 During the year he also bought four pounds of green tea at eight shillings a pound and one pound of hyson at eleven shillings.

22 For any one type of tea, the quality and corresponding price could vary as much as 6d. In Melrose's advertisements, "fine" was quoted from 6s. to 6s. 4d. and higher; "good" from 5s. 6d. to 5s. 8d.

23 Grieve, thirty-five credit entries; Taylor, forty-eight.

24 The last entry in the Day Book (not necessarily the end of his account) is 19 May 1832.

25 One question remains unanswerable. Melrose stocked no flour or oatmeal. Did any of the three purchase such items elsewhere, or were their customers still buying most of their grains at the local market?

26 "Customers Ledger 1786–1791," Ms. F942, Manchester Public Library.

27 The amount is a very rough calculation. It does not include coal or drinks at the inn, that are sometimes debited to the accounts. The number of customers does not include those who purchased only coal or drinks.

28 Smith, *Wealth of Nations*, 342.

29 Small loaf of wheaten bread.

30 Several of the entries for flour are combined with other items and do not state the quantity. The amount is, therefore, an estimate, but it cannot be far off.

31 Loaf sugar was nine pence per pound, but there are too few entries to note changes over time.

32 "Penmorfa Shop Ledger," Bangor Ms. 82, Bangor, University of North Wales Library. The letters A to H are missing in the index.

33 Ibid.

34 See Mui, "Andrew Melrose," esp. 33–7.

35 Smith, *Wealth of Nations*, 342.

CHAPTER TWELVE

1 Jefferys, *Retail Trading*, 37.

2 Defoe, *English Tradesman*, 205–8.

3 Alexander, *Retailing*, 204.

4 *Voyage en Angleterre, 1728*, fol. 29, quoted in Braudel, *Wheels of Commerce*, 69–70 and George, *London Life*, 162.

5 Jefferys, *Retail Trading*, 5; Alexander, *Retailing*, 173.

6 Stowe Papers, "Wotton Household Accounts," Box 1748–1799, Bundle 1783–9, Huntington Library. In 1784 William Winter had in stock 732 pounds of tea.

7 "Dunham Housekeeping Book, 1758–1836," Ms/Br/F640/D6, Manchester Public Library.

8 Francis Cust to Sir John Cust, 27 December 1739, quoted in Twining, *Two Hundred and Twenty-Five Years*, 13.

9 Bishop of Exeter to R. Twining, 31 January 1805, Add. Ms. 39,931, fol. 168, BM.

10 David Pugh and Company to Sir Robert Menzies, 28 April 1802, Archives of David Lloyd, Pigott and Company. The writers wish to thank the firm for permitting them to see their extant records. Sir Robert was still purchasing his groceries from the firm in 1811. See bill in Patent Office Library for 2 March 1811.

11 See the letter from Mrs William of 75 Gloucester Place. She ordered five pounds of hyson "the same as she always had, packed in four one pound canisters for going abroad." Davison Newman Papers, Ms. 8631/1, Guildhall Library.

12 BM, Add. Ms. 36, 666, fols. 24, 46, order for 1777.

13 William Calder, grocer of Edinburgh and Charles Cowan and Company, grocer, Leith. "Household Accounts (1795–1839) of the Rev. Thomas Laurie," Mss. 1930–1934, National Library of Scotland.

14 Ibid.

15 *Leeds Mercury*, 16 May 1769. Advertisement by James Donaldson, grocer and teaman, Leeds. A variation of this type was appended to many advertisements.

16 Jefferys, *Retail Trading*, 4, 37.

17 Heal, *Tradesmen's Cards*, plate XCII.

18 Twining, *Two Hundred and Twenty-Five Years*, 12–13.

19 Ibid., 17.

20 See Jefferys, *Retail Trading*, 4.

21 McKendrick, "Josiah Wedgwood," 412.

22 Ibid., 423.

23 See the notice in the *London Gazette*, 7 November 1706, of a meeting of a Commission of Bankruptcy "at Tom's Coffee-house." Such a notice must have pleased young Tom who had barely opened his coffee-house, Twining, *Two Hundred and Twenty-Five Years*, 4.

24 Whether Tom Twining travelled to the house every day is not known, but his family was in residence there.

25 *Whitehall Evening Post*, 13–15 May 1756 in Twining, *Two Hundred and Twenty-Five Years*, 17

26 *Ipswich Journal*, 18 October 1766 in ibid., 17.

27 Richard Twining, *Observations; Remarks*; and *An Answer*.
28 For a more extended discussion of the controversy with the East India Company and the subsequent flurry of advertising, see Mui, "William Pitt," 457–9.
29 *Morning Post*, 18 January 1785.
30 Photography of a broadsheet among the Dent papers, reproduced in Willan, *Abraham Dent*, 18–19.
31 *Leeds Mercury*, 12 March 1751. For earlier advertisements, see Cranfield, *Provincial Newspapers*, 221–2, 250, and 197–206 for the distribution area of provincial newspapers. For advertisements of medicines in Bath, see P.S. Brown, "The Venders of Medicines," 19: 352–69.
32 *Leeds Mercury*, 15 January 1751.
33 Ibid.
34 For Steel's specific cake, see ibid., 26 February 1751. For John Newberry and others, see Cranfield, *Provincial Newspapers*, 250 and Young, *Toadstool Millionaires*, esp. 3–16.
35 *Leeds Mercury*, 10 July 1770.
36 Jefferys, *Retail Trading*, 6.
37 Willan, *Abraham Dent*, 17.
38 *Leeds Mercury*, 5 March 1751.
39 Ibid., 14 May 1751.
40 See the advertisement for a *Map of Manchester* in the *Leeds Mercury*, 21 May 1751. Among other places listed as selling the map was "Mr Lord, bookseller in Wakefield and at his shops in Barnsley and Pontefract."
41 Cf. Redlich, "Some English Stationers," 93–7.
42 See the advertisements in the *Leeds Mercury*, 26 September and 30 October 1786.
43 *Leeds Mercury*, 21 May 1751.
44 Ibid., 23 May 1769.
45 Willan, *Abraham Dent*, 16, 32, 40.
46 Ibid., 15.
47 *Leeds Mercury*, 14 May 1751. He claimed to be the maker.
48 *Public Advertiser*, 18 February 1769, quoted in George, *London Life*, 371.
49 *Leeds Mercury*, 17, 24, 31 May 1774.
50 Ibid., 16, 23 May 1769; 15, 22, 29 May, 30 October, 6, 13 November 1770. (Our microfilm copy of the *Leeds Mercury* has no issues from July 1751 to 1769.)
51 Ibid., 22, 29 June, and 6 July 1773.
52 Ibid., 29 June, 6, 27 July 1773.
53 Ibid., 27 February 1781.

54 See ibid., 28 November 1769 (William Townsend, "Grocer, Tea Dealer and Tobacconist"); 13 July, 21, 28 December 1773 (John Lofthouse and Peter Milner, both grocers in Leeds); 8 March, 10 May 1774 (J.C. Reinhardt of Wakefield); 3, 10 May 1774 (John Proctor, grocer and tea dealer of Leeds).

55 Ibid., 14 May 1751.

56 Ibid., 16 May 1769. See also the advertisements by John Thompson, mercer in Hornby, ibid., 22 and 29 May 1770, and others.

57 Ibid., 8, 15 March, 5, 12 April, 3, 10, 17, 31 May, 7 June, 18 July 1774. There is a gap in the collection of the *Leeds Mercury* from 1770 to 1773 and a frustrating gap from 1774 to 1779 – that is, in the collection we used.

58 Ibid., March, April, and May 1774.

59 McKendrick, *Consumer Society*, chap. 2.

60 Cranfield, *Provincial Newspapers*, esp. 169–77.

61 *Leeds Mercury*, 12 November 1782, bankruptcy notice. Of the several creditors of the bankrupt "shopkeeper" in Pudsey, Yorkshire, two, Joseph Ross and Thomas Sherbrook, were active in business at Leeds.

62 Ibid., 3, 10 May 1774.

63 Ibid., 18 July 1774.

64 Ibid., 8, 15, 22 June 1773; 26 April, 10 May 1774.

65 *York Courant*, 27 January 1778.

66 Ibid., 18 August 1778.

67 Ibid., 24 February 1778.

68 Sales to country shopkeepers were not always an asset. In 1782, Joseph Ross and Thomas Sherbrook were among the creditors of a bankrupt draper in Pudsey, Yorkshire. See above note 61.

69 The advertisements of shopkeepers cited in this paragraph can be found in *Leeds Mercury*, 7 September 1779; 12 September 1780; April and May 1782 for Joseph Ross; 7 May 1782, William Wigglesworth; 24 April, 1 May 1781; 3, 10, 17 May 1785; 25 April 1786, Sanderson; 6 July 1784; 10 October 1785; 16 May 1786, Thomas Skegg; 26 July 1785, W. Tatham; and *York Courant*, 7 February 1786, R. Hindley. W. Tatham may have had two shops, one in Leeds and a second in York. On 24 January 1786 he advertised in the *York Courant* a sale at the "west end of the Minster Yard." He used the same advertising ploy, "10 percent and many 20 percent cheaper than at any sale or shop whatever," and, of course, all prices were fixed.

70 See, for example, advertisement of J. Achinson, *Leeds Mercury*, 28 December 1779; 26 June 1781 and that of Stridewick, ibid., 16 December 1783; 17 May 1785.

71 *York Courant*, 2 February 1779.

72 *Leeds Mercury*, 17 March 1789. The firm also advertised their India Muslin Warehouse in the *Times*, 18 January 1790.

73 *Leeds Mercury*, 13, 20, 27 September, 11 October 1791, and *Times*, 7, 15, 18, 22 January 1790.

74 *Leeds Mercury*, 27 September 1791.

75 Ibid., 20 December 1791.

76 Ibid., 2, 9, 16 March 1793.

77 *Times*, 17 March 1790.

78 The above advertisements can be found in ibid., 1, 7, 12 January, 5, 13, 17 March, 24 April, 3 July 1790.

79 Robert Owen, *Life*, 1: 12.

80 Corfield, *English Towns*, 8.

81 Heal, *Tradesmen's Cards*, plate XXXIV. The trade cards provide ample evidence of the large variety of ready-made clothing sold by drapers and others.

82 See, for example, *Leeds Mercury*, 1 May 1770 (John Bowling, hatter); 22 March 1774 (John Daniel, hatter of Halifax); 10 May 1774 (David Cresswell, hatmaker of Wakefield); 15 June 1773, 3 May 1774 (Kay, hatter and perukemaker).

83 See, for example, Elizabeth Reynolds's notice in *Leeds Mercury*, 31 May 1774.

84 Ibid., 16 November 1793. He was still advertising in 1796.

85 Vaisey, *Diary of Thomas Turner*, 14, 60, 278.

86 Willan, *Inland Trade*, 31, 56, 79.

87 George, *London Life*, 198.

88 Sutton, "Marketing of Ready Made Footwear," 93–112.

89 *Leeds Mercury*, 5 December 1786, 2 January 1787.

90 Ibid., 19 July, 2 August 1791.

91 Ibid., 30 August, 18 September 1791.

92 Ibid., 11 October 1791.

93 Lord Macaulay in the *Edinburgh Review*, April 1830 (from "Mr. Robert Montgomery's Poems"), quoted in Jefferys, *Retail Trading*, 4, note 2.

94 By the 1780s, the style of the firm was Warham, Potts and Smith, later Warham, Potts and Company. The firm bought files from Peter Stubs. See Ashton, *Peter Stubs*, 52, 59.

95 *Leeds Mercury*, 18 April 1788.

96 The advertisements of shopkeepers cited in this paragraph can be found in *Leeds Mercury*, 1 February 1774 for John Fothergill; 28 July, 9, 19 August 1785, William Horsfall and Arthington Wilson; 5, 12 September, 5 December 1785, Sheffield Repository; 18 April

1788, Warham; 19 July 1791, Thomas Marriott. *York Courant*, 17 January 1786, William Sturdy who had been one of the small group of ten in 1775 sued by the City of York to take up their freedom. At the time he had a "pot shop." See York House Book, 44, fols. 403–4.

97 See *Times*, 5 February 1790 and other issues for the same year.

98 Ibid., 5 March, 2 April 1790. Tipper and Company claimed to have been the first to lower the price of coal which they sold at thirty to thirty-four shillings a chaldron, "delivered anywhere in town or out free."

99 *Leeds Mercury*, 29 May 1770; 12 April, 10 May 1774; 16 June 1781 for William Armitage; 21, 28 July 1774, J. Riley; 1 February, 28 March 1774, T. Bradford.

100 Ibid., 16 October 1781.

101 Ibid., 19 April 1791.

102 Smith, *Wealth of Nations*, 243.

103 Such articles also served a practical purpose as a form of collateral on which money could be raised at the pawn shop. See George, *London Life*, 370, note 47.

104 *Times*, 5 January 1790 and *Leeds Mercury*, 1 May 1770, the notice of James Fieldshaw.

105 *Leeds Mercury*, 11 June 1751 for London liquor dealer; *York Courant*, 1 September 1778, David Evans & Co.; 15 December 1778, Genuine Jamaica Rum Warehouse; 23 October 1787, Mathers Todd.

106 *Leeds Mercury*, 6 May 1780.

107 Ibid., 18 June 1782.

108 Ibid., 19 February 1788.

109 Ibid., 26 April 1791.

110 *Times*, 21 January 1790.

111 Ibid., 3, 4 March 1790.

112 Ibid., 2 April 1790.

113 *Leeds Mercury*, 30 October 1770 for Clifton; 17 May 1774, E. Dickson; see also 27 November 1770 for B. Tinsdall.

114 Ibid., 15 May, 5 June 1770, and 1 February 1774.

115 Ibid., 4 September 1781. A number of advertisements by coal dealers appeared in earlier issues.

116 Ibid., 11 June 1751. The seedsmen had apparently cooperated in placing the advertisement. Those listed as selling the seed included: one firm in Leeds; three in Wakefield, one of whom also had a shop in Barnsley; and one each in Sheffield, Rotherham, and Hull. Other announcements by seedsmen appeared in later issues.

117 For a description of his advertising techniques, see Mui, "Andrew Melrose," 42–5.

CHAPTER THIRTEEN

1 *Whitehall Evening Post*, 13–15 May 1756, quoted in Twining, *Two Hundred and Twenty-Five Years*, 17.

2 Twining, *Observations*, 21–4.

3 "Account of Aitcheson of Edinburgh," 8 January 1785, Melville Castle Muniments, GD 51/3/249, fols. 1–2, SRO. For a description of the methods of the Smugglers, see Mui, "Smuggling," 44–73.

4 It should be noted that the figures in "Account of the Quantities of Tea Retained for Home Consumption in the U.K.; the Rates of Duty Chargeable Thereon, and the Net Receipt of Duty by the Customs and Excise, in each Year from 1740 to 1844 Inclusive, 46 (191), *PP 1845*, are somewhat misleading. In the first place, the figures for quantities include those exported to Ireland on which, until 1819, the dealers obtained the full drawback. But more confusing are the figures for duty. The Commutation Act of 1784 reduced the rate of duty (excise and customs) on tea, but placed an additional tax on windows. The law stated that if the produce of these two taxes exceeded a certain stated sum the "surplus was to be paid over to Excise and applied to the duties on tea." In 1794, for example, the surplus amounted to £325,422 3s. 5.25d., "Quantities, Rates and Amounts of Excise Duties, 1684–1798," Excise Accounts, fol. 77, No. 11863, HMCL. That surplus has been included as a duty on tea, giving a net receipt of £671,974. A portion of that sum was, of course, paid not by the tea dealers but by householders. No figures are available for the surplus in 1806 but it appears to be roughly similar to that of 1794. In 1796 it was as high as £375,477 14s. 8.75d.

5 For a description of the controversy, see Mui, "William Pitt," 447–65.

6 Ashton, *Iron and Steel*, 177–85; Clapham, *Economic History*, 1: 198–205.

7 The above is drawn from various sources. See Twining, *Observations*, esp. 34–44; Letter to Robert Preston, 26 January 1785, quoted in *An Answer*, 73–5, also 3–4, 11–15; Anon., *Tea Purchaser's Guide*; Anon., *Tsiology*, esp. 39–49, 110, 116; "1st Rept. R.C. on Excise Establishment (Tea Permits and Surveys)," 21 (417), *PP 1833* for the evidence of tea dealers to the commission. Particularly revealing is the statement of Mr Gibbs, London tea broker, describing the traditional methods of the trade, 146–7. His account is corroborated by Mr Dean of Excise, 95, on the business practices of tea dealers and the changes occurring in the trade.

8 Francis Garratt to Dundas, 22 July 1800, Melville Papers, Ms. 1063, fol. 173b, National Library of Scotland.

9 Two advertisers gave no proprietor's name, styling themselves "Grocery Warehouses"; three claimed to be new warehouses opened to provide the public with pure tea. The tabulation was made from the *Morning Post, Morning Chronicle, Morning Herald, St James Chronicle, London Chronicle*, and *General Advertiser.*

10 *Morning Chronicle*, 2 February 1785.

11 Ibid., 6 September 1784. *Tea Purchaser's Guide* referred to by Hodgson is a well-drawn up description of the different types and qualities of teas used in England.

12 See, for example, *Morning Herald*, 6 October 1784 (Jenken's Warehouse); 4 November 1784 (Mundy and Walker). *Morning Chronicle*, 6 October 1784 (John Hodgson).

13 See especially, *Morning Herald*, 4 November 1784 (Mundy and Walker); 23 December 1784 (Hodgson). *Morning Chronicle*, 2 February 1785 (Antrobus and Seaman). *Morning Post*, 18 January 1785 (P. Constable); 27 January 1785 (Hodgson); 31 January 1785 (Samuel Yockney).

14 *Morning Chronicle*, 31 January 1785.

15 *Morning Post*, 31 January, 1, 2, 4, 7, 11 February 1785.

16 Ibid., 18 January 1785.

17 *Morning Herald*, 29 November 1784.

18 *Morning Post*, 27 January 1785.

19 Ibid., 3 February 1785.

20 *Morning Herald*, 29 November 1785.

21 Ibid., 15, 27 October 1784; *Morning Post*, 12 March 1785.

22 See, for example, *Morning Post*, 17 January 1785 (P. Constable); 31 January 1785 (S. Yockney); 4 February 1785 (Thomas Newland). *Morning Chronicle*, 26 April 1785 (Mundy and Walker).

23 *Morning Post*, 7 February 1785.

24 Ibid., 31 January 1785.

25 *Morning Chronicle*, 2 February 1785.

26 See, for example, *St James Chronicle*, 5 February 1785 (John Smith and Son) and the *Morning Chronicle*, 2 February 1785 (Antrobus and Seaman).

27 *Morning Chronicle*, 27 January 1785.

28 See, for example, *Morning Post*, 18 January 1785 (James Maund); 22 January 1785, (Committee of the Tea Trade signed by R. Twining, A. Newman, W. Palmer, John Pinhorn, N. Robinson, T. Rutton, T. Travers); 31 January 1785 (J. Smith and Son); 2 February 1785 (John Davidson); 4 February 1785 (J. Brownell, T. Newland); 7 February 1785 (Blakiston and Company); 9 February 1785 (Theomarty Crane); and the *Morning Chronicle*, 9 February 1785 (Richard King).

29 *Morning Post*, 1 February 1785.

30 See *Morning Chronicle*, 29 January 1785 (T. Lussingham); 18 January 1785 (P. Constable); 24 January 1785 (E. Eagleton); 31 January 1785 (S. Yockney); 28 January 1785 (Mundy and Walker); and the *Morning Herald*, 27 October 1784 (Mr Will).

31 *General Advertiser*, 7 February 1785.

32 *Morning Post*, 1 February 1785.

33 Ibid., 18 January 1785.

34 *Morning Herald*, 23 December 1784.

35 *Morning Post*, 18 January 1785.

36 Ibid., 7 February 1785.

37 See *London Chronicle*, 19 April 1785 and Thomas Morton, *Report* and *Further Report*, both published by the East India Company.

38 Twining, *Observations*, 38–41; *An Answer*, 3–4.

39 See *Morning Herald*, 4 November 1784 (Mundy and Walker).

40 *General Advertiser*, 17 March 1785. Constable, a former silk broker, was introduced into the December 1784 East India auction to facilitate Pitt's aim to reduce tea prices. See Mui, "William Pitt," 453–8; Dermigny, *La Chine*, 3: 1035–7, and Ehrman, *Younger Pitt*, 242–5.

41 *Morning Post*, 22 March 1785.

42 *Leeds Mercury*, 19 April 1785.

43 *York Courant*, 7 February 1786.

44 *Felix Farley's Bristol Journal*, 6 January 1787 *et. seq.* In the provincial newspapers, advertisements appeared in several successive issues. The dates indicate only the first advertisement noted.

45 Ibid., 20 January 1787; *Bath Chronicle*, 4 January 1787.

46 *Bath Chronicle*, 1 February 1787.

47 Ibid., 4 October 1787.

48 *Felix Farley's Bristol Journal*, 1 December 1787.

49 *Bath Chronicle*, 2 August 1787.

50 Ibid., 4 January 1787.

51 Ibid., 11 January 1787.

52 See *Felix Farley's Bristol Journal*, 19 May 1787 (William Lewis); 23 June (M. Carr); 13 October (Mary Browne).

53 *Leeds Mercury*, 19 October 1784.

54 Ibid., 25 January 1785.

55 Ibid., 5 May 1789.

56 Ibid., 6 July 1784.

57 Ibid., 4 May 1793.

58 For a description of the distributive methods adopted in Scotland, see Mui, "Smuggling," 56–60.

59 For an account of Melrose's early business career, see Mui, "Andrew Melrose"; for his activities as a tea merchant, Mui and Mui, eds., *William Melrose*. For a brief description of James Richardson, see ibid., xlii–xlv; of William Law, ibid., 25, note 2; 107, note 2.

60 Andrew Melrose, Sheppard's former apprentice, was also an avid advertiser and used handbills even more extensively. One suspects that Sheppard and the other shopkeepers were also using handbills. Melrose's handbills were usually longer and more specific than newspaper advertisements. It is unfortunate that so few eighteenth-century handbills have survived. They would have provided a far more vivid and clearer picture of the advertising techniques of shopkeepers.

61 *Edinburgh Advertiser,* 11 March 1791. The advertisers repeated their notices in several successive issues. Only the date of the first advertisement is cited here.

62 Ibid., 5 April, 8 July 1791.

63 Ibid., 18 January, 15 February, 12 August, 14, 25 October 1791.

64 Ibid., 18 January, 1 February, 22, 29 April, 3 June 1797.

65 Ibid., 5, 29 April, 14 October 1791.

66 Ibid., 18 January, 5, 19, 29 April, 12 August, 25 November 1791.

67 See, for example, Ibid., 4 October 1791.

68 Ibid., 5, 19 April, 3 May 1791.

69 Ibid., 23 March 1798.

70 Ibid., 27 April 1798. Sheppard's announcement was timed to follow the newspaper's report of Pitt's budget speech which included a new tax on tea.

71 Ibid., 17 April 1798. The increase in prices at the March Sale was probably due to the buyers' eagerness to purchase as large a quantity as possible before the forthcoming increase in duty.

72 Ibid., 8 July 1791.

73 Ibid.,, 15 February 1791.

74 Ibid., 2 May 1791.

75 Ibid., 26 April, 24 May, 6 December 1791.

76 Twining, *Two Hundred and Twenty-Five Years,* 22.

77 Correspondence and Trade Circulars, Mennell (Tuke) Archives. Reproductions in our possession.

78 Ibid.

79 BM, Add. Ms. 36,666, 26 March 1791, fol. 43.

80 "Memorial of John Waddington," 29 December 1788, E/T, 24: 154–6, HMCL.

81 Jones, *Two Centuries,* also, "Memorial of David Pugh and Company," November 1798, E/T, 30: 481–3, HMCL, concerning tea sent to Newton, Montgomeryshire, without a permit.

82 As late as 1833 traditional firms were expressing their fears and apprehensions about the possible effect on demand of the introduction of low quality free-trade tea. See "1st Rept. R.C. on Excise Establishment," 21 (417), *PP 1833.*

83 In a billhead dated 1778 of "Edward Eagleton, Tea Man at the sign of the Grasshopper," 9 Bishopsgate, Humphrey Morice Esq., paid £4

10s. for twelve pounds of superfine singlo, Gow White Archives, London tea merchants and brokers.

84 Edward Eagleton to Pitt, 26 July 1784, 30/8/293, fols. 57–58b, PRO. He described the tea dealers as "very opulent" who "can lead a great many of the trade to accord in what they do or say." This set of men, by buying tea "in combination," had bid up the prices unnecessarily high in the March 1784 Sale. "Bohea put up by the East India Company at 2s. 3d., they bought for 2s. 10d. to 3s. 2d.; Congou and Souchong [put up at 2s. 3d.] from 4s. 8d. to 9s.; Singlo put up at 2s. 6d. ... at 3s. 10d. to 5s. 6d."

85 *Felix Farley's Bristol Journal*, 5 January 1782.

86 *Leeds Mercury*, 7 November 1786.

87 *Leeds Mercury*, 7, 21 November; 5, 19 December 1786; 2 January 1787.

88 *Morning Chronicle*, 14 February 1787.

89 *Leeds Mercury*, 14 November 1786.

90 It was an excellently drawnup chart as the following sample shows:

Sort of tea	Deposit £	No. of Chests	Net Weight lbs.	Duty per cent	Cost of Lot £
Bohea	12	3	1000	12½	90 to 100
Congou	10	5	400	12½	60 to 90

91 *Leeds Mercury*, 14, 28 November, 12 December 1786. Observe that the dates of the advertisements addressed particularly to dealers alternated with those primarily designed for retail customers and small shopkeepers. It should also be noted that his statements concerning the terms and methods of sale at the auctions are accurate.

92 *Norfolk Chronicle*, 12 January 1793. The towns listed were: Birmingham, Worcester, Leicester, Derby, Bath, Evesham, Gloucester, Pershore, Winchcombe, Newbury, Liverpool, Manchester, Chester, Winchester, Southampton, Andover, Gosport, Exeter, Ramsey, Basingstoke, Lymington, Stockport, Monmouth, Hereford; Brechon in Wales; and Glasgow and Edinburgh in Scotland.

93 *Manchester Mercury*, 13 October 1795.

94 See *Leeds Mercury*, 15 April 1797. It was a half-column notice.

95 *Manchester Mercury*, 30 June 1795. In 1818, a "Winter" was a well-established London dealer and member of the Committee of the Tea Trade.

96 For the firm's activities in 1818, see below, p. 275. An Edward Eagleton was one of a number of principal tea dealers who testified at the

Royal Commission on Tea Permits in 1833. He may well have been
the same person. He stated that his trade with country dealers was
not so large as it had been formerly.

97 Miscellanies [Letters Out], 57 (1 October 1818), no. 1179: 91–151 10.

98 On the trials, see HMCL Customs and Excise Trials, 610: 101–121;
612: 1–109, 681–692; 614: esp. 419–425: 615: 105–222; 622: 313–
424. HMCL, E/T, 81: 42–8; 82: 15–17, 26–8, 31–7, 273–5; 85: 32–54,
281–8. On rumours, see *Times*, 16, 18 March 1818 and R. Twining,
Jr. to Court of Directors, 18 March 1818, Court Books, 125–A: 1187,
10. On public outcry, and dealers' actions, *Times*, 16 March, 18, 29,
30 May, 9 December 1818; *Manchester Mercury*, 31 March, 7 April,
12 May, 30 June 1818; *Leeds Mercury*, 31 March 1818 *et. seq.*; *Edinburgh Advertiser*, 22, 29 May, 11 December 1818.

99 HMCL, E/T, 82: 16 and 10, *Court Books*, 125–A: 1187.

100 Frederick Gye (1781–1869), MP for Chippenham, 1826–30, purchased Vauxhall Gardens in 1821 and launched a wine company on
the same principles as his tea company. The latter was successful,
but Vauxhall, although it provided good entertainment including
Paganini's single-string performance, proved a pecuniary drain. In
1836 the wine company collapsed and by 1840 both Vauxhall and
the tea company were liquidated. *DNB* and Vizetelly, *Glances Back*,
1: 18–22. The author was the son of a friend of Gye.

101 *Times*, 30 October, 2, 3, 4 November 1818.

102 Vizetelly, *Glances Back*, 18–19.

103 Reports in *Times*, 3, 4, 5, 6, 7, 9, 10, 14, 17, 20 November 1818.

104 Ibid., 5, 20 November 1818.

105 Sparrow was an old established dealer and a member of the committee appointed at the general meeting. He may have had reason to
feel particularly aggrieved as Gye opened his first shop right next
door to his. *Times*, 2 November 1818.

106 Report in ibid., 7 December 1818.

107 Ibid., 28 September 1819.

108 *York Herald*, 2 October 1819.

109 *Manchester Herald*, 26 September 1820.

110 *Leeds Mercury*, 31 March 1821.

111 Ibid., 10 November 1821.

112 For example, *Manchester Herald*, 26 September 1820, Sparrow.

113 *Leeds Intelligencer*, 2 January 1823, London Genuine Tea Company.

114 *Leeds Mercury*, 10 November 1821, Long.

115 *Manchester Herald*, 26 September 1820.

116 Ibid., 3 June 1823 and *Leeds Mercury*, 27 January 1821.

117 *Leeds Mercury*, 4 August 1821. The firm of J. & T. Crossley, Coleman
Street, London, advertised continuously throughout the year.

118 "Memorial of Frederick Gye and Co., 23 Ludgate Hill, London," 6
November 1823, E/T, 109: 181–2, HMCL. Gye stated that in February
1823 his company had sent to their agent, Mr Andrew Sievwright at
Edinburgh, 1,424 pounds of black and 420 pounds of green tea,
made up in packages from a quarter pound to one pound each,
sealed and labelled. Since then, Sievwright informed Gye that 257
pounds of black and 155 pounds of green were not suitable for the
Edinburgh market – "totally unsaleable." The agent now wished to
return the teas. The regulations on the request were originally designed to restrict the movement of illicit tea and therefore very strict.
See 21 Geo. 3, c. 55, sec. 24.

119 *Edinburgh and Leith Advertiser*, 8 October 1825.

120 *Leeds Intelligencer*, 3 April 1823, A Warmoll & Co., a London
firm.

121 "The accounts of J. Allan and of Larken, Varnham and Hamilton,"
Personal Ledger, 1815, Andrew Melrose Archives. From 1816,
Allan of Penicuik had a running account with Melrose. For over a
year, from 1822, Allan obtained all his tea from Gye's company by
means of Melrose. Almost every month from October 1822 to January 1824, the account was credited "by cash paid F. Gye & Co. £21"
and debited the same or following day "to cash paid F. Gye & Co.
£21," or "to order sent Gye & Co." No charge for the service was
debited to the account. Melrose was a native of Penicuik. Presumably
he was acting out of kindly motives towards an old acquaintance.
Melrose purchased no tea from Gye.

122 Tea sold by East India Company in 46 (191), *PP 1845*.

123 *Leeds Mercury*, 15 December 1821; *Manchester Herald*, 3 June 1823,
and Vizetelly, *Glances Back*, 19–21.

124 *York Herald*, 27 February, 13 March, 2, 30 October, 27 November,
25 December 1819. Only the date of the first announcement is
given.

125 HMCL, E/T, 76: 421–3, 22 May 1821.

126 *Leeds Mercury*, 16 June 1821; *Times*, 28 March 1826.

127 HMCL, E/T, 109: 183, 6 November 1823.

128 Cf. Jefferys, *Retail Trading*, 6, who dates this "revolution in the distributive trade" to the latter half of the nineteenth century.

129 The five included J. Sandford, the Crossleys, the China Tea Co., the
East India Tea Co., and A. Warmoll.

130 HMCL, E/T, 80: 115–32, 188–96. The memorials are dated from June
to October 1818 from: Barnsley (thirty-seven signatures), Bradford
(sixteen), Halifax, Leeds, and Wakefield (twenty-eight), Bolton,
Manchester (three grocers and sixty-six others); Salford, Warrington
(eighteen); Birmingham and Nottingham (fifteen).

131 See above, chap. 4.

132 Many laws governed the sale and movement of tea. The most rele-
vant were 10 Geo. 1, c. 10, secs 10,15; 12 Geo. 3, c. 46, sec. 5; 19
Geo. 3, c. 69, secs 18, 22; 20 Geo. 3, c. 35, secs 14, 16; 48 Geo. 3
c. 84, sec. 7. For interpretations on this issue, see Hawking Coach
Office to Treasury, 21 August 1818, E/T, 80: 191, HMCL and
Excise to Treasury, 16 October 1818, 131–32.

133 Ibid., 189, esp. memorial from Nottingham.

134 Letter of 21 November 1818, Excise General Letters, Northwich Collection, 1804–19; 10, HMCL.

135 Memorial from Fry, Coleby & Richardson and from Sanderson &
Barclay, 3 October 1821, E/T, 91: 396–8, HMCL.

136 Anon., *Tsiology*, 35–40. The author was probably William Smith, MP,
a partner in the firm of Smith, Travers, Kemble and Co. until 1813,
and then in that of Smith and Kemble until 1823 when he retired.
Both firms did a big business, mainly wholesale, in tea and were old
established dealers. The book gives an accurate account of the history of the trade and a vivid description of the current problems in
the domestic trade. The author was obviously intimately acquainted
with all aspects of the trade. William Smith was a Unitarian who held
strong moral and political views. For an account of his business and
political activities see Anon., *Chronicles of Cannon Street*, 11, 17–21,
23–4.

137 The information concerning Nicholson's activities was drawn primarily from: *Johnstone's London Commercial Directory* (1817); Robson's *London Commercial Directory* (1822 *et. seq.*); Anon., *Tsiology*, esp. 110–16;
NCG, a weekly first published by John Nicholson on 7 April 1832
and continued until at least December 1834. The latter, as does
Tsiology, gives numerous references to Nicholson's quarterly *Tea Book*
and *Sale List* first published in December 1823. However, no extant
copies of the earlier issues (22 December 1823 to December 1831)
have been unearthed.

138 For a description of the practices of brokers in examining and evalu-
ating tea see in particular: "Papers Concerning the London Tea
Market, 1783–1817," Davison, Newman and Company Papers, Ms.
8611, Guildhall Library; Francis Baring to Henry Dundas, 3 February 1787, Melville Papers, Ms. 1069, fols. 214–19, National Library
of Scotland; Report, S.C. on Affairs of the East India Company," 7
(122): 563–7, *PP 1812–13*, evidence of Thomas Styan, a tea broker
for thirty years; "1 st Report, S.C. on the China Trade," 5 (644):
482–3, 491, *PP 1830*, evidence of tea brokers, John Layton and
W.J. Thompson; Anon., *The Tea Trade*, published by "several influential members of the tea trade," 10–11.

139 *NCG*, 1: 1 (7 April 1832); 50: 400 (16 March 1833); 103: 94–95 (22 March 1834. Nicholson frequently quoted from his earlier publications and continued to level accusations against the London wholesale dealers.

140 Ibid., 103: 95 (22 March 1834).

141 Richard Twining to Treasury, 15 April 1818, E/T, 51: 348–52, HMCL. Twining described the rate as "the fair profits of trade." His estimate of profit concerned his company's supply of tea, coffee, and chocolate to three ships on the North Pole Expedition. The 10 percent was suggested as a rough method to calculate a proper drawback on this particular re-export. The tea had been shipped from his stock and not directly from the East India Company's warehouse. There was no clear record of its cost at the auction.

142 Anon., *Tsiology*, 114–15.

143 Ibid., 112–15.

144 This would seem to be the implication of the statements in ibid., 114.

145 *NCG*, 103, 22 March 1834; 137, 15 November 1834, and others.

146 Recorded letter from Edward Venn, tea broker, reporting three meetings of tea brokers and their resolution; 10, Court Books, 132 (6 April 1825): 761; court drafted letter to Venn giving the brokers a week to change their minds, 770; 12 April 1825, 780, recorded letter of 9 April from Francis Kemble, chairman of the Committee of the Tea Trade requesting court not to persist in its resolution of the sixth to print the *Tea Book* itself, giving reasons; recorded letter from Edward Venn, 12 April, chairman of the Committee of Tea Brokers agreeing entirely with letter of Committee of the Tea Trade and stating their reasons. The letters from the brokers and tea dealers to the court and the Warehouse Committee have not been preserved. The court's reply to "Edward Venn, tea broker" informing him of its decision is in 64 (6 April 1825), Miscellanies, 10.

147 10, Court Books, 132 (13 April 1825): 789. The court also recorded a "letter from S. Hooper suggesting a plan for the more equal distribution of the Tea Books among the brokers." Hooper, it would appear, was not a party to the Committee of Tea Brokers and may have served as broker for John Nicholson. The Warehouse Committee of the East India Company submitted to the court a "letter addressed to the Committee itself by Charles Varnham." The committee observed that all the letters "seemed to indicate a large portion of brokers being willing to follow their resolution."

148 Anon., *Tsiology*, 114.

149 10, Court Books, 133: 423 (9 November and 30 December 1825).

150 Court of Directors to Messrs John Garratt & Co., 31 December 1825, Miscellanies, vol. 64, 10 (no fols.).

151 HMCL, Excise Trials, 145, part 1 (1833): 90–1 and 151, the evidence in the case against Hall & Allison, London tea dealers, who were accused of fraudulently changing the teas in the chests and of counterfeiting the East India Company's seal.

152 Anon., *Tsiology*, 116–17 and *NCG*, nos. 1, 24, 44, 103.

153 *NCG* provided shopkeepers with somewhat similar information on a wide variety of groceries. The importance of these trade journals in enabling shopkeepers to control the charges of their suppliers has not been sufficiently explored. When Andrew Melrose opened his first ledger, he proudly recorded his subscription to *The London Price Current* from 1816, *Mauwades London Price Current* and *Nicholson's London New Price Current*, the latter two from 1817. See Mui, "Andrew Melrose," 38.

154 Statement of John Travers at a general meeting of tea dealers on the termination of the East India Company's monopoly, quoted in *NCG*, 40 (5 January 1833): 313 and evidence of Cadman Hodgekinson, a London dealer in "1st Report, R.C. on Excise Establishment (Tea Permits)," 21 (417): 143, *PP 1833*.

155 Evidence of Richard Gibbs who declared himself to have been "bred from infancy in the tea trade" as his father before him, "1st Report, R.C. on Excise Establishment (Tea Permits)", 21 (417): 147, *PP 1833*.

156 Ibid., 140, evidence of Robert Smith.

157 Ibid., 174, evidence of William Hugh Fenn, London dealer.

158 *Times*, 7 March 1834.

159 Since 1824, Excise had been warning Treasury of the loss to revenue by the prevalent practice of mixing lower quality tea with those of higher price. In 1833 two cases of well-known London dealers, caught in various forms of deception, appeared before the courts.

160 "1st Report, R.C. on Excise Establishment (Tea Permits), 21 (417): 146, *PP 1833* gives evidence of Richard Gibbs.

161 Ibid., 39–40.

162 See letter from the East India Company to John Freeling, Excise, 16 December 1830, Miscellanies, 69, no. 2986 10. The company wanted Excise to simplify the methods of clearing teas from the company's warehouses. The "great increase ... in clearing teas more in detail" to be sent directly to country dealers had occasioned bottlenecks in the usual procedure.

163 HMCL, Excise Trials, 145, part 1 (1833): 90–1.

164 Ibid., 151. Evidence presented in the court case against Hall and Allison, London tea dealers. These dealers were accused of fraudulently changing the teas in the chests and of counterfeiting the East India Company's seal.

CHAPTER FOURTEEN

1 Smith, *Wealth of Nations*, 342.

Bibliography

The following include only those sources most useful for the present study. Because information on the subject must be collected from widely scattered sources, the compilation of a comprehensive bibliography does not seem a promising or helpful project.

PRIMARY SOURCES

Manuscripts

Bangor: University of North Wales Library
    Account Book of (an unidentified) Shop near Bangor, 1784–1800, Bangor
        Ms. 416
    Penmorfa, Caerns, Shop Ledger, ca. 1788–1798, Bangor Ms. 82
California, San Marino: H.E. Huntington Library
    Stowe Papers, Wotton Household Accounts, Box 1748–1799
Edinburgh: National Library of Scotland
    Household Account Book of Rev. Thomas Laurie, Ms. 1934
    Melville Papers, Ms. 1063
Edinburgh: Scottish Record Office
    Andrew Melrose Archives
    Excise Revenue Accounts, vol. 14
    Melville Castle Muniments, Account of Aitcheson of Edinburgh, 8 January
        1785, GD 5/3/249
Exeter, Bishop's Court: W.E. Taylor & Son. Ltd Archives
    The Garratt Papers
Kew: Public Record Office, HM Customs and Excise Library
    Customs and Excise Trials
    Excise Accounts, no. 11863, "Quantities, Rates and Accounts of Excise
        Duties, 1684–1798"

Excise Accounts, England, E-600 (1788–1828)
Excise General Letters, Northwich Collection, 1804–1819
Excise Letter Books
Excise and Treasury
London: British Library
  Additional Manuscripts
    33,039 Newcastle Papers
    37,666 Order Book of W. Fenton, 1773–1794
    39,931, 39,932 Twining Family Correspondence
London: David Lloyd Pigott Co. Archives
  Correspondence and Trade Circulars
London: Gow White, London Tea Merchants and Brokers Archives
  Edward Eagleton Papers
London: Guildhall Library
  Davison Newman & Co. Papers
    Correspondence and Partnership Papers, Ms. 8630, 8631
    London Tea Market, 1783–1817, Ms. 8611
London: India Office Records and Library
  China: Court Letters
  Court Books
  Miscellanies (Letters Out)
London: Patent Office Library
  Sir Robert Menzies, Bill of 2 March 1811
London: Probate Office, Somerset House
  Will of Francis Garratt
London: Public Record Office
  Home Office 42/7, Tax on Shops, 1785
  Pitt Papers, 30/8 series, vols. 81, 280, 281, 283, 288, 290, 293, 294, 302
Manchester: Manchester Public Library
  Customers' Ledger of William Wood, F942/73955/D32
  Dunham Housekeeping Book, 1758-1836, Br/F640/D6
  Tea Licence of David Bullock of Manchester, Sept. 1811, no. 362
Oxford: Mui's Personal Collection
  Mennel (Tuke) Archives: Correspondence and Trade Circulars
Staffordshire, Sandon Hall: Harrowby Trust
  Excise Documents, Ms. 285, 525
York: York Public Library
  Freemen's Roll, 1743–1811, D.4
  York Corporation Records, House Book, vol. 44

Government Documents

Cobbett, William, ed. *Parliament.* (History of England ... 1066–1803).

Debrett, John, ed. *Parliament*. (History, debates and proceedings of both houses of parliament of Great Britain, 1743–74)

Great Britain. *House of Commons Journal*, esp. vols 28, 40, 41, 42, 44

Great Britain. Parliament. *Parliamentary Papers*.

  1812–13, 7 (122), "Rep't, S.C. on Affairs of East India Company"

  1824, 18 (194), "Hawkers and Pedlars; Number of Licences Granted Annually for the Last Seven years, 1 April 1824

  1830, 5 (644), "1st Rep't, S.C. on China Trade"

  1833, 21 (417), "1st Rep't, R.C. on Excise Establishment" (Tea Permits and Surveys);

  1834, 17 (518), "Rep't, S.C. on Tea Duties"

  1837, 25 (239), "Municipal Corporations in England and Wales";

  1837, 30, "19th Rep't, R.C. on Excise Establishment" (Excise Licences);

  1844, 22 (123), "Hawkers Licensed in 1800, 1810, 1820, 1830, 1840, and 1843";

  1845, 46 (191), "Account of the Quantities of Tea retained for Home Consumption in the U.K. ... , 1740 to 1844";

  1857, 83, "Tea and Coffee Dealers' Licences for England and Wales, Scotland and Ireland from 1781 to 1855."

Newspapers

Bath Chronicle
Cambridge Chronicle
Edinburgh Advertiser
Edinburgh Journal
Edinburgh and Leith Advertiser
Felix Farley's Bristol Journal
General Advertiser (London)
Gentleman's Magazine
Glasgow Courier
Ipswich Journal
Leed's Intelligencer
Leeds Mercury
London Chronicle
Manchester Herald
Manchester Mercury
Morning Chronicle (London)
Morning Herald (London)
Morning Post (London)
Nicholson's Commercial Gazette and Grocers' Register of Useful Knowledge
Norfolk Chronicle
St James Chronicle (London)

Times (London)
York Courant
York Herald

SECONDARY SOURCES

Books

Adburgham, Alison. *Shops and Shopping, 1800–1914*. London: George Allen
    & Unwin 1967.
Alexander, David G. *Retailing in England During the Industrial Revolution*.
    London: Athlone 1970.
Anon. *Chronicles of Cannon Street*. London: J. Travers & Sons n.d..
– *Duties of Excise: A Statement of the Mode of Charging and Collecting the Duties
    of Excise*. London: Commissioners of Excise 1830.
– *Tea Purchaser's Guide*. London: 1785.
– *The Tea Trade*. London: Effingham Wilson 1834.
– *The Trade of England Revised* (1681). In *Seventeenth-Century Economic Doc-
    uments*, edited by J. Thirsk and J.P. Cooper, 389–402. Oxford: Clarendon
    Press 1972.
[Smith, ?]. *Tsiology: A Discourse on Tea*. London: 1826.
Ashton, T.S. *An Economic History of England: The 18th Century*. London:
    Methuen 1955.
– *An Eighteenth-Century Industrialist: Peter Stubs of Warrington*. Manchester:
    Manchester University Press 1939.
– *Economic Fluctuations in England, 1700–1800*. Oxford: Clarendon Press
    1959.
– *Iron and Steel in the Industrial Revolution*. 3rd ed. Manchester: Manchester
    University Press 1951.
Bailey's Eastern Directory, 1784. London: J. Andrews.
Bailey's Western and Midland Directory, 1783. Birmingham: Pearon & Rollason.
Beeke, Rev. H. *Observations on the Produce of the Income Tax and on its Proportion
    to the Whole Income of Great Britain*. London: J. Wright 1800.
Blackman, Janet. "Changing Marketing Methods and Food Consumption."
    In *Our Changing Fare*, edited by T.C. Barker, J.C. McKenzie, and J. Yudin.
    London: Macgibbon & Kee 1966.
Braudel, Fernand. *The Wheels of Commerce*. New York: Harper & Row 1982.
Carey, John. *An Essay on the State of England in Relation to its Trade, its Poor
    and its Taxes* (Bristol, 1695). In *Seventeenth-Century Economic Documents*,
    edited by J. Thirsk and J.P. Cooper. Oxford: Clarendon Press 1972.
Chalklin, C.W. *The Provincial Towns of Georgian England*. Montreal: McGill
    Queen's University Press 1974.
Clapham. J.H. *An Economic History of Modern Britain*. Vol. I. Cambridge:
    Cambridge University Press 1939.

Coleman, D.C. *The Economy of England, 1450–1760.* Oxford: Oxford University Press 1977.

Colquhoun, Patrick. *A Treatise on Indigence.* London: J. Hatchard 1806.

Corfield, P.J. *The Impact of English Towns 1700–1800.* Oxford: Oxford University Press 1982.

Craig, James. *The Excise Officer's Pocket Companion.* Edinburgh: n.p. 1794.

Cranfield, G.A. *Development of the Provincial Newspapers, 1700–1760.* Oxford: Clarendon Press 1962.

Davies, David. *The Case of the Labourers in Husbandry Stated and Considered.* London: C.G. & J. Robinson 1795.

Davis, Dorothy. *Fairs, Shops, and Supermarkets: A History of English Shopping.* Toronto: University of Toronto Press 1966.

Deane, Phyllis & Cole, W.A. *British Economic Growth, 1688–1959.* Cambridge: Cambridge University Press 1967.

Defoe, Daniel. *The Compleat English Tradesman.* London: C. Rivington 1745.

Dermigny, Louis. *La Chine et L'Occident, Le Commerce a Canton aux XVIIIe Siècle, 1719–1833.* 4 tome. Paris: S.E.V.P.E.N. 1964.

Dictionary of National Biography. 2d ed. Oxford: Oxford University Press 1917.

Dowell, Stephen. *History of Taxation and Taxes in England.* Vol. 2. London: Longmans 1884.

Eden, F.M. *The State of the Poor.* 3 vols. 1797. Reprint. London: Cass 1966.

Ehrman, John. *The Younger Pitt.* London: Constable 1969.

Eversley, D.E.C. "The Home Market and Economic Growth in England, 1750–1780." In *Land, Labour and Population in the Industrial Revolution,* edited by E.J. Jones and G.E. Mingay, 206–259. London: Eward Arnold 1967.

Fay, C.R. *English Economic History Mainly Since 1700.* Cambridge: Cambridge University Press 1948.

Fisher, F.J. "The Development of the London Food Market, 1540–1640." In *Essays in Economic History,* vol. 1, edited by E.M. Carus Wilson, 135–151. London: Edward Arnold 1966.

George, M.D. *English Social Life in the Eighteenth Century.* London: Sheldon Press 1923.

– *London Life in the Eighteenth Century.* London: K. Paul, Trench, Trubner & Co. Ltd. 1925.

Glass, D.V. "Gregory King's Estimate of the Population of England and Wales, 1695." In *Population in History,* edited by D.V. Glass and D.E.C. Eversley, 159–220. London: Edward Arnold 1974.

Gray's Annual Directory, 1832. Edinburgh: John Gray.

Hartwell, R.M. "The Neglected Variable: The Service Sector." In *The Industrial Revolution and Economic Growth,* edited by R.M. Hartwell, 201–225. London: Methuen 1971.

– "The Service Revolution: The Growth of Services in Modern Economy."

In *Fontana Economic History of Europe: The Industrial Revolution*, vol. 3, edited by C.M. Cipolla. London: Collins/Fontana 1973.

Heal, Sir Ambrose. *London Tradesmen's Cards of the XVIII Century*. New York: B.T. Batsford 1968.

The Signboards of Old London Shops. New York: B.T. Batsford 1972.

Hoskins, W.G. *Industry, Trade and People in Exeter*. Exeter: Manchester University Press 1968.

Huie, James. *An Abrigement of All the Statutes now in Force, Relative to the Revenue of Excise in Great Britain*. Edinburgh: n.p. 1797.

Jefferys, J.B. *Retail Trading in Britain, 1850–1950*. Cambridge: Cambridge University Press 1954.

Jones, Hurford. *Two Centuries: The Story of David Lloyd Pigott and Company of London, Tea and Coffee Merchants 1760–1960*. London: Harley Publishing Company n.d.

Johnstone's London Commercial Guide and Street Directory, 1817. London: Barnard & Farley.

Kent's Directory, 1784. London: Richard & Henry Causton.

King, Gregory. *Natural and Political Observations and Conclusions Upon the State and Condition of England, 1696*. Edited by George Chalmer. London: John Stockdale 1804.

Krause, J.T. "Some Aspects of Population Change, 1690–1790." In *Land, Labour and Population in the Industrial Revolution*, edited by E.J. Jones and G.E. Mingay, 187–205. London: Edward Arnold 1967.

Lowndes's London Directory. London: T & W. Lowndes, 1784

Mathias, Peter. *The Brewing Industry in England, 1700–1830*. Cambridge: Cambridge University Press 1959.

– *Retailing Revolution. A History of Multiple Retailing in the Food Trades Based Upon the Allied Suppliers Group of Companies*. London: Longmans 1967.

McKendrick, Neil; Brewer, John; and Plumb, J.H. *The Birth of a Consumer Society: The Commercialization of Eighteenth-Century England*. Bloomington, Ind.: Indiana University Press 1982.

Mennell, Robert O. *Tea: An Historical Sketch*, London: Effingham Wilson 1926.

Minchinton, Walter. "Patterns of Demand, 1750–1914." In *Fontana Economic History of Europe: The Industrial Revolution*, vol. 3, edited by C.M. Cipolla, 77–186. London: Collins 1973.

Mitchell, B.R. and Deane, Phyllis. *Abstract of British Historical Statistics*. Cambridge: Cambridge University Press 1962.

Morton, Thomas. *Report of Proceedings Respecting the Sale and Prices of Tea*. London: East India Company 1784.

Morton, Thomas. *Further Report of Proceedings Respecting the Sale and Prices of Tea*. London: East India Company 1785.

Mui, Hoh-Cheung and Mui, Lorna H. *The Management of Monopoly: A Study*

of the English East India Company's Conduct of its Tea Trade, 1784–1833.
Vancouver: University of British Columbia Press 1984.

– eds. *William Melrose in China, 1845–1855.* Edinburgh: Scottish History
Society 1973.

Owen, Robert. *The Life of Robert Owen.* 2 vols. 1857. Reprint. New York:
Kelley 1967.

Paine, Thomas. *The Case of the Officers of Excise: With Remarks on the Quali-
fication of Officers.* London: W.T. Sherwin 1793.

Pigot, James, *London and Provincial New Directory for 1822–23.* London: J.
Pigot & Co.

Postlethwayt, Malachy. *Great Britain's True System.* 1757. Reprint. New York:
Kelley 1967.

– *The Merchant's Public Counting House.* London: John & Paul Knapton 1750.

Robson's London Commercial Directory, Street Guide & Carrier List for 1822.
London: William Robson 1822.

Schumpeter, Elizabeth. *English Overseas Trade Statistics, 1697–1808.* Oxford:
Oxford University Press 1960.

Smith, Adam. *An Inquiry into the Nature and Causes of the Wealth of Nations.*
Edited by E. Cannan. New York: First Modern Library 1937.

Society for Bettering the Conditions and Increasing the Comforts of the
Poor. *Reports.* Vol. 1. London: The Society 1798.

Stout, William. *Autobiography of William Stout of Lancaster, 1665–1752.* Edited
by J.D. Marshall. New York: Barnes & Noble 1967.

Symons. J. *Excise Laws Abridged.* London: J. Nourse 1775.

Thirsk, Joan, ed. *Agrarian History of England and Wales, 1500–1640.* Vol. 4.
Cambridge: Cambridge University Press 1967.

Tillott, P.M. ed. *Victoria County History, The City of York.* London: Oxford
University Press 1961.

Turner, George. *General View of Agriculture in Gloucestershire.* London: Board
of Agriculture 1794.

Twining, Richard. *An Answer to the Second Report of the East India Directors,
Respecting the Sale and Prices of Tea.* London: T. Cadell 1785.

– *Observations on the Tea and Window Act and on the Tea Trade.* London: T.
Cadell 1784.

– *Remarks on the Report of the East India Directors, Respecting the Sale and Prices
of Tea.* London: T. Cadell 1784.

Twining, Stephen H. *Two Hundred and Twenty-Five Years in the Strand: 1706–
1931.* London: R. Twining & Co. 1931.

– *The House of Twining, 1706–1956.* London: R. Twining & Co. 1956.

Universal British Directory. 1799.

Vaisey, David, ed. *Diary of Thomas Turner, 1754–1765.* Oxford: Oxford University Press 1985.

Vizetelly, Henry. *Glances Back Through Seventy Years, Autobiographical and other*

Reminiscences. Vol. 1. London: Kegan Paul & Co. 1893.

Wadsworth, A.P. and de L. Mann, J. *The Cotton Trade and the Industrial Revolution.* Manchester: Manchester University Press 1965.

Westerfield, R.B. *Middlemen in English Business, particularly between 1660 and 1760.* New Haven: Yale University Press 1915.

Willan, T.S. *An Eighteenth-Century Shopkeeper: Abraham Dent of Kirkby Stephen.* Manchester: Manchester University Press 1970.

– *The English Coasting Trade, 1600–1750.* Manchester: Manchester University Press 1967.

– *The Island Trade.* Reprint. New York: 1970.

Young, J.H. *The Toadstool Millionaires: A Social History of Patent Medicines in America before Federal Regulation.* esp. 3–16. Princeton: Princeton University Press 1961.

Articles

Blackman, Janet. "The Food Supply of an Industrial Town: A Study of Sheffield's Public Markets, 1780–1900." *Business History* 5, no. 2: 83–97.

– "The Development of the Retail Grocery Trade in the Nineteenth Century," ibid., 9, no. 2: 110–17.

Brown, P.S. "The Venders of Medicines in Eighteenth-Century Bath Newspapers. *Medical History* 19 (1975): 352–69.

Burley, K.H. "An Essex Clothier of the Eighteenth Century." *Economic History Review* (2nd ser.) 11, no. 2: 289–301.

Chartres, J.A. "Road Carrying in England in the Seventeenth Century: Myth and Reality." *Economic History Review* (2nd ser.) 30, no. 1: 73–94.

Cooper, J.P., "The Social Distribution of Land and Men in England, 1436–1700." *Economic History Review* (2nd ser.) 20, no. 3: 419–440.

Deane, Phyllis. "The Implications of Early National Income Estimates for the Measurement of Long Term Economic Growth in the United Kingdom." *Economic Development and Cultural Change* 4, no. 1: 3–38.

John, A.H. "Agricultural Productivity and Economic Growth in England 1700." *Economic History Review* (2nd ser.) 20, no. 3: 419–440.

Mathias, Peter. "The Social Structure in the Eighteenth Century: A Calculation by Joseph Massie." *Economic History Review* (2nd ser.) 10, no. 1: 30–45.

McKendrick, Neil. "Josiah Wedgwood: An Eighteenth-Century Entrepreneur in Salesmanship and Marketing Techniques." *Economic History Review* (2nd ser.) 12, no. 3: 408–33.

Mui, Hoh-cheung and Lorna H. "Andrew Melrose, Tea Dealer and Grocer of Edinburgh, 1812–1833." *Business History* 9, no. 1: 30–48.

– "The Commutation Act and the Tea Trade in Britain, 1784–1793." *Economic History Review* (2nd ser.) 16, no. 2: 234–53.

– "Smuggling and the British Tea Trade before 1784." *American Historical Review* 84 (Oct. 1968): 44–73.
– "Trends in Eighteenth-Century Smuggling' Reconsidered." *Economic History Review* (2nd ser.) 28, no. 1: 28–43.
– *"William Pitt and the Enforcement of the Commutation Act, 1784–1788." English Historical Review* 76 (July, 1961): 447–65.

Redlich, Fritz. "Some English Stationers of the Seventeenth and Eighteenth Centuries." *Business History* 8, no. 2: 86–102.

Robinson, E. "Eighteenth-Century Commerce and Fashion: Matthew Boulton's Marketing Techniques." *Economic History Review* (2nd ser.) 16, no. 1: 39–60.

Schwarz, L.D. "Income Distribution and Social Structure in London in the Late Eighteenth Century." *Economic History Review* (2nd ser.) 32, no. 2: 250–9.

Scola, Roger. "The Relationship between Food Markets and Shops in Manchester, 1770–1870." Paper read at the Annual Conference of the Urban History Group, 5 April 1974.

Sutton, G.B. "The Marketing of Ready Made Footwear in the Nineteenth Century." *Business History* 6, no. 2: 93–112.

Index

Adburgham, Alison, 4
Agar, Seth (York grocer and confectioner), 183, 184–5
Agar, William (York grocer and confectioner), 184–5
aledrapers, 133, 187
alesellers, 132–3; estimated numbers and income of, 141–2, table 26
Alexander, David, 4, 89 n54, 169n31, 172n33
Allison, Alexander (Perth tea dealer), advertisements by, 265
Alstonfield, Staffs., 75, 101–2
Archer, Edward (London draper), ready-money sales by mail order, 237
Armitage, William (Leeds cabinetmaker), advertisements by, 243
Arnold, William (London grocer), 174
artisan-shopkeepers, 36, 50–1
Ashburner, Mr Kendal (bookseller), 229, 230
Ashton, T.S., 152
Association of London Tea Dealers, 20
Atkinson, John (York confectioner), 185
Austen, Jane, 291

Aylesbury, Bucks., number and rental value of assessed shops (1785) in, appendix 2

Backbarrow Iron Company (Lancashire firm), 202
Bailey: compiler of commercial directories, 61–2; enumeration of shopkeepers, 64, 65, 122, 167–8
Bailey's Eastern Directory, table 30, 177
Bailey's Western Directory, table 30, 177
bakers, 52, 132, 156; income of, in York, table 24
bankruptcies: records of, 49–50, tables 3, 4, and 5, 52, 69–70; of shopkeepers and regional differences, tables 3, 4, 5, and 6, 52–5
Baring, Francis (financier), 138, 189
Barnard Castle, Durh., 12, 246
Barnstaple: excise collection of, 37; numbers of tea dealers in, 163
Barwick, Sara, and Son (dealers in coal, Leeds), 247

Bath, Som.: number and rental value of assessed shops (1785) in, 88, appendix 2; number of tea dealers (1784) in, tables 30 and 36; proportion of shopkeepers with tea licences in, table 36; shopkeepers of, 84, 260–2
Bath New Tea Warehouse, advertisements by, 261
Baxter, Robert (York grocer), 185
Beccles, Suff., number and rental value of assessed shops (1787) in, table 13
Beeke, Rev. H., 140
Benson, Jane (York tea dealer), 186
Bentley, Thomas, 18
Berry, John (Manchester grocer), 231
Bethnal Green (London), 174; shop tax assessment in, 92; proportional distribution of retail shops by income and assessment class in, 116–17, table 20, 120
Bills of Mortality: number of shops (1759) in, 36, table 2, appendix 1; in 1797, 108; ratio of